Sprawl Busting:

State
Programs
to
Guide
Growth

Sprawl Busting:

State Programs to Guide Growth

By
Jerry Weitz, AICP

PLANNERS PRESS
AMERICAN PLANNING ASSOCIATION
Chicago, Illinois
Washington, D.C.

122 S. Michigan Ave., Suite 1600, Chicago, IL 60603

ISBN (paperback edition): 1-884829-27-9
ISBN (hardbound edition): 1-884829-28-7
Library of Congress Catalog Number 99-72285
Printed in the United States of America

Interior composition by Joanne Shwed, Backspace Ink

Contents

List of Maps

List of Figures

List of Tables

List of Sidebars

List of Abbreviations

ALI	American Law Institute
APA	American Planning Association
APF	Adequate Public Facilities
APDC	Area Planning and Development Commission (Georgia)
ARC	Atlanta Regional Commission (Georgia)
ASPO	American Society of Planning Officials
CMSA	Consolidated Metropolitan Statistical Area
CRAG	Columbia Region Association of Governments (Oregon)
CZMA	Coastal Zone Management Act (United States)
DCA	Department of Community Affairs (Florida, Georgia)
DCD	Department of Community Development (Washington)
DCTED	Department of Community, Trade and Economic Development (Washington)
DLCD	Department of Land Conservation and Development (Oregon)
DNR	Department of Natural Resources (Georgia)
DOE	Department of Ecology (Washington)
DRI	Development of Regional Impact (Florida, Georgia)
EAR	Evaluation and Appraisal Report (Florida)
EDD	Economic Development Department (Oregon)
ELMS	Environmental Land Management Study (Florida)
FAC	Florida Administrative Code
GIS	Geographic Information Systems

GMA	Growth Management Act (Florida, 1985; Washington, 1990 and 1991)
ICE	Intergovernmental Coordination Element (Florida)
ISTEA	Intermodal Surface Transportation Efficiency Act (U.S.)
JLCLU	Joint Legislative Committee on Land Use (Oregon)
LCDC	Land Conservation and Development Commission (Oregon)
LUBA	Land Use Board of Appeals (Oregon)
LULU	Locally Unwanted Land Use
MSA	Metropolitan Statistical Area
NIMBY	Not In My Back Yard
OAR	Oregon Administrative Rules
OCP	Office of Coordinated Planning (Georgia DCA)
ODOT	Oregon Department of Transportation
OFM	Office of Financial Management (Washington)
OMB	Office of Management and Budget (United States)
OPB	Office of Planning and Budget (Georgia)
ORS	Oregon Revised Statutes
PUD	Planned Unit Development
PMSA	Primary Metropolitan Statistical Area
RCW	Revised Code Washington
RDC	Regional Development Center (Georgia)
RIR	Regionally Important Resource (Georgia)
RPC	Regional Planning Council (Florida)
RTPO	Regional Transportation Planning Organization (Washington)
TGM	Transportation and Growth Management Program (Oregon)
UGA	Urban Growth Area (Washington)
UGB	Urban Growth Boundary (Oregon)
UUC	Unincorporated Urban Community (Oregon)
WAC	Washington Administrative Code

Preface and Acknowledgments

I first became interested in urban planning in 1983 as an undergraduate senior at Emory University. Dennis Grady, who was teaching a course on state and local politics while he was earning his Ph.D. there in political science, had attended Georgia Tech's graduate city planning program. Through his course Grady introduced me to the politics of land use and zoning. Intrigued with planning, I completed the graduate city planning program in 1985. From there I took an entry-level position with the City of Roswell in the area where I grew up—North Fulton County. I also later held a staff planner position with Fulton County for a year. Seeking greater responsibility and career advancement, I took the position of zoning administrator for the Albany Dougherty Planning Commission in 1988.

In early 1989, while I was working as a zoning administrator in Albany and Dougherty County, Georgia (located south of what some call the "Macon-Dixie" line) and just before passage of the Georgia Planning Act, a local television reporter suggested to me that planning legislation would never pass in Georgia. Many people shared the reporter's skepticism; most informed outside observers did not expect planning legislation to pass in the local home rule environment of Georgia's politics. Gov. Joe Frank Harris, however, had been lobbying business groups and legislators to support growth strategies legislation, the Governor's Growth Strategies Commission had completed its consensus-building and technical work, and the planning act did pass the Georgia General Assembly in 1989.

At the time, I viewed (naively, I have to admit) passage of Georgia's new legislation as the "planners' full employment act." Having some interest in consulting, and having quickly received my fill of southwest Georgia politics (I like to say that I "did my time below the gnat line"), I resigned my zoning administrator position and moved back to the Atlanta region to try my hand at being a consulting planner. I wanted to prepare local comprehensive plans and hoped to make consulting wages in doing so. After sending out solicitations to most of the counties in the state to provide comprehensive planning services, however, I received enough responses to convince me that regional development centers (RDCs) were going to prepare most local plans. The new planning act had assigned major responsibilities to RDCs, including local comprehensive planning technical assistance. Hence, it was not the planning consultant full-employment act I had thought it would be. Much of the local comprehensive planning work would be done by RDC planners. That was where the action was going to be, I figured.

I took the position of regional planner for the Georgia Mountains RDC in December 1989. The RDC has jurisdiction in the 13-county northeast portion of the state and is headquartered in Gainesville. During nearly five years there, I observed and participated in Georgia's coordinated planning program. My work included local comprehensive planning, substate regional planning, and interaction with staff members of the Georgia Department of Community Affairs (DCA), specifically the Office of Coordinated Planning (OCP). I share in this book some of the implementation experiences and lessons I gained from participating in Georgia's planning program as a local and regional planner.

By 1994, after living for two-and-a-half years in a renovated historic residence in the small town of Gillsville, Georgia (between Gainesville and Commerce), my wife, Patti, and I were ready for a change. I had read John DeGrove's *Land Growth and Politics* (1984) during graduate school at Georgia Tech, and while living in Gillsville I had finished his second major work about state land use planning (1992). I was intrigued with Oregon's legendary statewide land use program, including regional planning in Portland, as described in those two books. Georgia's coordinated planning program seemed to pale in comparison with Oregon's planning and regulatory mandates, since it did not require local planning and did not mandate that local governments adopt zoning ordinances. How refreshing it would be, I thought, to work with or under a state mandate where local governments treated planning and land use regulation seriously. Having honeymooned in 1990 in the Pacific Northwest, Patti and I were mesmerized by the natural beauty and sense of adventure of what my father calls "God's Country."

When Patti got an offer to take a higher paying job in Portland, I was all in favor of moving to the area, given its national reputation as an innovative laboratory for regional planning (see DeGrove 1992; Oliver 1989). Also, Oregon was the undisputed pioneer in state land use planning. Portland State University had a good reputation, in my view, with its urban setting and the works of Professors Sy Adler, Carl Abbott, and Deborah Howe (now editors of the *Journal of the American Planning Association*). I told Patti that rather than letting my pride be hurt that she would become the major breadwinner of the family, I would take advantage of the opportunity and study for my Ph.D. if we moved to Portland. We both agreed to try and advance our careers and moved to Beaverton (in the west part of the Portland, Oregon, region) during September 1994. I had secured, just before moving to Oregon, a job-share position with Oregon's Department of Land Conservation and Development (DLCD) within its new Transportation and Growth Management (TGM) Program. In this book I share some experiences I had with Oregon's planning program while working as an urban growth management specialist in Oregon's TGM Program from 1994 to 1997. This view of a state growth management program as a staff member provides a perspective that balances the local and regional planning experience I gained from working with Georgia's program. My professional experience with DLCD is supplemented by academic work at Portland State and the perspectives of planning professors there about regional and state planning in Oregon.

In 1994 I was accepted into the urban studies Ph.D. program at Portland State but decided to wait until the 1995 academic year to begin so as to gain in-state residency and reduce tuition costs. Meanwhile, I had my job-share position at DLCD and also a temporary assignment there. I had saved little money for tuition, however, and was looking for a way to save some dollars for my second round of graduate school. I learned that Al Benkendorf, a planning consultant in Portland, was looking for a part-time planner to work with him on planning contracts he secured with the cities of Battle Ground and Washougal, Washington, (both in Clark County) and with the town of PeEll, Washington (in Lewis County). I thought working on development regulations and preparing a comprehensive plan for cities and towns in Washington would be a neat way to gain exposure to Washington's new Growth Management Act, while earning some extra tuition money. Benkendorf hired me, and, by working part time for his firm from October 1994 until March 1996, I gained some insider's knowledge of Washington's growth management program. I completed new zoning regulations and subdivision codes for Battle Ground and Washougal and a comprehensive plan for PeEll.

Upon completion of my graduate course work and advancement to candidacy at Portland State in the spring of 1997, I took a full-time position as planning division manager in Cowlitz County, Washington (immediately north of Clark County and the Portland region). Cowlitz County was on the verge of being mandated to plan under GMA, and I viewed this position as an opportunity to lead some tough, controversial, but nonetheless interesting and challenging GMA tasks of completing countywide planning policies, drawing urban growth areas, and managing a local comprehensive planning process. Although at the time of this writing Cowlitz County was still not mandated to plan under GMA, I share some of my experiences of working in southwest Washington.

This book is about state-sponsored land use planning in Florida, Georgia, Oregon, and Washington. Though I don't have experience in Florida, that state is included in my analysis for reasons that are explained in the introduction. The vast majority of this work is drawn directly from my doctoral dissertation, which I completed in one year (after knowing for some time my research interest) and defended in October 1998. Publication with APA required that I embellish my academic work with stories of planning practice, a task I was most pleased to accept. Indeed, I would have written the dissertation initially from more of a scholar-practitioner's perspective with stories of practice, but I perceived that the practitioner's perspective might not be wholly appropriate given my academic audience and the work's principal purpose of providing a scholarly contribution to state growth management program research. The stories of practice were inserted most conveniently as sidebars so as not to interrupt or complicate the flow established in my dissertation.

Sprawl Busting is intended to tell the story of state growth management in the four states through 1997. A couple of key study commission reports, however, were published in 1998 and are worth brief mentioning here. In Washington, the Land Use Study Commission issued its final report, which, among other findings and recommendations, suggests a consolidated land use code is desirable, but the consensus needed to develop and implement it does not yet exist. The Land Use Study Commission has now gone out of existence, but the agenda for regulatory reform in Washington remains unfinished. Lawmakers in Washington face the daunting task of trying to reconcile 1970s-era environmental statutes, such as the Shoreline Management Act and State Environmental Policy Act, with the growth management legislation of the early 1990s.

In March 1998, Georgia's Board of Community Affairs called for appointment of a task force to evaluate the effectiveness of the Georgia Planning Act of 1989 and its implementation during the last decade. In December 1998, the Growth Management Reassessment Task Force issued a report containing sweeping recommendations that will, if implemented, change the character and direction of Georgia's program for the management of growth and the mitigation of sprawl. The task force suggests that the governor lead the state beyond growth strategies to growth management, the state adopt a vision for desired growth patterns, the regional development centers be retooled to better address regional issues, state incentives be offered to encourage good growth management practices by local governments, state agencies mitigate policies and practices that encourage sprawl development, and consistency requirements be instituted so that local land use regulations will implement adopted comprehensive plans. In preparing its recommendations, the task force reviewed growth management practices in other states, including urban growth boundaries and minimum density zoning in Oregon. If mandate designers follow the recommendations of the task force, in addition to establishing the Georgia Regional Transportation Authority, Georgia will be well on its way toward instituting a sprawl busting program of its own.

I want to acknowledge the support of many folks that enabled me to complete this book. First, to my wife, Patti, and son, Jay, I regret the severe family time deficit that I accumulated in my academic and publishing pursuits. It is to Patti and Jay that I dedicate this work. To Gwen and Jim Hollcraft, I owe many thanks for hiring Patti at a good salary that enabled our relocation to Oregon, which advanced both of our careers.

As noted above, I owe thanks to Dennis Grady for introducing me to city planning as a profession. Roger Rupnow, professor emeritus of

Georgia Tech's graduate city planning program, was my mentor while I was in graduate school. My first exposure to state growth management was through his class, where we read and discussed John DeGrove's *Land Growth and Politics* (1984).

Dr. Sam Dayton, retired from his long-standing position as executive director of Georgia Mountains RDC, served as a Ph.D. practitioner role model while I was a regional planner. Larry Sparks, the RDC's director of planning, became a friend as well as a supervisor and was by my side in the local and regional planning efforts we completed. Larry and I shared many experiences about Georgia's program that helped to frame some of the stories that I offer here. I extend thanks to Mike Gleaton and Jim Frederick of Georgia's OCP, with whom I interacted during my employment with Georgia Mountains RDC and who offered interview time in 1997 to bring my perspective of Georgia's planning program up to date. James Quinn, Paul Noll, and Bob Dennis of the Florida Department of Community Affairs also deserve acknowledgment and thanks for affording me an interview and giving me access to all relevant state agency materials. With their assistance I was able to write an account of Florida's program without the benefit of personal experience.

In Oregon, I owe many thanks to John Kelly and Elaine Smith for hiring me to research urban growth management tools and contribute to policymaking with Oregon's TGM program. John Kelly deserves credit for the first part of the title of this book, for it was he who referred to the staff of the Oregon Transportation and Growth Management Program as "sprawl busters." The importance of that opportunity to conduct research and develop expertise about state and local growth management cannot be underestimated. With the TGM Program I had the unique opportunity of getting paid to do research that not only fulfilled DLCD's work programs but also coincided entirely with my own academic research interests. I want to thank other folks at DLCD for their support and confidence in my contributions, including but not limited to Dick Benner, Greg Wolf, Anna Russo, Mitch Rohse, Bill Adams, Sue Geniesse (who I still refer to as my better work-half, since she held the other half of my job-share position), and especially Jim Knight, with whom I engaged in some insightful discussions about the needs and directions of Oregon's planning program. The people of Oregon and Govs. Barbara Roberts and John Kitzhaber deserve much credit as well for supporting state growth management and for providing jobs devoted strictly to bettering urban growth management in Oregon.

As noted above, I owe thanks to Al Benkendorf for hiring me to do work that enabled me to gain insights into Washington's GMA. I also acknowledge Larry Frazier, director of Cowlitz County's Department of Building and Planning, for selecting me in 1997 to manage the county's planning division. Larry shared with me some of his perspectives of state growth management programs as a planning director in Florida, California, Oregon, and Washington.

My dissertation committee deserves special recognition. Sy Adler was my adviser throughout my enrollment at Portland State and chaired my dissertation committee. Sy was a major influence in the direction and content of this work. He kept me focused on my research questions when I strayed, and he thankfully did not agree when I asked to be relieved of writing one of my dissertation chapters (Chapter 11) when the work began to grow lengthy and the writing got tough. Besides Sy Adler I also want to thank the other two members of what I call the *Planning the Oregon Way* (1994) "trio" who are currently JAPA's editors: Carl Abbott, for helping me recognize that the structural analysis provided by my work was missing a discussion of politics that help explain the evolution of state growth management programs, and Deborah Howe, who provided early advice about state growth management program topics for my dissertation and helped to solidify my account of Oregon's planning program. Ethan Seltzer, Director of Portland State's Institute for Portland Metropolitan Studies, was also on my dissertation committee and offered constructive criticisms that were incorporated into my work. Gordon Dodds, chair of the history department, served as my committee's graduate office representative. I also want to thank Arthur "Chris" Nelson, star alumnus of Portland State's urban studies program, noted expert on growth management, and faculty member at Georgia Tech. Chris consulted with me about dissertation topics and would have been a member of my dissertation committee had it not been for the logistical problems that having an out-of-state dissertation committee member arrangement would have posed.

I owe major credit and many thanks to Stuart Meck, principal investigator for APA's Growing Smart Program. He helped launch my publications career and took initiative to share my dissertation with Sylvia Lewis, APA's director of publications. Had it not been for Stuart's initiative and confidence in my work, this book probably would not have been published. I must recognize the influence of Peter J. May, political science professor at the University of Washington. Peter's work on state mandate design (see Burby and May 1997; May 1994; 1993) has conceptualized a new field of study that provided inspirational guidance as I conducted my research.

My silent mentor and greatest source of inspiration for writing about state growth management programs is John DeGrove, former secretary of Florida's Department of Community Affairs and author of the two aforementioned books that helped to earn him the title of the "dean of state growth managers." While I never had the privilege of working or studying under DeGrove, his work provided me with the inspirational guidance needed to complete my dissertation and this work. It is in the tradition of DeGrove's two books that I offer this work, and I can only hope that it will be as equally well received as a contribution to the state growth management literature.

Jerry Weitz
Alpharetta, Georgia
July 24, 1999

CHAPTER

1

Introduction

This book provides a history and structural analysis of state growth management programs in Florida, Georgia, Oregon, and Washington between 1969 and 1997. State-sponsored land use planning has three principal structural components: the intergovernmental structures (i.e., local, regional, and state roles as established in statutes) and sequence of planning; state requirements for local land use planning (i.e., minimum planning standards established via statutes and rules); and state support functions for land use planning (i.e., grants, technical and educational assistance, provision of data, etc.). The formula for understanding the structure of state-sponsored land use planning is set forth below.

State-sponsored land use planning = f (structure, standards, support)

RESEARCH OBJECTIVES

My objectives in presenting this work are as follows. First, I want to tell the story (selected parts) of growth management program design and implementation in four growth management states from the perspective of a "mandate designer." A mandate designer is one charged with the responsibility of designing a state growth management program. I focus on the comprehensive planning mandate to learn how the programs are structured, what the rules are for preparing land use plans, how local governments have fared in their planning experiences, and what types of support the state has provided to meet the local comprehensive planning mandate. Second, I reveal lessons learned from analyzing program structures and implementation experiences in the four states. I provide a critique of state-sponsored land use planning based on what the literature says and the lessons drawn from a content analysis of state growth management program laws. I am ultimately interested in providing observations, methods of inquiry, and lessons that can be used by program designers to improve state-sponsored programs of land use planning, particularly with regard to minimum standards for local land use plans.

Noticeably absent from these research objectives is a desire to take into account the state-level politics that influence the content of state growth management legislation and the direction of program implementation. My intent is to provide a structural comparison of state growth management programs without significant references to state-level politics and policy processes. My research thus differs from the major works of the dean of state growth managers (DeGrove 1992, 1984) and certain scholars of Oregon's program (Abbott 1994; Knaap 1994), which focus on the politics of adopting state growth management statutes and implementing programs.

DEFINITION OF STATE-SPONSORED LAND USE PLANNING

I borrow Dennis Gale's (1992) nomenclature and definition of a "state-sponsored" growth management program. According to Gale, a state-sponsored growth management program includes the following characteristics, among others: (1) it is provided for under state legislative enactment; (2) the program mandates or encourages local (city and county) governments to prepare comprehensive plans and, in some states, requires or encourages regional entities to prepare plans; (3) it mandates or encourages plan submittal to the state and/or a substate body for review and comment, approval, or negotiation; and (4) it maintains a system of incentives and/or disincentives to encourage compliance or cooperation (Gale 1992).

Because Gale's definition of state sponsorship implies but does not specifically include the characteristic of areal comprehensiveness (all land area and all cities and counties in the state), I would add to the second characteristic above that most, if not all, cities and counties in the state are mandated or encouraged to plan. I could say that "all" local governments and "all" land area in the state are included, except for Washington, which does not mandate/encourage all counties (and cities within them) to adopt comprehensive plans. Gale's definition, with this slight modification, serves to further distinguish comprehensive state-sponsored growth management programs (such as those of the four states subject to this inquiry) from less-than-areally-comprehensive (substate) approaches characterized as state growth management. For example, New York's Adirondack Park Agency (Graham 1981; Liroff and Davis 1981) and the Tahoe Regional Planning Agency in California-Nevada (Strong 1984) are not statewide programs but instead establish local planning requirements only within a specific region of the state. Similarly, state mandates that local governments complete plans for environmentally sensitive subareas of the state (e.g., California Coastal Commission, New Jersey's Pinelands Protection Act, etc.) (Bollens 1992) do not constitute areally comprehensive programs of statewide growth management.

Second, I substitute the term "land use planning" for growth management. The term growth management is certainly appropriate here. I use the term land use planning, however, in a deliberate attempt to limit the scope of this work. I do not attempt to cover the full scope of local comprehensive plans and state growth management programs in the four states. That is, I narrow the scope of growth management and comprehensive planning (which, broadly defined, include economic development, public facilities planning, population forecasting, housing, and other elements) to the subject that is my true area of interest: urban land use planning. Passing references to other elements of local comprehensive plans, however, such as transportation and public facilities, are provided in certain instances.

SELECTION OF STATES

At least eight states have programs that meet the criteria for state sponsorship as described above (Gale 1992), too many to include in one research effort. Other states might qualify or come close to qualifying, such as Hawaii, California, and Maryland. Growth management scholars often exclude Hawaii from consideration because it is a unique and small island state. Maryland adopted a program in 1992 that might qualify as state-sponsored, but it was put in place after Gale's research was prepared. From the many growth management states, I chose four programs of state-sponsored land use planning: Florida, Georgia, Oregon, and Washington.

I chose those state programs for several reasons. First, I seek to combine two prominent programs (Florida and Oregon) adopted during the "quiet revolution" (Bosselman and Callies 1971) for which extensive literatures exist with two 1990s-style programs (Georgia and Washington) for which much less research has been completed. Second, state programs instituted during the quiet revolution served (purportedly) as principal examples or models for other states to use in establishing their programs. Specifically, Georgia supposedly used Florida's program as a basis of departure, while Washington drew heavily on Oregon's program in establishing its own. By examining Florida-Georgia and Oregon-Washington, and other cross-fertilization paths between pairs of states, I hope to discover the patterns of evolutionary learning between and among these four state growth management programs. Third, I have professional planning experience in three of these four states, which enables me to identify sources of information, contacts, and experiences that are appropriate to the stories told here. The four states I chose are geographically clustered in two regions (the Pacific Northwest, and the southeastern United States), which facilitates a comparison of growth management styles in two subnational regions. I also selected the four states in part because each of the programs has its own unique institutional structure and record of implementation. Analysis of four different state programs has merit because a broader range of approaches can be revealed and contrasted.

A HISTORICAL FRAMEWORK OF PROGRAM EVOLUTION

I describe the evolution of state growth management programs according to three distinct waves or eras of state-sponsored land use planning: the quiet revolution (1969-1976); the second wave (1980-1988); and the third wave (1989-1997). Chapter 2 is devoted to a description of the choice of this historical classification scheme and why it is used instead of an organizational framework that was initially applied. Chapter 2 also outlines various evolutionary themes and presents them in historical narratives. Chapters 3, 4, and 5 sketch the evolution of growth management program design and implementation during the three waves.[1] A central question of this research is, "For each of the three eras, what is distinctive about state growth management program evolution?" The description of growth management programs according to a three-era historical classification scheme also provides a foundation of descriptive information for more specific analyses in subsequent chapters.

The historical narratives (Chapters 3, 4, and 5) are constructed from a nearly exhaustive literature review. Scholarly attention to growth management during the quiet revolution is abundant. Programs in Florida and Oregon are especially well described and analyzed. Other scholars have paid equal attention to the birth of additional state growth management programs in the 1980s (i.e., the second wave of program evolution). Literature describing activities during the quiet revolution and second wave, however, deserves reconciliation, consolidation and critical reinterpretation (Weitz 1999).

Very little research describes the adoption and implementation of third-wave, 1990s-style growth management programs in Georgia and Washington. Few if any scholarly works describe and analyze state growth management program experiences during the past five years in any the four states selected for study. My research is intended to help fill this void.

STRUCTURE, STANDARDS, AND SUPPORT

I already presented a simple formula that identifies three major components of state-sponsored land use planning. Structure is the first of three major components of state-sponsored growth management programs. The intergovernmental structures of state growth management programs are described and analyzed by scholars in the fields of planning and policy analysis. Few studies, however, apply systematic, comprehensive methods. In Chapters 6, 7, and 8, I analyze the content of state statutes to describe the intergovernmental division of authority and responsibility legislators used to implement land use planning in the four states. The state statutes analyzed here are as follows:

- Florida's 1985 growth management act (Florida Statutes Chapter 163) and related statutes;
- Georgia's 1989 Planning Act and related statutes (House Bill 215, 1989 laws);
- Oregon's 1973 land use act and related statutes (Senate Bill 100, codified as ORS 197); and
- Washington's Growth Management Act (1990 and 1991) (Revised Code Washington 36.70A).

One of my objectives is to use the findings from the content analysis of state statutes as evidence that tends to support certain propositions about evolutionary paths of learning among the states. I give specific attention to identifying the roles of cities, counties, regional entities, and state agencies in the four state planning programs, and to the sequences of planning among these institutional actors.

In later chapters, I focus attention on the other two components of state-sponsored land use planning, standards (Chapter 9) and support (Chapter 10). Minimum planning standards for local comprehensive plans are included in administrative rules. I analyze selected sections of the following administrative rules:

- Florida Administrative Code Annotated Rule. 9J-5;
- Rules of the Georgia Department of Community Affairs, Chapter 110-3-2;
- Oregon's Administrative Rules, Chapter 660 (which include the statewide planning goals); and
- Washington Administrative Code 365-195.

I identify the various elements of comprehensive plans required by the four states but then focus in Chapter 9 on land use planning and urban growth management content requirements. Provisions designed to mitigate sprawl are emphasized. With the exception of general descriptions and overviews, few studies analyze the state-mandated requirements for local plans, particularly those for land use planning and urban growth management. One notable exception is Starnes's (1986) analysis of Florida's Rule 9J-5. Also, a team of scholars (including Ray Burby, Peter May, Linda Dalton, Philip Berke, Steve French, and Ed Kaiser) in several different works recently has analyzed the natural hazards elements of local plans as a topical focus to determine the effects of state mandates. The research presented in Chapter 9 adds a new dimension to the literature on state growth management by providing an in-depth inventory and comparison of land use and urban growth elements of the local comprehensive plans required in the four states.

Support functions, addressed in Chapter 10, comprise the third major component of the state mandates for land use planning. The state departments charged with implementing growth management in the subject states have structures and program features that support local and regional comprehensive planning. The responsible state agencies in the four states are as follows: the Florida Department of Community Affairs (DCA); the Georgia Department of Community Affairs (also known as DCA); the Oregon Department of Land Conservation and Development (DLCD), with its companion Oregon Land Conservation and Development Commission (LCDC); and the Washington Department of Community, Trade and Economic Development (DCTED), formerly Department of Community Development (DCD).

The support functions of individual state programs are manifested in departmental annual reports, program designs, budgets, organizational charts, work programs, and internal policy memoranda. Like the statutes and administrative rules for local planning, these descriptions of support functions for local planning (funding, technical assistance, etc.) lend themselves to some content analysis. Since the sources of data are much less readily apparent and available, however, the research method used in completing this work is much less standardized with respect to the four state programs.

With the possible exception of DeGrove (1992, 1984), scholars have not studied technical assistance components of state growth management programs to any significant degree. Technical assistance remains an underemphasized component of state growth management program design. Chapter 10 presents information that contributes another dimension to the challenge of state growth management program implementation and the study of state-sponsored land use planning. Specifically, it chronicles in historical perspective the efforts of the state administering agencies to establish technical assistance and funding programs to help local governments meet the local comprehensive planning mandate.

CRITICISMS, LESSONS, CONCLUSIONS AND LIMITATIONS

In Chapter 11, I summarize and critically reinterpret intergovernmental frameworks found in the literature that have been applied to state growth management programs. Based on the research presented here, I provide evidence that refutes these frameworks, though I present other findings that tend to support them. I hope that Chapter 11 is an important contribution to the literature, in that it critically reinterprets prior scholarly work based on a more detailed content analysis of state statutes than currently found in the literature.

A significant body of literature criticizes state growth management programs and prescribes certain reforms. Such works, however, amount to patchy, unorganized, less-than-comprehensive approaches to criticism and prescription. Only recently have state growth managers and land use planners begun to construct frameworks for critiquing state growth management programs and prescribing changes to improve program implementation (e.g., Deyle and Smith 1998; Baer 1997; Burby and May 1997). Chapter 12 offers program analysts and mandate designers a number of observations, lessons, criticisms, recommendations, and prescriptions to improve state growth management programs. These prescriptions are based on a synthesis of the criticisms and prescriptions found in the growth management literature and my own findings that flow from the content analysis and my professional experience. The recommendations offered here will help program designers to judge the suitability, adequacy, comprehensiveness, timing, and appropriateness of the three major components of state-sponsored land use planning (structure, standards, and support). The prescriptions in Chapter 12 should have value to practicing mandate designers and state program administrators, in that growth managers can draw on past experiences, learn from other states, improve existing programs, and develop new, better programs. This work should contribute to the literature by suggesting different ways to improve state-sponsored land use planning.

Chapter 13 summarizes the most important findings, themes, and conclusions from earlier chapters and highlights various limitations of this research. In this final chapter I present a four-stage model of intra-program evolution, speculate about the fourth wave of state growth management program history, and offer a research agenda for developing a more comprehensive theory of the evolution of state growth management programs.

CONTEXT: STATE ROLES IN LAND USE PLANNING

For decades, all states have implemented policies relating to local planning, zoning, and subdivision control. State policymakers have become increasingly concerned with the overconcentration of population in urban areas, the accelerated pace of suburban sprawl, and the environmental degradation that has accompanied rapid and haphazard development. Most states have responded to these problems by adopting, in a piecemeal fashion, a whole range of "single-purpose" (Burby and May 1997, 2) state land use control measures, including coastal zone protection, wetlands preservation, power plant siting, and wild rivers preservation, to name just a few.

Increasingly, policymakers in certain states also have increasingly recognized that collections of single-purpose statutes have not solved the problems associated with urban growth. Local government officials often are unable or unwilling to address the problems associated with growth and development without encouragement or mandate by states (Barrows 1982). The inability or unwillingness of local government officials to plan for urban growth has led some states to address the problems of growth by adopting "comprehensive planning approaches" (Burby and May 1997, 3) to legislation and implementing programs that include the three major components of state-sponsored land use planning: an intergovernmental structure of state, regional, county, and city planning and a mandate or incentive that some or all of the localities in the state develop a comprehensive plan; minimum statewide guidelines and standards (through legislation or by rule) that localities must meet in developing plans; and funding and assistance to support local and regional land use planning that meets the minimum planning standards. Again, these three components are summarized in the formula provided at the beginning of this chapter.

CONTEXT: PROGRAM EVOLUTION AND CHANGE

State-sponsored programs of comprehensive land use planning take several years to design and implement. Such programs evolve and change at many stages during the course of program design and implementation. Growth management statutes are adopted and implemented in political environments where policies and objectives are subject to debate and compromise. As noted earlier, I do not set out to tell the stories of political debates and compromises. An inquiry into the political influences surrounding program adoption and implementation activities would depart from my focus on structure.

In designing a state growth management program, the intergovernmental structure (e.g., an administering department or commission, regional planning agency, and local government) must be established. The administering agency may have to be created, and once in place, it takes time to design, equip with resources, and staff with the appropriate personnel. Contents and procedures for land use planning (i.e., minimum standards) also must be promulgated, via administrative rules of the state department or commission or by some other means. Advance and ongoing technical assistance for local planning is necessary. For example, data and maps are needed to support local land use planning and might have to be produced before local governments initiate land use planning programs. Once the institutional structure, standards, and resources are in place to support land use planning, the localities (and, in some cases, regional planning agencies) can initiate the multiyear process of preparing, adopting, implementing, amending, and updating comprehensive plans.

Programs of state-sponsored land use planning are rarely static during their lengthy processes of program development and implementation. Growth management programs go through processes of evolution and change. Growth management statutes get refined, compromised, or tinkered with by legislators for various reasons, and such changes in legislation necessitate or stimulate changes in the administration of existing programs. Again, I do not emphasize these political dynamics. Judicial reviews (both the courts and special appeals boards) also can significantly affect the direction and content of land use planning programs. Furthermore, changes in the principles of professional land use planning may precipitate updates in land use planning standards as the planning profession itself evolves.

Policymakers also inquire about the growth management programs of other states to determine lessons in establishing and improving their own. Learning by program officials can take place within a given state growth management program, or between growth management programs of states. Of the many possible explanations of how state growth management programs evolve (e.g., interest group politics, administrative behavior, etc.), I am most interested in identifying the paths of learning between pairs of states and the lessons that manifest themselves from that discovery.

GROWTH IN THE STATES

Since the topic is generally the management of growth (i.e., population and the land development that supports it), it is only fitting that I review population trends and the political geography of the four states.

Florida

Florida was the fourth most populous state in the United States, with almost 13 million people as of 1990 (see Table 1.1). With a land area of approximately 54,000 square miles, Florida is similar in size to Georgia. The capital is Tallahassee (population 124,773 in 1990). The most populous city was Jacksonville (672,971), which is consolidated with Duval County. The second largest city was Miami (358,548) (U.S. Department of Commerce 1991a).

With nine out of every 10 residents residing in metropolitan statistical areas (MSAs), Florida was the most urban of the four states (see Table 1.2). There are 20 MSAs in Florida, three of which exceeded one million population in 1990 (see Table 1.3). Florida's metropolitan areas have all witnessed rapid growth. The slowest-growing MSA in Florida from 1980 to 1990 was Pensacola (18.9 percent), while the fastest growing MSA was Naples (76.9 percent). Several of Florida's MSAs had 1980-1990 decennial population growth rates of more than 40 percent. With the exception of the Pensacola MSA, populations within the land areas outside of the central city in all other MSAs grew by more than 25 percent during the decade (see Table 1.3). Florida has 67 counties, 33 of which are located in MSAs.

Georgia

With approximately 6.5 million people, Georgia was the eleventh most populous state in the United States as of 1990 (see Table 1.1). The state's land area is approximately 58,000 square miles. The capital and most populous city was Atlanta (population of 394,017 in 1990). The second largest city was Columbus (179,278), which is consolidated with Muscogee County (U.S. Department of Commerce 1991a).

Approximately two-thirds of the state's population as of 1990 was located in eight MSAs (see Tables 1.2 and 1.3). With more than two million residents, the Atlanta MSA (encompassing 18 counties in 1991) was the most populous urban area in all four states. Three of Georgia's MSAs cross into abutting states (Augusta into South Carolina, Chattanooga into Tennessee, and Columbus into Alabama). Three MSAs (Albany, Chattanooga, and Columbus) had decennial population growth rates of less than two percent, while Atlanta received the lion's share of absolute population gain and percentage increase (32.5 percent). The population increase occurring outside the central city of Atlanta but inside the Atlanta MSA during the 1980s (42.5 percent) rivaled growth trends in some of Florida's MSAs. Georgia has 159 counties (see Map 1.2), 38 of which are located in the state's eight MSAs.

Oregon

Oregon's population in 1990 (2,842,321) made it the twenty-ninth most populous state in the United States as of 1990 (Table 1.1). Oregon has the largest land area of the four states included in this research (96,000 square miles). The capital is Salem (population of 107,786 in 1990). The most populous city was Portland (437,319), and the second largest city was Eugene (112,669) (U.S. Department of Commerce 1991a).

Approximately two-thirds of the state's population as of 1990 was located in the state's four MSAs (see Tables 1.2 and 1.3). Three of the metropolitan areas (Portland, Salem, and Eugene-Springfield) lie in the Willamette Valley, which encompasses much of the state's population and metropolitan land area. With the Vancouver, Washington, primary metropolitan statistical area (PMSA), the Portland PMSA formed a consolidated metropolitan statistical area (CMSA) as of 1991. In 1993 the CMSA was expanded to include the Salem MSA. None of Oregon's MSAs lies east of the Cascade Mountains. Oregon's MSAs witnessed population gains that were more modest than those of Florida (see Table 1.3). In fact, unlike Florida, three of Oregon's four MSAs (Eugene-Springfield, Medford, and Salem) had noncentral-city areas of the MSA grow more slowly (or in the case of Eugene-Springfield, actually lose population) than the growth rate for the MSA as a whole (see Table 1.3). Incidentally, I cannot help but wonder if urban growth boundaries have contributed to the slower growth rates outside of Oregon's major cities. Oregon has 36 counties (see Map 1.3), nine of which are located in MSAs.

Washington

Washington was the eighteenth most populous state in the United States as of 1990, with approximately four million people. The state's land area is 66,600 square miles. The capital is Olympia (33,840 population in 1990). The most populous city was Seattle (516,259), and the second largest city was Spokane (177,196) (U.S. Department of Commerce 1991a).

With eight out of every 10 state residents living in metropolitan areas, Washington's population was the second most urban of the four states. Washington contains nine MSAs, three of which are east of the Cascade Mountains (Richland-Kennewick-Pasco, Spokane, and Yakima). Those three MSAs grew modestly in population (less than 10 percent) during the 1980s, while the other six MSAs grew significantly (approximately 20 percent or more). Washington has 39 counties (see Map 1.4), 12 of which are located in MSAs.

Table 1.1. 1990 Population, Land Area, and Population Density: Florida, Georgia, Oregon, and Washington

State	Population	Land Area (square miles)	Density (persons per square mile)
Florida	12,937,926	53,997.1	239.6
Georgia	6,478,216	57,918.7	111.9
Oregon	2,842,321	96,002.6	29.6
Washington	4,866,692	66,581.9	73.1

Source: U. S. Department of Commerce, Economics and Statistics Administration, Bureau of the Census (August, 1991b). 1990 Census of Population and Housing. Summary Population and Housing Characteristics. Florida (CPH-1-11), Georgia (CPH-1-12), Oregon (CPH-1-39), and Washington (CPH-1-49). Table 15. Land Area and Population Density, 1990.

Table 1.2. Metropolitan Area Population, 1970-1990: Florida, Georgia, Oregon, and Washington

	Population in Metropolitan Areas				Percent Change	
State	1990	Percentage of total state population	1980	1970	1980-1990	1970-1980
Florida	11,754,000	90.8	8,884,000	6,213,000	32.3	43.0
Georgia	4,212,000	65.0	3,403,000	2,807,000	23.8	21.2
Oregon	1,947,000	68.5	1,763,000	1,415,000	10.4	24.6
Washington	3,976,000	81.7	3,322,000	2,752,000	19.7	20.7

Note: Population figures rounded to the nearest 1,000 by the original source.

Source: U. S. Department of Commerce, Economics and Statistics Administration, Bureau of the Census (August 1991a). *State and metropolitan data book 1991* (4th ed.). Table E.

Table 1.3. Population, 1980-1990, and Land Area: Metropolitan Statistical Areas in Florida, Georgia, Oregon, and Washington

Metropolitan Statistical Area	Land Area (square miles)	Population 1980	Population 1990	Percent Change, 1980-1990, metropolitan area	Percent Change, 1980-1990, outside central city
Florida					
Bradenton, FL	741.2	148,445	211,707	42.6	42.0
Daytona Beach, FL	1,105.9	258,762	330,762	43.3	52.8
Fort Lauderdale-Hollywood-Pompano Beach, FL PMSA	1,208.9	1,018,257	1,255,488	23.3	34.0
Fort Myers-Cape Coral, FL	803.6	205,266	335,113	63.3	58.4
Fort Pierce, FL	1,128.2	151,196	251,071	66.1	82.5
Fort Walton Beach, FL	935.8	109,920	143,776	30.8	37.3
Gainesville, FL	1,167.5	171,392	204,111	19.1	32.6
Jacksonville, FL	2,635.7	722,252	906,727	25.5	49.7
Lakeland-Winter Haven, FL	1,874.9	321,652	405,382	26.0	26.0
Melbourne-Titusville-Palm Bay, FL	2,767.1	272,959	398,978	46.2	34.9
Miami-Hialeah, FL PMSA	1,944.5	1,625,509	1,937,094	19.2	25.1
Naples, FL	2,025.5	85,971	152,099	76.9	93.9
Ocala, FL	1,579.0	122,488	194,833	59.1	79.1
Orlando, FL	2,537.9	699,906	1,072,748	53.3	58.9
Panama City, FL	763.7	97,740	126,994	29.9	43.8

Table 1.3. Population, 1980-1990, and Land Area: Metropolitan Statistical Areas in Florida, Georgia, Oregon, and Washington (Continued)

Metropolitan Statistical Area	Land Area (square miles)	Population 1980	Population 1990	Percent Change, 1980-1990, metropolitan area	Percent Change, 1980-1990, outside central city
Florida (continued)					
Pensacola, FL	1679.5	289,782	344,406	18.9	23.3
Sarasota, FL	571.8	202,251	277,776	37.3	47.9
Tallahassee, FL	1,183.0	190,329	233,598	22.7	29.3
Tampa-St. Petersburg-Clearwater, FL	2,554.5	1,613,600	2,067,959	28.2	42.6
West Palm Beach-Boca Raton-Delray Beach, FL	2,034.3	576,754	863,518	49.7	60.0
Georgia					
Albany, GA	685.5	112,394	112,561	0.1	16.6
Athens, GA	933.4	130,015	156,267	20.2	26.4
Atlanta, GA	5,121.5	2,138,143	2,833,511	32.5	42.5
Augusta, GA-SC	1,947.0	345,923	396,809	14.7	18.0
Chattanooga, TN-GA	2,090.6	426,443	433,210	1.6	9.3
Columbus, GA-AL	1,106.3	239,196	243,072	1.6	-7.7
Macon-Warner Robins, GA	1,171.7	263,591	281,103	6.6	22.4
Savannah, GA	919.9	220,553	242,622	10.0	33.2
Oregon					
Eugene-Springfield, OR	4,554.2	275,226	282,912	2.8	-1.9
Medford, OR	2,785.4	132,456	146,389	10.5	7.3
Portland, OR PMSA	3,743.0	1,105,750	1,239,842	12.1	19.1

Table 1.3. Population, 1980-1990, and Land Area: Metropolitan Statistical Areas in Florida, Georgia, Oregon, and Washington (Continued)

Metropolitan Statistical Area	Land Area (square miles)	Population 1980	Population 1990	Percent Change, 1980-1990, metropolitan area	Percent Change, 1980-1990, outside central city
Oregon (continued)					
Salem, OR	1,926.1	249,895	278,024	11.3	6.7
Washington					
Bellingham, WA	2120.1	106,701	127,780	19.8	24.1
Bremerton, WA	396.0	147,152	189,731	28.9	36.6
Olympia, WA	727.1	124,264	161,238	29.8	31.6
Richland-Kennewick-Pasco, WA	2,945.3	144,469	150,033	3.9	2.1
Seattle, WA PMSA	4,216.3	1,607,618	1,972,961	22.7	31.0
Spokane, WA	1,763.8	341,835	361,364	5.7	8.0
Tacoma, WA PMSA	1,675.6	485,667	586,203	20.7	25.2
Vancouver, WA PMSA	629.9	192,227	238,053	23.8	28.3
Yakima, WA	4,296.1	172,508	188,823	9.5	9.2

Source: U. S. Department of Commerce, Economics and Statistics Administration, Bureau of the Census (August, 1991a). *State and metropolitan data book 1991* (4th ed.). Table D.

Note

1. A fourth wave was not evident when I wrote my dissertation. As this book goes to press, a fourth wave is clearly evident, beginning with the "smart growth" movement popularized in 1998 (also see Weitz 1999).

Map 1.1. Counties and Selected Places, Florida

Map 1.2. Counties and Selected Places, Georgia

Map 1.3. Counties and Selected Places, Oregon

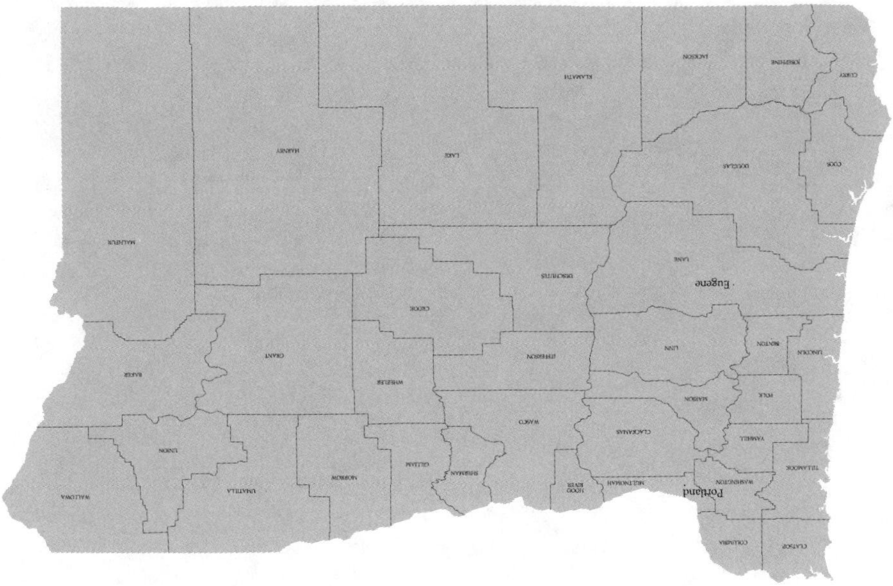

Map 1.4. Counties and Selected Places, Washington

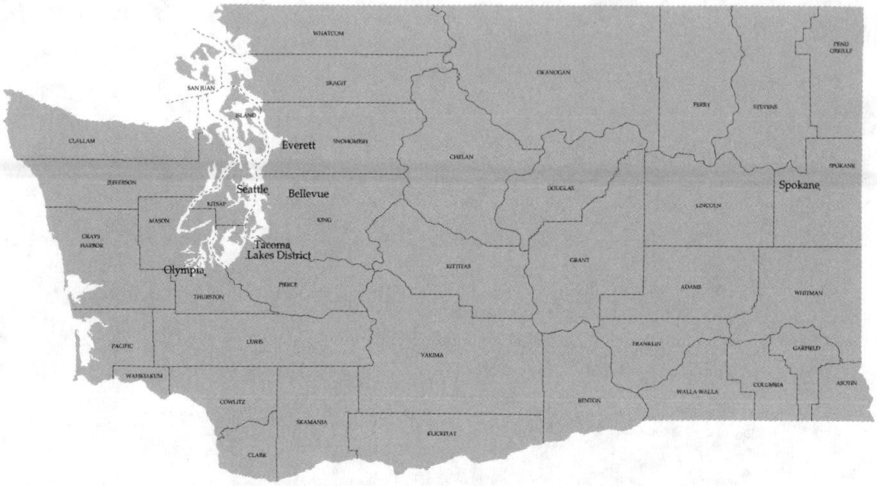

CHAPTER

2

Historical Framework

The organizational framework for presenting a historical narrative of the evolution of state growth management programs is an important consideration. Any historical classification of a subject must be justifiable with respect to the research objectives and the literature that support the inquiry. Before presenting the narrative, I evaluate alternative approaches to organizing the historical narrative and justify use of the framework selected.

AN INITIAL SCHEME FOR CLASSIFYING PERIODS OF GROWTH MANAGEMENT PROGRAM EVOLUTION

I initially proposed to use a framework that included five periods: Before 1972, 1972-1981, 1982-1987, 1988-1992, and 1993-1997. The use of these periods appears to have merit, because they encompass the entire 25-year history of state-sponsored growth management, from adoption to the present, and provide mostly equal units of time (i.e., five-year periods, with the exception of one that covers a decade) that divide the historical narrative into short and manageable time increments. I initially organized and presented the historical information based on that scheme. After preliminary review of the historical narrative organized that way, however, the principal reviewer of this work suggested that I should reconsider the historical classification scheme with respect to its appropriateness given research objectives and available alternatives. That advice prompted me to critique the initial historical classification scheme, identify purposes of the historical framework, formulate alternatives for organizing the historical narrative, review literature for guidance, and select an alternative for organizing and presenting the historical narrative.

CRITIQUE OF THE INITIAL HISTORICAL CLASSIFICATION SCHEME

A primary consideration in presenting historical information is that the organization has to be logical for the case studies included in the research. The only distinction that appears to be essential is the division between the two eras during which state growth management programs were adopted (i.e., Florida and Oregon during the quiet revolution of the early 1970s and Georgia and Washington in the late 1980s and early 1990s). The division of state growth management program history into first and second waves is pervasive in the state growth management literature (DeGrove 1993, 1992, 1989; DeGrove and Metzger 1993; Fulton 1991, 1989; Meeks 1990; Niebanck 1986).

I discovered some gaps in the story of state growth management program evolution. For example, little state growth management program activity occurred in Washington between 1977 and 1988, at least as evidenced in the literature. A rigid application of my proposal for organization might force me into researching unimportant periods just to "fill in the gaps." Furthermore, I hoped for an alternative to the rather monotonous, period-by-period framework for organization. Surely, I could find a more interesting way to deliver the historical narrative, I suspected. After constructing an initial five-category proposal, I discovered that there was no clear rationale for the classification based on context and themes important to the subject inquiry, so I began a search for information that would help me construct a better historical framework.

THE SEARCH FOR AN ALTERNATIVE HISTORICAL FRAMEWORK

One alternative for organizing the historical narrative is to tell the stories of program evolution by individual states in separate chapters. Such an approach has been popular with DeGrove (1992, 1984) and avoids the "back and forth" nature of a simultaneous, comparative method. Separate chapters of program evolution by state, however, would necessitate a fifth chapter that wove the evolution of programs of individual states into a unifying perspective. I rejected this alternative, because my main purpose is to draw conclusions at different points in time that cut across all four states. Only a simultaneous, comparative approach can satisfy that objective.

While a historical classification scheme must be logical for all four states included, it also should be consistent with program evolution in the universe of growth management states. For example, 1969 is a watershed year in the quiet revolution because the states of Maine and Vermont adopted legislation (as did Oregon with Senate Bill 10 and Florida with its earliest planning statute) involving statewide land use control (Mann and Miles 1979). I considered reviewing the literature of other growth management states and selecting a historical classification scheme that represented the "best fit" for describing all state growth management programs, but that task would draw me away from a focus on four states.[1] Furthermore, I feared that such additional research was likely to reveal only what other scholars of state growth management programs already have concluded—that first and second waves of program evolution exist. Nonetheless, the historical framework must be logical with respect to the universe of state growth management programs unless histories of the four state programs specifically dictate that the classification deviate from that found in the literature.

A framework for state growth management program evolution might be found in the policy analysis literature. The historical narrative might be organized on the basis of distinctive steps in the policymaking process (e.g., a softening-up period, adoption of statute, implementation, policy reformulation, and so forth). The policy analysis literature is relevant to my research, and the policymaking process certainly has an influence on the choice of organizing the historical narrative. A literature review of the policy analyst's perspective to support the historical framework, however, would unnecessarily depart from my research objectives.

The historical classification scheme could be based on analyses of various contexts important to the inquiry. Several contextual realms have influenced other scholars of planning and public policy and could be considered, such as the national political environment (e.g., states as subsets of national policymaking), changes in approaches to federalism (e.g., intergovernmental relations under the Reagan Administration), and the evolution of planning practice and theory and their influence on state growth management programs (e.g., the American Law Institute's *Model Land Development Code*). Because this idea sounded promising, I sought additional guidance from literature to help determine a historical classification scheme that would be, if possible, more accommodating of these contextual realms.

To describe the evolution of state growth management programs according to historical periods, Doug Porter's (1989) research agenda suggests a comparison of phase I (1970 to 1976) and phase II (1980 to 1988). The 1970-1976 period also is similar to DeGrove's (1989) identification of the first wave of growth management as the 1970 to 1975 period. Given the passage of time, Porter's suggestion if nothing else needs to be updated. I also found it puzzling that Porter did not account for all years of state growth management program implementation—he omitted 1977-1979 from his recommended eras of comparison. With all due respect to Porter, who has to be considered the dean of local growth managers, I could not initially accept his scheme because it did not include certain years. After my own research, however, I agree that there is a good reason to confirm Porter's historical classification and exclude 1977-1979: The only significant activity during that period (which I call an interlude) was in Florida and Oregon. Florida adopted an advisory state plan and amendments to the state planning act (1978); Oregon's program continued with modifications, but no landmark legislation was adopted. A whisper of activity is noted in Washington during the period. State-sponsored land use planning did not exist between 1977 and 1979 in Georgia, and it appears to have been in a period of dormancy elsewhere. I initially discarded Porter's framework because of its lack of comprehensiveness, but given the dormancy of growth management during this interlude, I subsequently concluded it would be prudent to accept Porter's scheme and build on it to include activities in subsequent years. Before I could fully accept Porter's scheme, however, I needed to review other literature that classifies the history of growth management programs.

Stuart Meck, principal investigator for the American Planning Association's Growing Smart℠ program, provides a short history of state planning and zoning enabling legislation that is also useful in determining key dates for classifying state growth management program evolution (Meck 1996). Meck's narrative is especially important with respect to its discussion of events in the 1960s. Although he does not specify a historical framework per se, Frank Popper's (1989; 1988) discourse provides additional insight into classifying periods of land use regulation. The works of McDowell (1986) and the American Planning Association

(1996a; 1989) also are useful in determining the status of state, regional, and local planning during different periods. The following sections of planning history are included to help justify selection of the historical framework. These sections attempt to build a description of various planning contexts within which the reader can view the evolution of (and change in) state-sponsored land use planning. The following sections are important also because they set up a summary of themes in the evolution of state growth management that are then carried into subsequent chapters.

Regional planning in the 1960s

The year 1965 was a landmark for metropolitan and multistate regionalism. The Housing and Urban Development Act of 1965 made councils of governments eligible for planning funds. Regional economic development commissions also were established in 1965. The 1960s was an important decade in the evolution of metropolitan planning agencies, which were tapped by legislation in 1966 and by the administration in 1968 (Office of Management and Budget Circular A-95) to review and comment on development projects in areas funded with federal grants (McDowell 1986).

Recommendations for state planning in the 1960s

The American Society of Planning Officials' *New Directions in Connecticut Planning Legislation* (1966) contained one of the first recommendations to give state and regional planning agencies authority to review local plans. A survey of state planning one year later reported that 40 states had assigned local planning assistance to state planning agencies and 35 state agencies had performed local planning assistance activities (Beyle, Seligson and Wright 1969). The National Commission on Urban Problems (also known as the Douglas Commission) published a report titled *Building the American City* (1968), which recommended a state requirement for a local development guidance program and establishment of a state agency for development planning and review. Also in 1968, several private and federally funded studies called for reforms of existing land use planning and regulatory systems. By the late 1960s, the United States had enough experience with land use regulation to be critical of flaws (Meck 1996).

Land use planning and regulation in the 1970s

State, regional, and local planning practices have an influence on the choice of a historical classification scheme. If the content and scope of local comprehensive plans fall into distinct time divisions, then such divisions might need to be incorporated into the historical framework. By the late 1960s, a new set of environmental problems had come into being because of rapid urbanization, and local governments were relatively powerless to solve such problems. Healy (1983, 237) finds that 1971 was the year when a new environmental focus came to dominate land use planning thought; the 1970s are aptly called the "environmental decade." American land use regulation began to be centralized at regional, state, and federal government levels in the early 1970s. There was a burgeoning regulatory environment at the federal level, including the 1969 National Environmental Policy Act, 1970 Clean Air Act, 1972 Clean Water Act, and the 1972 Coastal Zone Management Act, among others. A National Land Use Policy bill was introduced every year between 1968 and 1975. In 1974, the Senate passed a land use act by a wide margin, but the House rejected it by seven votes (Popper 1989, 1988; McDowell 1986).

At the state level, between 1965 and 1975, at least 20 states had new environmentally oriented land use laws, and 37 states had new programs of statewide planning or regulation at the regional level (Popper 1988). McDowell (1986) recognizes 1965 to 1975 as a distinct period in the evolution of state planning. The literature on state and regional growth management also blossomed during the early 1970s; a notable, representative example is *The Quiet Revolution in Land Use Control* (Bosselman and Callies 1971). The excitement of the land use community in the early 1970s, including the near-passage of federal land use legislation, probably helped to stimulate adoption of state growth management laws in Florida (1972) and Oregon (1973) and attempts to pass planning laws in Georgia and Washington during that time (Popper 1988).

Although not published in final form until 1976, the *Model Land Development Code* (American Law Institute 1974) represented a critical rethinking of American planning law. Drafts of Article 7 of the code, state land development regulation, were influential in designing growth management programs in Florida and Oregon years before the model code was finally published. The quiet revolution in land use control appears to have ended rather abruptly in the mid-1970s when the national land use bill was not revived. By 1976, all states had some type of overall state-coordinated planning, and public administration theory specified that planning was an important management function of governors (McDowell 1986). Hence, McDowell's discussion confirms 1975 or 1976 as a year of demarcation (i.e., the end of an important period).

By the 1970s, several new ideas had "taken root" in the "stalwart family tree" of urban land use planning (Kaiser and Godschalk 1995). The land use design was a descendant of the general plan concept that was pervasive in the 1950s and 1960s (see Kent 1990). The land classification plan, or a general map of growth policy areas, was already in existence by 1961 in Hawaii. The land classification plan evolved further, however, in the 1970s on the basis of Ian McHarg's *Design With Nature* (1969) and Oregon's land use law (1973), with its requirement to draw urban growth boundaries (Kaiser and Godschalk 1995).

Influence of the Reagan Administration in the 1980s

The early 1980s is another break point in the evolution of state and regional planning, or better yet, a new beginning as Porter's historical framework implies. The year 1981 appears to be a watershed: "701" planning assistance from the U.S. Department of Housing and Urban Development ended, and "Title II" multistate river basin commissions were abolished. Federal regional councils were abolished in 1983 (McDowell 1986). A critique by the President's Commission on Housing (1982) of overregulation by local government provides another example of the new federal context that evolved under the Reagan Administration (Meck 1996). In its early years the Reagan Administration emphasized cutting regulation and rolling authority back to the states, a change that represented the beginning of a profound shift in the federal public policy milieu. The federal context undoubtedly had some influence on the evolution of state growth management programs. Lacking federal grants-in-aid and given the Reagan Administration's unfavorable view of regulation, the early 1980s in the United States were certainly not an incubator time period for new local, regional, and state land use regulation. Indeed, state land use reform efforts briefly subsided in the early 1980s (Burby and May 1997), and substate regionalism went into a period of decline (Bowman and Franke 1984).

Planning practice in the 1980s

The environmentally based land use paradigm of the 1970s ran out of steam in the early 1980s (Healy 1983), and it appears that new approaches and concepts replaced the emphasis on the environment. Peter Hall (1988) finds the 1980-1989 period was characterized by "ecologically conscious NIMBYism." Both Healy and Hall therefore seem to echo Porter's (1989) suggestion that 1980 to 1988 is an appropriate period for studying state growth management programs. Characterizations of 1980s land use planning practice also suggest that the 1980s is a distinctive period in growth management history.

Frank So (1984) finds that as early as 1970, the field of planning abandoned the traditional map-oriented planning model. Other scholars find that during the 1960s city planning departments began to give up the traditional planning document in favor of policy plans (Hollander and colleagues 1988). The shift in emphasis on policy over maps appears even stronger, however, in the 1980s, when local planners responded to Harvey Perloff's (1980) call for policy plans, rather than the mapped, end-state versions popularized earlier. The emphasis on policy rather than physical plans represented an important shift in planning practice. Shorter-range (three- to 10-year) development management plans, which have roots in the environmental and state growth management movements, also became popular during the 1980s because of their emphasis on specific courses of action. Hence, two variations of urban land use plans—policy plans and development management plans—garnered strength during the 1980s (Kaiser and Godschalk 1995; Kaiser, Godschalk and Chapin 1995).

Other important changes that occurred by the 1980s: the recognition that local land use decisions, especially those regarding locally unwanted land uses ("LULUs") (Popper 1981), have regional and statewide effects; a growing awareness of abandoned properties, underused infrastructure and the need for infill and redevelopment in central cities and suburbs; and a growing partnership between state and local governments (Gage 1990; Hall 1989; DeGrove 1983; Healy 1983; Popper 1981). Furthermore, the introduction of strategic plans and specific (rather than general) plans signaled significant changes in local planning practice during the 1980s (Bryson and Einsweiler 1988; Cornish 1987). The advent of computer-aided drafting and design and geographic information systems during the 1980s ensured that traditional land use mapping functions would maintain their ascendancy (Zotti

1987; Castle 1986). Negotiation, mediation, and dispute resolution techniques began to be incorporated into planning practice.

New planning directions in the 1990s

The founding of the National Growth Management Leadership Project by 1000 Friends of Oregon in 1989 signaled an increase in attention paid to comprehensive planning at the state level. The American Planning Association's "Growing Smart" program, which began in 1994, represented another important example of an emerging new wave of interest in statewide comprehensive planning (Salkin 1993). Adoption by Congress of the Clean Air Act Amendments of 1990 and the Intermodal Surface Transportation Efficiency Act of 1991 represented a watershed in American planning history. Federal legislation in the early 1990s set the stage for a new era of integrated transportation and land use planning (Jeff 1996). Local and regional agencies across the country (Freilich and White 1996), especially those in Oregon (Adler 1994; Moore and Thorsnes 1994), have responded to the call for making the transportation and land use link (Kelly 1994). Urban land use planning practice in the 1990s also has been characterized by the preparation of hybrid plans encompassing design, policy, and management. Technological advances in the applications of geographic information systems during the 1990s helped tie land use design plans, land classifications systems, and policy plans together (Kaiser and Godschalk 1995).

Visioning exercises also have found favor in local planning processes during the 1990s in the Atlanta region (Helling 1998), Maryland (Callies 1994), Oregon (Ames 1993), and elsewhere. Applications of best development practices (Ewing 1996) and efforts to encourage livable, sustainable communities are hallmarks of 1990s planning practice. Publication of recent model approaches to state planning (American Planning Association 1996a, 1996b) and local regulation (Freilich and Schultz 1995) indicates some renewed interest in land use reform that perhaps has not existed since the early enthusiastic use of the draft *Model Land Development Code*. Though it emerged in the 1970s and was firmly entrenched by the 1980s, fiscal impact analysis appears to have gained additional prominence in 1990s planning practice (Bunnell 1997; Burchell 1993). Finally, program evaluation, via benchmarking and other effectiveness measurement tools, has been applied increasingly to growth management and planning programs during the third wave (Oregon Progress Board 1994; Burby and colleagues 1993). Hence, the developing intersection of growth management with the field of policy evaluation (Weitz and Moore 1998; Baer 1997; Burby and May 1997; Talen 1996a, 1996b; Berke and French 1994; Burby and Dalton 1994; Burby and colleagues 1993; Dalton 1990; Alexander and Faludi 1989) represents another important characteristic of a third wave in state growth management program history.

Summary

The literature shows that the quiet revolution was being planned and started to evolve between 1965 and 1970. It erupted around 1970 and then abruptly ended by 1976. A short period of relative dormancy followed (1977-1979). The election and initiation of the Reagan Administration in 1980-1981 marked a change in the climate for state and regional planning. Federal regulation, new planning tools and techniques, new programs of growth management leadership, and efforts to reform state planning enabling statutes in the early 1990s mark the beginning of yet another era in state and regional planning.

SELECTION OF A HISTORICAL CLASSIFICATION SCHEME

Events in the four states must take precedence over general historical classification schemes. In fact, the state with the most complex history tends to dictate the organizational scheme selected. John DeGrove (1989) identifies the first-wave period of growth management history in Florida as occurring between 1972 and 1975. Allan Wallis (1993) divides Florida's growth management history into first and second waves, the second wave beginning in 1982 with the appointment of the Environmental Land Management Study II. Wallis's historical classification scheme appears to have gained acceptance only by a minority of scholars.

Other scholars describe growth management in Florida according to three major periods: the pre-1975 responding period; the 1975-1985 implementing and reassessing period; and the post-1985 comprehensive system period (Liou and Dicker 1994; DeGrove 1991, 1989; Turner, 1990a). This historical classification scheme generally fits the evolution of growth management in the state with the most complex history, matches the historical accounts of the quiet revolution, and appears to be consistent with changes in land use planning practice. With slight adjustments, the intersection of the Florida program historical classification scheme with Porter's framework can be made consistent with all major events in the history of growth management programs in the other three states. All that is left to complete the historical framework is to summarize the modified scheme and use it to describe the evolution of growth management in all four states.

The first period (1969-1976) is the quiet revolution, which has no clearer genesis in the four states than Oregon's Senate Bill 10 (1969). The quiet revolution abruptly ended around 1975-1976, after Florida adopted its local comprehensive planning act (1975) and Oregon adopted its last statewide planning goals (1976). Those are two prominent reasons to designate 1976 as the end of the quiet revolution and thereby apply Porter's recommendation. Because there was very little activity on the growth management front during 1977-1979, that period can be excluded, as Porter's recommended framework implies. The second period of evolution began in 1980 and extended through 1988, again consistent with Porter's recommended framework and also corresponding with the Reagan Administration's influence. In the end, the historical classification scheme I have chosen simply builds on Porter's (1989) framework by adding a third period (1989-1997), which includes 1990s-style adoption and implementation of growth management programs in Georgia and Washington. In the concluding chapter, I also identify signs of a fourth wave of state growth management program history.

ORGANIZATION OF THE HISTORICAL NARRATIVE

Each of the three periods (1969-1976, 1980-1988, and 1989-1997) is presented in its own chapter (3, 4, and 5, respectively). The information presented in those three chapters is purposefully limited to description. The narratives are organized chronologically because such an organization enables the comparison of state programs and their status during different periods. The historical account places emphasis on the following features: state, regional, and local planning and related legislation, whether successful or unsuccessful; the status of local planning; and state implementation experience.

Growth management activity in the four states does not suggest the existence of a distinct period before 1969; state planning legislation was not significant in any of the four states. Important regional planning activities, however, occurred during the 1960s that deserve inclusion in the discussion of the quiet revolution. Therefore, major regional planning events are included in Chapter 3. Planning enabling legislation in the four states also is described to some extent in Chapter 3, because such laws establish the legal framework for planning and land use regulation. Attention is paid to the influence of the *Model Land Development Code* and the extent to which it has been used by legislative committees and program designers. I attempt to provide an overarching view of the evolution of state, regional, and local planning that serves as a springboard for more specific analyses. Conclusions about the evolution of planning in the four states, the status of local plans, and how the states compare are provided at the end of the historical narratives in Chapters 3, 4, and 5.

At this point, I have only descriptive (i.e., what?) questions in mind: What growth management legislation was adopted in the four states? What types of conferences and study commissions preceded or followed legislation? Once growth management laws were passed, what was required to implement the laws, and how did state implementing officials occupy their time? What are the most important characteristics of the three major program components (structure, standards, and support) of state-sponsored land use planning at the state, regional, and local levels? As state growth management programs evolved during the three eras, what are the program characteristics that distinguish growth management practice from earlier eras? What was the status of local plans, and how satisfied were state implementing officials with the results obtained? Those are the principal descriptive questions that frame the narratives in the next three chapters.

SUMMARY OF PROGRAM EVOLUTION AND CHANGE

Here, I provide an overview of the findings, themes, and conclusions presented in Chapters 3, 4, and 5. The description of contextual realms provided earlier in this chapter has set up this discussion of evolution and dynamics. Each subsection introduces a theme and highlights distinctive activities within each of the three waves of state growth management program history. These evolutionary themes become more apparent as one reads the next three chapters on program history.

Influence of the *Model Land Development Code*

The American Law Institute's model code was highly influential before its final publication in 1976, and remnants of the model remain in at least two of the four state growth management programs today. The model code was used specifically in designing first-wave growth management programs in Florida and Oregon. In the third wave, Georgia's program implemented two major programs recommended by the model code: areas of critical state concern (called regionally important resources in that state) and developments of regional impact (DRIs). Washington did not follow the model code but instead put in place its own unique, 1990s-style approaches to addressing critical areas and regional impacts. While Florida's DRI program suffered some during the third wave, the legacy of the model code remains to some extent in the four states.

State mandate designs and the status of local planning

I seek to determine the status of local comprehensive planning during the three waves of state growth management program history. The local comprehensive plan is, in essence, the centerpiece of each of the four state growth management programs and is thus the focus of much attention in the three chapters that follow. The story of local planning based on state mandates is clear. Florida and Oregon instituted "coercive"-type state mandate designs for local comprehensive planning, and they had their difficulties during the quiet revolution. Local planning took much longer in these states than expected, and both Florida and Oregon experienced local compliance problems. Local plans did not get produced as quickly as program designers had hoped. The quality of local plans produced and their relationships with state and regional plans were considered substandard. Florida's and Oregon's programs during the quiet revolution lacked sets of standards that outlined the states' expectations for the content and substance of local comprehensive plans. In short, Florida and Oregon experienced both compliance delays and consistency problems. Despite these lessons of the quiet revolution, second-wave modifications to state mandate designs appear to have been equally overambitious with respect to compliance deadlines.

The second wave of state growth management program evolution is characterized by the adoption of state standards via administrative rules, as a way to further enunciate statutory goals and intentions, and by increased favor for technical assistance and capacity-building approaches over the continuation of coercion-based approaches. During the 1980s, Florida developed standards for local plans, and Oregon gradually put in place a complex set of statutes, rules, goals, guidelines, decisions, and interpretations to guide the development of local comprehensive plans and development regulations.

When Georgia and Washington joined Florida and Oregon as growth management states during the third wave of program history, some of the same problems with respect to local compliance with planning mandates continued. Local plan compliance seems to have improved, however, based in part on mandate designs that favored (or at least included, in Washington's case) capacity- and commitment-building features and formal programs of technical assistance. That is, it appears that designers of third-wave programs learned from Florida and Oregon—they limited application of the coercive approach in favor of an empowerment strategy. Although neither Georgia nor Washington has been entirely successful, the third-wave-style approaches have achieved faster compliance records than Florida and Oregon attained initially. The faster rate of compliance, however, has come with its own setbacks and compromises, as the reader will see. Over time, state growth management programs in the four states have relied less on the consistency doctrine or have at least relaxed (in the cases of Florida and Oregon) interpretations of consistency requirements.

Public facilities planning

While my principal interest is land use planning, public facilities planning has become one of the more emphasized elements of both comprehensive planning and state growth management program designs. As numerous scholars (particularly DeGrove 1991) have noted, the quiet revolution was dominated by an interest in protecting the environment. During the second and third waves of program evolution, however, state interest in assuring adequate public facilities to accommodate development at the local level increased progressively. Oregon's program was modified during the second wave to be more accommodating to economic development and to provide support (via the provision of urban land served with public facilities) for new urban growth. Florida's well-known concurrency mandate was established in the mid-1980s.

Third-wave state growth management programs reflect greater understanding of the important interrelationship between public facilities and land use. Washington exhibited attention to public facilities planning with its mandate for local governments to implement transportation concurrency and capital improvement programs. Besides fine-tuning its concurrency requirements, Florida modified its growth management laws in the 1990s to strengthen intergovernmental coordination elements (ICEs) of local plans. Oregon also strengthened its growth management program with respect to public facilities and intergovernmental service delivery with new statutory provisions in the 1990s. Statutes and activities in Georgia during the 1990s also confirm that public facilities and intergovernmental service delivery issues have gained a significant amount of attention in the coordinated planning program.

Regional planning

My research confirms that the 1960s were the heyday of federal- and state-sponsored substate regionalism in the four states. Nationally, regional planning went through a period of decline and identity crisis during the second wave, only to rebound under the rubric of governance and problem solving in the 1990s. (For a literature review of regional planning, see Weitz and Seltzer 1998.)

Georgia was an early leader in regional planning, and metropolitan and regional planning of some variation were strong in each of the four states before the quiet revolution. Florida's mandate designers instituted substate regional planning as part of its growth management program during the quiet revolution, while Oregon's lawmakers attempted but then compromised away a multicounty regional planning proposal in adopting Senate Bill 100. During the second wave, within the context of the Reagan Administration's influence, substate regional planning declined. During this time, however, Florida retained its regional planning councils and even reinvigorated them as an integral component of state-sponsored land use planning.

Land use monitoring and information systems

During the quiet revolution, state growth management programs placed surprisingly little emphasis on standards for classifying land uses, although Hawaii's land classification is an important exception. Washington's failed legislative attempt during the early 1970s is another exception; the State Land Planning Commission recommended a statewide land information data base that was never developed. During the early 1980s, there was a growing understanding of the importance of land supply monitoring and land information systems for planning. In Oregon, that understanding was stimulated in part by an economic recession and changes to statutes requiring public facilities plans and inventories of industrial lands. In Oregon and Georgia, during the early years of the second wave, there were calls for the creation of state-sponsored land information systems. Those calls went unanswered. Only Georgia's third-wave program contains a program component to produce a statewide planning database using geographic information systems. In the Pacific Northwest, permit streamlining was a more pressing task during the second wave in Oregon and during the third-wave period in Washington.

Urban sprawl and livable communities

Each of the four states had some general concerns about urban form during the quiet revolution, though only Oregon and Florida acted legislatively to address those concerns. Concern over the costs of urban sprawl was a central issue that surfaced along with the quiet revolution of the early 1970s. Each state had single-purpose environmental mandates, and Florida, Oregon, and Washington were all pioneers with respect to environmental statutes. Florida and Oregon adopted land use programs with the objectives of environmental protection more than the goal of compact urban form. Oregon's urban containment strategy, however, was highly advanced in that it served to achieve multiple objectives of protecting farm and forest lands and containing urbanization while purportedly minimizing public service costs.

The rampage of land development in the Sunbelt and the Pacific Northwest during the 1980s and 1990s brought new attention to problems of urban sprawl and to land use planning as a mechanism for mitigating undesirable growth patterns. Florida revamped its program in the 1980s to better address urban sprawl. Washington developed a third-wave program that enunciated the goal of preventing sprawl. Oregon redirected its program emphasis during the third wave of program evolution to promote improved urban growth management, livable communities, and integrated transportation and land use planning. Georgia's program remains relatively silent with respect to urban sprawl and does not suggest that there are desirable patterns of development (though the Growth Strategies Reassessment Task Force recommended in December 1998 that the state should enunciate desirable patterns of development). All four states have addressed to some extent the question of how livable their urban areas are or at least have pondered the extent to which they are achieving smart development goals.

Program reexamination and assessment

To its credit, Florida is the only one of the four states that has institutionalized a continuous assessment and monitoring system as part of its growth management program. The three Environmental Land Management Study Committees (ELMS) and other examples, cited in the chapters that follow, clearly indicate that Florida's planners and lawmakers engaged in examinations of their state growth management program. What is more important, Florida's lawmakers acted on those assessments and modified their growth management program accordingly. Florida added to its valuable reassessment institution (i.e., ELMS) with studies of the costs of urban development patterns and other assessment efforts during the third wave of program history.

Oregon, after initiating its land use program during the quiet revolution, did relatively little to fine-tune or otherwise redesign its system. There are some examples of critical re-examination and program evaluations in Oregon that occurred during the second wave of state growth management program history. Those efforts, however, were largely either ignored or unfunded. The third wave, however, brought major new attention to program evaluation in Oregon, with urban growth management studies, benchmarking by the Oregon Progress Board, and related efforts. Washington has not necessarily equaled Florida's efforts but has attempted to build assessment and monitoring tasks into its growth management program. Georgia's program designers have not specifically integrated monitoring into their program, but weaker signs of attention to monitoring are nevertheless apparent in that state. Hence, an accumulating understanding of the need for program evaluation is a characteristic of the third wave of state growth management program history.

I now move to the task of telling the stories of growth management program evolution and change in the four states.

Note

1. Based on a literature review of all state growth management programs (Weitz 1999), I conclude that the four-wave classification fits reasonably well. When looking at all the relevant states, however, I believe the classification's weakest feature is its sharp distinction between the end of the second wave and the beginning of the third. Other scholars have determined that programs in Georgia and Washington actually belong to the second wave.

CHAPTER

3

The Quiet Revolution in State-Sponsored Planning: 1969-1976

At the beginning of the quiet revolution in 1969, only Oregon (via Senate Bill 10) had adopted a state requirement that local governments prepare and adopt land use plans. Florida also had a land use planning statute in 1969, but it was not implemented. Florida adopted legislation to manage land and water resources and prepare a state plan (1972) and to require local government planning (1975). Georgia led other states in regional planning during the 1960s, passed metropolitan river protection (1972), and attempted but failed to pass critical areas (1973) and vital areas legislation (1974). Oregon passed its Land Conservation and Development Act (1973), established regional planning in the Portland metropolitan area (1973), and adopted statewide planning goals (1974-1976). Washington created a State Land Use Commission (1971), passed a Shorelines Management Act (1971), and prepared but failed to pass mandatory land use legislation (1973).

Figure 3.1 provides a summary of major legislation and events during the quiet revolution in the four states.

FLORIDA

Before the quiet revolution, the Florida state government's interest in land use was focused on promoting development, not restricting or

Figure 3.1. Study Committees, Activities, and Legislation, 1960-1976

	1960.......... 1965 .... 1970.......... 1975
Florida	County and Municipal Planning for Future Development (1969)
	Governor's Conference on Water Management in South Florida (1971)
	Governor's Task Force on Resource Management (1971)
	Environmental Land and Water Act (1972); Comprehensive Planning Act (1972); Land Conservation Act (1972); Water Resources Act (1972)
	Florida 2000 Governor's Conference on Growth and the Environment (1973)
	Local Government Comprehensive Planning Act (failed 1974) (1975)
Georgia	Atlanta Region Metropolitan Planning Commission Act (1960)
	Area Planning and Development Commissions (APDCs) formed (1960)
	APDCs redrawn to include entire state (1970)
	Atlanta Regional Commission established (1971)
	Metropolitan River Protection Act (1972)
	Governor's Planned Growth Commission (1973)
	Critical Areas Act (failed 1973)
	Vital Areas Council established (1974)

Figure 3.1. Study Committees, Activities, and Legislation, 1960-1976 (Continued)

	1960 .... 1965 .... 1970 1975
Oregon	Columbia Region Association of Governments formed (1967)
	Conference on Future Land Use in the Willamette Valley (1967)
	Senate Bill 10 (1969)
	Coastal Conservation and Development Commission (1971)
	Senate Bill 100 (1973)
	Senate Bill 769 (CRAG) (1973)
	LCDC's statewide planning goals adopted (1974)
	LCDC's coastal goals adopted (1976)
	Report of the Joint Legislative Committee on Land Use (1976)
Washington	Regional Conferences authorized (1965)
	State Land Planning Commission created (1971)
	Initiative 43, Shorelines drafted (1971)
	Shorelines Management Act (1971)
	Land Development Control and Planning Act (failed 1973)

Source: Compiled by the author from various sources as referenced in the text.

managing it. The state had a century-long policy of promoting growth (Kelly 1993, 113). "No one gave a tinker's damn about growth in Florida until 1971" (McCahill 1974, 211). It had done little to stimulate localities to adopt land use regulations. It was one of the last states to extend zoning powers to local governments, and counties in Florida lacked land use regulatory authority as late as 1967.

The state's growth promotion policy changed at the beginning of the quiet revolution when the legislature passed 41 environmental protection bills (Wallis 1993) and in 1969 passed local planning legislation. Before the quiet revolution, Florida's law contained only single-purpose, environment-focused programs. Florida eventually determined that its piecemeal approach to environment and growth would not suffice and moved to the forefront of state growth management during the quiet revolution (Burby and May 1997, 48-50, 65).

Early planning legislation (1969)

Florida's legislature kicked off the quiet revolution in 1969 when it enacted a statute (County and Municipal Planning for Future Development, Florida Statutes Chapter 163) that provided for local planning and zoning programs. The 1969 legislation left to local government discretion whether planning and zoning programs would be implemented. Adoption of a comprehensive plan was a prerequisite to implementing a local zoning program, but the local comprehensive plans were virtually ignored because of the act's weak consistency requirement.

Regional planning

During the 1960s in Florida, four multicounty regional planning agencies were organized as voluntary councils of elected officials. The regional planning agencies had only advisory authority. Funding came from Title, I, Section 701, of the U.S. Housing Act of 1954, and from city and county matching contributions. Regional planning in Florida was given a boost by the Environmental Land and Water Management Act of 1972 (discussed below), which required guidelines to review and evaluate developments of regional impact (DRIs).

Since only four multicounty regional planning agencies existed, the Division of State Planning (part of the Department of Administration) assisted or coerced all counties to form 10 regional planning councils (RPCs) to implement the 1972 law's provisions. RPCs had limited authority to review local plans prepared under the Local Government

Comprehensive Planning Act of 1975 (discussed below) but had few resources, and no regional plans existed to facilitate regional review of local plans. After the 1975 act, the major role for RPCs continued to be review of DRIs; this development review authority gave RPCs important power and a real presence in the state planning program. For various reasons over the years, boundaries were adjusted to include 11 rather than 10 RPCs (Starnes 1993, 77-78, 82-83).

Governor's Conference on Water Management in South Florida (1971)

A major step toward state involvement began with Gov. Reubin Askew's call in 1971 for a conference (chaired by John DeGrove) on land and water management (Burby and May 1997, 50; Starnes 1993, 78; Wallis 1993, 1; Healy and Rosenberg 1979, 132-133; Carter 1974, 125; McCahill 1974). The Governor's Conference on Water Management in South Florida in 1971 was an important event in Florida's efforts to manage land and water resources. The conference issued a report that called for limits on population densities in the south Florida region and proposed a comprehensive policy framework at the state and regional levels. The carrying capacity concept of land use was the foundation of the conference's recommendations. Also in 1971, the governor appointed a Task Force on Resource Management (again headed by John DeGrove) to develop land use control legislation for consideration by the state legislature in 1972 (Burby and May 1997, 50; Wallis 1993, 1-2; DeGrove 1984, 107-108; Carter 1974, 126-127; Myers 1974, 12-13).

Florida considers Hawaii's program and the model code

At this time, only two approaches existed to provide guidance in preparing state legislation: Hawaii's state planning law (1961) and the American Law Institute's draft *Model Land Development Code*. Chicago lawyer Fred Bosselman had experience with both, and Gov. Askew called on Bosselman and other experts to help address the pending growth crisis in Florida (McCahill 1974). Florida rejected Hawaii's approach to statewide zoning on grounds of a lack of institutional capacity. Florida had many more local governments than Hawaii, and the states differed broadly in objectives and physical characteristics. State land classification, like Hawaii's approach, was found to be too time consuming since it would require a state land use plan to implement.

The Governor's Task Force on Resource Management presented draft legislation that included the requirement that local governments prepare comprehensive plans. Askew, however, believed a legislative mandate for local planning was too much for the legislature to take on in one sitting and thus recommended that it be dropped until later. The task force then produced a legislative package of four bills, one of which resembled (with modifications) the "big cases" (Article 7) approach of the *Model Land Development Code* relative to "areas of critical state concern" and "developments of regional impact" (Kelly 1993, 113; Pelham 1993, 1979; Wallis 1993, 3; DeGrove 1984, 109; Healy and Rosenberg 1979, 133; Godschalk 1975; Carter 1974, 131-133). According to McCahill (1974, 212), Bosselman suggested to the committee that the *Model Land Development Code* be used, and "ultimately, they did in fact use Article 7 of the ALI code."

Land and water legislation (1972)

In 1972, the Florida Legislature passed four bills related to land and water management: the Environmental Land and Water Management Act of 1972 (Senate Bill 629–1972 Florida Laws Chapter 72-317–Florida Statutes Chapter 380); the State Comprehensive Planning Act of 1972 (Florida Statutes Chapter 23)[1]; the Land Conservation Act of 1972 (Florida Statutes Chapter 250); and the Water Resources Act of 1972 (Florida Statutes Chapter 373) (Wallis 1993, 3; DeGrove 1984, 110-116; Pelham 1979, 9; Godschalk 1975; Carter 1974, 133; McCahill 1974; Myers 1974, 13). The 1972 legislature also established a study group, the Environmental Land Management Study (ELMS), to suggest further policy directions and get the new environmental land and water management law off the ground (Lawlor 1992; Healy and Rosenberg 1979, 165; Myers 1974, 19).

The Environmental Land and Water Management Act established two programs in the spirit of the *Model Land Development Code*: areas of critical state concern and developments of regional impact. The State Comprehensive Planning Act created a new agency containing a Division of State Planning charged with preparing a long-range comprehensive state plan. The Water Resources Act established the state's five water management districts, and the Land Conservation Act provided for state purchase of sensitive lands (Healy and Rosenberg 1979, 165; Pelham 1979, 152; Wallis 1993, 3).

Status of local planning and zoning (1974-1975)

At the time the Environmental Land and Water Management Act was passed, local governments were "ill-prepared to cope with land and growth-management problems" (DeGrove 1984, 161). DeGrove (1984, 162) cites a 1974 Florida League of Cities survey finding that only 29 of Florida's 67 counties had zoning ordinances, and Carter (1974, 316) cites 1973 ELMS committee findings that 60 percent or more of the state's land area had yet to come under any comprehensive planning program. Similarly, Healy and Rosenberg (1979, 132-133) found that in 1973 fewer than half of the counties exercised land use controls of any kind and more than 50 percent of the state's land area was without local development controls of any kind. Godschalk's (1975) finding that 28 of 67 counties and one-third of the cities in Florida lacked local zoning and subdivision controls appears to conflict with the findings of Carter, Healy and Rosenberg, and the Florida League of Cities relative to the status of county zoning ordinances in Florida.

Environmental Land Management Study (ELMS) and legislative proposals

The Governor's Conference on Water Management in South Florida was so successful as a policy-initiating device that it was convened again in 1973 as the Florida 2000 Governor's Conference on Growth and the Environment (DeGrove 1984, 129). In 1974, ELMS was given a broad mandate to propose legislative changes, to review and comment on the effectiveness of RPCs, and to study almost anything else related to land and water management. The ELMS committee proposed several new laws, including the Local Government Comprehensive Planning Act, which would have required every city and county in Florida to prepare and adopt a comprehensive plan within three years. A 1974 legislative proposal, which would have authorized $50 million in state aid to finance local planning, cleared House and Senate committees but failed to pass the legislature. The defeat of the local comprehensive planning bill, which was the ELMS committee's top priority, came as a surprise (Burby and May 1997, 51; Wallis 1993, 3-4; DeGrove 1984, 123-129; Healy and Rosenberg 1979, 166-167; Healy 1976; Myers 1974, 33).

Local Government Comprehensive Planning Act (1975)

In 1975, the Florida Legislature voted overwhelmingly to adopt the Local Government Comprehensive Planning Act (Florida Statutes §

163.3161 to § 163.3211). The law was based in part on laws passed in 1969 and 1971 (Lawlor 1992). The 1975 act mandated adoption of local comprehensive plans in accordance with statutory requirements no later than July 1, 1979. The 1975 law also removed the state funding for local planning that had been included in the bill prepared in 1974. According to the local plan content requirements of the law, local governments had to complete comprehensive plans containing nine elements (including a future land use element) and satisfying several general requirements. Local land development regulations were required to be consistent with adopted comprehensive plans. The 1975 act, however, allowed local comprehensive plans that did not contain land use maps (Starnes 1993, 82), and local plans developed pursuant to the act varied widely in quality (Burby and May 1997, 51).

Under the 1975 act, the Division of State Planning could review and comment on, but could not change, local plans. If local plans were not completed within four years, however, the Division of State Planning could designate itself as the local planning agency and prepare plans at local expense or have the county plan govern. The division assigned the lead role for regional review of local plans to the newly assembled RPCs. The act did not, however, specify evaluative criteria for review of local plans. Although a consistency requirement was included in the act, local plans did not have to be consistent with the state plan, and regional plans were not required (Pelham 1993, 1979; Wallis 1993, 10; DeGrove and Juergensmeyer 1986).

Status of local planning

The 1975 planning act required 458 local governments (391 municipalities and 67 counties) to plan. Though comprehensive plans were not due until July 1, 1979, by December 1976 DCA had received plans or portions of plans from 26 local governments for state review. Nearly all (370) municipalities met the July 1, 1976, requirement for designating a local planning agency (Florida DCA 1976a). By April 1977, 33 local governments had submitted one or more comprehensive plan elements to the state for review, but only two were submittals of complete comprehensive plans. Also at that time, two counties and 12 cities needed extensions to meet the act's requirements of designating local planning agencies (Florida DCA 1977a).

GEORGIA

Planning enabling legislation and state planning

In 1957, via the Planning and Zoning Enabling Act, Georgia authorized municipal and county planning commissions, conferred zoning powers, and created a state planning commission. The state planning commission was authorized to prepare a general plan for the overall development of the state, including recommendations on the most desirable land use patterns. In 1959, the state planning commission was abolished and its duties transferred to the Department of Commerce. State responsibility for planning shifted to different agencies over time. The State Planning and Programming Bureau, part of the Executive Department, had responsibility for planning functions beginning in 1967. In 1970 this bureau's name changed to the Bureau of State Planning and Community Affairs. It was abolished in 1972 (Kundell, Campbell, Heikoff, et al. 1989, 15-16).

An early leader in regional planning

The 1957 Planning and Zoning Enabling Act also provided for the establishment of Area Planning and Development Commissions (APDCs). One of Georgia's practicing planners notes that Georgia's experience with substate districting originated at least as early as 1946 or 1947, when Atlanta's metropolitan planning commission was established. The commission was supposedly the first publicly supported multicounty planning agency in the United States (DeGrove 1992, 140; Stuebing 1987). Citing work of the Advisory Commission on Intergovernmental Relations, Starnes (1993) notes that in 1959 Georgia became the first state in the nation to organize nonmetropolitan multicounty planning and development agencies. The voluntary approach of 11 counties in the Coosa Valley region of northwest Georgia in 1959 proved successful and served as an example of what might be done throughout the state (Steubing 1987).

In 1960, the Georgia General Assembly passed the Atlanta Region Metropolitan Planning Commission Act, creating the agency that succeeded the Metropolitan Planning Commission and adding three counties to its jurisdiction (DeGrove 1992, 140; West 1992). Kundell and colleagues (1989, 18) indicate that APDCs were created in 1960 and became important sources of technical assistance for cities and counties without planning staffs. In 1961, the state government began providing financial assistance to APDCs on a matching and contract basis (Kundell et al. 1989, 19).

APDCs originally did not include all of Georgia's 159 counties. In 1970, however, the 1957 planning enabling legislation for APDCs was amended to require that APDC boundaries be redrawn to include all counties in the state (DeGrove 1992, 140). In mid-1971, the Georgia State Planning and Community Affairs Policy Board established formal APDC substate district boundaries, recognizing 17 APDCs and the Atlanta Regional Commission (Starnes 1993).[2]

The Atlanta Regional Commission was established under Georgia Laws, 1971, Act 5, with broader powers than the APDCs (DeGrove 1992, 140; West 1992; Kundell et al. 1989, 19). Act 5 of 1971 established the Atlanta Regional Commission as the region's comprehensive planning agency for land use, transportation and other services (DeGrove 1992, 140).

Status of local planning (1970)

Kundell and colleagues (1989) have compiled statistics for planning in Georgia by cities and counties for various years. In 1970, only 20 of Georgia's 159 counties and only 90 of approximately 536 cities reported having comprehensive plans. Zoning ordinances existed in only 48 counties and 75 cities that same year (Kundell et al. 1989, 24).

Metropolitan River Protection Act (1972)

The Metropolitan River Protection Act was passed by the Georgia General Assembly and signed into law by Gov. Jimmy Carter in 1972. The act provided for the Atlanta Regional Commission to prepare a comprehensive plan for a section of the Chattahoochee River corridor and required local government actions to be consistent with the plan as determined by the commission through a review and comment procedure (DeGrove 1992, 141).

Failure of Critical Areas and Vital Areas legislation (1972-1975)

In 1972, the Local Zoning and State Land Use Policy Subcommittee of the House State Planning and Community Affairs Committee found a need for regulation of geographical areas of critical state concern and drafted the Critical Areas Act of 1973 (HB 467). The proposed legislation was introduced in the 1973 session of the Georgia General Assembly and would have designated critical areas along mountain tops and major rivers as well as within 1,000 feet of major highway rights-of-way and interchanges. The State Office of Planning and Budget (OPB) would have been charged with developing standards and guidelines for use of critical areas and review of local government plans. Under the proposed legislation, OPB could prepare, adopt, and enforce its own plan for critical areas if local governments failed to produce acceptable plans. When the 1973 act stalled in committee, supporters succeeded in establishing a Vital Areas Council.

The council drafted the Vital Areas Act of 1974, and a senate version of the bill was introduced in January 1974. Though much less ambitious than the 1973 Critical Areas Act, the 1974 legislation also failed to pass. The State Land Use Subcommittee continued efforts during 1975 but to no avail (Kundell et al. 1989, 88-89).

An effort to establish growth policies (1973)

In 1973, Gov. Jimmy Carter named a Planned Growth Commission, but no policy changes resulted from the commission's effort (DeGrove 1992, 102). Patton and Patton (1975) indicate that Georgia had a state land use planning program under way as of September 1, 1974. Pelham (1979, 8) notes, however, that in 1974 Georgia's legislature (along with many other states at about the same time) rejected a proposal for state land use legislation. These scholars were likely referring to the failed attempt at passing critical/vital areas legislation.

On a multistate regional scale, Georgia was one of 15 southern states participating in the Southern Growth Policies Board. The Board was organized to determine alternatives for growth in the multistate region and forestall undesired development patterns in the coming decades (Scott, Brower and Miner 1975, 316).

Status of local planning (1976)

Local governments at the time were receiving technical assistance from APDCs because of significant funding from federal agency activities, including the Department of Housing and Urban Development's well-known 701 program. Given the available technical and financial assistance and heightened popular concern as a result of new federal environmental laws, the status of local planning improved remarkably in Georgia compared to 1970 levels of activity. By 1976, 90 of Georgia's 159 counties (56.6 percent) and 253 of approximately 536 cities (47.2 percent) had adopted land use or comprehensive plans (Kundell et al. 1989, 24-26).

OREGON

Enabling legislation and state planning

Oregon's municipal planning and zoning enabling legislation originated as early as 1919. Although some zoning ordinances were guided by comprehensive plans, most of the local government land use regulations that were adopted during the five decades after adoption of state enabling legislation were not guided by plans. Planning and zoning authority was extended to counties in 1947. Oregon had minor land use planning programs from 1935 to 1939 and again in 1955. By 1963, 16 counties (mostly in the Willamette Valley) had zoning ordinances, but only eight counties had land use plans (Abbott, Howe and Adler 1994, xi; Sullivan 1993; Knaap and Nelson 1992, 16, 37).

Portland region and Willamette Valley planning

In 1967, the Columbia Region Association of Governments (CRAG) was formed by the counties of Clackamas, Columbia, Multnomah, Washington, and Clark (in Washington) as a voluntary organization to coordinate planning efforts (Leonard 1983, 98). Also in 1967, a conference on future land use in the Willamette Valley helped to spread awareness about urban encroachment onto the valley's farmlands (Abbott, Howe and Adler 1994, xii).

Senate Bill 10: The birth of statewide planning goals (1969)

The origins of Oregon's planning program lie in changing social and economic trends during the 1950s and 1960s and in the environmental ethic of the 1960s (Knaap 1994; Howe 1993; DeGrove 1984, 237-238; Leonard 1983, 133). Senate Bill 10, passed in 1969, was a simple directive that mandated local governments to adopt comprehensive plans and zone their land. The law provided that the governor shall prepare land use plans and enforce zoning on all areas not subject to local regulation (Knaap and Nelson 1992, 20, 35; Leonard 1983, 7; Little 1974, 10; RuBino and Wagner 1972). The law also established the nation's first set of statewide planning goals, the concepts of which were affirmed by voters in a statewide referendum in 1970 (Governor's Task Force on Land Use 1982). Senate Bill 10, however, was considered ineffective and fatally flawed (Howe 1993; Little 1974, 10). The law did little to change prevailing development patterns, lacked state oversight, failed to provide funding and technical assistance, and did not require coordination, consistency, and conflict resolution between local jurisdictions (Sullivan 1993; DeGrove 1984, 239; Governor's Task Force on Land Use 1982; Leonard 1983, 7).

Coastal planning

In 1971, the legislature passed the Oregon Coastal Zone Management Act, which created an Oregon Coastal Conservation and Development Commission to prepare a comprehensive plan for preserving and developing the coastal area. The commission's plan would supersede local plans. The coastal commission did not complete such a plan, but it did prepare a report to the legislature in 1975 and inventories that were subsequently used for planning. The coastal commission was eventually absorbed into the larger statewide planning program (Knaap and Nelson 1992, 21-22; DeGrove 1984, 238; Leonard 1983, 5; Joint Legislative Committee on Land Use 1976; Little 1974, 9).

Preparation and adoption of Senate Bill 100 (1972-1973)

In 1972, Gov. Tom McCall convened his fifth Conservation Congress, during which land use was discussed. A report on the future of the Willamette Valley, prepared by Lawrence Halprin, also helped to set the stage for adoption of state-sponsored land use planning in Oregon (Abbott, Howe and Adler 1994, xiii). Late in 1972, Sen. Hector Macpherson's land use policy action group was finalizing what would become Senate Bill 100, Oregon's comprehensive, statewide planning legislation. According to Macpherson, who is considered the father of Oregon's land use planning program, Bosselman and Callies' *The Quiet Revolution in Land Use Control* (1971) served as the bible for preparing new land use planning legislation (Abbott, Howe and Adler 1994, xiii). The original version of Senate Bill 100 followed ALI's *Model Land Development Code* in certain respects (Knaap 1994; Rosenbaum 1976).

The original Senate Bill 100 would have established 14 regional planning districts. Regional planning represented a nonlocal decision-making process that raised fierce opposition because of the issue of local home rule. The regional planning provisions were excised from the bill and replaced with a structure whereby counties would coordinate all planning activities affecting land uses within them (Abbott,

Howe and Adler 1994, xiv; DeGrove 1984, 241; Leonard 1983, 14; Little 1974, 18).

Senate Bill 100 passed the Oregon Senate in 1973 by an 18 to 10 margin and the House by a vote of 40 to 20 (Little 1974, 14-21). It was signed by the governor May 29, 1973 (Sullivan 1993) and became effective October 5, 1973. Scholars have noted that the vote on Senate Bill 100 was split along geographic lines, with the Willamette Valley heavily in support and all other geographic areas of the state in opposition (Knaap and Nelson 1992, 197; DeGrove 1984, 244; Little 1974, 30). Popular support for Oregon's land use program has remained sharply divided by region (Knaap 1994).

Senate Bill 100's planning requirements

Senate Bill 100 required every local government to prepare a comprehensive plan, consistent with statewide planning goals, for the land within its jurisdiction and to prepare and adopt regulations to implement its comprehensive plan (Knaap 1994; Knaap and Nelson 1992, 1; Lawlor 1992; DeGrove 1984, 245). Before Senate Bill 100, most cities and counties in Oregon had never written local plans (Oliver 1992). Authority over local land use decisions was officially retained until local plans were acknowledged and until the Land Conservation and Development Commission (LCDC) could prepare and enforce its own land use plan and regulations in cities and counties without acknowledged plans (Knaap and Nelson 1992, 23-24).

Regional planning in the Portland area

In 1969, the Metropolitan Service District was formed to address solid waste disposal issues and to assume operation of the region's zoo. Other regional entities also were created that year, including the Tri-County Metropolitan Transit District and the Portland Metropolitan Area Local Government Boundary Commission (Kent 1983). In 1973, the Oregon Legislature passed Senate Bill 769, which empowered CRAG to coordinate regional planning in the three-county Portland area.[3] Leonard (1983, 98) notes that in 1973 CRAG was the first regional body to be granted statutory authority to require local governments to conform land use decisions to regional planning standards. The legislation made membership of Clackamas, Multnomah, and Washington counties (and the cities within them) in CRAG mandatory (Kent 1983). In its 1976 final report, the Joint Legislative Committee on Land Use suggested the possibility of restructuring CRAG during the 1977 legislative session (Joint Legislative Committee on Land Use 1976), and the 1977 Oregon Legislature proposed that CRAG be abolished and replaced with a new special district to provide services as well as planning coordination.

In May 1978, voters of the three-county Portland region approved (by a three-county majority of 55 percent) the creation of a reconstituted Metropolitan Service District (Metro), the first popularly elected regional government in an interjurisdictional metropolitan area in the United States (Leonard 1983, 99-100; Kent 1983). DeGrove (1992, 146-147) notes that Metro was created in 1979 via amendments to the Metropolitan Service District Act of 1969. Metro's statutory responsibilities included adoption of regional urban growth goals and objectives, review and coordination of all land use activities within the district, and adoption of various functional plans (Kent 1983). Metro assumed the regional planning role of (i.e., merged with) CRAG in 1979 (Sullivan 1994).

Adoption of statewide planning goals (1974-1976)

After nearly 100 public hearings and workshops attended by more than 10,000 Oregonians, a questionnaire randomly distributed to 100,000 voters, and television programs viewed by 100,000 Oregonians, LCDC adopted 14 statewide planning goals in December 1974. The goals became effective January 1, 1975, and required every city and county to prepare a comprehensive plan in compliance with the goals within one year. LCDC adopted a greenway goal in December 1975 and four coastal goals in late 1976 (Abbott 1994; Knaap and Nelson 1992, 25; DeGrove 1984, 251-252, 280; Leonard 1983, 12; Governor's Task Force on Land Use 1982; Joint Legislative Committee on Land Use 1976). The Department of Land Conservation and Development distributed a land use handbook in December 1975 to assist local governments in measuring comprehensive plans against statewide requirements. During 1975 and 1976, however, LCDC did not press local governments for compliance with statewide planning goals (Leonard 1983, 15).

Also in 1975, 1000 Friends of Oregon was established privately to oversee implementation and achieve the full realization of Senate Bill 100 and the statewide planning goals (DeGrove 1984, 278; Leonard 1983, 20; Governor's Task Force on Land Use 1982). Oregon's land use program owes its continued existence in part to 1000 Friends, according to

Gordon Oliver (1992). Former LCDC member Tom Walsh has indicated that without 1000 Friends, the state planning law would have fallen to one of the repeal efforts (Oliver 1992).

Status of local planning (1976)

In October 1976, a legislative committee reported on the progress of Senate Bill 100 (Joint Legislative Committee on Land Use 1976). The committee's staff observed LCDC's meetings, received annual progress reports from local planning officials, and attended various meetings in the Willamette Valley and on the coast. All local governments were supposed to have plans acknowledged by January 5, 1976 (Governor's Task Force on Land Use 1982). The committee's 1976 final report notes that, by the first week of 1976, nearly all (245 of 278) of the state's cities and counties had requested one of three kinds of extensions to the planning mandate (Joint Legislative Committee on Land Use 1976).

WASHINGTON

Enabling legislation

Washington has one of the most confusing sets of planning and zoning enabling legislation in the United States (Burby and May 1997, 72; Settle 1983, 4). Washington's first planning enabling statute (RCW 35.63), sometimes called the Planning Commission Act, was adopted in 1935. If localities exercised planning powers, the city or county was required to create a planning commission. The 1935 act did not require adoption of a comprehensive plan unless a zoning ordinance was adopted. The act provided broad guidelines (containing no required elements) if a locality prepared a comprehensive plan. An alternative planning enabling statute for municipalities (RCW 35A.63), known as the Optional Municipal Code, applied to all noncharter municipalities and charter cities of more than 10,000 population. Cities that established planning agencies under the code were required to develop comprehensive plans containing a land use element and a circulation element. Counties exercising planning under the Planning Enabling Act (RCW 36.70) were required to establish planning agencies and develop comprehensive plans containing a land use element and a circulation element (Haworth and Anderson, Inc. 1976, 4-11).

Regional conferences and metropolitan corporations

Besides local planning, a 1965 state act (codified as RCW 36.64) allowed counties and cities to permit contiguous general-purpose units of local government to form regional conferences, better known today as councils of government. Regional conferences could study a wide variety of facilities and problems, including land use. A regional conference could prepare and adopt a comprehensive plan for its area, but no provision was made in the law for regulations to implement a regional plan. For populous metropolitan areas, metropolitan municipal corporations could be established to provide services, including comprehensive planning, if authorized by metro constituents. Metropolitan municipal corporations so authorized could prepare comprehensive land use plans and review plans and ordinances of component local governments. As of 1976, only Snohomish County had a metropolitan municipal corporation exercising authority over comprehensive planning (Haworth and Anderson, Inc. 1976, 23-27).

Status of local planning (1970)

Efforts to establish statewide legislation for local comprehensive planning in Washington originated in the early 1960s. A citizens advisory committee reported to a legislative committee that urban sprawl needed to be curbed and a state comprehensive plan was needed. No legislation, however, resulted from the committee's recommendations (Burby and May 1997, 73). Local planning thus was carried forward without the benefit of state sponsorship.

The Department of Community Development (DCD) in 1976 determined the status of individual cities and counties with respect to comprehensive planning and the dates the local plans were adopted. These data enable a determination of the status of local planning at earlier times. As of the end of 1969, 24 of the state's 39 counties (61.5 percent) and 83 out of 266 cities (31.2 percent) had adopted comprehensive plans (Haworth and Anderson, Inc. 1976, 78-88).

Initiative 43 and shorelines management (1970-1971)

As did Oregon's, Washington's involvement in land use grew out of the environmental movement of the 1960s. The state legislature passed environmentally oriented legislation in 1967, 1969, and 1970. A scenic rivers act was introduced in 1967, and shorelines management acts were proposed in 1967, 1968, and 1970, but all failed (Settle 1983, 130; Bish 1982, 86).

The state of Washington's Shorelines Management Act (SMA) of 1971 is not often viewed as a comprehensive planning mandate. It is considered instead a "single purpose" mandate (Burby and May 1997, 75). The statute's jurisdiction over shorelines hardly qualifies as a comprehensive planning program, but the plans and regulations adopted under SMA were important precursors to later planning efforts. The story of SMA is worthy of attention here as it relates to local government planning and regulation.

In 1970, after failing in its attempt to get a Seacoast Management Bill passed, the Washington Environmental Council sponsored Initiative 43, known as the Shorelines Protection Act (Washington Department of Ecology 1994; Bish 1982). The initiative reflected severe distrust of local government and placed responsibility for preparing and administering a shoreline plan with the state Department of Ecology (DOE). The state would administer all substantial development permits. Also, instead of local government input, the initiative suggested preparation would proceed through regional citizens' councils.

Knowing that Initiative 43 would be submitted to voters in 1972, the governor and legislature acted in 1971 to provide a substitute to the "anti-local and single-interest" initiative. The state's version of a shorelines bill maintained local government control over shorelines planning and permit administration but gave DOE preemptive authority to regulate shorelines if local government efforts were inadequate. The legislature passed the Shorelines Management Act of 1971 and began implementation June 1, 1971, even though the popular vote on Initiative 43 was not scheduled until 1972. The statewide voting results were 68 percent in favor of SMA over Initiative 43 (Bish 1982, 86-88).

State Land Planning Commission (1971-1973)

In 1971, the Washington Planning and Community Affairs Agency (1971) developed a report that recommended four legislative alternatives for land resource management. One was establishment of a State Land Use Commission that would designate settlement, conservation, and agricultural districts (RuBino and Wagner 1972, 30). This alternative appears to resemble the land classification system initiated in Hawaii a decade earlier.

Washington joined other states during the early 1970s in creating a land use commission to prepare comprehensive plans and studies to modernize state land use regulatory programs (Bosselman and Callies 1971, 300). The State Land Planning Commission was created by legislation in 1971 (Engrossed House Bill No. 865; 1971 Wash. Laws, Chapter 27). The commission's principal functions were to study the state's land use laws and recommend "land use changes which have impact beyond the physical boundaries" of governmental jurisdictions. The commission was specifically directed to look at the *Model Land Development Code* and other private and public studies.

Of greater significance to this research, the commission was given the tasks of: (1) formulating recommendations as to planning criteria and guidelines for preparing local land use plans and (2) developing a statewide land use data bank or alternative system to assist in formulating, evaluating, and updating long range goals and policies for land use, urban expansion, and other factors that shape statewide development patterns (Bosselman and Callies 1971, 300-302). The commission could not achieve its mandate because it was "severely handicapped by the lack of professional staff in the early stages and the necessity of educating many of its members" (Bagne 1975, 345). Furthermore, the commission appears also to have been handicapped by a lack of resources; its budget for fiscal year 1972-1973 was only $91,000 (Bosselman and Callies 1971, 302). A legislative drafting committee of the commission, however, developed a draft land use bill that the commission approved and circulated throughout the state. The commission found the idea of a statewide land use data bank raised fears of "big brother," so instead the commission recommended a central information center to inventory existing sources of land use information and distribute information to the public (Bagne 1975, 344).

House Bill 791 (1973): Failure of state and local planning legislation

In the early 1970s, a Land Development Control and Planning bill was recommended by the State Land Planning Commission. Other bills were introduced in the legislature based on the recommendations of the commission but were rejected (Burby and May 1997, 73). One of these proposed acts, House Bill 791, was introduced in 1973 and passed the house but died in the senate. The final version of the bill ran some 150 pages and was based on the *Model Land Development Code,* although there were significant departures from it. The bill included nine major sections including provisions on local land use planning, state participation in local land use regulation, and state and regional land use planning (Bagne 1975). Subject to certain exemptions and with limited state review, the bill would have required every county and city to adopt a land use plan and ordinance. It is interesting to note that the required local land use plan was a policy process rather than a traditional physical plan. That is, local land use plans envisioned by the act were required to contain goals and objectives supported by findings but not the maps and illustrations of a traditional physical plan. If a local government failed to prepare and adopt a plan, the state land planning agency (created under the act within the office of the governor) would prepare a plan for that locality (Bagne 1975).

House Bill 791 (1973) described a state land use plan and process in greater detail than the local planning process. Consistent with the *Model Land Development Code*, the state plan was intended to include provisions regarding areas of critical state concern and developments of regional impact. The state plan would have required the approval of the state land planning agency and could have been vetoed by either the governor or the legislature. No state land use ordinance was proposed, although the state agency was required to prepare short-term state land programs to guide state land activities. Regional planning bodies could be established either by localities or the state to review local plans for consistency with regional plans and designate lands of regional significance (Bagne 1975).

Implementation of shorelines management

Meanwhile, DOE implemented the 1971 Shorelines Management Act. Final guidelines, published by DOE in June 1972, provided that each local government prepare a detailed shorelines inventory and master program for anticipated future development. The master program, much like a comprehensive plan but only for shorelines jurisdictions, had to be submitted to DOE for approval. If it rejected the program, DOE could prepare its own alternative for shorelines of statewide significance. Local governments were required to develop a procedure for administering shoreline "substantial development" permits. Local implementation was difficult, due to a lack of data for land use inventories and insufficient and unskilled local government staffs. The state's shorelines management program, however, was easily adapted to federal requirements of the 1972 Federal Coastal Zone Management Act

(CZMA), and in 1976 Washington's program was the first approved under CZMA (Bish 1982, 89-98). Hence, even though the shorelines planning program involved only small portions of land area and was not a comprehensive planning requirement for all land in all local jurisdictions like Oregon's, Washington had a state-mandated planning program in place with much the same potential for preemptive state authority before Oregon's Senate Bill 100.

Status of local planning (1976)

In 1976, the legislature created the Planning and Community Affairs Agency to provide financial and technical assistance in community planning and development (Haworth and Anderson, Inc. 1976, 49). Planning activity increased significantly over levels of activity in 1970. By 1976, 33 of the state's 39 counties (84.6 percent) and 83 of the state's 266 cities (31.2 percent) had adopted comprehensive plans. Also at that time, all but six counties were members of regional planning organizations (Haworth and Anderson, Inc. 1976, 78-88). As in Georgia, the increase in local planning activity is probably attributable to the availability of federal financial assistance and heightened popular support for environmental regulation.

CONCLUSIONS

Several conclusions can be offered regarding the quiet revolution in the four states. First, regional planning programs preceded state-sponsored programs of local land use planning. Each of the states provided some sort of authority to form multicounty planning entities, spurred in part by federal support. Georgia was an early leader in regional planning, and both Florida and Georgia attained comprehensive statewide coverage with regional planning boundaries by the end of the quiet revolution. The drafters of Oregon's Senate Bill 100 tried but failed to impose a multicounty regional framework on local government planning efforts. Washington authorized regional conferences to plan but gave them no significant statutory authority over local government. Special planning legislation was passed for the largest metropolitan regions in Georgia (Atlanta) and Oregon (Portland).

Second, as growth management scholar John DeGrove (1991) suggests, environmental considerations were the most important feature of state land use planning programs during the quiet revolution. Environmental considerations also dominated local comprehensive planning.

Washington failed to pass a state mandate for local land use planning but passed a series of important single-purpose environmental laws, including SMA, which contains a strong state mandate for local planning in shorelines jurisdictions. Georgia twice attempted to pass critical areas legislation that would have required land use planning for several areas of the state. Georgia's legislators, however, succeeded in passing only a metropolitan river protection bill for the major river (Chattahoochee) in the Atlanta region. Florida's land and water management legislation preceded its local planning mandate, and, once established, the local planning legislation appears not to have influenced land use as much as other statutes. Oregon was the first of the four states to pass a local planning mandate. In Oregon, however, as in other states, environmental protection activities such as coastal planning preceded local comprehensive planning mandates.

During the quiet revolution in the four states, the most popular example available for drafting state planning laws was the *Model Land Development Code*. Scholars specifically note that the model code was influential in Florida and Washington. In addition, there is evidence that Hawaii's land classification approach also was considered by program designers in Florida and Washington. Given that Bosselman and Callies' work (1971) was the bible used by the father of Oregon's land use planning, the model code was undoubtedly used in establishing Oregon's planning legislation. Judging by the nomenclature and reported content of Georgia's legislative attempts during the quiet revolution, the model code was probably applied in that state as well. The model code's provisions for areas of critical state concern were, in summary, incorporated to some extent into the planning laws passed in Florida and Oregon and the laws that failed to pass in Georgia and Washington during the quiet revolution.

A coercive or state preemption model was commonly used in legislation that passed in Florida and Oregon and in others as well (Burby and May 1997). Oregon's Senate Bill 10 allowed the governor to plan and control land uses if local governments failed to act, and Senate Bill 100 retained state control via LCDC at least until plans were acknowledged as conforming to statewide planning goals. Similarly, in Florida the state land planning agency could designate itself as a local planning agency if a local government failed to meet the state's local planning deadline. Washington's SMA and unsuccessful land use legislation were based on a preemption model where the state retained control if

Table 3.1. Status of Local Planning, 1970 and 1976

	Florida		Georgia		Oregon		Washington	
	1970	1977	1970	1976	1970	1976	1970	1976
Cities	N/A	N/A	95	253	N/A	1	83	153
% of all	—	—	17.6%	46.8%	—	0.4%	31.2%	57.5%
Counties	N/A	N/A	20	90	N/A	1	24	33
% of all	—	—	12.6%	56.6%	—	2.8%	61.5%	84.6%
TOTAL	N/A	2	115	343	N/A	2	107	186
% of all	—	—	16.4%	49.0%	—	0.7%	34.0%	59.0%

Notes: N/A means not available. According to Florida's Department of Community Affairs (1977a), only two local governments had submitted complete local comprehensive plans by April 1977, although 33 local governments had submitted one or more elements of the comprehensive plan to the state.

Sources: Florida Department of Community Affairs (1977a); Hawarth and Anderson, Inc. 1976 (Washington); Joint Legislative Committee on Land Use 1976 (Oregon); Kundell et al. 1989 (Georgia).

local governments failed to act according to state mandate. Georgia's critical areas act also appears to have contained a similar state preemption device. Hence, authority of the state to direct or perform local planning in cases where local governments failed to do so is a hallmark of the quiet revolution in the four states.

Finally, state mandates for local land use planning were not highly successful in the four states, at least by the end of the quiet revolution in 1976. After adoption of statewide planning goals, Oregon allowed only one year to complete local plans that complied with the goals. Few local governments had plans that complied with statewide goals by 1976. The unsuccessful local planning act drafted in Florida during 1974 would have allowed only three years for local governments to plan. Florida provided a four-year period for local governments to comply with its 1975 local planning mandate. By the end of the quiet revolution in 1976, local governments with adopted comprehensive plans were the exception rather than the rule.

Table 3.1 provides a summary of the status of local planning in the four states near the beginning (1970) and end (1976) of the quiet revolution. To the extent they can be determined, Table 3.1 indicates the number of cities, counties and total local governments with local comprehensive plans. Most of the counties in Georgia and Washington had land use plans by 1976. During the quiet revolution, local planning mandates in Florida and Oregon were not having much effect. Two years after adoption of Florida's 1975 planning act, and four years after adoption of Senate Bill 100 in Oregon, very few cities and counties had completed local comprehensive plans as required by state law.

Notes

1. DeGrove and Juergensmeyer (1986, vi) cite the Florida State Comprehensive Planning Act of 1972 as Florida Statute Chapter 186. Perhaps it was later codified differently.

2. Kundell et al. (1989, 18-19) indicate that 19 APDCs existed as of 1970. These authors also suggest that it was 1972 (rather than 1971) that APDCs officially came into being.

3. Sullivan (1994) finds that it was Senate Bill 100 that in 1973 established authority of CRAG to perform regional planning within the Portland metropolitan area. Also, according to Kent (1983), CRAG was created as a voluntary organization as a result of a government reorganization study in 1963 sponsored by the Oregon legislature. Note that Kent's finding conflicts with Leonard's (1983) finding mentioned earlier, that CRAG was formed in 1967.

CHAPTER

4

Evolution of State-Sponsored Land Use Planning During the Second Wave: 1980-1988

As mentioned in Chapter 2, Porter's (1989) research agenda implies and this research confirms that not much was happening in the four states between 1977 and 1979. During this interlude (1977 to 1979) between the quiet revolution and the second wave of growth management that began in 1980, some growth management activity did occur in Florida and Oregon. This activity and minor activity in Washington deserve brief attention here.

STATE-SPONSORED PLANNING DURING THE INTERLUDE (1977-1979)

Planning in Florida during the interlude

Preparation of a state plan pursuant to the Florida State Comprehensive Planning Act of 1972 was delayed by the daunting scope of the legislative mandate. The State Planning Division devoted almost two years to the development of the state plan. The governor approved and the legislature adopted the State Comprehensive Plan in 1978, six years after passage of the State Comprehensive Planning Act. The completed state plan, which was an advisory document only, contained 14 elements, including one on land development (DeGrove and Juergensmeyer 1986; Healy and Rosenberg 1979, 136, 168; O'Connell 1986; Pelham 1979, 153).

In 1978 the Florida legislature substantially revised the State Comprehensive Planning Act of 1972 (1978 Florida Laws, Chapter 78-287) (Pelham 1979, 181).[1]

Regarding the status of local planning, Pelham (1979, 168) finds that by 1978, 102 governments had submitted plans or parts of plans to the state for review. DeGrove (1984, 162) notes, however, that only 62 localities (51 municipalities and 11 counties) had submitted plans or elements of plans for state review. In April 1979, only 190 of Florida's 527 local governments had submitted complete or partial plans to the Division of State Planning for review. Extensions had to be granted to at least 176 local governments to complete plans. Hence, local planning moved slower in Florida than anticipated given that most plans were due by this time.

Legislation in Oregon during the interlude

In 1977, via Senate Bill 570, the Oregon Legislature repealed LCDC's preemptive authority to prepare and administer local comprehensive plans if cities and counties failed to act, another symbol of the end of the quiet revolution. The preemption provision of state law was replaced with authority to issue enforcement orders (Knaap 1994; Sullivan 1994; Knaap and Nelson 1992, 29; DeGrove 1984, 246; Leonard 1983, 11; Governor's Task Force on Land Use 1982). LCDC used its enforcement powers several times between 1977 and 1980 (DeGrove 1984, 263; Leonard 1983, 15). The formal "acknowledgment" process, which provided the procedures for LCDC to approve local plans, was added by the Oregon Legislature in 1977 (Sullivan 1993, 1994). In 1979, the Land Use Board of Appeals was created by the Oregon Legislature as a means to consolidate review of local government land use decisions (Sullivan 1994; Knaap and Nelson 1992, 34; Leonard 1983, 19; DeGrove 1984, 257). By the late 1970s, the land use program's emphases had become clear: preserve rural lands, institute urban growth boundaries, and facilitate urban development (Leonard 1983, 18, 33). Between 1977 and 1981, LCDC turned down some city and county comprehensive plans because of a failure to comply with state goals or to achieve consistency between plans of cities and counties (Leonard 1983, 42).

Oregon's land use program was not implemented smoothly during the 1970s. One of the obstacles to implementation was referenda on Senate Bill 100. Attempts to rescind or curtail the scope of state involvement in land use again were launched in 1978. Also, there were concerted attempts in the 1977 and 1979 legislatures to alter, dilute, or underfund the state program. Each time that opposition surfaced, a large amount of staff time and some of LCDC's meeting time was devoted to refuting charges made by the program's opponents (DeGrove 1984, 248; Leonard 1983, 35-37).

A whisper of activity in Washington

Briefly, there was one effort to stimulate state-sponsored land use planning in Washington during the interlude between the first and second waves of growth management. In 1978, Gov. Dixie Lee Ray appointed a Working Group on Growth Management that identified among other things the need for local authority to manage growth. No legislation was proposed, however, as a result of that group's effort (Burby and May 1997, 73).

OVERVIEW

During the second wave of growth management (1980-1988), Florida strengthened regional planning councils (1980), studied its implementation record (1982-1984), comprehensively reexamined and then overhauled its growth management program with new legislation (1985), and prepared a second state comprehensive plan (1985). Georgia's first efforts to initiate growth strategies were hampered (1982, 1984), but later a growth strategies commission was created and succeeded (1987). Oregon studied its implementation record with a governor's task force (1982), finally achieved acknowledgment of all local comprehensive plans (1986), and entered the postacknowledgment phase of its program. The literature does not indicate any significant events or activities in Washington. Major committees, activities, and legislation are summarized in Figure 4.1.

FLORIDA

In 1980, the Governor's Resource Management Task Force concluded that, for various reasons, the Local Government Comprehensive Planning Act of 1975 had not achieved its objectives (DeGrove and Juergensmeyer 1986; O'Connell 1986; Stroud 1983). Weaknesses in the state's 1970s growth management laws were readily apparent by the end of the decade (Koenig 1990; DeGrove 1986). The growth management program put in place during the quiet revolution consisted mostly of a system of environmental protection, with a relatively weak local planning mandate.

Figure 4.1. Study Committees, Activities, and Legislation, 1980-1988

	1980 ....1981 ....1982...........1933...........1984...........1985...........1986...........1987...........1988
Florida	Regional Planning Council Act (1980)
	Governor's Resource Management Task Force (1980)
	Environmental Land Management Committee II (1982)
	State and Regional Planning Act (1984)
	Omnibus Growth Management Act (1985)
	State Comprehensive Planning Act (Second state comprehensive plan) (1985)
	Local planning standards (Rule 9-J5) (1986)
Georgia	Georgia Commission on State Growth Policy (1982)
	Georgia 2000 Project (1984)
	Governor's Growth Strategies Commission (1987)
	Land Information Study Commission (1987)
	Mountain Protection Act (failed 1988)
Oregon	Governor's Task Force on Land Use (1982)
Washington	No committees, activities, or legislation noted.

By 1981, most local governments had completed comprehensive plans that had been reviewed by the state. The Department of Community Affairs (DCA), however, conducted an evaluation of local plans and found them to be inadequate in their ability to address growth problems. Florida's local governments had little capacity to address the impacts of development, and an infrastructure crisis was developing in the state due to overdevelopment (Wallis 1993, 6-7).

Regional Planning Council Act (1980)

The recommendations of Gov. Bob Graham's Resource Management Task Force included the strengthening of the state's regional planning councils (RPCs), and most of its recommendations were approved in 1980 when the Florida Legislature passed the Regional Planning Council Act (Stroud 1987). This legislation strengthened RPCs, required that all RPCs in the state be reorganized, added a requirement that one-third of their membership be composed of persons appointed by the governor, and mandated the preparation of comprehensive regional policy plans (Starnes 1993; DeGrove 1984, 128, 173; Stroud 1983).

Lance deHaven-Smith (1984) indicates that local plans were required to be consistent with adopted regional policy plans. In 1981, executive directors of RPCs agreed to employ a common format and method for preparing regional plans in an attempt to secure funding from the legislature. When that funding request was not approved, RPCs were reluctant to proceed with regional planning (Stroud 1983).

Status of local planning (1982)

By mid-1982, 419 of 461 cities and counties had adopted comprehensive plans that had been reviewed and commented on (approval not required) at the regional and state levels (DeGrove 1984, 162; Healy and Rosenberg 1979, 167-168; Pelham 1979, 166-179).[2] Since there was no plan enforcement mechanism provided in the 1975 local planning law, however, haphazard development continued at a rampant pace (Koenig 1990). While most cities and counties adopted local plans, it was widely recognized that the local comprehensive plans varied greatly in quality and had not been reviewed for consistency with regional and state plans (DeGrove 1984, 172).

Environmental Land Management Study II (1982-1984)

By the early 1980s, there was consensus that Florida's land use laws needed an overhaul. In 1982 the second Environmental Land Management Study Committee (ELMS II) was appointed by Gov. Graham to make recommendations for legislative reforms. Between 1982 and 1984, ELMS II operated as a centerpiece for reexamination of Florida's growth management system. The committee's report, issued in 1984, found that local plans were ineffective because of the absence of strong state and regional plans. The ELMS II report also concluded that weaknesses of local comprehensive planning included inadequate funding, a lack of consistency requirements, minimum quality standards, and insufficient guidance by state and regional policy plans. ELMS II recommended strengthening coastal elements of local plans guided by state standards for coastal development. The ELMS II committee's findings and recommendations led directly to the 1985 Omnibus Growth Management Act, in which the idea of top-down review (i.e., vertical consistency) became a centerpiece of growth management (DeGrove 1994; Pelham 1993; Wallis 1993, 8; Koenig 1990; Lawlor 1992; DiMento 1986; O'Connell 1986).

State and Regional Planning Act (1984)

In 1984, the Florida legislature passed the State and Regional Planning Act (Florida Statutes Chapter 186) which required the governor's office to prepare and submit to the legislature a state comprehensive plan. The act provided a new statewide planning framework and tied the framework to a legislatively adopted comprehensive plan prepared by the governor. As distinguished from the first state plan, which was lengthy, verbose, and prepared late, the directive to prepare a new state plan was more specific. The new plan would be submitted to the 1985 legislature, could only be composed of goals and policies in jargonless terms, and could not include a land use map. The state comprehensive plan was adopted by the Administration Commission (the governor and cabinet) and then by the legislature during the 1985 session (DeGrove and Juergensmeyer 1986; O'Connell 1986). The act also mandated comprehensive regional policy plans be adopted by RPCs and local plans be reviewed by the RPCs for consistency with the applicable regional plans. Comprehensive regional policy plans were scheduled to be completed within 18 months after adoption of the state plan (O'Connell 1986), and each RPC had adopted a regional plan by 1987 (DeGrove and Metzger 1993).

Omnibus Growth Management Act and a new state plan (1985)

In 1985, Gov. Bob Graham and John DeGrove, then secretary of Florida's DCA, hesitated to propose more than a modest growth management reform package. The governor sought approval of a state plan, stronger coastal elements in local plans, and an improved process of reviewing DRIs. DeGrove was concerned about advancing any sweeping proposals for fear they might jeopardize more modest reform packages. The governor, however, proposed and senate and house leaders supported a package of growth management laws. To secretary DeGrove's surprise, the "sweeping" legislation was approved by the legislature (Wallis 1993, 9).

Two major acts were approved by the Florida Legislature in 1985: the Omnibus Growth Management Act (Chapter 85-55, Florida Laws)[3] and a companion bill titled the State Comprehensive Planning Act, (Chapter 85-57, Florida Laws) that adopted the State Comprehensive Plan and fulfilled the requirements of the State and Regional Planning Act of 1984 (DeGrove 1994; Kelly 1993, 114; DeGrove and Juergensmeyer 1986). The Growth Management Act, also known as the Local Government Comprehensive Planning and Land Development Regulation Act, was a major rewrite of the 1975 Local Government Comprehensive Planning Act (O'Connell 1986).

The new State Comprehensive Plan did not create any regulatory authority. A performance standard in the state plan draft prepared by the governor's office suggested that "85% of new population growth from 1985 to 1995 occur in existing urban areas," but this standard was dropped by the legislature. The State Comprehensive Plan estimated an additional $52 billion would be needed by the year 2000 to fund infrastructure needs (Wallis 1993, 16-17; DeGrove and Juergensmeyer 1986; O'Connell 1986; also see Weitz and Moore 1998).

Adoption of the 1985 growth management law was preceded by a "well-timed and masterfully planned" professional Conference on Managing Megagrowth. From this conference came recommendations incorporated into legislation passed in 1985. In addition, preparation of the state plan served to focus attention of legislators on growth management (O'Connell 1986). The new growth management laws resulted from "extraordinary" attention given by blue ribbon committees (ELMS I and ELMS II), a supportive governor, special legislative conferences, and interested legislators (Stroud and O'Connell 1986).

Requirements of the Growth Management Act

The 1985 Omnibus Growth Management Act (GMA) added concurrency, consistency, and compact development requirements (the three "Cs," as DeGrove has dubbed them), strengthened RPCs, and gave DCA authority to review and, if necessary reject, local comprehensive plans. The act required that counties revise local plans in accordance with state requirements before December 1, 1987; plan revisions for coastal municipalities were due prior to December 1, 1988, while all other municipalities had until December 1, 1989, to complete comprehensive plan revisions. Local governments were required to adopt or amend land development regulations within one year after a revised local plan was submitted for review. To enforce the planning and regulation mandates, the Administration Commission could direct state agencies to withhold infrastructure funds from local governments if their plans were not in compliance with state requirements (Kelly 1993, 115; O'Connell 1986).

Minimum local planning standards: Rule 9J-5 (1986)

The Local Government Comprehensive Planning and Land Development Regulation Act (Omnibus GMA) required DCA, the state land planning agency, to adopt rules establishing minimum criteria for review and determination of compliance of local plan elements required by the act (Wallis 1993, 13; O'Connell 1986). On February 15, 1986, DCA adopted Rule 9J-5. Legislative approval of Rule 9J-5 was required and was received in 1986 (Wallis 1993, 17).

Rule 9J-5 set forth types of data and analyses and several goals, objectives, and policies that had to be incorporated into local plan elements. The state land planning agency was also required to provide model comprehensive plans and local land development regulations. Furthermore, if requested to do so, the agency was required to assist local governments in local plan adoption and implementation (DeGrove and Juergensmeyer 1986). Of interest to this inquiry, the act specified that the rule had to include criteria to determine whether elements identify mechanisms and procedures for monitoring and evaluating plan implementation, including specific measurable objectives (O'Connell 1986).

Revisions to local plans

As described above, the first step in the overhauled growth management program was for the state to prepare its own comprehensive plan.

Next, 11 multicounty RPCs developed plans, then Florida's 461 cities and counties followed with comprehensive plans.[4] By this time, most of the cities and counties in Florida already had comprehensive plans and basic land use regulations, so the new legislation resulted for the most part in a plan revision process. One significant addition to local planning requirements was the preparation of capital improvement elements to ensure adequate public facilities were provided at acceptable levels of service. Another important emphasis of the 1985 local planning law was stronger coastal plan elements, which had been required since 1975. Coastal cities and counties were required to prepare/revise comprehensive plans first, followed by local governments in the interior, then those located in the northern part of the state. The Omnibus GMA also required that all local land development regulations be consistent with the adopted local plan (i.e., what I term later as "implementation consistency"). Compliance requirements of the legislation set dates beginning in 1988 for local governments to submit plans for state review. The last local plans were not required to be completed until July 1991 (DeGrove 1994; Wallis 1993, 24; Koenig 1990; DeGrove and Juergensmeyer 1986; Stroud and O'Connell, 1986).[5]

State funds could be withheld from local governments that failed to comply with the requirements of GMA. Such a sanction could apply if the local plan was late, internally inconsistent, or inconsistent with state and regional plans. For local governments that failed to produce a plan, DCA could authorize the RPC to develop the local comprehensive plan (Wallis 1993, 18). Hence, unlike Oregon, which repealed the preemptive authority of LCDC in 1977, Florida maintained the provision for DCA to force planning on recalcitrant local governments.

Addressing concurrency

It appears as if much of the time of program administrators was consumed in determining how to administer the concurrency requirements of GMA. Neither the Omnibus GMA nor Rule 9J-5 specifically defined concurrency. In March 1988, Thomas Pelham, secretary of DCA, issued the basic principles that the department would follow in implementing the concurrency requirement of GMA (Wallis 1993, 24).

Quality of local plans (1988)

The quality of local plans at the close of the second era of state-sponsored planning was not as great as state officials desired. Robert

Nave (1988), then chief of DCA's Bureau of Local Planning, described some of the common problems found in local comprehensive plans submitted to the state for review. Nave observed that future land use maps suffered in certain respects, including the failure of plan goals, objectives, and policies to provide for measurable and specific guidance in plan implementation. Nave also noted inconsistencies between land use analyses and information presented in existing and future land use maps. The quality of maps was also considered to be a common problem. One local government submitted a series of photographs as its required land use maps (Nave 1988). DCA also noted that some local comprehensive plans took, verbatim, the goals, objectives, and policies from the various model elements prepared by DCA. DCA found such a practice objectionable because the goals and policies of the model plan elements were not all prepared for the same locality and were therefore, not necessarily internally consistent (Florida DCA 1989i).

GEORGIA

Renewed attempts to prepare growth strategies (1982-1984)

In 1982, Georgia Act 1530 established the Georgia Commission on State Growth Policy. The principal charge of the commission was to advise state government on the roles of state and local governments in growth and development. The commission adopted a work program and analyzed community preparedness for growth and development. It never fully addressed the issue of land use, however, and the commission was not continued (Kundell et al. 1989, 11-12). The issues of preparedness for planning and land use control were left to a later governor to implement (DeGrove 1992, 102).

Another attempt to address growth management issues was the "Georgia 2000" project sponsored in 1984 by the Cooperative Extension Service at the University of Georgia. This project was led by a 50-member blue ribbon committee charged with considering alternatives for the state's future. The committee had a land and water subcommittee that issued recommendations for land use planning and technical and financial assistance to undertake planning and zoning activities. That subcommittee specifically recognized the need to address regional impacts of development and to identify areas of statewide interest (Kundell et al. 1989, 12-13), apparently in the tradition of the *Model Land Development Code*.

Status of local planning (1985)

Kundell and colleagues' (1989) statistics indicate a sharp decline in the number of city and county comprehensive plans between 1976 and 1985. Only 52 counties, or one-third of the total counties in the state, reported having a comprehensive or land use plan in 1985. Similarly, only 166 or 33 percent of all cities had land use or comprehensive plans in 1985. The decline in the number of comprehensive plans reported by cities and counties between 1976 and 1985 is attributed to a reduction in state and federal funding which eliminated planning and zoning staffs employed by APDCs. Also at this time, more local governments adopted zoning ordinances, but there were a significant number of cities and counties that adopted their first zoning ordinance without a formal plan on which to base the zoning (Kundell et al. 1989, 24-26).

Birth of the Growth Strategies Commission (1987)

Creation of a Growth Strategies Commission in Georgia was proposed by Gov. Joe Frank Harris in a speech to the Georgia Conservancy in 1986. The governor announced his growth strategies initiative in his "state of the state" address in January 1987. That year, the Georgia House of Representatives passed House Resolution 77, which formally urged the Governor to create a Governor's Commission on Growth Strategy. The governor then appointed a 16-member advisory group, which recommended a broad mission statement and a set of goals and objectives for the Growth Strategies Commission (Costa 1987). In June 1987, Gov. Harris appointed a Growth Strategies Commission to analyze growth issues and make recommendations (DeGrove 1992, 102-103; Kundell et al 1989, 13; Broussard 1987). The commission included 36 members composed of state legislators, city and county officials, business persons, two academicians, and private citizens.[6] Local planning commissioners and professional planners were not represented on the Growth Strategies Commission. The commission was chaired by Joel Cowan, who also chaired Gov. Jimmy Carter's Planned Growth Commission in 1973. The Growth Strategies Commission later divided into four task forces, including one on land use and another on natural resources. The commission held 19 public hearings throughout the state and produced three reports that laid the foundation for the 1989 Georgia Planning Act (Bohlen, McGuire and Meck 1996; DeGrove 1992, 102-104; Silverman 1988; Broussard 1987; see especially Governor's Growth Strategies Commission 1988).

Legislation and related efforts (1987)

Because creation of a Growth Strategies Commission was pending, the Georgia General Assembly in 1987 did not debate planning legislation. According to Dick Lane, vice chairman of the House State Planning and Community Affairs Committee, all land use bills during the 1987 session were to be held in committee pending appointment of the Growth Strategies Commission. Rep. Lane told a group of planners in January 1987 that land use and zoning had been under the home rule power of local governments for a long time and that this situation would be difficult to change (Silverman 1987). Indeed, Georgia in 1987 was an unlikely setting for a growth strategy encompassing a state role in the land use planning process. Georgia was known for its posture of aggressive economic development and its strong tradition of home rule (DeGrove, Roberts and Nelson 1990).

One of the only legislative actions of planning significance passed in 1987 was Senate Resolution 92, which created a Land Information Study Commission. The purpose of this commission was to study the possibility of creating a statewide land information system on tax appraisals, zoning, and land use planning for use by local and state officials (Georgia Chapter APA 1987).

Mountain protection fails (1988)

On February 2, 1988, the Georgia Senate unanimously approved the Georgia Mountains Protection Act. The bill's passage in the Senate was engineered by Lieutenant Gov. Zell Miller, who presided over the senate. The bill would have limited development on mountains of 2,200 feet or more above sea level having slopes of 25 percent or more. Local governments would have been required to develop land use plans and permit procedures for regulating construction on the mountains. This bill, however, failed to pass the House of Representatives (Georgia APA 1988).

OREGON

In 1981, Oregon's economy was in a recession, and the state witnessed an unprecedented net loss of population (Knaap and Nelson 1992, 165). Given an unfavorable economic climate, the land use program was the brunt of some of the blame for the state's economic woes. Oregon's land use program weathered yet another challenge by ballot initiative in 1982, and the program would have faced additional challenges in 1984 and 1986 but initiative petitions fell short of the required number of signatures (Knaap and Nelson 1992, 189). Although the early- to mid-1980s were not favorable to the objective of advancing a growth management agenda in Oregon, some significant legislation nevertheless passed during the second wave of growth management (1980-1988).

Legislation (1981)

In 1981, the legislature approved procedures for the Land Conservation and Development Commission to review local comprehensive plan amendments and instituted the process of periodic review (Sullivan 1994). The amendment to Oregon's land use act required local governments to notify LCDC of all plan amendments, but not all amendments necessarily had to be submitted according to the law (Knaap and Nelson 1992, 31). In the wake of the 1981 economic recession, Oregon modified its planning program to include economic development by focusing local plan reviews on the quantity and quality of industrial land supplies (Knaap and Nelson 1992, 165, 174).

Governor's Task Force on Land Use (1982)

In May 1982, Gov. Vic Atiyeh appointed a 12-member Task Force on Land Use to investigate four issues: the length of time required to complete local plans, inefficiencies in state and local permit processes, problems of plan implementation and the continuation of financial assistance to local governments, and land use litigation. The task force held a series of public hearings around the state that attracted more than 1,000 citizens. Testimony filled seventy tape recordings and seven loose-leaf notebooks.

The task force's final report, issued September 30, 1982, recommended replacing the Land Use Board of Appeals (LUBA) with a new land use court, flexibility in dealing with cities and counties with unique and disparate characteristics, and withholding of state-shared revenues from local governments failing to meet a final plan acknowledgment deadline of January 1, 1984. The task force suggested that computerized inventories of industrial lands be established and encouraged local governments to place greater emphasis on economic development and public facilities planning. The task force's report also recommended consideration be given to establishing standards of education and experience for professional planners (Governor's Task Force on Land Use 1982; Knaap and Nelson 1992, 179).

Status of local planning (1982)

By 1982, some local comprehensive plans were still not acknowledged by LCDC. Only 151 local government plans, or 54 percent of the total, had been acknowledged by the state (Governor's Task Force on Land Use 1982; Leonard 1983, 126).[7] By the fall of 1982, all 241 cities had completed comprehensive plans, and only five county plans remained to be submitted to LCDC (Leonard 1983, 125-126). Local comprehensive plans were almost never acknowledged on the first submission (DeGrove 1984, 264). The 278th and final local comprehensive plan was acknowledged by LCDC in 1985 (Knaap and Nelson 1992, 1, 32; Nelson 1990a). Knaap and Nelson (1992, 13) and William Fulton (1991) note that the last local comprehensive plan was acknowledged in 1986. Senate Bill 100 was silent on what would happen to LCDC after local plans were acknowledged (Leonard 1983, 25).

Legislation (1983)

Following the recommendations of the Governor's Task Force on Land Use, the Oregon legislature approved bills that accelerated the acknowledgment process of local comprehensive plans and streamlined the land use permitting process. By 1983, LCDC had adopted a stance of allowing substantial (less than total) compliance with the statewide planning goals. Legislation in 1983 also was directed at promoting economic development via local comprehensive plans. Certain sections of law (ORS § 197.707 to § 197.717) indicate an intent by the legislature to enhance economic development and define it as vital to the welfare of the state (Knaap and Nelson 1992, 180). Local plans submitted after the 1983 legislation had to provide adequate supplies of commercial and industrial land.

Public facilities planning rule (1985)

To further implement Goals 9 (economic development) and 11 (public facilities), and in part to facilitate better growth management, LCDC adopted a public facilities planning rule. The administrative rule required local governments containing urban areas with 2,500 persons or more to develop public facilities plans (Knaap and Nelson 1992, 104-106).

Postacknowledgment (1986)

Eleven years after adoption of the initial statewide planning goals, all local comprehensive plans were finally acknowledged by LCDC. Entering the late 1980s, DLCD and LCDC elaborated and codified most of the goals and guidelines into statutes and administrative rules. Attention shifted in the postacknowledgment period to implementation of local plans (Knaap and Nelson 1992, 200).

Economic development (1986-1988)

In 1986, LCDC adopted an administrative rule for implementing Goal 9. Oregon's Economic Development Department (EDD) in 1986 produced an extensive volume of data to help local governments prepare economic development elements of local comprehensive plans. In 1988, Goal 9 was rewritten and retitled economic development. The intent of these efforts was to foster economic development through local land use planning (Knaap and Nelson 1992, 180-181).

Program evaluations

In 1980, DLCD received funds pursuant to the federal Coastal Zone Management Act of 1972 to prepare (via a consultant) an evaluation design. The proposed evaluation framework suggested definable objectives and measurable indicators for statewide planning goals. However, the state's economic recession limited the state's political willingness to undertake the evaluation design's recommendations. In 1983, DLCD hired another consultant to design a comprehensive plan monitoring system (Richard Ragatz Associates, Inc. 1983). Although Ragatz Associates' report was completed and distributed, local governments did not receive any funds for implementing the suggested comprehensive plan monitoring system, and the consultant's study was largely forgotten. Preparation by the University of Oregon's Bureau of Governmental Research and Service in 1987 of a prospectus and cost estimate for an evaluation design represented a third attempt to evaluate Oregon's land use program during the 1980s (Howe 1994, 275-276).

WASHINGTON

The literature does not reveal any significant planning and growth management conferences, legislation, or other relevant growth management activities in Washington during the second wave. Chapter-length accounts of growth management in Washington (Smith 1993; DeGrove

1992) do not identify any historical developments preceding adoption of the Growth Management Act (GMA) in 1990. This gap in the literature raises the question whether the inattention was due to lack of scholarly interest. It is likely that scholars paid no attention because there was little going on in Washington during this time. Prior to implementation of the Columbia Gorge Scenic Area Act (described below), Washington's role in land use was limited, local planning was optional, and one county in the gorge did not have any land use controls (Adler 1990, 316-319).

For consistency in the narrative, I would talk about events in Washington at this point. However, there were none. The absence of a historical account of growth management in Washington during the second wave provides an opportunity to insert here a brief discussion of an important development in bistate regional planning during this time period.

In the latter part of the 1980s, the states of Washington and Oregon and local governments located in the Columbia River Gorge were engaged in a unique bistate scenic area protection program that preceded Washington's growth management program. I turn to that topic briefly, with particular attention to the status of local planning in counties on the Washington side of the Columbia River Gorge.

Bistate regional planning in the Columbia River Gorge

Regional planning for the Columbia River Gorge in Washington and Oregon dates back to the 1930s with the work of the Pacific Northwest Regional Planning Commission. In 1953, the Oregon Columbia River Gorge Commission was established, and Washington set up its own state Columbia Gorge Commission in 1959. Both state commissions were supposed to educate and advocate for protection of the scenic qualities of the gorge (Abbott, Adler and Abbott 1997, 35-37).

In 1986, Congress passed Public Law 99-564, known as the Columbia Gorge National Scenic Area Act. Abbott, Adler, and Abbott (1997) provide an account of the legislative efforts leading up to passage of the 1986 scenic area law. The act declared a national interest in the scenic qualities of the Columbia River Gorge and created a national scenic area along an 83-mile stretch of the Columbia River from the Deschutes River westward to the mouth of the Sandy River near Portland. By passing the law, Congress expressed its consent for an interstate compact between Oregon and Washington for regional land use planning mandated by the federal government. The scenic area act was signed by President Reagan in 1986 (Abbott, Adler and Abbott 1997; Adler 1990).

Public Law 99-564 created an intergovernmental planning system including a bistate commission, six county governments (three in each state), and 13 urban areas. The six counties were mandated to adopt ordinances to implement the scenic area designation. The Columbia Gorge Commission was responsible for planning for less-sensitive lands and approving implementing ordinances prepared by counties. The scenic area act required the states of Oregon and Washington to fund the regional commission. Like other land use regulations preceding it, agencies leading the planning effort for the gorge scenic area (the United States Forest Service and the Gorge Commission) could impose ordinances on counties if the counties failed to adopt acceptable regulations (Adler 1990). The scenic area act's implementation record generally has followed the concepts of Oregon's land use act with the goals of preserving farm and forest lands and containing urban development in selected areas (Abbott, Adler and Abbott 1997). Just recently, the Gorge Commission and its regulatory authority has been in the Oregon news with the "Bea House" controversy. Though not relevant to the second wave of state growth management program history, it is nonetheless of sufficient interest that it be summarized here. See Sidebar 4.1 for the story of the Bea House controversy.

Status of planning in Washington's gorge counties

Most of the Washington side of the gorge lies within two counties—Skamania and Klickitat. The 1986 national scenic area legislation was spawned in part by Skamania County's approval during the early 1980s of subdivisions in the viewshed across the Columbia River from Multnomah Falls (Adler 1990). Skamania County's record of land use planning and regulation was poor enough during the 1980s for scholars of the scenia area program to conclude that the county "scandalized conservation-minded Oregonians through the 1980s by deciding to live without county zoning or any other basic form of growth management." Indeed, the Columbia River Gorge National Scenic Area originated for the most part from an effort to solve the problem of the residential subdivision of gorge lands in Washington, and most of the private land in the Gorge was on the Washington side of the river. Skamania County during the 1980s had refused to participate with Clark and Klickitat counties in an effort to establish regional planning and

Sidebar 4.1. Columbia River Gorge Scenic Area: The Bea House Controversy, 1998-1999

After receiving a permit from Skamania County, Washington in May 1997, Brian and Jody Bea began to construct their three-story, 37-foot high dream house in the Prindle area with a view of the Columbia River across from Multnomah Falls. All new development in the Columbia Gorge National Scenic Area must be reviewed for consistency with the scenic area act to ensure that structures do not clutter the landscape. The Beas's land use application for a house with a barn and a shop. was approved by the county subject to 33 conditions. Skamania County's approval of the Beas's home was challenged by the Columbia River Gorge Commission because the home is visible from Multnomah Falls and Interstate 84 and would therefore purportedly mar the scenic views of the gorge.

Executive Director Jonathan Dougherty has argued that the house should be demolished, and the Gorge Commission has the authority to order the house demolished or moved. The Gorge Commission has been criticized for entering the process too late, after the Beas's house was nearly constructed. When the commission reviewed the county's 1997 decision, it failed to raise any concerns about the visibility of the Bea House. Skamania County planners testified before a contested case hearing in December 1998 that the Beas violated permit conditions and development regulations by wiping out trees to expand their view, by grading more area than was permitted to be excavated, by locating the house on an unapproved location on the lot, and by laying out the foundation for the house prior to receiving a building permit. The record purportedly shows, however, that Skamania County's decision to approve the Bea House contains flaws and contradictions and that the county has repeatedly failed to enforce scenic area rules, including those applicable to the Beas' home site. According to writer Brent Walth (1998), the Beas, Skamania County, and the Gorge Commission are all to blame for the controversy. The Bea House might have been allowed to stand in its disputed location, but it could be years before the Beas could get the house screened sufficiently from view to meet scenic protection standards.

On January 25, 1999, the Columbia River Gorge Commission issued an enforcement order giving Skamania County six months to bring the Bea house into compliance with scenic area laws. The Beas brought suit against the Columbia River Gorge Commission and Skamania County asking that the enforcement order be dismissed. Skamania County brought suit against the commission, seeking a ruling that it lacks jurisdiction. Court proceedings were scheduled for late July 1999 (Sources: Senior 1999a, 1999b, 1999c, and 1999d; Thomson 1998; Walth 1998).

zoning on the Washington side of the gorge. Had Skamania County adopted effective land use plans and zoning in the early 1980s, it might have derailed the effort to adopt federal regulation establishing the gorge as a national scenic area. When the scenic area act was passed in 1986, Skamania County flew the United States flag at half-mast (Abbott, Adler and Abbott 1997).

Klickitat County was relatively active in land use planning during the early 1980s and instituted regulations that included a gorge scenic protection overlay zone. The county was sued during the 1980s, however, by a gorge watchdog group for allegedly violating its own law. Furthermore, in 1986 after passage of the scenic area act, Klickitat County refused on principle to take part in the implementation of the scenic area act (Abbott, Adler and Abbott 1997). Klickitat and Skamania counties are probably representative of the general status of land use planning and regulation in counties outside the Puget Sound region (and perhaps other metropolitan areas) of Washington during the 1980s.

CONCLUSIONS

What is distinct about state growth management programs during the second wave of program evolution? Several conclusions can be drawn from the legislation and implementation experiences of the second wave of state program evolution. Unfortunately, those conclusions must be drawn only from Florida and Oregon since Georgia and Washington had not yet developed state-sponsored programs of land use planning. The primary objective here is to summarize parallel developments occurring in Florida and Oregon that collectively characterize 1980s-style state growth management. To a much lesser extent, conclusions are based on observations in Georgia, where there were early efforts to create a statewide growth strategy. Some of the conclusions are cumulative in the sense that they incorporate observations about the quiet revolution which occurred a decade earlier. Also, certain themes developed

Table 4.1. Status of Local Planning, 1982 and 1986

	Florida		Georgia		Oregon		Washington	
	1982	**1986**	**1982**	**1986**	**1982**	**1986**	**1982**	**1986**
Cities	N/A	N/A	162	166	N/A	242	N/A	N/A
% of all	—	—	30.3%	33.7%	—	100%	—	—
Counties	N/A	N/A	54	52	N/A	36	N/A	N/A
% of all	—	—	34.0%	33.6%	—	100%	—	—
TOTAL	419	N/A	216	218	151	278	N/A	N/A
% of all	90.9%	—	31.2%	33.6%	54%	100%	—	—

Sources: DeGrove 1984 (Florida); Governor's Task Force on Land Use 1982 (Oregon); Knaap and Nelson 1992 (Oregon); and Kundell et al. 1989 (Georgia).

during the second wave were duplicated in the 1990s-style programs of Georgia and Washington that developed in the third wave.

Influence of the model code

Provisions of the *Model Land Development Code,* areas of critical state concern, and developments of regional impact, were maintained and strengthened in Florida during the second wave. Though not discussed in the foregoing narrative, significant literature exists on Florida's establishment of critical areas such as the Big Cypress Swamp and sponsorship of a more effective DRI process (e.g., DeGrove 1988). Oregon maintained LCDC's authority to designate areas of critical state concern, though the commission never elected to utilize that authority during the 1980s. The Georgia 2000 Committee's recommendations called for attention to regional land use impacts and thus also mirrored provisions of the model code regarding areas of critical state concern and developments of regional impact.

Ambitious local plan preparation deadlines

Table 4.1 provides a summary of the status of local planning in the four states during the 1980s, to the extent it can be determined. Recall that Oregon initially allowed only one year for local governments to prepare comprehensive plans consistent with statewide planning goals. It took 11 years before all local plans in Oregon were acknowledged. Florida's 1975 local planning act allowed four years for the preparation of plans but, by 1979, less than half the local governments had adopted comprehensive plans. All of the plans of local governments in Florida were still not complete by 1982.

Florida's 1985 Omnibus GMA gave counties just two years to revise local plans to be consistent with state and regional plans and only one year after completing plans to bring development regulations into compliance with local plans. RPCs were given only 18 months to bring comprehensive regional policy plans into compliance with the state comprehensive plan. Those and other examples of plan compliance deadlines clearly indicate that program designers were ambitious, and perhaps a bit unreasonable, in setting such short time frames to complete planning activities. The failure of local governments (and regional agencies in Florida) to meet compliance deadlines raises two important questions: Why could local governments not meet the plan deadlines imposed? What were the obstacles to local plan preparation and certification of compliance?

Inconsistency and enforcement

Oregon's land use act and Florida's GMA both mandated vertical consistency between statewide goals/plans and local comprehensive plans. Clearly, the consistency doctrine (DiMento 1980) is a centerpiece of 1980s-style state growth management. Unfortunately, vertical consistency remained an elusive goal during the second wave. Plan review experience in the two states reveals inconsistencies between state goals and local plans. As a result, both Florida and Oregon had to use sanctions and exercise enforcement powers against local governments to achieve compliance. The limited success of top down (state to local) planning mandates begs the question of whether centralized planning schemes with strong state mandates are the most appropriate way to structure a successful planning process. The debate over regulation versus incentives (or coercive versus empowerment approaches) is addressed in Chapter 12, which focuses on criticisms and prescriptions of state growth management programs.

The growing recognition that local governments were slow to comply with state planning mandates appears to have resulted in some softening of the application of such mandates. For example, Oregon's Task Force on Land Use (1982) suggested that the state's program requirements needed to be applied with some flexibility. Also, Oregon's program administrators began to seek substantial rather than total compliance with statewide planning goals. Late in the 1980s, Florida began to negotiate compliance agreements with local governments, in recognition of the need to apply state planning requirements in a flexible manner on an individual basis.

Local planning standards

One probable reason for poor plan compliance records by local governments in Florida and Oregon is that state program administrators did not adequately communicate their expectations. Oregon's statewide planning goals, by definition, are general. Although more specific voluntary guidelines also exist as part of the goals, neither the goals nor the guidelines provide objective standards upon which to determine the consistency of local plans with statewide goals. Florida's 1975 local planning act described the local plan elements required for a comprehensive plan but did not specify any standards by which compliance could be determined.

By the 1980s, this lack of local planning standards became evident to program administrators. The Florida Legislature in 1985 directed the preparation, as part of the Omnibus GMA, of local planning standards for determining plan compliance. Changes in Florida's growth management program during the second wave focused on more specific, measurable standards on which to base decisions about local comprehensive plan compliance with state mandates. Also during the 1980s, Oregon's LCDC incrementally put in place the administrative rules needed to interpret the statewide planning goals and guide local plan preparation and review. Hence, the advent of rulemaking to provide specific standards for local plans and determinations of compliance is a characteristic that distinguishes 1980s-style state growth management from the quiet revolution.

It is also worthy to note that the Oregon Governor's Task Force on Land Use (1982) recommended minimum standards for the experience and education of planners. Although this recommendation was not implemented in Oregon, minimum standards for regional planners were implemented a decade later in Georgia.

Technical assistance and capacity-building

Another likely explanation of the poor track records of local planning in Florida and Oregon during the second wave of program evolution is that local governments did not have the capacity and technical capability needed to complete plans according to state mandates. There are relatively few examples of local planning technical assistance by Oregon and Florida state governments during the quiet revolution. For exceptions in Florida, however, see Florida DCA (1976a) and KRS Associates, Inc. (1976). Both states provided grants for local planning, and there were some references found that indicate some intentions to provide models to guide local planning activities. These references, however, do not appear to constitute comprehensive approaches to providing local planning technical assistance. As noted earlier, there was a growing recognition in Florida during the early 1980s that local governments had (despite implementation of the 1975 local planning act) little capacity to address growth problems. Program administrators had just begun to recognize the importance of building the capacity of local governments for planning and problem solving. For example, Georgia's State Commission on Growth Policy (1982) explored the community preparedness of local governments for planning.

Land information systems

A growing recognition of the need for statewide databases is another hallmark of 1980s-style state growth management. The Oregon Governor's Task Force on Land Use (1982) recommended that a state land use inventory and data base be compiled. When Oregon's land use program shifted emphasis toward economic development in the 1980s, legislation and subsequent rules called for inventories of industrial lands. Georgia's legislators exhibited a similar recognition of the need for a state role in compiling land use information when it approved the formation of a Land Information Study Commission in 1987. Though during the second wave of program evolution neither Oregon nor Georgia implemented a comprehensive land information system, the recognition of the need for land information set a precedent for later efforts in Georgia.

A new emphasis on public facilities planning

During the 1980s, there was growing concern over the aging condition of infrastructure in the nation's communities. Unprecedented growth in suburban areas and the strains such development placed on existing infrastructure prompted Florida's legislators in 1985 to add concurrency and local capital improvement program requirements as major tenants of that state's growth management program. In the wake of an economic recession, and in part to better manage urban growth, the Oregon legislature required local public facility plans. LCDC followed with an administrative rule detailing the requirements of local public facility plans. Though apparently for different reasons, both Florida and Oregon added public facilities planning as major components of 1980s-style state growth management.

Permit streamlining

Much of the attention paid to Oregon's land use planning program during the early 1980s was focused on streamlining a complicated development process. Liberal provisions for appeals of development decisions in Oregon slowed down local development processes. As indicated in the next chapter, Washington struggled with regulatory reform in the mid-1990s in much the same way as Oregon did during the 1980s.

Reexamination and evaluation

Florida appears to have perfected a model of near constant reexamination of its growth management program. Program reformers in Florida used well-timed conferences and committees composed of a broad spectrum of stakeholders to debate, prepare, and pass growth management legislative reforms. Such a model of consensus building was subsequently used in Georgia to gain the passage of the 1989 Georgia Planning Act. With the exception of the Governor's Task Force on Land Use (1982), and perhaps some work of the Joint Legislative Committee on Land Use (JLCLU), Oregon did not engage in much legislative reexamination of its state land use program. On the other hand, academicians continued to study the effects of Oregon's planning program (Daniels and Nelson 1986; Leonard 1983; Porter 1986; Stroud and DeGrove 1980).

Other efforts began to materialize during the 1980s in Oregon with respect to administrative evaluation of the land use program. Program evaluation efforts were initiated but not completed in Oregon during the 1980s. In Florida, the 1986 administrative rule for local plan contents specifically included a local plan monitoring and evaluation requirement. Hence, a trend toward reexamination, monitoring, and evaluation of planning began in the 1980s and constitutes another characteristic that distinguishes 1980s-style planning from the quiet revolution.

Notes

1. It looks probable that the Florida Legislature's 1978 actions to amend the state comprehensive planning act of 1972, and adoption of the state plan itself were part of the same legislation. However, that cannot be verified here.

2. Pelham (1979) places the number of local governments required to plan in 1978 to be 529, while DeGrove (1984) finds the number of total local governments required to plan to be 461. DeGrove (1984, 122) also notes that the state as of 1978 had some 400 cities, 67 counties, and numerous special districts. Hence, the difference in the numbers may be that Pelham included special districts in his tally.

3. Cited by one source as (Chapter 85-55, Florida Laws). But see DeGrove and Juergensmeyer (1986) who indicate the Growth Management Act of 1985 amended at least twelve chapters of the Florida Statutes, most importantly chapters 163, 161, 380, 186, and 193.

4. Pelham (1993) finds the number of local governments required to plan is 458, including 67 counties. Wallis (1993, 24) finds that there were 467 plans that would be reviewed.

5. This information conflicts with research described earlier. Perhaps the local plan compliance deadlines in Florida were extended by DCA.

6. DeGrove (1992, 142) notes that the Growth Strategies Commission consisted of 31 appointed members.

7. DeGrove (1984, 263) finds that as of March 1982, only 134 local plans had been acknowledged. Further, he finds that another 84 plans had been reviewed but 30 local governments had submitted no plan at all. By July 1982, 256 of 278 local plans had been submitted to the LCDC. Only 12 of 42 coastal cities and counties had acknowledged plans in July 1982 (DeGrove 1984, 282).

CHAPTER

5

State-Sponsored Land Use Planning in the Third Wave: 1989-1997

During this time period, Florida established a Task Force on Urban Growth Patterns (1989), initiated a third Environmental Land Management Study Committee (ELMS III), achieved local government compliance with the Omnibus GMA's local planning requirements, substantially modified the requirements of GMA (1993), took a hard line against urban sprawl, and initiated pilot projects for sustainable communities (1997). Georgia passed its planning act (1989), adopted and significantly amended minimum planning standards (1990 and 1992, respectively), established programs for review of DRIs and designation of regionally important resources (RIRs), nearly completed local plans and began to prepare regional plans (1995), and passed a law requiring local service delivery strategies (1997). Oregon initiated a study of urban development patterns, passed a transportation planning rule (1991) that encouraged integration of land use and transportation in local plans, strengthened local tools for urban growth management, passed and implemented buildable lands and housing needs legislation (1995), and initiated pilot programs for regional problem solving. Washington passed growth management legislation (1990, 1991); prompted local governments toward implementation of the growth management act's critical areas, resource lands, and comprehensive planning requirements; passed a regulatory reform act (1995); and established a Land Use Study Commission (1995) to integrate the growth management act and environmental planning. Figure 5.1 provides a summary.

FLORIDA

State land development plan (1989)

In March 1989, DCA published a revised state land development plan (Thompson and Meck 1996; Florida DCA 1989a). The purpose of the plan is to guide implementation of the state comprehensive plan's goals and policies related to land development issues. The land use and development guidelines specified in the state land development plan are intended but not required to be used by local governments in preparing comprehensive plans and by RPCs in developing regional plans (Florida DCA 1989b).

In practice, the state land development plan, which has been updated over time, has had only a limited impact on policymaking. The state land development plan was envisioned by John DeGrove and Gov. Bob Graham's administration as an "integrating" feature between the state comprehensive plan and regional plans. The state land development plan is one of three functional growth management plans (the others are water and transportation). The state land development plan has never been fully connected with state and regional plans, and its only legal authority is under Chapter 380, Florida Statutes, where it is supposed to guide policy for DRIs (Quinn and Noll interview, 2/18/98).

Governor's Task Force on Urban Growth Patterns (1989)

In 1988, Gov. Bob Martinez appointed a 22-member task force to study the state's urban growth patterns. The task force formed four subcommittees, including one on local government that was chaired by DeGrove. As part of the task force's efforts, DCA sponsored a study on encouraging compact development and another that analyzed state and regional programs to determine if they encouraged urban sprawl (Florida DCA 1988a). The task force also was guided by reports prepared by the consulting firm of James Duncan and Associates and others (1989a; 1989b). These reports were significant in that they provided data on the capital costs associated with compact, contiguous, satellite, scattered, and linear urban forms via case studies of developed areas (Kelly 1993, 170). The final report of the Governor's Task Force on Urban Growth Patterns (1989) was presented to the governor on June 30, 1989. It contained

Figure 5.1. Study Committees and Legislation, 1989-1997

	1989	1990	1991	1992	1993	1994	1995	1996	1997
Florida	State Land Development Plan (1989)								
	Governor's Task Force on Urban Growth Patterns (1989)								
			Environmental Land Management Study Committee III (1991)						
					Anti-sprawl policy (1993)				
					Growth Management Act (1993)				
							Land Use and Water Planning Task Force (1995)		
									Sustainable Communities Demonstration Projects (1997)
Georgia	House Bill 215 (Georgia Planning Act) (1989)								
		Minimum planning standards (1990)							
			House Bill 643 (Mountain and River Corridor Protection Act) (1991)						
				Minimum planning standards (amended) (1992)					
					Government Efficiency Act (1993)				
							Future Communities Commission (1995)		
								Minimum standards for regional plans (1996)	
									House Bill 489 (Service Delivery Strategy Act) (1997)

Figure 5.1. Study Committees and Legislation, 1989-1997 (Continued)

	1989 ....1990 ....1991...........1992...........1993...........1994...........1995...........1996...........1997
Oregon	Urban Growth Management Study (1989)
	Task Group on Development Inside Urban Growth Boundaries (1991)
	Transportation Planning Rule (1991)
	Transportation & Growth Management Program (1993)
	House Bill 2709 (Buildable Lands and Housing Needs (1995)
	Regional Problem Solving (1995)
Washington	Executive Order 89-08 Growth Strategies Commission (1989)
	House Bill 2929 (Growth Management Act I) (1990)
	House Bill 1025 (Growth Management Act II) (1991)
	Minimum planning standards (1992)
	Substitute Senate Bill 1724 (Regulatory Reform Act) (1995)
	Land Use Study Commission (1995)
	Engrossed Senate Bill 6094 (Buildable Lands) (1997)

Source: Compiled from various sources as indicated in the text.

43 recommendations to address the goal of stopping urban sprawl, including establishment of urban service areas (DCA 1989c). Incidentally, on November 6, 1989, Florida's DCA also sponsored a conference on urban sprawl in Orlando (Florida DCA 1989d). The concern over urban sprawl also manifested itself in other actions of DCA.

Defining and limiting urban sprawl

Some scholars believe that urban sprawl was exacerbated by the growth management program's transportation concurrency requirements, because urban development has been implicitly encouraged to locate in the outlying areas of regions where road capacity is available (Weitz 1997a; Wallis 1993, 29; Koenig 1990). DCA worked toward flexibility of the concurrency mandate while strictly enforcing the law's antisprawl requirements. Plans for Charlotte and Citrus counties were rejected by DCA secretary Thomas Pelham for promoting urban and rural sprawl. In the case of Charlotte County's plan, DCA argued it had authority to find that a plan that promoted sprawl was not in compliance based on the state plan. When DCA was challenged on the finding of noncompliance, an administrative hearing officer found that combating sprawl was an emerging policy rather than a rule and was therefore not ripe for a rule challenge. DCA's approach to urban sprawl was upheld when the Florida Division of Administrative Hearings ruled in favor of DCA in consolidated cases brought by Charlotte County and homebuilders associations (Florida DCA 1990a).

In 1991, the District Court of Appeals upheld DCA's authority to define urban sprawl on the basis of existing language in the GMA. The court further upheld DCA's interpretation of sprawl. Secretary Pelham found the order to be a great victory, supporting DCA's authority to combat sprawl. In 1993, DCA was working on legislation that would further define and limit urban sprawl (Wallis 1993, 30-31; Koenig 1990).

ELMS III and legislation (1991-1992)

In November 1991, Gov. Lawton Chiles appointed 51 members to a third environmental land management study committee (Shelley 1993). ELMS III investigated whether the state's land use laws were working and, more specifically, Florida's record with respect to containing urban sprawl, protecting farm and forest lands, and promoting affordable housing (Murley, Draper and Durrence 1992). The committee issued a final report including 174 recommendations for improvements to the growth management system. Two of the more important recommendations included: reauthorization of RPCs to focus on planning and coordination roles and termination of the DRI program after implementation of local plans enhanced by intergovernmental coordination elements (ICEs) (Shelley 1993).

An important role was played by 1000 Friends of Florida in thwarting efforts to weaken Florida's land use laws during the 1992 legislative session. At Gov. Chiles's urging, virtually all of the major decisions about the state's growth management laws were to be deferred until 1993 and the work of ELMS III (Murley, Draper and Durrence 1992). However, the 1992 legislative session resulted in a "fine-tuning" law that included, among other things, the requirement that DCA make recommendations about whether the DRI program should be replaced, repealed, or incorporated into the comprehensive planning process. Another bill (HB 1061) called for the sunset of RPCs in October 1993 and established a thorough review of the role of RPCs by the state Advisory Council on Intergovernmental Relations and ELMS III. Unless reenacted by the Florida legislature, portions of the State and Regional Planning Act (Florida Statutes Chap. 186) would be repealed by HB 1061 (Murley, Draper and Durrence 1992). Major attacks on state land use legislation were expected again in the 1993 session (DeGrove 1994; Lewis 1992).

Status of local planning (1989-1992)

By November 1989, approximately 120 local governments had adopted local comprehensive plans pursuant to the 1985 act (Florida DCA 1989e). By 1990, DCA had reviewed about half of the local comprehensive plans submitted by Florida's 457 local governments. By August 1990, DCA had made 225 compliance determinations: 114 plans were found to be in compliance, 39 were still not in compliance, and 72 were found to be not in compliance but the local governments involved had entered into stipulated settlement (negotiated compliance) agreements with DCA. All local comprehensive plan reviews were expected to be completed by the spring of 1992, and by July 1992, all local governments were expected to have land development regulations adopted (Florida DCA 1990b).

McKay (1991) notes that as of August 1991, all 459 of Florida's local governments had submitted comprehensive plans to DCA for review. More than one-half (268) of the local plans were in compliance (by original submission or through negotiated compliance), while 64 were not in compliance and 127 plans were under review in September 1991. Many small cities and some of the rural counties have resisted the state mandate to meet minimum statutory requirements, but once found not in compliance most were subsequently willing to comply with the state's growth management laws (McKay 1991).

According to DCA's secretary William Sadowski (1992), by February 1992, all 457 local governments had filed comprehensive plans with DCA. Of those, 276 had been found in compliance with the 1985 growth management act, 33 were the subject of final or pending compliance agreements, 101 were found not in compliance, and the reminder were somewhere in the review pipeline. Other sources present compliance statistics that appear to conflict with the secretary's findings.[1]

Status of regional planning

Florida's regional planning councils have been viewed by some as ineffective and by others as an unnecessary additional layer of authority to review local plans. Prior to the passage of the Omnibus Growth Management Act (1985), RPCs were weak in both technical capacity and political authority. The Omnibus GMA authorized funds for preparing regional policy plans. It also authorized the councils to develop local plans if local governments elected the RPC to do so or if local governments refused to develop their own plans. One observer finds that RPCs made significant progress in helping to implement the state comprehensive plan, and that as of 1991 each of the councils had submitted amendments to its regional policy plan to the state for review (McKay 1991). DCA's newsletter confirms this point. During the first six months of 1991, 10 of the 11 RPCs were expected to submit amendments to their comprehensive regional policy plans for state review (Florida DCA 1991b).

Nevertheless, few, if any, of the RPCs are widely respected by their member local governments. The councils have not demonstrated effectiveness in coordinating local comprehensive plans within their jurisdictions. The directors of RPCs are not officially at the bargaining table when DCA negotiates compliance agreements with local governments (Wallis 1993, 40-41).

As noted previously, given the widespread criticism of RPCs, the Florida Legislature passed a bill (Chapter 92-182, Section 1, 1992 Florida Laws) that would end the RPC legislation if it was not affirmatively retained by the 1993 legislature. ELMS III was also required to evaluate RPCs and to submit recommendations by November 1, 1992 (Pelham 1993). Hence, going into the 1993 legislative session, serious questions were being raised locally and in the legislature about the desirability of continuing the RPCs in their current roles.

Growth Management Act (1993)

The 1993 legislative session was expected to be controversial with the legislative recommendations of ELMS III due. The legislature passed the Growth Management Act of 1993 (CS/HB 2315), which marked the culmination of a year-long review of the state's growth management laws by ELMS III (Murley, Powell and Draper 1993). The act (Chapter 93-206, Florida Statutes) also is known as the "ELMS III legislation" (Shelley 1993). This title is fitting because approximately 130 of ELMS III's 174 recommendations are reflected in the statute (Murley, Powell and Draper 1993).

Growth management element of the state plan. Significant changes were made to the content of Florida's state comprehensive plan by the 1993 act. Because the state comprehensive plan had not been reviewed and revised since its adoption, the 1993 act made the plan subject to biennial review and revision. The revised state plan was specifically required to include measurable objectives that were not part of the state plan at the time the legislation was adopted. Of specific interest to this inquiry, the 1993 act also required preparation of a growth management element of the state comprehensive plan (Murley, Powell and Draper 1993). The growth management element, however, has never been prepared, due in part to opposition from the Governor's Office and its strategic planning unit (Quinn and Noll interview, 2/18/98).

Changes in regional planning. The 1993 Growth Management Act made significant changes to the Regional Planning Council Act. RPCs were scheduled to sunset in 1993 based on 1992 legislation already described. ELMS III recommended that the 11 RPCs be retained but that changes be made regarding their legal authority. Essentially, the planning and coordination roles of RPCs were made more explicit, while their regulatory authority was minimized. For instance, RPCs were stripped of their authority to appeal development orders for DRIs. RPCs were also required by the 1993 act to establish dispute resolution and "cross-acceptance" processes to resolve inconsistencies between regional and local plans. Furthermore, each RPC was required to adopt new "strategic regional policy plans" (e.g., see Northeast Florida Regional Planning Council 1996) containing only five elements but excluding land use, thus replacing the comprehensive regional policy plans of the earlier era. To ensure broad local support of the regional plans, a two-thirds vote of the RPC's governing board was required for plan adoption (Murley, Powell and Draper 1993).

Intergovernmental coordination element (ICE). The Growth Management Act of 1993 resulted in the first major changes to the Local Government Comprehensive Planning and Land Development Regulation Act (Omnibus GMA) since it was passed in 1985. The 1993 act revised three mandatory elements of local comprehensive plans: housing, transportation, and intergovernmental coordination, the latter being the most significant. The intergovernmental coordination element (ICE) of a local comprehensive plan (due December 31, 1997) and resulting regulatory process were envisioned to replace the DRI program, which had been recommended by ELMS III for termination under certain conditions. Certain small and rural local governments could retain the DRI program, but completion by most local governments of ICEs and subsequent steps would lead to termination of the DRI program in their jurisdiction (Murley, Powell and Draper 1993). Indeed, ELMS III saw ICEs as a mechanism for "withering away" the DRI program (Quinn and Noll interview, 2/18/98). The 1993 ELMS III legislation reflected this intention to phase out the DRI program and shift responsibility for review of large scale developments to local governments through revised ICEs (Florida DCA 1995).

Jim Quinn, chief of DCA's Bureau of State Planning, and Paul Noll, senior management analyst in the state planning bureau, indicate that the ICE has not replaced the DRI program (Quinn and Noll interview, 2/18/98). The idea was that the extraterritorial view of DRI reviews could be imbedded in ICE, but putting that notion into practice has been difficult. Furthermore, the development community, ironically, favored the DRI process to what was evolving out of the implementation of ICEs, such as the identification of "regionally significant resources." In practice, the ICEs are weak, nearly impossible to enforce, and do not adequately address extrajurisdictional impacts as originally intended. Furthermore, it is the RPCs rather than local governments that have developed expertise in regional impact reviews. Hence, while local governments will still be required to prepare and maintain ICEs, the "new" ICE provisions (relative to replacing DRIs) will be excised from the rule (Quinn and Noll interview, 2/18/98).

Other results of the 1993 Act. Several other activities were spawned by the 180-page ELMS III legislation. These included: (1) a study, prepared by Gov. Chiles's office, of regional planning agency boundaries; (2) publication of an administrative rule to guide rewrites of regional strategic policy plans; (3) preparation of amendments by DCA to Rule 9J-5 for presentation to the 1994 legislature; (4) a streamlining of the local plan amendment process, and (5) refinements to the areas of critical state concern program (Murley, Powell and Draper 1993).

Status of planning (1993-1995)

By July 1993, more than 90 percent of local governments in Florida had obtained compliance or had compliance agreements with DCA (DeGrove 1994). In 1995, a bill was proposed, but not enacted, that would have designated the state comprehensive plan as the "state planning document," thus subjecting the judicial branch to the state strategic planning process (Henderson, Drake and Ross 1995).

Land Use and Water Planning Task Force (1995)

In November 1993, Gov. Chiles appointed a Land Use and Water Planning Task Force that was initially recommended by ELMS III and included in the 1993 ELMS III legislation. Its final report in 1995 contained 29 recommendations to enhance the state's land and water policies. These recommendations included, after considerable debate, the repeal of the legislative requirement for a growth management element of the state comprehensive plan and substitution in its place of three state-level agency plans (water, land, and transportation) (Shelley 1995).

Sustainable communities demonstration projects (1997)

The Governor's Commission for a Sustainable South Florida was created to address the task of recommending how to restore the ecosystem and promote a sustainable economy and quality communities. In its report to the governor, the commission recommended creation of "sustainable communities" in which sprawl would be curtailed by urban development boundaries and whose urban centers would provide an economically vibrant lifestyle. The Florida Legislature acted on these recommendations with the passage of the Florida Sustainable Communities Demonstration Project, codified as Florida Statutes § 163.3244.

Five communities were designated as pilot projects, three of which were required to be in the South Florida Water Management District: Boca Raton, Martin County, Ocala, Orlando, and Tampa/Hillsborough County. Limiting urban sprawl is one of six broad principles of sustainability defined by the program, and sprawl is to be contained by instituting urban development boundaries in the pilot projects (Florida DCA 1997a, 1997b). At the time of this writing, it was too early to speculate about the success of these pilot projects.

GEORGIA

The Georgia Planning Act (1989)

Gov. Joe Frank Harris convened the 1989 legislative session with the charge to pass growth strategies legislation. There were numerous skeptics because three prior efforts to produce and pass growth management legislation had never been accepted politically. The governor met with wavering legislators and directed his entire staff to work for adoption of the legislation. During a two-week period in 1988, Gov. Harris himself made personal appeals for support of the growth strategies legislation at 15 business forums. The governor's effort won him an award from the American Planning Association in 1990 for distinguished leadership by an elected official (Walker 1990).

Requirements of the Georgia Planning Act

Georgia's three-tiered statewide comprehensive growth management legislation (House Bill 215) was passed in 1989 with a unanimous vote from the senate and a 155 to 13 vote in the politically conservative house (DeGrove 1992, 106; DeGrove, Roberts and Nelson 1990; Thornton 1990; Walker 1990). Georgia's planning law provides a unique experiment in bottom-up planning. Georgia DCA's Office of Coordinated Planning (OCP) notes that "lawmakers and planners realized that a state-mandated, Oregon-style growth management system would never fly in Georgia, a home rule state with strong opinions on local government autonomy and private property rights" (Georgia DCA 1996a).

The 1989 Georgia Planning Act requires regional planning, provides incentives for local planning, and establishes procedures for identifying regionally important resources (RIRs) and reviewing DRIs (Frederick 1992). Local governments are not required to prepare and adopt local comprehensive plans. Failure to adopt a state-approved plan, however, results in decertification of the local government, or in more precise terms, loss of qualified local government status. Local governments without qualified local government status are ineligible to receive certain grants and loans available from DCA, the Department of Natural Resources (DNR) and other authorities (Georgia DCA 1996a). The act was deliberately short on penalties for local governments that do not plan, but incentives to plan are provided (Lawlor 1992). DCA was reorganized with OCP to provide technical assistance and databases, and to otherwise implement the planning law (Walker 1990).

Minimum standards for local plans (1990)

DCA formed a Coordinated Planning Implementation Committee and an Implementation Issues Policy Task Force to assist in the early implementation of the 1989 Georgia Planning Act. The Georgia Chapter of APA was represented on the Implementation Committee but was not given a seat on the task force (Kirk 1990). DeGrove (1992, 109) notes that implementation by DCA began after it received a letter from the governor in October 1988 requesting assistance, and work teams were established to develop planning standards and procedures, construct a data network, and determine the proper distribution of grant money.

Georgia Code § 50-8-7.1 directs DCA to establish minimum standards and procedures for coordinated and comprehensive planning. Those minimum planning standards were adopted by the Board of Community Affairs on January 10, 1990. The Georgia Planning Act (Georgia Code § 50-8-7.1) required ratification of the initial minimum standards and procedures by the Georgia General Assembly, which the legislature accomplished via House Resolution 638 (Resolution 77, Georgia Laws, 1990 Session) on April 4, 1990.

The Georgia Planning Act also required minimum standards and procedures for protection of natural resources, the environment, and vital areas of the state. The Board of Natural Resources adopted those standards and procedures on December 6, 1989. The Georgia Planning Act (Georgia Code § 12-2-8) also required general assembly ratification of the initial environmental planning criteria (known as the "part five" standards because they were encompassed within part five of the 1989 Georgia Planning Act). The Georgia General Assembly ratified those environmental planning standards via Senate Resolution 331 (Resolution 63, Georgia Laws, 1990 Session) on March 28, 1990.

Mountain and river corridor protection (1991)

The Mountain and River Corridor Protection Act (House Bill 643) was passed in 1991. This legislation was much weaker than the 1988 bill (see Chapter 4) that Lieutenant Gov. Miller succeeded in guiding through the Senate, but which ultimately failed (Weitz 1992; Georgia APA 1991).

Capital facilities, impact fees, and new standards

In 1990, the Georgia General Assembly passed the Georgia Development Impact Fee Act (House Bill 796). This act authorizes cities and counties with adopted comprehensive plans that include capital facilities elements to impose development impact fees (Dillard and Dingle 1990). On April 9, 1992, the Board of Community Affairs adopted revisions to the minimum planning standards for local comprehensive plans (see Sidebar 12.3). The revised standards were effective October 1, 1992, and applied to plans submitted for regional review after September 30, 1992. The amended standards incorporated the requirements of the Development Impact Fee Act and Mountain and River Corridor Protection Act (Doyle 1992; Georgia APA 1992a; Georgia DCA 1992a).

Related legislation (1992-1993)

Also in 1992, the general assembly passed Senate Bill 660, which gave RDCs authority to set up nonprofit lending programs. The councils were already exercising this function, perhaps without the appropriate legal authority. The general assembly also passed two other bills related to coordinated planning. House Bill 1389 deleted all aspects of the Shore Assistance Act and created the Marshland Protection Act (Georgia APA 1992b). Senate Bill 590 changed the composition of the Governor's Development Council (attached to DCA for administrative purposes) to include commissioners of various state departments and five private sector members (DeGrove 1992, 114; Georgia APA 1992b).

In 1993, the Georgia General Assembly passed the Government Efficiency Act, which provided funds for studying or implementing local service or service-provider consolidation. This law's implementation provided a timely complement to the Georgia Planning Act because local governments discovered through public facilities planning and capital improvement programming that there were opportunities for service consolidation (Georgia DCA 1996a).

Status of local planning in the 1990s

Local plan preparation proceeded according to a staggered schedule prepared by OCP after recommendations from RDCs. The first local plans, including prototypes prepared by RDCs with financial support from DCA (see Sidebar 10.1), were due in 1991 and the last local government plans were due to be adopted by September 30, 1995. Despite the lack of a local planning mandate, local plans were as of the early 1990s being prepared by most if not all local governments (Lawlor 1992), at least by those that were scheduled by their RDC and DCA to plan.

It is surprising to some that Georgia's local governments have prepared local plans under the voluntary system of coordinated planning. For example, Mike Gleaton, director of OCP, suggested at the concept stage that a 75 percent participation rate would be a great achievement (Georgia DCA 1996a). By the end of 1995, virtually all of Georgia's 700 cities and counties obtained the status of "qualified" local government (DeGrove 1996). By 1997, 680 (including all 159 counties) of Georgia's 692 local governments (98.3 percent) had adopted comprehensive plans consistent with minimum planning standards adopted pursuant to the Georgia Planning Act (see Table 5.2). The high degree of compliance by local governments is probably attributed to the state's selection of an appropriate combination of carrots and sticks, including: incentives (e.g., authorization to adopt development impact fees); disincentives (e.g., loss of eligibility for certain grant funds); less detailed planning standards than those found in Florida; partial funding of some plans through RDCs; and the availability of technical assistance from the state and regions (e.g., preparation of planning guidebooks and assistance by regional planners).

Implementation of environmental planning standards

On the other hand, DCA's report on local implementation of the more specialized land use and environmental standards in Georgia is not very positive. Database analysis by DCA indicates that, for a variety of reasons, less than two-thirds (62 percent) of the 313 local governments with one or more water supply watersheds in their jurisdiction commit in their plan to implement protection standards promulgated by DNR. The percentage of local governments with jurisdiction intending to implement mountain protection standards is even lower. Of 22 local governments with jurisdictions containing protected mountains, only 58 percent indicate in plans the intent to implement some or all of the recommended protection measures. Accuracy of available protected mountain maps is cited as a chief factor limiting local implementation.

The prospects for local plan implementation of the requirements for river corridor protection are brighter. Of 187 local governments with jurisdictions containing protected rivers, 73 percent have plans that indicate an intent to implement all or some of the protection measures recommended by the Mountain and River Corridor Protection Act and promulgated by DNR (Georgia DCA 1996a).

Implementation of capital improvement programs

Only 17 local governments had by 1996 adopted capital improvement plan elements that met minimum planning standards. Such elements are required for local governments to be eligible to charge impact fees under the 1990 Development Impact Fee Act. DCA attributes the low number to the significant administrative and financial burdens imposed by the impact fee act. Legislative proposals to simplify the planning and regulatory requirements have so far been unsuccessful (Georgia DCA 1996a).

A new era of regional planning

With local planning nearly completed, the coordinated planning program shifted its emphasis to the preparation of regional plans. Regional planning required by the Georgia Planning Act has been sidetracked by political debates and legislative proposals for realignment of the boundaries of RDCs. Some of the complications arose with Gov. Miller's proposal for a Council of Economic Development Organizations (i.e., regional economic development districts), while others grew out of fiscal mismanagement by certain RDCs. Given opposition from a majority of RDCs, the Georgia Board of Community Affairs on January 10, 1995 voted not to comprehensively realign RDC boundaries into a recommended 12-district configuration resembling the governor's regional economic development districts. Instead, the board opted for an incremental, locally driven approach and approved the combination of two RDCs and the transfer of certain counties between RDCs (Georgia DCA 1996a).

Despite the conflict and mistrust generated by the debate over boundaries of the RDCs, regional planning is now under way. Minimum standards for regional planning were adopted by the Board of Community Affairs in May 1996. That same year, DCA funded 11 of the state's 17 RDCs to begin regional planning. In two cases, pairs of RDCs combined to produce regional plans (Georgia DCA 1996a).

Implementation of a statewide database

One of the successes that DCA can boast about is that Georgia is the only state to have collected existing and future land use data statewide according to a unified coding system. Given OCP's emphasis on the use of geographic information systems (GIS) in local and regional planning, land use maps can be overlaid on community facilities and other layers of data. A chief benefit of this system is the edge the data may give the state in its economic competition with other southern states (Georgia DCA 1996a). Georgia's vision of a three-tiered system of coordinated planning cannot be completed until RDCs finish the mandated regional plans and the state itself completes and adopts a state plan.

Georgia Future Communities Commission (1995)

Independent of but related to coordinated planning is the work of the Georgia Future Communities Commission. The Georgia General Assembly established the commission by resolution in 1995 to investigate problems related to economics, governance, and quality of life in Georgia's communities. The commission had four work groups, one of which was charged with economic development and land use issues. That work group heard expert testimony on growth management, planning, and zoning issues. The Commission was introduced to land development tools such as urban growth boundaries (UGBs) and transferable development rights (TDR). It was charged with proposing recommendations for the problems found, and the commission worked with the University of Georgia's Carl Vinson Institute of Government to develop a benchmarking process to measure local government progress (Georgia APA 1996). By the summer of 1996, the commission concluded that service duplication, overlap, competition, and conflict had fostered inefficient service delivery systems (Association County Commissioners Georgia et al. 1997, foreword).

Service Delivery Strategy Act (1997)

The Georgia General Assembly in 1997 passed House Bill 489, which requires each county and the cities within the county to adopt a "service delivery strategy" by July 1, 1999.[2] The law does not define what is meant by local government services, and this omission was apparently intentional. The bill and three companion bills that passed the General Assembly were signed by Gov. Miller. In the spirit of Georgia's local home rule tradition and consistent with the bottom-up design of Georgia's planning program, the approach to service delivery strategies recommended by the city and county associations and adopted as law in Georgia is a locally controlled process. The legislation is intentionally vague to maximize the discretion of cities and counties in the development of their service delivery strategies (Association County Commissioners Georgia et al. 1997).

Each county was required to initiate development of a service delivery strategy between July 1, 1997, and January 1, 1998. The bill specifies that each service delivery strategy must include an identification of services provided by various entities; assignment of responsibility for the provision of services and the location of service areas; a description of funding sources; and an identification of contracts, ordinances and other measures necessary to implement the service delivery strategy. Adoption by resolution of a service delivery strategy is required by the county, the county seat city, all cities over 9,000 population, and 50 percent or more of all other cities over 500 population in the county.

Georgia's DCA is assigned responsibility for verifying local adoption of service delivery strategies in compliance with the act. According to the law, however, DCA shall neither approve nor disapprove the specific elements or outcomes of service delivery strategies. Criteria for service delivery strategies include elimination of unnecessary duplication, arbitrary water and sewer rate differentials, and double taxation.

Sanctions for noncompliance include, as with the Georgia Planning Act, ineligibility of local governments to receive DCA-administered grants and state-administered permits. Also, projects inconsistent with an adopted strategy will not be eligible for state funding or permits. Updates of service delivery strategies must be completed according to DCA's schedule for local comprehensive plan updates (Association County Commissioners Georgia et al. 1997). Georgia's lawmakers displayed good forethought in anticipating the need to integrate service delivery strategies into local comprehensive plans at a future date most convenient and reasonable for local governments.

Of special interest to this inquiry are the act's provisions regarding land use plans. The law requires that local governments must amend their land use plans to eliminate conflicts and ensure compatibility. The intent of these provisions is to protect citizens near borders of local government jurisdictions from land use conflicts. This effort indicates Georgia's further interest in the 1990s in securing horizontal coordination (see Chapter 8). Adoption of a single land use plan for the entire county, including incorporated areas, is an alternative to amending individual local land use plans. House Bill 489 also requires that extraterritorial water and sewer services by any jurisdiction must be consistent with applicable land use plans and ordinances. Furthermore, processes must be established by July 1, 1998, to resolve land use classification disputes when a county objects to a municipal annexation within its jurisdiction (Association County Commissioners Georgia et al. 1997). According to Larry Sparks, director of planning for the Georgia Mountains RDC, there is a movement among cities and counties to try and do away with the provisions of House Bill 489 in the 1999 session of the Georgia General Assembly (Sparks interview, December 26, 1998).

OREGON

Urban growth management study (1989)

By the late 1980s, with local comprehensive plans acknowledged, the emphasis of the program and its watchdog group, 1000 Friends of Oregon, shifted from protection of farm and forest lands to a focus on more efficient development within UGBs to contain sprawl (Oliver 1992). In the 1990s, the Department of Land Conservation and Development continued to recognize that it should undertake evaluations and investigate growth management innovations by other growth management states (Abbott, Howe and Adler 1994, xxii; Howe 1991a). In 1989, the Oregon Legislature approved funding for, and DLCD sponsored preparation of, a comprehensive urban growth management study and a study of farm and forest lands (Weitz and Moore 1998; DeGrove 1992, 150; Knaap and Nelson 1992, 58). The urban growth management study included preparation of four case studies that quantified development trends inside and outside of UGBs (Oregon DLCD 1992; ECONorthwest et al. 1991). In 1991, the Oregon Legislature curtailed DLCD's request for additional funds to follow up and complete the 1990-1991 urban growth management study (Abbott 1994). DLCD then formed a Task Group on Development Inside Urban Growth Boundaries composed of local planners and stakeholders. The task group described several urban growth management problems and recommended additional tools to address the problems of urban development inside UGBs (Oregon DLCD 1992; also see Weitz and Moore 1998).

Transportation planning rule (1991)

In 1991, LCDC adopted the transportation planning rule (OAR § 660-12). This rule requires each local government with a population of 2,500 or more to prepare and implement a transportation system plan. With respect to land use, the rule requires that local governments in metropolitan regions reconsider all existing land use designations and densities to determine if they support multiple modes of travel. Local governments are also supposed to amend their ordinances to encourage infill development. DLCD, in collaboration with the Oregon Chapter of the APA, prepared an 18-minute video describing the rule. The transportation planning rule won an award in 1993 from APA for planning implementation by a large jurisdiction (Morris 1993).

Transportation and Growth Management Program (1993)

The Oregon Department of Transportation (ODOT) and DLCD created Oregon's Transportation and Growth Management (TGM) Program in 1993 in part to promote improved urban growth management in Oregon's urban areas and to develop additional urban growth management tools for inclusion in the state's planning program (Weitz and Moore 1998; Cortright, Gregor, Kelly et al. 1993). In 1994, the TGM Program sponsored a technical evaluation and a handbook of the 11 growth management tools (ECONorthwest and colleagues 1995a, 1995b) that the 1992 Task Group on Development Inside Urban Growth Boundaries had recommended (Oregon DLCD 1992). The TGM Program also sponsored preparation in 1995 of a method for conducting case studies of development inside UGBs. I was Oregon's project manager for those two efforts.

As distinguished from the 1991 case studies, the 1995 case studies focused only on development patterns inside UGBs. The case studies method was designed to present empirical evidence (tables and maps) that would confirm or deny the task group's finding of dispersed development inside UGBs. Depending on the amount of dispersion the case studies might show, LCDC might require, via administrative rules, local implementation of additional urban growth management tools. The case studies demonstrated, however, that recent urban development had proceeded largely in conformance with Oregon's land use policies (Weitz and Moore 1998). Another case study, one I prepared personally but which has not been reported previously, is a time series analysis of development patterns in the Bend UGB (see Sidebar 5.1).

Sidebar 5.1. Bend, Oregon: The Epitome of Urban Sprawl?

One of the projects I worked on as an urban growth management specialist for the state of Oregon was a time-series analysis of development trends in the Bend UGB (located in central Oregon). It was intended to confirm or deny the dispersed development hypothesis as applied to the Bend UGB. This exercise was undertaken to substantiate the perception of the TGM Program staff that the Bend UGB exhibited a prime example of development dispersal (sprawl, leapfrogging, discontinuous and discontiguous development). The work was intended to complement other case studies of development inside UGBs (for the results of those case studies see Weitz and Moore 1998).

The Bend study largely confirmed the concerns of the Task Group on Development Inside UGBs and the TGM Program. Dispersed development existed early in the history of the Bend UGB. In fact, the UGB itself was drawn in the late 1970s to include an already dispersed pattern of urban development approvals. Though the dispersed development pattern of the early 1970s set the stage for subsequent sprawl, a continued pattern of development dispersal was evident in each of the time periods studied. Bend in 1962 had a compact grid development pattern of approximately two square miles. By 1981, after 20 years of extensive urban growth, development in the Bend UGB had spread out in a discontinuous pattern approximately five miles in an east-west direction and eight miles in the north-south direction.

Development during 1981-1985 was also highly dispersed, with hardly any residential development locating contiguous to the central urban core. Although most of the development during this period was contiguous to or within dispersed residential subdivisions, smaller subdivisions occurred in even more isolated and remote locations. By 1985 a discontinuous urban commercial strip along US Highway 97 of approximately five miles in length had emerged.

During 1985 to 1991 residential development occurred in almost every section of the UGB. While the pattern of new development was one of general infilling of vacant land among other subdivisions, there was nevertheless a continuing scatter pattern of development. Nonresidential development occurred mostly as infill within the discontinuous commercial strip of US Highway 97, although commercial and industrial development also moved into nonhighway locations during this period.

The 1991-1995 period was characterized mostly by construction of golf course residential developments in the western and northwestern sections of the UGB. Multifamily developments were built in new locations, thus resulting in limited dispersal of what was until 1991 a fairly concentrated multifamily development pattern. Nonresidential development followed a pattern of infilling the (by now) contiguous and nearly continuous commercial strip along US Highway 97, although some institutional, commercial and light industrial development continued in nonhighway locations of the UGB.

Several factors contributed to the dispersed development pattern in Bend. Local (particularly those of Deschutes County) and state policies on public facilities and land use are probably the single most important contributing factors. Deschutes County's policies permitted the development of dispersed residential subdivisions in the UGB without connection to sanitary sewer, but state environmental policy facilitated local policy until the early 1970s. Indeed, the county's local public facilities and land use policies were acknowledged as consistent with state land use policy. Another factor leading to development dispersal in the Bend UGB is the existence of nonurban and "interim" development. Urban residential subdivisions "leapfrogged" over larger undeveloped properties and lower density residential properties. Another factor contributing to development dispersal was the lack of availability of certain lands in the UGB, due principally to the concentration of vacant land in larger parcels controlled by a few owners who would not release the lands for urban development.

Earlier and stronger growth management could have avoided the problem of dispersed development in the Bend UGB. Substantiating the existence of dispersed development in Bend and identifying the probable causes of the development dispersal lend additional credibility and urgency to the task group's recommendations for strengthened urban growth management. It is never too late to apply new tools that will retrofit dispersed urban development patterns into the transportation-efficient livable communities the TGM program is committed to achieving.

Source: Oregon Transportation and Growth Management Program. 1995a. Problem Documentation Case Study: Bend Urban Growth Boundary Development Time Series Analysis, 1985-1995.

The TGM Program designed and implemented a local government grant program and technical assistance (see Figure 10.3) to carry forth its objectives of multimodal transportation system plans and the application of new and improved urban growth management by local governments. Much of the program's budget is derived from Intermodal Surface Transportation Efficiency Act (ISTEA) funds, and local grants constitute the vast majority of the program's budget. In addition to local grants (see Sidebar 10.2), the TGM program has conducted various analyses and studies to develop state policy. As one example, the TGM program sponsored a consultant study to develop methods and case studies by which transportation accessibility can be measured (JFK and Associates, Pacific Rim Resources and SG Resources 1996).

Buildable lands and other legislation

In 1993, the Oregon Legislature passed House Bill 3661B which allows housing to be built on certain rural lots of record created before 1985. The bill was generally considered to be an attack on, and a weakening of, Oregon's land use program. That same year, DLCD's budget was cut to a figure of some $400,000 less than that proposed by the governor (APA 1993). However, due to the election in November 1994 of a supportive governor, John Kitzhaber, major adjustments made by the 1993 Oregon legislature to the state land use program have been implemented without weakening the system (DeGrove 1996). A massive assault was made on land use laws by the Oregon Legislature in 1995. In April 1995, 1000 Friends of Oregon was actively opposing 57 proposed land use bills. However, the efforts by Republican legislators to weaken former Gov. Tom McCall's land use legacy either failed or were vetoed by Gov. Kitzhaber (DeGrove 1996; Liberty 1996).

A significant piece of legislation passed by the Oregon Legislature in 1995 is House Bill 2709 (ORS § 197.296). This legislation was introduced by the Metropolitan Portland Homebuilders Association and was designed to facilitate expansion of UGBs. Through compromises generated by a working group including 1000 Friends of Oregon, the bill actually evolved into legislation codifying existing planning practices and providing new mechanisms to implement the state's affordable housing and growth management policies. Under this new legislation, the long-accepted practice of drawing UGBs to provide 20-year supplies of land was codified. The law also required that city and county population forecasts be coordinated (ORS § 195.036). Certain urban local governments must inventory their supplies of buildable residential lands based on actual mixes of housing types and densities and project their housing needs.

In cases where the actual densities and land supplies fall short of residential development needs projected for the 20-year planning period, those governments must expand their UGBs or adopt measures (e.g., minimum residential development densities) that demonstrably increase the likelihood that the appropriate mixes and densities of residential development will occur inside existing UGBs. The bill met with the approval of the homebuilders because it gave them some reassurance that UGBs would not be drawn too tightly to accommodate the residential housing market (also see Sidebar 7.1). It met with DLCD's approval because it codified some long-standing planning principles for urban development (e.g., 20-year supplies of land in UGBs) and diverse, affordable housing (e.g., housing needs assessments). House Bill 2709 passed both the house and senate by wide margins (Liberty 1996). DLCD worked during the two years following adoption of this law to guide implementation by local government, and a guidebook was published in 1997 (Oregon TGM Program 1997).

Regional problem solving (1995)

A second significant piece of legislation passed in 1995 was a regional problem-solving bill (House Bill 3548) attached to a light rail funding bill and passed during a one-day special session held July 28, 1995. The regional problem-solving program was designed to introduce some flexibility in the application of statewide planning goals in cases where regional problem-solving strategies were developed and approved by DLCD. The program provided funding for four pilot projects, and DLCD hired new staff members to administer the pilot projects. The pilot projects selected for funding were, incidentally, of intracounty areas rather than multicounty regions. The notion of regional problem solving drew opposition from 1000 Friends of Oregon, because it viewed problem-solving as a mechanism for large scale rezoning of farm and forest lands in conflict with statewide land use goals. However, Gov. Kitzhaber assured staff members of 1000 Friends that the regional problem-solving legislation would not be used to weaken the land use program (Liberty 1996).

Transportation and growth management (1997)

The TGM Program's budget for the 1997-1999 biennium increased substantially as a result of strong support for growth management and transportation system planning by Gov. Kitzhaber. The budget increase came as a surprise to many observers, given the heightened concern over state spending and local property tax limitations as well as biennial threats to DLCD's budget (Weitz 1997b). The increase in budget has enabled the TGM program to add several grant managers' positions and increase local grant budgets. TGM staff also continue to review local transportation system plans and implement programs that support "smart development" (see Oregon TGM Program 1998) and remove local regulatory obstacles to quality, multimodal, mixed use development. The TGM Program also expanded its "quick response" program to save smart development projects from jeopardy during local review processes, participated in activities of the governor's community solutions team, and continued to develop urban growth management policy.

Of special interest is DLCD's recent analysis and proposal to further enunciate Goal 14, Urbanization. As an employee of DLCD and the TGM Program (1994-1997), I participated in precursor efforts to revise and further enunciate the state's urbanization goal. In support of these objectives, the TGM Program sponsored a consultant study of Goal 14 (Cogan Owens Cogan 1997). Also, DLCD has recommended to LCDC that Goal 14 technical assistance, rules, goal amendments, and if necessary legislation become a high priority for the remainder of the biennium (DLCD 1997). DLCD has convened working groups to amend Goal 14 (DLCD 1998). Also of significance is the recent reelection of Gov. Kitzhaber, who has pledged to maintain and even strengthen the state's land use laws.

WASHINGTON

In the late 1980s, *The Seattle Times* hired urban affairs journalist Neal Peirce to examine growth management in the Puget Sound region. Peirce prepared a series of reports that concluded there was no growth management in the region (Corr 1990).

Growth Strategies Commission (1989)

Washington's Gov. Booth Gardner vetoed a legislative action in 1989 that, if not vetoed, would have required the chief executive to appoint a Growth Strategies Commission, because he viewed it as an improper invasion by the legislature into executive affairs. The governor appointed the Growth Strategies Commission during August 1989 via Executive Order 89-08. The purpose of the commission was to provide recommendations for preserving the environment and quality of life while maintaining economic development and growth in all regions of the state (Kelly 1993, 122; DeGrove 1992, 120).

DeGrove (1992, 121-128) summarizes the work of the Growth Strategies Commission which took place between 1989 and 1991, including its efforts following adoption of the first Growth Management Act (GMA I). The commission had five subcommittees, including one on land use, each of which completed its own report in early 1990. As the commission worked, the legislature was debating and passing GMA I. A July 1990 draft interim report suggested that all state agencies and local governments should plan. Local plans would be composed of several elements including land use/infrastructure linkage, housing, environmental management, parks and open space, and character and design. In the interim report, the commission also recommended substantive and procedural planning requirements for each level of government (DeGrove 1992, 121-122).

Pursuant to GMA I, the Growth Strategies Commission went back to work to develop the state oversight role lacking in GMA I and to address certain other weaknesses in the program. The commission issued a final report (Washington State Growth Strategies Commission 1990) that recommended modifications to GMA I's statement of goals and additional efforts to strengthen planning at all government levels. Of particular interest, the final report addressed issues of urban growth patterns and called for strong measures to combat urban sprawl. The commission also suggested that the local requirement for concurrency be extended from transportation facilities to several other facilities (DeGrove 1992, 125-128).

Adoption of the Growth Management Act (1990-1991)

The Washington Legislature adopted the Growth Management Act (House Bill 2929, or GMA I) in 1990 and strengthened its requirements with a second Growth Management Act in 1991 (House Bill 1025, or GMA II). GMA I and GMA II are referred to here collectively as, simply, GMA. (For a meticulous account of the complex enactment processes of GMA I and GMA II, see Settle and Gavigan 1993). While the state placed its own twist on its growth management legislation, it borrowed UGBs (called urban growth areas in Washington) from Oregon, concurrency from Florida, and the notion of flexibility from Georgia (Callies 1994; DeGrove 1994; Lewis 1992). The legislature, however, deliberately avoided the top-down planning system found in Oregon (Reinert 1996).[3] A growth management division within the Department of Community Development (now Community, Trade, and Economic Development, or DCTED) was established to administer the program.

The enforcement mechanism for planning is the system of three Growth Management Hearings Boards based in Seattle, Olympia, and Yakima, which can order local governments to comply with the law and request that the governor impose fiscal sanctions (see Sidebar 8.2 for an example of enforcement in Clark County). Gov. Gardner appointed the three members of each of the three boards, and the boards began their work May 15, 1992 (Planning Association of Washington 1994; Lewis 1992; Washington DCD 1992b).

The Growth Management Act's requirements

GMA I mandated requirements for all cities and counties. Only counties with a population of 50,000 or more with 10 percent decennial population growth, or counties of any size with a 20 percent decennial growth rate, were mandated to prepare comprehensive plans (see Table 7.1). GMA was subsequently amended (Washington Laws 1995, Chapter 400) to raise the 10 percent figure, applicable to counties with populations of 50,000 or more, to 17 percent, based on a proposal by legislators representing Cowlitz and Grays Harbor Counties. This mandate meant that only 16 of the state's 39 counties, and cities within them, were required to prepare and adopt local comprehensive plans consistent with 13 state goals. Local governments were also mandated to prepare and adopt regulations to implement their comprehensive plans. In addition to those counties mandated to plan, 10 other counties volunteered to plan under GMA by 1992. Local plans were supposed to be finished by July 1993 and the regulations to implement them were due one year later.

Critical areas and resource lands

Within one year (by July 1, 1992) all local governments in the state, not just those mandated to prepare local comprehensive plans, were required to adopt ordinances protecting critical areas and classifying resource lands.[4] For a description of implementing critical area regulations in Cowlitz County, see Sidebar 6.1 in the following chapter. According to Mike McCormick, then the assistant director for growth management, almost half of the local governments met the deadline for designating resource lands and protecting critical areas. Some local governments did not complete the designation of resource lands and protection of critical areas, because they engaged in controversial discussions and needed more time to involve citizens in decision making. Hence, the growth management division appears to have been more interested in good progress being made toward the objective than strict compliance with the deadline. July 1, 1992, was also the deadline for those counties engaged in planning to complete their countywide planning policies (Washington DCD 1992b). Countywide planning policies were Washington's solution to the need for a regional approach preceding local planning. It appears similar to Oregon's approach, which substituted counties for regional planning councils during the debate over Senate Bill 100 in 1972 and 1973.

Agency implementation and support for local planning

In 1990, DCD sponsored a study to design a strategy for meeting the data needs of local governments planning under GMA I. The study, which was based on a detailed questionnaire mailed to all counties and 49 cities in the state, identifies the range of data needed to prepare plans, indicates what data resources are available, outlines gaps in data available for local plans, describes an approach to automating growth management data into a statewide system, and recommends actions to allow state agencies to meet the needs of local jurisdictions. The study received input from the growth management division's Technical Advisory Group (Dye Management Group 1990).

The Dye Management Group's report (1990) indicates the status of data collection and obstacles to planning by local governments in 1990. The report concludes that: (1) existing critical area inventories were virtually nonexistent, especially those of fish and wildlife habitats, aquifer recharge areas, and geologic hazards; (2) subcounty demographic and employment data were largely unavailable; (3) little coordination of public facilities provision had taken place between planners, utility providers, finance departments, and public works agencies; and (4) a lack of local planning capacity existed due to shortages of staff, financial resources, and information systems.

Based on those and other findings, the Dye Management Group recommended that an information systems strategy be implemented to help local governments develop the capacity to access, generate and utilize planning data. The group also found that "how to" methodological guidance was urgently required in rural counties and smaller cities, and it recommended rapid development of a resource manual and the dispatch of growth management action teams to jurisdictions in need of assistance (Dye Management Group 1990).

Of particular interest to my investigation is the Technical Advisory Group's assessment of the minimum types of land use data considered necessary for planning. These included: (1) existing land use by general type of use (residential by density, commercial, industrial, agricultural, and others); (2) the intensity of use (current parcel development in accordance with zoning); (3) characteristics of parcels (location, area, and natural features); and (4) suitability of land for development (including a value ratio of land to improvements) (Dye Management Group 1990, 19).

The state's original local planning grant appropriation in 1992 of $8.6 million was cut to $6.8 million. McCormick notes that DCD's budget was cut 13 percent, while the growth management division's funding was reduced 26 percent and resulted in the loss of four positions. Budget cuts eliminated funding for DCD's environmental planning pilot projects, but the department began work on the program anyway. The central objective of the pilot projects was to determine how to integrate growth management planning with the State Environmental Policy Act. Despite budget cuts, each county planning under GMA received a base grant allocation of $100,000 (Lewis 1992; Washington DCD 1992a).

Legislation and funding (1992)

The state legislature recognized almost immediately after adopting GMA that additional work needed to be done to fine-tune the system. Few legislative changes to GMA were proposed in 1992, however. An effort to add new wetlands requirements to local government plans failed, and Gov. Booth Gardner vetoed a bill that would have allowed the siting of industry outside urban growth areas (Washington DCD 1992a).

Though legislation during 1992 was virtually insignificant, the legislature appropriated $150,000 to the University of Washington and a planning consultant to "plug the holes" in GMA and recommend possible changes to local land use regulations. The University of Washington also established a Growth Management Planning and Research Clearinghouse that completed a survey of growth management trends in 150 cities and tracked local planning progress under GMA (Lewis 1992).

Meanwhile, the growth management division announced it would evaluate its technical assistance program based on input from cities, counties, planning directors, and its own advisory committee. Further, DCD sponsored an Interagency Work Group on Growth Management which held several meetings to coordinate growth management policies and activities.

Adoption of local planning standards (1992)

In June 1992, DCD's growth management division announced that it would complete the procedural criteria for preparing comprehensive plans by the end of that summer. Another set of administrative rules—the minimum guidelines for classifying agricultural, forest, mineral lands, and critical areas—was completed with the assistance of other state agencies (Washington DCD 1992a).

Status of local planning in the 1990s

Planning by local governments in accordance with GMA progressed at a slower pace than originally envisioned and with greater variation than desired (Burby and May 1997, 74; Pivo 1993). As of 1994, GMA applied to 26 of the state's 39 counties, and the cities within those counties (DeGrove 1994). Another source, however, indicates that 29 counties were planning under GMA by May 1994 (Planning Association of Washington 1994). The state's growth management watchdog group, 1000 Friends of Washington, reports that as of 1996 more than 100 Washington cities and counties have plans that comply with GMA, and more than 85 percent of the state's cities and counties have complied with the requirement to adopt critical area regulations (1000 Friends of Washington 1996).

Also as of 1996, there are 21 adopted local comprehensive plans that have already been amended (Washington State DCTED and League of Women Voters 1997). As of the beginning of 1997 nearly 150 communities, including 14 counties, have adopted growth management plans, while 33 of 39 counties have designated agricultural resource lands. As of September 16, 1997, 161 of the 213 cities (75.6 percent) mandated or in a county opting to plan had adopted comprehensive plans in compliance with GMA requirements, while slightly less than half of such cities had adopted all or part of the required development regulations. Table 5.1 provides a status report of plans and regulations mandated to be adopted by counties (Washington DCTED 1997).

Table 5.1. County Compliance With Washington GMA Requirements: September 16, 1997

GMA Requirement	Number of Counties in Compliance	Total Number of Counties Required or Opting to Comply	Percentage
Classify resource lands of long term significance	32	39 (*)	82.1
Identify and regulate critical areas	31	39 (*)	79.5
Adopt county wide planning policies	29	29	100
Designate and adopt urban growth areas	22	28	78.6
Adopt comprehensive plans	17	28	60.7
Adopt development regulations	24	29	82.8

* Mandatory for all counties in Washington State

Source: Washington Department of Community, Trade and Economic Development 1997.

Technical assistance

As of 1994, DCTED published more than 41 monographs and guidebooks on growth management (Planning Association of Washington 1994). Washington's technical assistance program paralleled Georgia's program, which also produced several "how to" planning guidebooks (also see Figure 10.4).

Regulatory reform and the Land Use Study Commission (1995)

In 1995, the governor established a Task Force on Regulatory Reform, and the Washington Legislature passed regulatory reform legislation (Senate Bill 1724). The purpose of this legislation, which became effective June 1, 1995, was to connect state environmental laws with growth management and reduce the time required for issuing local development permits. The state's regulatory reform initiative echos efforts undertaken in Oregon some 13 years earlier. Many local governments in Washington have reduced permitting time by revising regulations to conform to the Regulatory Reform Act (Washington DCTED and League of Women Voters 1997). The Regulatory Reform Act also established the Land Use Study Commission, which worked to integrate aspects of the State Environmental Policy Act, the Shorelines Management Act, and GMA. The governor announced appointment of the Commission members on September 28, 1995. The 14-member commission was established with the overall mission to integrate land use and environmental laws into a single manageable statute. The study commission's other tasks included determining methods to provide for greater certainty in the planning process and evaluating funding mechanisms for local governments to recover the costs of integrated planning and environmental analysis (Durkan 1996; Reinert 1996; Wells 1996).

Legislation (1996-1997)

During 1996, the Washington Legislature passed two bills that would have weakened GMA. 1000 Friends was, however, according to its own account instrumental in persuading the governor to veto the bills. One bill would have given vested status to projects under an illegal comprehensive plan. The other would have allowed urban-scale subdivisions and other development in rural areas as part of a master planned resort (1000 Friends of Washington 1996a, 1996b).

Two amendments to GMA in 1997 relate to this inquiry: provisions for greater flexibility for counties in the planning for and regulation of rural lands outside UGAs; and a mandate for six counties (Clark, King, Kitsap, Pierce, Snohomish, and Thurston) to adopt, in consultation with cities, review and evaluation programs to determine if they are achieving urban densities within their urban growth areas. Cities took a position against the mandate to evaluate urban densities because of limited funding. Numerous other amendments to GMA were either defeated or vetoed by the governor. In its position statements on land use for the 1998 legislative session, the municipal association opposed granting unilateral authority to counties to alter or opt out of GMA responsibilities without advice from and the concurrence of cities (Association of Washington Counties 1997).

CONCLUSIONS

I conclude that second wave trends were continued and amplified during the third wave of state growth management program evolution, but that some distinctive program emphases appeared during the 1990s.

Pervasiveness of the model code

ALI's *Model Land Development Code* is evident in Georgia's and Washington's growth management programs. Georgia adopted two provisions reminiscent of the model code, DRIs and areas of critical state concern (the latter dubbed "regionally important resources" in Georgia). Washington adopted its own version of critical areas protection that had, in one sense, more comprehensive areal coverage than other programs. Each local government in Washington was required to adopt regulations protecting several types of critical areas (wetlands, groundwater recharge areas, etc.) as defined by GMA. On the other hand, in Florida, the 1990s brought about a formal reconsideration of the DRI program in light of discontent with the state's RPCs. The DRI program survived, however, and the legacy of the model code still remains.

Local plan compliance deadlines

Washington's deadlines for the adoption of local plans that comply with state goals and standards were as ambitious as the compliance deadlines set in Florida and Oregon during the first and second waves of program evolution. Both Florida and Oregon experienced significant delays with respect to local plan preparation and adoption (Bollens 1993b). Washington set unrealistic deadlines for local governments to classify resource lands and adopt regulations protecting critical areas, then followed that mandate with an ambitious requirement to complete comprehensive plans and development regulations in a short period of time. Not surprisingly, Washington experienced some of the same delays in completing local plans as Florida and Oregon did.

Table 5.2 summarizes the status of local planning in the four states during the 1990s. In each case, the data refer to plans reviewed and approved (or acknowledged) by the state. In the case of Florida, the data pertain to plans "or parts of plans," and the 1993 figure shows that more than 90 percent of Florida's cities and counties had achieved local plan compliance or had compliance agreements in place. The 1997 figures for Washington are for those counties and cities within those counties that were required to or opted to plan under GMA.

Georgia and Washington both apparently learned from Florida to institute a staggered schedule for local governments to prepare comprehensive plans. As described earlier, Georgia based its decisions of when local plans should be due on input from RDCs, which studied the readiness of individual local governments for planning. Washington failed to produce universal compliance with its local planning mandate, while Georgia's voluntary, incentives-based approach nearly achieved universal compliance in fewer years.

Another important parallel between early programs and third wave programs is the way in which compliance is measured and applied.

Table 5.2. Status of Local Planning, 1993 and 1997

	Florida		Georgia		Oregon		Washington	
	1993	1997	1993	1997	1993	1997	1993	1997
Cities	N/A	N/A	445 of 533	521 of 533	Since acknowledgment (1986), all cities and counties in Oregon have had comprehensive plans.		N/A	161 of 213
% of all	—	—	83.5	97.7			—	75.6
Counties	N/A	N/A	142 of 159	159 of 159			N/A	17 of 29
% of all	—	—	89.3	100			—	58.6
TOTAL	N/A	N/A	587 of 692	680 of 692			N/A	178 of 242
% of all	90+	—	84.8	98.3			—	73.6

N/A means not available.

Sources: Personal communication with Jim Frederick, assistant director, Office of Coordinated Planning, Georgia Department of Community Affairs, December 31, 1997; Washington Department of Community, Trade and Economic Development, 1997 (data as of September 16, 1997). Other sources as noted in text.

Washington became more concerned with demonstrating good progress, not strict compliance. Expectations for plan mandate compliance were also more realistic in Georgia and Washington, given their propensity to promulgate more detailed standards and to implement more comprehensive programs of state support than those initially found in Florida and Oregon.

Florida continued to experience problems with local plan noncompliance during the early 1990s. New transportation system plans in Oregon were rarely accepted by the state's plan review team on their first submittal for review, and local plans in Georgia were also routinely turned back to the plan makers with comments for revision. These observations about plan compliance in Oregon and Georgia are based on my experience as an employee of Oregon's TGM Program in 1997 and as a regional planner in Georgia from 1990 to 1994. In Washington, local planning and critical area regulation lagged behind the compliance deadlines established by the state program.

Inconsistency and enforcement

Third wave programs in Georgia and Washington have moved away from the principle of consistency and a visible mechanism for enforcement, although horizontal coordination has been strengthened (see Chapter 8). Georgia did not require consistency between local plans and land development regulations (i.e., implementation consistency as described in Chapter 8). In fact, Georgia did not mandate that local governments adopt zoning to implement plans or even to prepare plans. Since regional plans and a state plan are not yet developed, Georgia has not exercised top-down, vertical consistency like Florida and Oregon. Both Georgia and Washington, however, require that plans be internally consistent. An analysis of the consistency doctrine in state growth management statutes is alluded to in Chapters 6 and 7 and more specifically described in Chapter 8.

With respect to enforcement of state mandates, Georgia avoided the mandate altogether by opting for an incentive-based approach to local planning. The only sanction or disincentive for not planning in Georgia is that local governments become ineligible to receive certain state grants and loans. Washington produced a stronger mandate than Georgia, because it forced certain local governments to plan, but it, too, encouraged other local governments to plan through funding, technical assistance, and authorization to adopt development impact fees. Unlike Florida and Oregon, Washington did not give the administering state agency any authority to enforce compliance with local planning mandates. Instead, that role was given to the three substate regional Growth Management Hearings Boards. Georgia and Washington have more or less eschewed the coercive style used in Florida and Oregon in favor of capacity- and commitment-building approaches (Burby and May 1997). Hence, 1990s-style programs in Georgia and Washington are characterized by a looser consistency framework, less of a top-down structure, more flexibility in program administration, and a less strong and visible compliance-based approach.

Technical assistance and capacity building

Growth management programs in Georgia and Washington appear to overshadow those in Florida and Oregon in their technical assistance programs for local planning. I conclude in Chapter 10, however, that Florida's technical assistance program of the second wave served as a benchmark for third wave programs to achieve. Washington's DCD hired a consultant (Dye Management Group 1990) to analyze the capacity of local governments to plan. The consultant's report included an inventory of data requirements and concluded that methodological guidance was needed. Both Georgia and Washington produced several "how to" guidebooks to help local governments plan. Even Oregon, without a statutory mandate to provide local planning technical assistance, modified its program in the 1990s to increase local outreach. Formal programs of local planning technical assistance and specific attention to the capacity of local governments to plan are hallmarks of 1990s-style state growth management.

Land information systems

Georgia developed technical standards for data systems and mapping and funded GIS hardware purchases by RDCs to provide an automated planning information network that could integrate local, regional and state plans. The Dye Management Group's report for Washington includes an outline of a similar framework. Requirements to prepare buildable lands inventories in Oregon (1995) and Washington (1997) further underscore the importance of developing land information systems via local comprehensive plans. Hence, development of statewide databases has been given greater emphasis during the third wave of state growth management program evolution.

Public facilities planning

Recall that local planning requirements were strengthened during the mid-1980s with requirements for concurrency in Florida and public facilities plans in Oregon. Concerns continued in the 1990s about the ability of local governments to finance infrastructure for growth. Washington borrowed Florida's concurrency concept and applied it to transportation facilities. Both Washington and Georgia used their authorization to assess development impact fees as an incentive for local governments to plan. Capital facilities plans and improvement programs were required by Florida along with concurrency requirements. Oregon required public facilities plans but still does not formally require capital improvement programs, unless the local government wishes to assess system development charges (i.e., impact fees). Transportation system plans in Oregon, however, require financing components.

Via the 1989 planning act, Georgia required community facilities and services elements and short-term work programs for comprehensive plans. A formal capital improvement program is not required, however, unless a local government desires to assess development impact fees. Georgia's Government Efficiency Act (1993) also demonstrates further interest by the state in improving service delivery, and that interest was confirmed with passage of the Service Delivery Strategy Act of 1997. Washington's rules require local capital facilities plans, and land use elements must be reconsidered by local governments if they experience funding shortfalls. Hence, the concern over public facilities planning in Florida and Oregon seems to have been recognized and amplified in programs adopted during the third wave of program evolution.

Furthermore, Georgia followed a path similar to the other three states with respect to public facilities planning. The requirements of Georgia's Service Delivery Strategy Act (1997) are substantially similar to the intergovernmental service coordination requirements passed by Oregon's legislature in 1993 (ORS 195). Florida and Washington, with their provisions regarding capital facilities planning, intergovernmental coordination, and concurrency, had a jump on Georgia and Oregon in addressing issues with respect to intergovernmental conflict and local provision of public facilities and services.

Reexamination and evaluation

As noted in Chapter 4, Florida appears to have perfected a model of nearly continuous program reexamination. Other states did not take such a comprehensive approach, although Washington immediately recognized the need to fine-tune its growth management program. Georgia made periodic additions to its planning program, as did Oregon, but neither state benefited from an institutional mechanism for routinely revisiting program progress. Georgia has recently changed that, however, with appointment of a Growth Strategies Reassessment Task Force.

Nevertheless, the interest in evaluation during the 1980s in Florida and Oregon appears to have been dwarfed by the popularity of program evaluation in the 1990s in each of the states. Florida evaluated the efficiency of its urban growth patterns while Oregon assessed the effectiveness of its UGBs. In Florida, ELMS III took on a role that was more evaluation oriented than reform proposal minded. Just a few years into its program, Washington evaluated its technical assistance program. Oregon instituted its Benchmarks program in the early 1990s. Georgia's Future Communities Commission investigated the notion of benchmarking. Washington recently extended the concept of benchmarking to an analysis of urban densities via 1997 legislation. Given these examples, monitoring, evaluation, and benchmarking hold a much more prominent place in third wave state programs than in the second wave of growth management programs.

Regional planning: new directions

There are some mixed signals from the four states about how regional planning has fared in the 1990s. The roles of RPCs in administering DRIs continue in Georgia but have diminished in Florida. In both states, there continues to be some lack of confidence in the roles and contributions of regional planning entities. Florida passed legislation in 1992 that would sunset RPCs, and in 1993 the state redirected the authority of RPCs. In Georgia, fiscal mismanagement prompted greater scrutiny over the public management of RDCs. With proposals for realignment of RDCs in Georgia, for a while it appeared as if RDCs would play second fiddle to Gov. Miller's Council of Economic Development Organizations.

Despite some drawbacks, regional policy plans exist in Florida, and regional comprehensive plans are being developed in Georgia. It is interesting to note that Florida redefined the title, content, and role of regional plans from "comprehensive" to "strategic" in 1993. This change of labels is indicative of a trend toward reconstitution of regional entities for purposes different from traditional land use planning.

Though it discards the multicounty approach of RPCs in Florida and RDCs in Georgia, Washington's GMA requires countywide planning policies which must be adopted prior to local planning. In Oregon, the regional problem-solving pilot programs hint at new possibilities for intergovernmental coordination and planning. In Washington, multicounty watershed-based planning is being funded. Hence, regional planning in the 1990s survived in Florida and Georgia and is taking on new directions in the Pacific Northwest.

Urban sprawl, compact development, and livable communities

All state growth management programs, including those not studied here, contain provisions that are designed to some degree to combat urban sprawl and promote compact urban development patterns (DeGrove and Metzger 1993). However, 1990s-style growth management is characterized by an increasing interest in containing urban sprawl, promoting compact development, mitigating the costs of inefficient growth patterns, and encouraging multimodal, livable, sustainable communities.

The style of growth management in the 1990s also must contend with new development trends in exurban areas and address quality of life issues (Burchell 1993). This concern for discouraging urban sprawl and promoting efficient growth patterns is illustrated in study efforts in Florida (1989) and Oregon during the 1990s. Florida followed its study of urban growth patterns with an antisprawl policy. Based on task force recommendations, Oregon developed new tools for improving urban growth management and established the TGM Program to link land use and transportation. More recently, DLCD has discussed the need to prepare an administrative rule on urbanization (Goal 14). Washington's Growth Strategies Commission took a hard line on urban sprawl in its final report to the legislature. The legislature in Washington heeded the commission's recommendations and adopted a state goal that specifically discourages sprawl, then adopted legislation limiting rural sprawl. Georgia has a planning law that is neutral with respect to urban form, yet even Georgia investigated the notion of creating quality communities.

Other trends are emerging that may point to an even greater level of distinction for the third wave of growth management program history. Georgia's Future Communities Commission may signify a greater acknowledgment of the interrelationship between local systems of governance and growth management issues. The increasing awareness of interrelationships between transportation and land use also marks a substantial change from 1980s planning practice. A watchdog organization (1000 Friends) has existed for two decades in Oregon and has gained strong footholds in Florida and Washington. The existence of active watchdog organizations in three of the four states may signal to growth management program observers that interest group oversight of growth management programs is becoming a necessity in the 1990s. Finally, Washington's struggle with integrating and/or reconciling 25 year old environmental statutes with 1990s growth management practices promises to be a challenge characteristic only of the third (and fourth) wave(s) of program evolution.

Notes

1. Bollens (1993b, 152) and Pelham (1993) provide compliance statistics that contain certain inherent conflicts with the secretary of the Department of Community Affairs's findings described in an official publication (see Sadowski 1992). Therefore, results from the official source are presented in favor of those found in the literature.

2. This bill (codified primarily as Georgia Code § 36-70-21 through § 36-70-28, with amendments to other sections) is not included in the content analysis of Georgia's statutes provided in Chapters 6, 7, and 8.

3. Given certain striking similarities with Oregon's approach, it is difficult for me not to take issue immediately with this finding. The debate over top-down versus bottom-up approaches and the specific structures of Oregon's and Washington's programs are addressed in later chapters.

4. The original deadline for jurisdictions to identify and adopt guidelines for critical areas was September 1, 1991 (Dye Management Group 1990).

CHAPTER

6

The Structure of State-Sponsored Land Use Planning: State Roles

In Chapters 6, 7, and 8, I analyze the content of state statutes to describe and compare the intergovernmental division of authority and responsibility used by legislators to implement land use planning in the four states.[1] This chapter and the two that follow are interrelated. Chapter 6 provides an overview of the typical sequence of state growth management program activities, describes some hypotheses about paths of program evolution, and analyzes and compares state-level (e.g., state comprehensive planning) responsibilities in land use planning. Chapter 7 analyzes and compares statutory provisions on substate regional planning and local comprehensive planning. Chapter 8 takes a look at the structures and principles of reviewing local comprehensive plans, then provides conclusions about three hypotheses of program evolution based on evidence presented there and in the two previous chapters.

An investigation of state growth management program structure can be organized at least two different ways: according to the chronology of program developments over time (i.e., state framework first, followed by regional plans, etc.) or according to the roles and responsibilities of the participants (i.e., state agency, regional entity, local government). Programs unfold first at the state level and then increasingly involve regional and local governments once certain state program features are developed.

My research attempts to describe and compare state growth management programs according to the first alternative for organization, the chronological approach. Table 6.1 illustrates a top-down mandate and sequence like that found in Florida's program. I describe the statutory responsibilities of the states, regions, and local governments and present program activities as they are believed to develop over time, based on logic, analysis of the content of statutes, and my own experience. Table 6.1 serves as an organizing framework for the content analysis. I do not follow the chronological approach entirely, because I prefer to discuss plan review structures (for both regional and local plans) and principles in a separate chapter rather than according to the sequence in which they unfold.

It is recognized that the chronological approach is not valid in all respects. State program components evolve simultaneously in many cases and do not lend themselves entirely to description as a linear process as suggested in Table 6.1. Note that Table 6.1 attempts to accommodate the simultaneous evolution of program activities by showing some overlap in the various stages of program development (i.e., the range of years the activity occurs overlaps the program phases). Furthermore, the sequence of planning activities also differs among the states, especially between Florida and Georgia. The sequence of planning activities in Georgia's program is generally the reverse of that shown in Table 6.1. I revisit Table 6.1 in Chapter 13 under the discussion of a "stage theory" of the evolution of state growth management programs.

HYPOTHESES ABOUT PROGRAM LEARNING AND EVOLUTION

The questions that drive the inquiry of state-sponsored land use planning program structure are derived from my own research interests as summarized in Chapter 1. These questions include: how state planning mandates compare; what the various roles are assigned to governments, agencies and entities in the intergovernmental system; what the required contents are for local comprehensive plans; and what types of support programs are specified and implemented.

I am interested in the evolution of state growth management programs. Evolution refers here to the historical development of state growth management programs. I suggest that designers of new programs look to existing programs for guidance, and that they identify

Table 6.1. General Chronology of State Growth Management Program Development Assuming a Top-Down Structure

Phase of Program	Program Activities (Responsible Participant)	Range of Years the Activity Occurs
State Planning	• State comprehensive planning (state)	0 - 1
	• Statewide planning goals (state)	
	• Critical areas of the state (state)	
Regional Planning	• Regional planning standards (state)	
	• Funding/ technical assistance for regional planning (state)	
	• Metropolitan planning (regions)	1 - 2
	• Regional planning (regions)	
	• Coordination of local activities (counties)	
	• Developments of regional impact (regions, localities)	
	• Review of regional plans (state)	
Local Planning	• Local planning standards (state)	
	• Funding/ technical assistance for local planning (state, regions)	1 - 4
	• Local comprehensive planning (localities, regions)	
Post—local planning implementation	• Review of local comprehensive plans (regions, state)	
	• Funding/ technical assistance for local development regulations (regions, state)	4 - 6
	• Sanctions for noncompliance with local planning mandates (state)	
	• Updates of local comprehensive plans (localities, regions)	
	• Review of local plan updates/ amendments (regions, state)	

certain features of existing programs and retain, reject, or modify them. I expect to find similarities (i.e., components retained) and differences (i.e., features that are rejected or modified) in the structures of state growth management programs as they develop over time. Similarities and differences are both considered to be "learning," because similarities can represent an affirmation by subsequent program designers that certain existing structures are desirable, while differences can represent a choice to reject a particular structural component of the program because it is found to be undesirable for one reason or another.

Evolution occurs within an individual state program (i.e., intraprogram evolution). I am more interested at this point, however, in identifying the evolutionary paths of learning between pairs of states (i.e., interprogram evolution). I believe that certain paths of learning are more important than others in determining how state growth management programs evolve over time. I expect to find evidence supporting three different hypotheses about the structural evolution of state growth management programs: cross-sectional convergence, regional longitudinal convergence, and longitudinal divergence. These hypotheses are illustrated in Figure 6.1 and more fully described below.

The cross-sectional convergence hypothesis predicts that programs developing during the same period of program history move toward similar growth management mandate structures. To some extent, I expect that Florida and Oregon have similar program structures because they developed during the same time period. This hypothesis is complicated, however, by the fact that Florida overhauled its program during the second wave of state growth management program history. Another example of cross-sectional convergence is the simultaneous development of third-wave programs in Georgia and Washington.

The regional longitudinal convergence hypothesis suggests that programs of states in the same subnational region will have similar mandate structures. Specifically, I predict that two patterns of regional convergence can be found: Georgia used Florida's growth management program, created in 1985, as a model or example; and Washington, in establishing its own program, drew heavily on Oregon's state land use program as it has evolved since 1973. A corollary to the regional convergence hypothesis is that programs in different subnational regions diverge from one another, or put simply, that the southern states have different ways of doing things than states in the Pacific Northwest do. In sum, regions diverge, while states within regions converge.

The longitudinal divergence hypothesis is another way of stating the evolutionary theme suggested in earlier chapters. It predicts that there will be discernible differences in mandate structures because the state growth management programs were developed during different periods. Specifically, third wave programs (Georgia and Washington) are

Figure 6.1. Hypothesized Paths of Learning in the Interprogram Evolution of State-Sponsored Land Use Planning

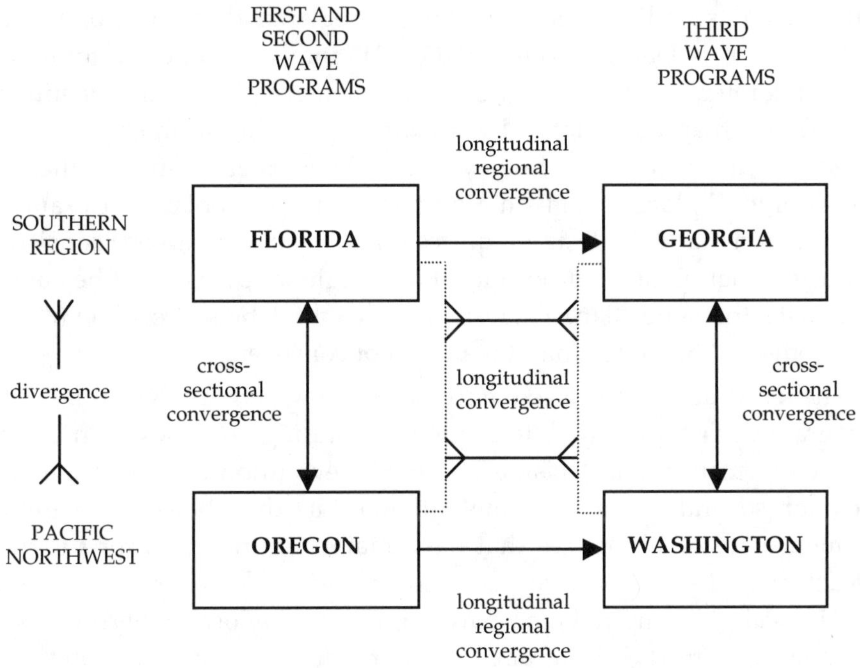

expected to have mandate structures that are different from first and second wave programs (Florida and Oregon).

Application of these three hypotheses suggests that four of the six possible cross-fertilization paths between states are more important than the others. I recognize, however, that other evolutionary paths are possible, such as Florida's influence on Washington's program design. I now compare the structures of the four states and look for patterns that tend to support or refute the three hypotheses about the evolution of state growth management programs.

SEQUENCE OF PLANNING IN MANDATE DESIGNS

Here, and by other scholars (Porter 1997; Starnes 1993, 86-87; Kelly 1993, 121-122; DeGrove 1992), state-sponsored land use planning programs are frequently characterized as top-down and bottom-up approaches to growth management. This way of characterizing state growth management mandate designs has already been alluded to in earlier chapters, and it receives more specific attention in Chapter 8. The terms "top-down" and "bottom-up" deserve further elaboration here.

Top-down and bottom-up describe different types of state mandate designs, specifically in terms of vertical consistency (i.e., the division of authority descending from the state to regional then local plans and activities). Eric Damian Kelly (1993, 121) indicates that "bottoms up" planning refers to the building of comprehensive plans from constituencies rather than as dictated by a central planning authority (i.e., the state). He also recognizes, however, that the term encompasses the synthesis of local plans in a given region into a regional plan. For example, a top-down mandate design requires that local plans must be consistent with regional plans, and both local and regional plans must be consistent with the state plan. There is more to the labels, "top-down" and "bottom-up," however, than the notion of consistency.

The terms also imply a sequence of planning activities. The choice by program designers of how to sequence planning activities is an important one because that decision guides the evolution of program activities for several years to come. Inherent in the choice of planning sequence are other choices that have major ramifications for program structure and evolution. For example, mandate designers are likely to ask if local plans are to be prepared first, will the local governments be capable and ready? Program designers may advocate a bottom-up approach because it is considered politically necessary, from a local home-rule perspective, that local plans be prepared before any mandates for policy consistency are instituted by higher levels of government. Alternatively, state growth management mandate designers may favor a top-down approach because they believe they can mobilize support for legislative action, or because they contend that state policy guidance is essential given the diversity of local government approaches to planning.

Once a choice is made regarding how planning will be sequenced, that choice is virtually irreversible—the program is committed to the direction chosen and all its implications. Despite the important implications of the choice to sequence planning in a top-down or bottom-up fashion, the ramifications of such choices have at best received only passing discussion by scholars of growth management programs.

States can prepare and adopt a state comprehensive plan followed by regional and then local planning, as in the case of Florida's program (i.e., the top-down approach of vertical consistency). Another option, which was chosen by Georgia, is to prepare local plans first, then follow with regional plans and ultimately a state plan (i.e., a bottom-up approach). Program designers in Florida and Georgia made distinctly different choices in their approaches to consistency and the intergovernmental sequencing of planning. This evidence suggests that Florida's program was not followed in its entirety by Georgia's program designers, but it does not necessarily show that the hypothesis of longitudinal regional convergence is invalid. The difference in planning sequence may suggest that evolutionary learning has occurred, since Georgia may have discovered that Florida's planning sequence was inappropriate and then deliberately discarded it.

STATE COMPREHENSIVE PLANNING

By state comprehensive planning, I refer to an overarching process and resulting document prepared by either the governor (with administrative assistance) or the state legislature. In describing state comprehensive planning, I do not refer to the role of state agency coordination and the adoption of state agency plans. The state agency coordination task is one that all four programs employ to some extent.

Florida's program is the only one in the four states that specifies the intent, role, content, and process of preparing and adopting a state comprehensive plan. Florida adopted a separate statute on state comprehensive planning, and the state comprehensive plan itself is adopted as a general law. Georgia's program also specifies a state plan, but legislative provisions are few regarding the state plan, and the state has not after 10 years prepared such a plan. This difference in the levels of detail devoted to state comprehensive planning between Florida and Georgia is explained by the facts that there are two Florida statutes devoted to state comprehensive planning while the few provisions relating to state comprehensive planning in Georgia are integrated into the 1989 Planning Act.

Georgia's program of state comprehensive planning, not yet implemented, is similar to Florida's only in that it provides for adoption of a state comprehensive plan. The sequence of state planning is markedly different in the two states, and the role of the state comprehensive plan in Florida is much more developed than in Georgia's statute. These are major differences, suggesting that Georgia departed significantly from Florida's state comprehensive planning mandate. The fact that both Florida and Georgia provide for a state plan provides some evidence for the hypothesis of longitudinal regional convergence. The differences in state comprehensive planning, however, tend to refute that hypothesis. The differences can be attributed in part to different preferences in the two states on how to sequence planning.

State growth management programs in Oregon and Washington do not include a state comprehensive plan. Instead, their programs rely on an alternative approach, statewide planning goals, which is discussed in the following section. I now describe in greater detail the differences between the provisions of growth management statutes on state comprehensive planning in Florida and Georgia.

Florida's State Comprehensive Planning Act sets forth a specific mandate for state comprehensive planning, as the excerpt below indicates.

> The preservation and enhancement of the quality of life of the people of this state require that a state comprehensive plan be adopted by the Legislature to provide policy direction for all state and regional agencies and local governments (Florida Statutes § 186.002). "State comprehensive plan" means the goals and policies contained within the state comprehensive plan initially prepared by the Executive Office of the Governor and adopted pursuant to s. 186.008 (§ 186.003). The Governor is the chief planning officer of the state . . . (§ 186.004). The Executive Office of the Governor shall . . . prepare . . . the state comprehensive plan (§ 186.006). [The] proposed state comprehensive plan . . . provides long-range guidance for the orderly social, economic, and physical growth of the state. The plan shall be composed of goals, objectives, and policies (§ 186.007).

The statutory excerpt above emphasizes the authority in Florida to prepare and adopt a state comprehensive plan. The state plan is prepared by the governor, who is the state's chief planning officer, making state planning an administrative function. The state comprehensive plan requires the establishment of policy and adoption of those policies in a plan by the state legislature, so the state plan clearly serves a legislative function as well. Florida's legislation regarding the state comprehensive plan goes beyond the adoption process to require biennial updates prepared by the governor's office and adopted by the state legislature, as indicated below. Note that the state plan preparation and adoption process has an intermediate step, consideration by an Administration Commission (defined as the governor and cabinet in a separate statutory provision, Florida Statutes § 163.3164).

> On or before October 1 of every odd-numbered year beginning in 1995, the Executive Office of the Governor shall prepare, and the Governor shall recommend to the Administration Commission, any proposed revisions to the state comprehensive plan deemed necessary. All amendments, revisions, or updates to the plan shall be adopted by the Legislature as a general law (Florida Statutes § 186.008).

Florida adopted the state comprehensive plan by statute (Florida Statutes, Chapter 187). Of special interest to this inquiry is the finding that Florida's state comprehensive plan is mandated to include a growth management element that guides urban form on a statewide basis.

> The growth management portion of the state comprehensive plan shall . . . identify metropolitan and urban growth centers . . . set forth and integrate state policy for Florida's future growth as it relates to land development . . . [and] provide guidelines for determining where urban growth is appropriate and should be encouraged . . . (Florida Statutes § 186.009).

As I note elsewhere, this statutory provision has not been implemented, and it is expected that this provision will be repealed by the legislature (Quinn and Noll interview, 2/18/98).

Georgia's program is described as a bottom-up approach that includes a state comprehensive plan. Starnes (1993, 87) finds that Georgia's Planning Act mandates a "state policy plan." Starnes's observations may stem in part from a reading of the final report of the Georgia Governor's Growth Strategies Commission (1988), which provides some of the rationale for policy choices that is absent in the statute itself. Kelly (1993, 121) also indicates that a mandate to prepare a state plan exists in Georgia's law. Kelly cites Georgia Code § 45-12-201 in support of his finding, which defines terms including "planning" by the Governor's Development Council as the "the process of determining actions which state agencies shall take."

The Governor's Growth Strategies Commission (1988, 13) specifically recommended a coordinated planning process that is "bottom-up" in focus. Yet, ironically, the commission clearly used Florida's top-down program as a basis for departure in designing its coordinated planning program. The commission's final report, which provided direction in drafting the 1989 Georgia Planning Act, indicates the following relative to the sequence of planning and the role of a state plan:

> The state begins the process by putting a "framework" in place . . . once the framework is in place, planning will begin at the local level. Local governments will be responsible for their own plans, and regional plans will be compiled from local plans. . . . The governor would become the state's chief planner, with ultimate responsibility for integrating local, regional, and state agency plans into a comprehensive statewide policy plan, updated annually and tied to the state budget . . . a state planning commission would be created by reconstituting the board of the current Department of Community Affairs. The reconstituted board would . . . [assist] the governor in compiling the statewide plan . . . (Georgia Governor's Growth Strategies Commission 1988, 14-15).

As specified above, Georgia's process was intended by the commission to begin with a state framework. The state planning framework, when it is the first sequential step in the program like in Florida, appears to defy or violate the notion of a bottom-up mandate design. After all, the state is the one that is taking the initiative and designing a system to guide other intergovernmental entities to plan. In this sense, the label "bottom-up" is either a poor description, or it results in confusion when applied to Georgia's program. Another explanation why Georgia's program is so labeled is that politically it needs to be described that way.

The program structure implemented by Georgia's planning act follows the bottom-up sequence of planning that was recommended by the Growth Strategies Commission. Although the commission specifically recommended a bottom-up approach, there is surprisingly little evidence of intent for such in Georgia's planning act. Moving away from the intent conveyed by the Growth Strategies Commission to a content analysis of Georgia's law, I find only two provisions that provide guidance on the sequence of local planning and a state comprehensive plan, as provided below.

> The department [of Community Affairs], utilizing the comprehensive plans of qualified local governments, shall assist the Governor in coordinated and comprehensive planning on the state level and throughout the state, including, but not limited to, assistance in the development of a comprehensive plan for the state (Georgia Code § 50-8-7.1).
>
> The [Governor's Development] council, at the direction of the Governor and subject to this article, shall perform the following functions . . . Coordinate, supervise, and review planning by state agencies. This shall include, but shall not be limited to, coordination of long-range planning and coordination of the location and construction of public facilities on the basis of

state, regional, and local considerations identified in the comprehensive statewide plan developed by the Governor with the assistance of the Department of Community Affairs (Georgia Code § 45-12-204).

These provisions clearly indicate that the state plan shall be prepared by the governor (with administrative assistance) and should take into account local comprehensive plans. Local plans must logically already be complete for the state plan to take them into account, but this hint of planning sequence does not specifically enunciate a sequence for regional planning. Georgia's legislation does not specify in any detail the intended sequence of planning, and as argued earlier, the sequence of planning has important ramifications with respect to state program design.

The sections excerpted above provide the only references in Georgia's law to preparation of a state comprehensive plan. Other sections do not integrate the notion of a state plan. For example, the definition of "coordinated and comprehensive planning" is defined as "planning by counties and municipalities and by regional development centers in accordance with the minimum standards and procedures" (Georgia Code § 50-8-2). This overarching definition of coordinated and comprehensive planning does not include a reference to preparation of a state comprehensive plan.

If Florida's and Georgia's programs have similar structures, as the regional convergence hypothesis suggests, then Georgia's state comprehensive plan mandate and process would have many of the same characteristics as Florida's approach to state comprehensive plan making. Recalling the final report of the Georgia Governor's Growth Strategies Commission, there are major similarities between Georgia's program, as initially conceived, and Florida's approach. The commission's suggestion that "the governor would become the state's chief planner" is the same as Florida's law (Florida Statutes § 186.004).

Indeed, Georgia's state planning function is similar to Florida's in that both specify a state comprehensive plan prepared by the governor. Both state planmaking processes include participation by the governor's top administrative officials. Hence, putting aside differences in plan sequencing between the two states, the underlying design of Georgia's state comprehensive planning component has some similarities with Florida's. This provides evidence that supports the longitudinal

Figure 6.2. State Plan Making Processes

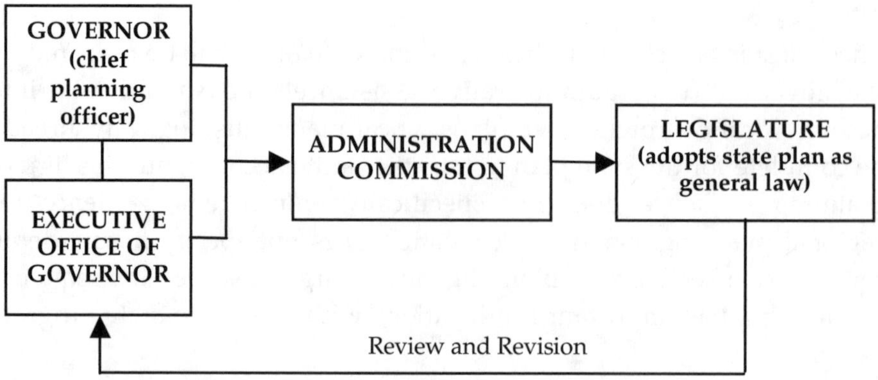

Florida's Continuous State Plan Making Process

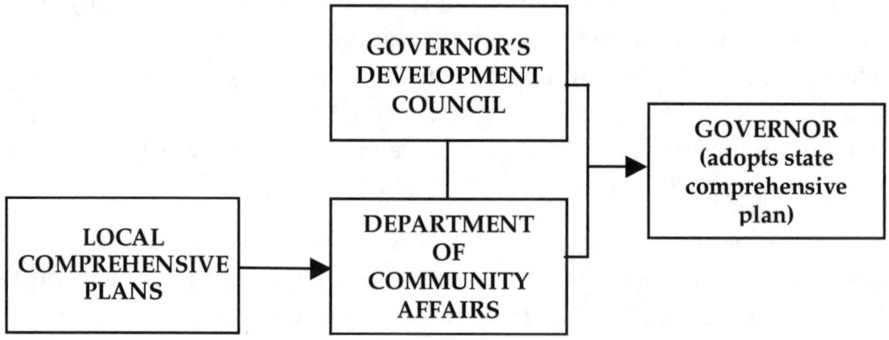

Georgia's State Plan Making Process

regional convergence hypothesis in the case of the southern states, but other notable differences also exist as illustrated in Figure 6.2.

Florida's approach specifically requires adoption of the state comprehensive plan by the legislature as a general law. In Georgia, the governor's adoption of the state comprehensive plan is final, and the plan is the governor's executive document. Another notable difference between the state comprehensive planning processes of Florida and Georgia is that Florida's process is continuous with biennial updates, while Georgia's state planning process receives virtually no description in the 1989 planning act. Figure 6.2 illustrates these differences inherent in Florida's and Georgia's state comprehensive plan making processes.

The processes of state comprehensive planmaking in Florida and Georgia have some major differences as noted above. Florida's legislators maintain authority over the state comprehensive plan (i.e., it is a statute), while Georgia's legislators appear to have no similar control (i.e., the plan is exclusively an executive function). Given the Georgia Planning Act's requirement that initial local planning standards had to be ratified by the Georgia General Assembly, it is worth pondering whether the legislature would also be interested in participating in a state comprehensive planmaking process if not reserving altogether the final authority to adopt a state plan.

Florida's choice in 1985 to revamp the growth management program with a vertical consistency requirement based on a state-regional-local planning sequence was probably made easier by the fact that most local governments had already completed some planning via the prior mandate (1975). Furthermore, the choice was also probably based in part on the poor track record and dissatisfaction associated with the first state comprehensive planning effort.

In Georgia's case, many governments did not have a history of land use planning and regulation, or of comprehensive planning for that matter. Authors of Georgia's planning statute undoubtedly drew on the state's strong home-rule tradition, including the fear of centralized land use authority, in rejecting Florida's plan sequencing model. Georgia's lawmakers may also have concluded that getting local planning underway was the most desirable initial outcome of the state-sponsored planning program.

It appears likely that the designers of Georgia's Planning Act envisioned the role of the Governor's Development Council, and any state plan it might adopt, as more of a coordinating mechanism than an instrument for policy guidance as Starnes (1993) seems to suggest. The guiding intent of the section of the planning act pertaining to the Governor's Development Council is "to provide for the coordination of planning, at the direction of the Governor" (Georgia Code § 45-12-200). Given the relative weakness of Georgia's mandate to prepare a state comprehensive plan (if one could even characterize the statutory language as a mandate), and the other differences outlined above, I conclude that state growth management programs in Florida and Georgia differ remarkably with respect to the provisions for (and processes of) state comprehensive planning. These findings provide evidence against the regional convergence hypothesis. I do not reject this hypothesis outright, however, for to do so would overlook the fact that both states mandate a state plan. In other words, the differences are in the details of how the state plan is processed and sequenced in relation to local and regional planning. The differences between state comprehensive planning approaches in Florida and Georgia are summarized in Table 6.2.

Table 6.2. Comparison of State Comprehensive Planning: Florida and Georgia

Characteristic of State Comprehensive Plan or Plan Process	Florida	Georgia
State comprehensive plan is required	✔	✔
Top down sequence: state plan is prepared first	✔	
Plan is legislative: adopted as a general law	✔	
Plan is executive document prepared by Governor	✔	✔
DCA has lead agency role in plan making		✔
Multiple state agencies are involved in planmaking	✔	✔
The state planmaking process is continuous	✔	

STATEWIDE PLANNING GOALS

Legislators in Oregon and Washington elected not to provide for a state comprehensive planmaking process and product. Instead, the practice in the Pacific Northwest is to adopt statewide planning goals in lieu of a state plan. This similarity represents a finding that provides support for the longitudinal regional convergence hypothesis in the case of Oregon and Washington (see Figure 6.1). While the state plans in Florida and Georgia are different from the approach of adopting statewide planning goals as found in Oregon and Washington, both the state comprehensive planmaking and state goal-setting approaches constitute top-down planning structures and sequences. Like Oregon and Washington, Florida's program provides a framework of state goals. Georgia's program also enunciates goals in advance of local planning.

Florida specifies its goals in a state comprehensive plan adopted by the legislature as general law, rather than via a state commission (as in Oregon). Georgia specifies five highly general goals as part of the Department of Community Affairs' administrative rules (Georgia DCA Rule § 110-12-1-.04(2)). Washington takes yet a different approach that specifies goals (but not a plan) within the statute itself. Hence, program

Table 6.3. Comparison of Statewide Planning Goals: Florida, Georgia, Oregon, and Washington

Goal	Florida	Georgia	Oregon	Washington
Land Use and Growth Management				
Land Use (planning)	✔	✔	✔	
Urbanization (urban growth)			✔	✔
Reduce Sprawl				✔
Agriculture (lands) (natural resource industries)	✔		✔	✔
Forest Lands (natural resource industries)			✔	✔
Mining	✔			
The Economy (economic development)	✔	✔	✔	✔
Housing	✔	✔	✔	✔
Downtown Revitalization	✔			
Property Rights	✔			✔
Permits				✔
Natural Resources and the Environment				
Water Resources	✔		✔	
Coastal and Marine Resources	✔		✔ (4 goals)	
Natural Systems (natural resources) (environment) and Recreational Lands (open space)	✔	✔	✔	✔ (2 goals)
Air Quality	✔		✔	
Energy (conservation)	✔		✔	
Areas Subject to Natural Disasters and Hazards			✔	
Hazardous and Nonhazardous Materials and Waste	✔			
Willamette River Greenway			✔	
Public and Community Facilities				
Public (community) Facilities (and services)	✔	✔	✔	✔
Transportation	✔		✔	✔
Education	✔			

Table 6.3. Comparison of Statewide Planning Goals: Florida, Georgia, Oregon, and Washington (Continued)

Goal	Florida	Georgia	Oregon	Washington
Public and Community Facilities (Continued)				
Health	✔			
Public Safety	✔			
Cultural and(or) Historic Resources (preservation)	✔	✔	✔	✔
Recreational Needs			✔	✔
Tourism	✔			
Governmental Efficiency	✔			
Other				
Children	✔			
Families	✔			
The Elderly	✔			
Employment	✔			
Citizen Involvement (participation and coordination)			✔	✔
Plan Implementation	✔			

Sources: Florida Statutes Section 187.20; Rules of the Georgia Department of Community Affairs; Oregon's Statewide Planning Goals and Guidelines, 1995 Edition; Revised Code Washington, Chapter 36.70A, § 36.70A.020.

designers in each state begin with a top-down framework of state goals to guide local and (in Florida and Georgia) regional plans but then implement the structure of that mandate in their own unique way.

Table 6.3 summarizes and compares the content of statewide planning goals adopted by the four states. Florida specifies 26 goals in its state plan. Georgia has only five goals as part of DCA's administrative rules. Oregon has 19 different statewide planning goals adopted by LCDC. Washington adopted 13 goals as part of the Growth Management Act (GMA). Both Florida and Washington adopted goals within the law itself, while Oregon and Georgia provided goals by rule. The trend toward fewer goals in third-wave programs represents evidence that supports the longitudinal divergence hypothesis and may signal that Georgia and Washington learned that having many goals introduced too much complexity to the mandate.

From Table 6.3, the goals of the various programs are compared by constructing indexes of similarity. I calculate proportions of the number of goals common to each pair of states and the total number of goals specified by either or both of those states (see Table 6.4). For example, to determine how comparable the goals of Georgia and Florida are, I count from Table 6.3 the number of goals that both states specify (the numerator) then divide that number by the total number of goals enunciated by at least one of the states in the pair (the denominator). The indexes of similarity exclude, from Table 6.3, the Willamette River Greenway goal and those goals classified as "other" given that these goals are highly individualized to Oregon and Florida, respectively.

Table 6.4. Similarity Indexes of Statewide Planning Goals: Florida, Georgia, Oregon, and Washington

	Florida	Georgia	Oregon	Washington
Florida		0.286 (6 of 21)	0.440 (11 of 25)	0.269 (7 of 26)
Georgia			0.375 (6 of 16)	0.357 (5 of 14)
Oregon				0.526 (10 of 19)

Source: Calculated from data in Table 6.3.

The highest similarity index is that calculated from a comparison of Oregon's and Washington's goals. It is the only index of the six possible pairs of states that has more than one-half (0.526) of the goals held in common. This finding provides evidence that supports the hypothesis of longitudinal regional convergence, or, in other words, programs in the same subnational region tend to have similar structures even if they are adopted at different times. On the other hand, the low similarity index between Florida's and Georgia's goals (0.286) provides evidence that tends to refute the regional convergence hypothesis.

The goals of Florida and Oregon exhibit some similarity according to the index (0.440) when compared with other pairs of states. This provides some evidence for the cross-sectional convergence hypothesis. However, the cross-sectional convergence hypothesis would also suggest a high similarity index between Georgia and Washington, which is not found. The lowest goal similarity index is between Florida's and Washington's goals (0.269), which provides evidence that the path of learning between those states is less important and justifiably excluded from Figure 6.1.

Returning to Table 6.3, each of the growth management states has the following statewide goals in common: economic development, housing, natural resources, public facilities, and historic resources. Three of the four states provide a land use goal; Washington does not have a goal titled "land use" but has, more significantly, specified the goal of reducing sprawl. For all intents and purposes, therefore, land use is a goal that is common to all four growth management programs.

Both Washington and Oregon have goals regarding urbanization/ urban growth. Also, recall prior discussion about the growth management element of Florida's state comprehensive plan, which if implemented would have required the state to direct urban growth. Note also that Florida has its antisprawl rule which implements state urbanization policies. Florida and Washington have goals relative to property rights, and Washington also provides a goal on development permits. Georgia is the only one of the four states that does not specify a transportation goal. Florida's state plan goes beyond the other three states by specifying human service goals (see "other" in Table 6.3).

It is important to note how these state goals apply to regional entities and local governments. Each of the four states provides that local comprehensive plans, whether mandated or not, must be consistent with the state-enunciated goals. Excerpted below are the specific requirements for the four states.

> The rule [minimum criteria for the review and determination of compliance of the local government comprehensive plan elements, or FAC 9J-5] shall include criteria for determining whether . . . the local government comprehensive plan elements are consistent with the state comprehensive plan . . . (Florida Statutes § 163.3177).
>
> The department [DCA] has established statewide goals . . . Goals developed in local plans shall be consistent with these initial statewide goals . . . (Georgia DCA Rules § 110-3-2-.04).
>
> The department [DLCD] shall prepare and the commission shall adopt goals and guidelines for use by state agencies, local governments and special districts in preparing, adopting, amending and implementing existing and future comprehensive plans (ORS § 197.225).
>
> The following goals are adopted to guide the development and adoption of comprehensive plans and development regulations of those counties and cities that are required or choose to plan . . . (RCW § 36.70A.020).

Goals established in Florida's state comprehensive plan are mandatory for all regional policy plans and local comprehensive plans. Georgia's administrative rules apply to each local government that chooses to plan. Oregon's goals apply to all local governments because each local government is required to plan. Washington's goals apply to countywide planning policies and to all local governments that are required to or volunteer to prepare local plans. Unlike the mandate designers in the other three states, Oregon's legislators anticipated the possibility that statewide goals will need revision over time; only its law specifically provides for amendments to statewide goals (ORS § 197.040 and § 197.245).

CRITICAL AREAS OF THE STATE

In addition to establishing a framework for state and local (and in Florida and Georgia, regional) planning, legislation of each state provides in some manner for establishing areas of critical state concern (i.e., critical areas). Florida's law provides for establishment of areas of critical state concern in the tradition of the *Model Land Development Code.* The state land planning agency may from time to time recommend, and in practice has recommended, to the Administration Commission that specific areas of critical state concern be established (Florida Statutes § 380.05). Similarly, Georgia's DCA is required to develop (and has adopted) planning procedures for regionally important resources (Georgia Code § 50-8-7.1). Regionally important resources are generally considered to be significant on a statewide basis and this term, though implicitly regional in scope, is considered to be just a different name for areas of critical state concern. This similarity in structure of programs in Florida and Georgia confirms the earlier conclusions that the model code is still pervasive. This similarity in structures also suggests support for the regional convergence hypothesis.

Oregon's LCDC has authority to recommend to the Joint Legislative Committee on Land Use the designation of areas of critical state concern (ORS § 197.040 and § 197.405). Unlike Florida and Georgia, however, Oregon elected not to designate areas of critical state concern. On paper, if not in practice, the inclusion of state authority to designate critical areas in Oregon confirms my conclusion about the pervasiveness of the model code. While Oregon has never elected to use these powers, it has never chosen to delete that authority. What is more, the existence of state authority over critical areas in both Florida and Oregon provides evidence that supports the hypothesis of cross-sectional convergence of programs initiated during the quiet revolution.

Washington has a unique approach to critical areas. The state's Growth Strategies Commission was specifically directed to recommend the designation of areas of critical state concern. State law provides that the Growth Strategies Commission shall "recommend to the legislature and the governor by October 1, 1990, a specific structure or process that . . . addresses lands and resources of statewide significance" (RCW § 36.70A.800). Again, this provision confirms my conclusion that model code provisions are pervasive in growth management mandate designs. Washington's GMA establishes a statewide framework for identifying and protecting certain specific critical areas and then requires local governments to designate and protect those critical areas. DCTED was required by law to adopt guidelines no later than September 1, 1990, to guide the classification of critical areas by local governments (RCW § 36.70A.050). Critical areas are defined as: wetlands; areas with a critical recharging effect on aquifers used for potable water; fish and wildlife habitat conservation areas; frequently flooded areas; and geologically hazardous areas (RCW § 36.70A.030). Hence, rather than requiring state involvement in the designation and management of individual critical areas that may be applied inconsistently across the state, Washington decided that there were five general types of critical areas and that each local government in the state (not just those required to plan) must identify and adopt regulations to protect those areas (see Sidebar 6.1 for an example of implementation in Cowlitz County).

Another important difference between the approach to critical areas taken in Washington, and those of other states, is that it requires the designation and protection of specified critical areas before local planning. Note that this is another conscious choice regarding the sequence of planning.

Although Washington's approach to providing standards for critical areas appears from the prior discussion to be unique, it has at least one similarity with Georgia's program; both require state rulemaking for critical areas. Georgia directs the Board of Natural Resources and Department of Natural Resources (DNR) to prepare and adopt rules for the protection of the natural resources, environment, and vital areas of the state, including, but not limited to the protection of: mountains; river corridors; watersheds of streams and reservoirs which are to be used for public water supply; the purity of ground water; and wetlands.

Sidebar 6.1. Protecting Critical Areas in Cowlitz County, Washington

Cowlitz County, with a population of about 90,000, was not initially mandated by GMA to adopt a comprehensive plan, and at the time of this writing had not reached a decennial population growth rate sufficient that it be required to do so. Each city and county in the state, however, was required by GMA in the early 1990s to adopt an ordinance protecting critical areas. The initial state deadline came and went, and so did the extended deadline, without passage by the county of a critical areas protection ordinance. Cowlitz County finally adopted a critical areas ordinance in June 1996. The cities within Cowlitz County were even slower to comply with this state mandate. Because there was no visible state agency enforcement of the mandate, the county and cities did not make it a priority to comply. Upon petition, the Growth Management Hearings Board could have found cities and counties without an adopted critical areas ordinance not in compliance with GMA.

As with other local governments participating in the National Flood Insurance Program, Cowlitz County already had a flood hazard area ordinance. With regard to this critical area, it simply referenced that ordinance in the critical areas ordinance. For aquifer recharge areas, the ordinance required that certain types of development such as junkyards obtain a critical area permit and that other uses be evaluated for potential impacts on recharge areas. Cowlitz County's critical areas ordinance provisions for fish and habitat areas have never really come into play, although that is likely to change soon given the listing of salmonids pursuant to the U. S. Endangered Species Act.

The section of the critical areas ordinance pertaining to wetlands was more significant in practice. It classified wetlands by types and established buffer requirements based on soils. Smaller wetlands remained unregulated unless their value was classified as regionally significant. While the wetland protection provisions have been useful in mitigating impacts in Cowlitz County, they afford only a small increment of additional protection over what already existed via federal permit requirements and/or what could have been achieved under the State Environmental Policy Act (SEPA).

Of greatest significance was the county's requirements for geologically hazardous areas. Most of the developable land in the county had already been used, and residential subdivisions were beginning to push their way up the many hillsides in the county. If maps showed that a particular development proposal would be located in an area of historic or potential landslide, or in an area of unstable slopes or severe erosion hazard, a geotechnical assessment was required to be prepared by a qualified expert. If that assessment showed evidence of landslides, a more detailed geotechnical report was required prior to issuance of a critical areas permit.

On rare occasions the geological hazard area provisions had some effect on the location of development, but the ordinance has not prohibited development to any significant degree. In practice, qualified experts have simply walked and visually inspected the site and certified site stability without conducting subsurface explorations of the site in question. As the administrator of that ordinance, I pushed for "tightening the screws" on the geotechnical requirements because of a large active landslide within the City of Kelso (not subject to the county's ordinance) that had already destroyed dozens of single family residences and was threatening major additional losses. Whether implementation of a critical areas ordinance in Kelso prior to subdivision development would have prevented this catastrophe is anyone's guess, though I remain skeptical that such an ordinance would have prevented the subdivision from locating on a geologically hazardous site.

This sidebar illustrates that, while on paper the critical area provisions of Washington's law appear to have many benefits, actual implementation of this GMA mandate in practice has not been fully enforced, and where implemented it has added only incrementally to existing environmental protection regulations.

Such standards are required to be used by local governments in preparing and implementing local comprehensive plans (Georgia Code § 12-2-8). Hence, this finding provides some evidence for the cross-sectional convergence hypothesis. Recall, however, that Georgia does not mandate local planning and so regulatory protection of these specific vital areas is therefore not necessarily required. For instance, a local government could adopt a plan but not include the implementation of the environmental planning standards in the plan and neglect to adopt and enforce critical areas ordinances, as indeed was found and discussed earlier.

Oregon's law specifically requires adoption by local governments of wetland conservation plans (ORS § 197.279) and plans and regulations consistent with a state goal regarding groundwater resources (ORS § 197.283). Given that Florida requires comprehensive plans to contain

Table 6.5. Critical Areas Protection: Florida, Georgia, Oregon, and Washington

Critical Area Provision	Florida	Georgia	Oregon	Washington
Designation and management of areas of critical state concern	✔	✔ (regionally important resources)	✔ (not exercised)	
State agency adoption of rules related to critical areas	✔	✔	✔	✔
Mandatory local designation and protection (by ordinance) of critical areas prior to local comprehensive planning				✔
Mandatory local plan elements related to critical areas	✔	✔ (for those choosing to plan)	✔	

Source: Compiled from state laws (see text discussion for citations).

elements relative to natural groundwater aquifer recharge and the conservation, use, and protection of natural resources in the area (Florida Statutes § 163.3177), its program has basically the same requirements as those in Oregon and Washington. This finding lends some support for the hypothesis of longitudinal regional convergence. Furthermore, the finding that all states to some degree address critical areas suggests that a general convergence over time has occurred, contrary to the longitudinal divergence hypothesis. Table 6.5 summarizes the various approaches to critical areas designation and protection in the four states.

Table 6.5 shows that all states except Washington have a state role for designating areas of critical state concern. Again, this finding supports earlier conclusions about the pervasiveness of the *Model Land Development Code*. Program officials in Florida and Georgia have exercised state authority to designate and manage areas of critical state concern, and they build on that approach by adopting critical area standards for local plans to follow. This finding supports the hypothesis of longitudinal regional convergence of state growth management programs. Oregon's approach is virtually the same but LCDC has never exercised its authority to recommend areas of critical state concern. Washington's program, again, is unique in that it: does not provide separate state authority to designate areas of critical state concern; and mandates, prior to the local planning process, the local designation and protection of critical areas.

I now turn to an analysis of the structure of regional and local planning, and the extent to which those structures tend to evolve along the paths predicted in the aforementioned hypotheses about program learning.

Note

1. Florida Statutes: Chapter 163, Part II, Intergovernmental Programs, County and Municipal Planning and Land Development Regulation, known and cited as the "Local Government Comprehensive Planning and Land Development Regulation Act;" Title XIII, Planning and Development, Chapter 186, State and Regional Planning, Sections 186.001-186.031, 186.801-186.911 known and cited as the "Florida State Comprehensive Planning Act of 1972;" Sections 186.501-186.513, known and cited as the "Florida Regional Planning Council Act;" and Chapter 187, known and cited as the "State Comprehensive Plan" (1995 version). The Georgia Planning Act of 1989, codified as Georgia Code Sections 37-70, 45-12, and 50-8 (1996 version via Internet), Oregon Revised Statutes, Chapter 197, Comprehensive Land Use Planning Coordination (1995 Edition). State of Washington's Growth Management Act, Revised Code of Washington (RCW) 36.70A. (1996 update via Internet). The description was supplemented in a few cases by rules of the administering agency.

CHAPTER

7

The Structure of State-Sponsored Land Use Planning: Regional and Local Roles

In this chapter, I continue the analysis of the content of state statutes. The regional and local planning structures of the four states are compared in order to determine patterns that confirm or refute the three hypotheses about program evolution and learning.

REGIONAL PLANNING STRUCTURE

Regional planning is a fundamental component of all four state growth management programs in some capacity or another. Recall from Chapter 1 that three of the four states have dominant metropolitan areas: Atlanta, Georgia; Portland, Oregon, and Seattle, Washington. Florida has 20 metropolitan statistical areas and is not dominated by any single urban center. Not coincidentally, the three states with dominant metropolitan regions also have planning legislation that specifically and uniquely pertains to those populated metropolitan areas.[1]

Metropolitan planning

Georgia has a law that establishes metropolitan area planning and development commissions (i.e., metropolitan commissions) in each area of the state with a population of more than 1,000,000 (Georgia Code § 50-8-82). Metropolitan commissions have all the powers of regional development centers (RDCs) plus additional powers (Georgia Code § 50-8-83). Georgia's RDCs were, before the 1989 planning act, called area planning and development commissions (APDCs). Metropolitan commissions are required to prepare and adopt "comprehensive development guides" for their areas (Georgia Code § 50-8-92) and to engage in a continuous program of research, study, and planning. These powers include land use (Georgia Code § 50-8-97) but specifically exclude zoning (Georgia Code § 50-8-92). Currently, Georgia's mandate to establish metropolitan commissions applies only to the metropolitan Atlanta region.

In Oregon, Portland's regional urban growth management program, sponsored by the state, is well known and does not require elaboration here (see Ehrenhalt 1998; Oliver 1996; 1992; 1989; Metropolitan Service District 1994a; 1994b; Poracsky and Houck 1994). The Metropolitan Service District recently approved the first major expansion of the Portland region UGB in 20 years, which is summarized in Sidebar 7.1.

Seattle's Municipality of Metropolitan Seattle, which is Seattle and King County's federation of local governments, undertook regional sewerage treatment in 1958. In 1972, the federation assumed responsibility for regional transportation services. The federation has had a successful history in fostering intergovernmental cooperation and long range planning (Peterson 1990). The Puget Sound Regional Council has also worked in the 1990s to link transportation and land use planning as part of its Vision 2020 plan (Watterson 1993). Washington requires that multicounty planning policies be adopted by "two or more counties, each with a population of 450,000 or more, with contiguous urban areas" (RCW § 36.70A.210). This requirement applies only to two counties in the Seattle metropolitan area, but multicounty planning policies may be adopted by other counties. The mandates for the Portland and Seattle metropolitan areas to plan for urban growth are the only significant references in Oregon's and Washington's land use laws relative to multicounty regional planning.[2] Oregon and Washington do not provide for comprehensive areal coverage of the state with multicounty regional planning councils. Both Florida and Georgia, on the other hand, do establish boundaries of regional planning councils that achieve statewide coverage.

Sidebar 7.1. Metro Expands the Portland Region UGB

Oregon law has since 1973 required that all cities adopt urban growth boundaries (UGBs) and since 1995 has required via House Bill 2709 (ORS § 197.296) that certain urban areas provide for a 20-year supply of urban land for development within UGBs. The new mandate to provide a 20-year land supply required that Portland's regional government, the Metropolitan Service District (Metro), push cities to accept more housing units and/or expand the region's UGB. Metro had prior to this law's passage already begun to consider concepts for future growth in the region (Metropolitan Service District 1994a). Metro chose a planning horizon of 50 years (i.e., the year 2040) and for some years had been immersed in debates about the future of the boundary. Homebuilders wanted an expanded UGB because rising real estate prices were attributed to the land constraints resulting from the UGB. Don Morrisette, homebuilder and one of Metro's elected officials, used his own funds in 1996 to hire some Portland State University planning professors to present an economic rationale for UGB expansion (see Mildner, Dueker and Rufolo 1996). Indeed, land prices inside the region's UGB have tripled in some areas (Franzen and Hunsberger 1998). On the other hand, downtown Portland interests, environmentalists, and many local leaders in the inner suburbs of the region constitute an anti-growth machine that views any expansion of the UGB as a magnification of sprawl (Ehrenhalt 1996).

Metro elected to follow a strategy of development densification inside the Portland region UGB so that future growth could be accommodated there (Ehrenhalt 1996; Metropolitan Service District 1994a; 1994b) with only modest expansions of the boundary. Average lot sizes in the Portland region have decreased from 13,000 square feet when the UGB was first effectuated (1979) to 6,700 square feet during the past few years. In December 1995, the Metro Council approved its Region 2040 plan. It also established urban reserves in anticipation of expanding the UGB. In 1997, Metro adopted its functional (i.e., land use) plan which among other things required local governments in the region to plan for increased housing densities. Then in 1998, pursuant to law, Metro was required to approve an expansion of the Portland region's UGB by 3,500 acres in 1998 and a comparable amount the following year to maintain the required 20-year supply of urban land. On December 3, 1998, Metro's governing council voted to expand the Portland region's UGB by approximately 5,100 acres. With the recent expansion the regional UGB will now contain some 375 square miles (Nokes 1998a; 1998b).

The decision by the Metro Council to expand the UGB was actually a series of votes on specific properties to be included in the UGB. Opponents have vowed to appeal some of the UGB decisions to the state Land Use Board of Appeals (LUBA). Oregon's DLCD sent a letter to Metro prior to the vote, suggesting that one of the properties proposed for inclusion in the UGB (i.e., a 4,000-acre parcel known as "St. Mary's") is unlikely to meet state law for preserving prime farmland. The state's land use watchdog group, 1000 Friends of Oregon, has indicated it will appeal the decision to include the St. Mary's property (in Washington County) within the UGB, and certain decisions designating certain areas considered ripe for UGB expansion (i.e., urban reserves) are already being appealed. Another boundary expansion is expected in 1999 (Franzen and Hunsberger 1998; Nokes 1998a; 1998b).

This difference between the Pacific Northwest and the southeastern United States is most likely attributed to the size of the counties in the states of both regions. Counties in the Pacific Northwest are geographically large compared to those in Florida and Georgia. For example, Washington covers its 66,581 square miles of area with 39 counties, while Georgia (not substantially smaller with almost 58,000 square miles, see Table 1.1), is divided into 159 counties. More than in the large counties in Oregon and Washington, urban growth patterns (and problems) in Florida and Georgia tend to spill across small county boundaries, enough to prompt legislators in these southern states to mandate multicounty regional land use planning. An interesting historical tidbit (source unknown) about why Georgia has so many counties is that state legislators did not want its rural citizens to be located more than a day's horseback ride to their county seat.

Mandatory multicounty regional planning councils

Florida and Georgia require all counties in the state to participate in coordination functions and planning at the multicounty regional level. Florida's Regional Planning Council Act articulates the need for multicounty regional planning councils (RPCs) and mandates that they plan, as excerpted below.

> There is a need for the establishment at the regional level of clear policy plans . . . It is the declared purpose of this act to establish a common system

> of regional planning councils . . . The regional planning council is recognized as Florida's only multipurpose regional entity that is in a position to plan for and coordinate intergovernmental solutions to growth-related problems on greater-than-local issues, provide technical assistance to local governments, and meet other needs of the communities in each region (Florida Statutes § 186.502).

Florida mandates counties, but not cities, to be members of RPCs, as noted in the excerpt below:

> Nothing contained in this [the Regional Planning] act shall be construed to mandate municipal government membership or participation in a regional planning council. However, each county shall be a member of the regional planning council created within the comprehensive planning district encompassing the county (Florida Statutes § 186.504).

Florida's RPCs act in an advisory capacity, conduct studies of the region, provide technical assistance to local governments on growth management matters, and prepare strategic regional policy plans (Florida Statutes § 186.505). Florida's legislation does not specifically authorize RPCs to prepare local plans. Rather, RPCs are authorized only to perform a coordinating function in a local planning effort.

Georgia's 1989 planning act also establishes a statewide system of multicounty planning agencies (RDCs). For a map of the boundaries of Georgia's RDCs, see Map 7.1. Each RDC is mandated to prepare and adopt a regional plan and submit it to DCA, after taking into consideration the local comprehensive plans within the region (Georgia Code § 50-8-35). Similar to Florida, Georgia's local governments (including cities) are mandated to be members of the RDCs for the regions in which they are located (Georgia Code § 36-70-4 and § 50-8-33).

Besides providing local planning technical assistance, Georgia's RDCs can under contract prepare local comprehensive plans. Subject to approval by Georgia's DCA, individual RDCs may require that local comprehensive plans include elements in addition to those established by DCA (Georgia Code § 50-8-35). However, this provision of the Georgia Planning Act has not been exercised to my knowledge.

Map 7.1. Boundaries of Georgia's Regional Development Centers

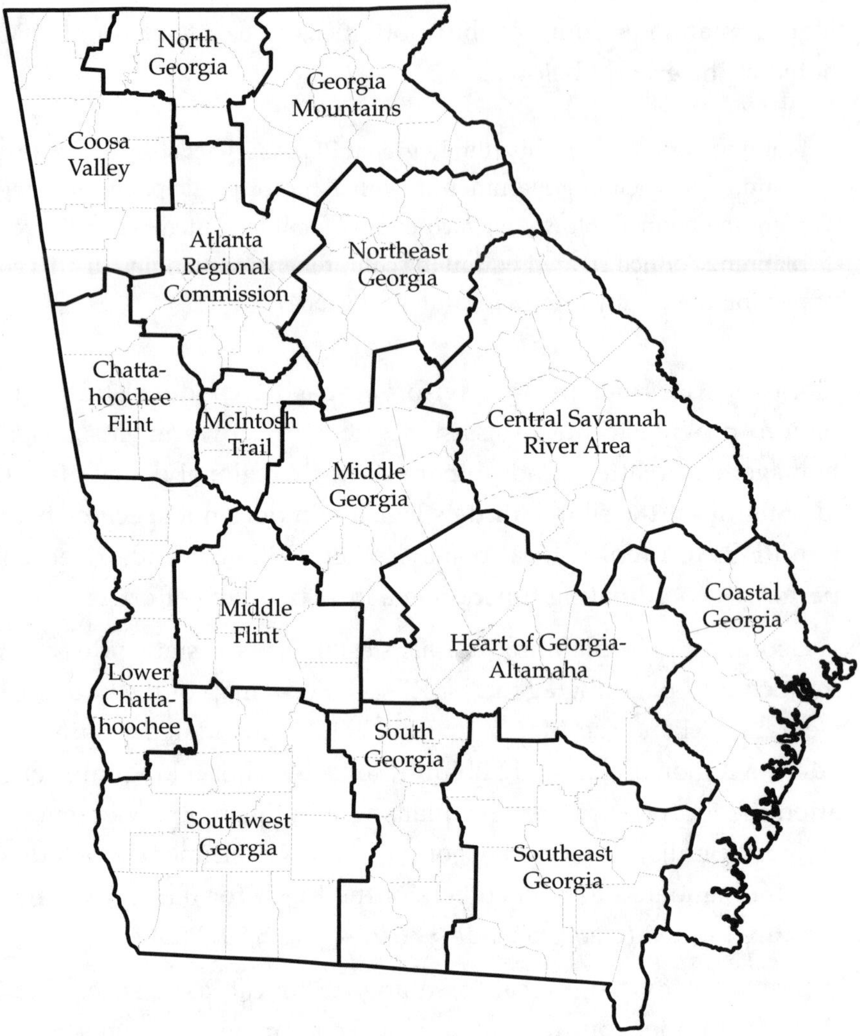

The two southern states differ from their Pacific Northwest counterparts in that they provide for development of regional impact (DRI) programs. I turn to that topic briefly.

Developments of regional impact

In the tradition of the *Model Land Development Code*, Florida implemented a DRI program. Georgia followed with an approach substantially similar to that process implemented by Florida. The statutory excerpts below indicate that laws in both Florida and Georgia provide for state adoption of rules to guide such processes:

> The Administration Commission shall by rule adopt statewide guidelines and standards to be used in determining whether particular developments shall undergo development-of-regional-impact review (Florida Statutes § 380.06).
>
> The department [DCA] shall develop planning procedures . . . for planning with respect to developments of regional impact . . . The department shall determine, in its judgment and for each region, what shall constitute developments of regional impact (Georgia Code § 50-8-7.1).

While not generally recognized as such, Washington's program of identifying "essential public facilities" can be viewed as a 1990s-style version of a DRI system (RCW § 36.70A.200). Local plans in Washington must include a process for identifying and siting certain regional facilities that would otherwise be difficult to site because of the not-in-my-backyard (NIMBY) and locally unwanted land uses (LULU) syndromes. The state Office of Financial Management (OFM) has a role in the process, as indicated in the passage below:

> The comprehensive plan of each county and city that is planning under this chapter shall include a process for identifying and siting essential public facilities. Essential public facilities include those facilities that are typically difficult to site. . . . The office of financial management shall maintain a list of those essential state public facilities that are required or likely to be built within the next six years. The office of financial management may at any time add facilities to the list. No local comprehensive plan or development regulation may preclude the siting of essential public facilities (RCW § 36.70A.200).

Legal provisions regarding essential public facilities in Washington do not address large scale private developments (e.g., a 500-lot residential subdivision), as DRI programs in Florida and Georgia do. Though the provisions on essential public facilities do not constitute a DRI program, they are designed to provide for the siting of difficult-to-locate facilities and fill the role of a state-regional-local coordinating mechanism in the same ways that Florida's and Georgia's DRI programs do. Both the DRI programs and essential public facilities provisions include state supervision of, and local participation in, a development issue of regional significance. Washington's essential public facilities program therefore has some important parallels with the DRI programs implemented in the southern states.

Senate Bill 100 authorized LCDC to review and approve proposals for siting certain types of facilities, termed "activities of statewide significance," but LCDC has never used that authority and it was subsequently repealed (Rohse and Watt 1994, 150-154). Oregon does not have a system of controlling difficult-to-site regional developments like other states do.

Regional planning standards

Florida's statutes provide two sources of standards for regional planning: the state comprehensive plan, and rules adopted by the Executive Office of the Governor, as excerpted below.

> The adopted state comprehensive plan shall provide, in addition to other criteria established by law, standards and criteria for the review and approval of . . . strategic regional policy plans (Florida Statutes § 186.007).
>
> The Executive Office of the Governor shall adopt by rule minimum criteria to be addressed in each strategic regional policy plan and a uniform format for each plan. Such criteria must emphasize the requirement that each regional planning council, when preparing and adopting a strategic regional policy plan, focus on regional rather than local resources and facilities (Florida Statutes § 186.507).

The governor's office, not DCA, adopts rules for regional plans. Florida's system provides for direct executive and legislative authority over regional planning. Florida's governor directs regional planning with the power of appointment of persons to RPCs and via authority as the state's chief planning official. Florida's legislature also guides regional planning via the adopted state comprehensive plan.

Georgia's statute requires DCA to develop and establish standards and procedures for coordinated and comprehensive planning (Georgia

Code § 50-8-3 and § 50-8-7.1). Coordinated and comprehensive planning is defined to include RDCs (Georgia Code § 50-8-2), and DCA has adopted standards for regional planning.

State funding of regional planning councils

Statutes in Florida and Georgia provide for state funding of regional planning. Florida law provides that "financial and technical assistance of the state should be provided to regional planning agencies" (Florida Statutes § 186.502). Georgia's DCA is specifically mandated to establish a minimum funding amount for RDCs (Georgia Code § 50-8-33). Both Florida's and Georgia's programs involve substate regional planning as an integral component of intergovernmental coordination and planning. Georgia elected to provide funding for local comprehensive planning through RDCs rather than directing state funds to local comprehensive planning efforts, as did Florida, Oregon, and Washington.

State review of regional plans

Florida and Georgia specifically require that regional entities prepare plans and submit them for review to the state for compliance with the regional planning standards already described. The passages below identify the specific provisions of law:

> Each regional planning council shall submit to the Executive Office of the Governor its proposed strategic regional policy plan on a schedule adopted by rule by the Executive Office of the Governor (Florida Statutes § 186.508).
>
> Each [regional development] center shall prepare and adopt a regional plan and submit the regional plan to the department [of Community Affairs]. The regional plan shall take into consideration local plans within the region (Georgia Code § 50-8-35). The department shall examine and analyze plans of state agencies, comprehensive plans of regional development centers, and comprehensive plans of municipalities and counties, undertaken as part of the coordinated and comprehensive planning process ... (Georgia Code § 50-8-7.1).

Georgia's law does not follow Florida's lead in requiring the periodic revision and review of multicounty regional comprehensive plans. Florida's law specifies that the regional planning process shall be continuous and ongoing and that RPCs must prepare evaluation and appraisal reports (EARs) on their strategic regional policy plans every five years. RPCs must assess the successes or failures of their regional plans and address changes to the state comprehensive plan as needed (Florida Statutes § 186.511). Florida's law ensures that regional planning will receive continuous attention by requiring that each RPC prepare and furnish an annual report on its activities (Florida Statutes § 186.513). Georgia's law also requires reports from RDCs, but those reports are required to ensure financial accountability, not consistency of regional plans with state plans.

Summary comparison of Florida and Georgia

Florida's and Georgia's approaches to regional planning have major similarities, including: (1) comprehensive areal coverage by multi-county regional planning councils; (2) a mandate for counties to maintain membership in multicounty entities; (3) a mandate to prepare regional plans and to submit those plans to the state for review; (4) DRI programs; (5) state rulemaking for DRIs and regional plans; and (6) statutory references to funding of regional planning agencies. Georgia's multicounty regional planning structure is substantially similar to Florida's, suggesting that Georgia used Florida's regional planning framework as a model in developing its own program design. These similarities confirm the regional convergence hypothesis.

There are, however, some notable differences between the two states' regional planning structures. Georgia reversed the planning sequence required in Florida and prepared local plans before regional plans. Other differences between regional planning in Florida and Georgia relate to the oversight of regional planning. In Florida, oversight of regional planning and coordination is assigned to the governor's office through promulgation of rules, review of plans, and appointments to RPC boards. In Georgia, the governor does not make appointments to RDC boards and has little if any direct authority over regional planning. Similar to its state comprehensive planning process, Florida requires a more-or-less continuous regional planning process. Georgia's law does not mandate that regional planning occur on an ongoing basis.

On balance, the striking similarities outweigh the differences, and I conclude that Florida's regional planning structure served as a model for Georgia. The similarities between regional planning structures in Florida and Georgia provide strong evidence for the hypothesis of longitudinal regional convergence.

Counties as regional planning entities

Oregon and Washington, in contrast to the southern states, do not mandate DRI programs (but recall that Washington's essential public facilities component serves a similar purpose), nor do they mandate an areally comprehensive system of multicounty RPCs and specify a role for them in the coordinated planning process. Instead, Oregon and Washington require counties to serve in the same intergovernmental coordination and planning capacities that multicounty RPCs do. This similarity in approaches to regional planning provides evidence that supports the regional convergence hypothesis.

Recall from Chapter 3, however, that the founders of Oregon's land use law initially proposed that 14 multicounty regional planning districts be established. Given the political turmoil connected with multicounty regional planning in Oregon during the 1970s, the state opted for a county-as-regional-entity approach in lieu of the otherwise favorable multicounty regional planning approach.[3] Oregon's land use statute does not clearly enunciate the counties-as-regional-entities approach (see generally Bollens and Caves 1994). Oregon counties, however, play a coordination role with respect to comprehensive planning, urban services and facilities agreements (ORS § 195.065) and, more recently, population allocations within and outside urban areas.

Perhaps more pointedly than Oregon's law, Washington's GMA enunciates this county coordination approach to regional planning. As the passage below indicates, the countywide planning policy in Washington serves much the same regional role as the multicounty planning efforts in Florida and Georgia do. Similar to Florida but in contrast to Georgia, Washington's countywide planning policy process occurs prior to local planning.

> The legislature recognizes that counties are regional governments within their boundaries. For the purposes of this section, a "county-wide planning policy" is a written policy statement or statements used solely for establishing a county-wide framework from which county and city comprehensive plans are developed and adopted pursuant to this chapter. The legislative authority of a county that plans under RCW 36.70A.040 shall adopt a county-wide planning policy in cooperation with the cities located in whole or in part within the county (RCW § 36.70A.210).

Instead of a multicounty regional planning structure, Washington requires countywide (regional) policies that precede local planning.

This sequence of regional (if one accepts that term) and then local planning in Washington mirrors the sequence in Florida where local plans must be consistent with regional policy plans.

The finding that Washington followed a counties-as-regional-entities model substantially similar to Oregon's regional structure provides evidence supporting the proposition that the Oregon-Washington evolutionary path is important (i.e., the longitudinal regional convergence hypothesis). The similarity in sequence between Washington's county-wide policies approach, which precedes local planning, and Florida's top-down consistency approach of state-regional-local planning, may suggest that the evolutionary path of learning between Florida and Washington is more important than I expected.

LOCAL PLANNING STRUCTURE

Excerpts of the local planning mandates highlight some interesting differences between and among the states. Florida and Oregon both require all cities and counties to plan, as specified in the excerpts below.

> Each local government shall prepare a comprehensive plan of the type and in the manner set out in this act or shall prepare amendments to its existing comprehensive plan to conform it to the requirements of this part in the manner set out in this part (Florida Statutes § 163.3167).
>
> City and county governments are responsible for the development of local comprehensive plans (ORS § 197.005). Cities and counties shall exercise their planning and zoning responsibilities . . . each city and county in this state shall . . . prepare, adopt, amend and revise comprehensive plans in compliance with goals approved by the [Land Conservation and Development] commission (ORS § 197.175).

It is noteworthy that both Florida and Oregon laws also mandate action by special districts. Florida requires that public facility reports of special districts be filed with local governments. Oregon's law requires plans and activities of special districts to be consistent with statewide planning goals. The following statutory excerpts describe these requirements for special districts.

> Each independent special district must submit a public facilities report to the appropriate local government as required by s. 189.415 (Florida Statutes § 163.3177).

Table 7.1. Applicability of Washington's Planning Requirements for Counties

Percent Population Increase, Last 10 Years	Counties With Population of Less than 50,000	Counties With Population of 50,000 or More
20% or more	Must plan but may opt out by resolution prior to December 31, 1990	Must plan
17% or more but less than 20%	Not required to plan	On or after May 16, 1995, must plan
10% or more	Not required to plan	Until May 16, 1995, must plan
Less than 10%	Not required to plan	Not required to plan
Opt-In alternative	May adopt a resolution to have GMA apply	May adopt a resolution to have GMA apply

Source: Derived from Revised Code Washington, 36.70A.040.

> . . . all plans, programs, rules or regulations affecting land use adopted by a . . . special district shall be in compliance with the goals within one year after the date those goals are approved by the commission (ORS § 197.250).

The finding that both Florida and Oregon mandate all local governments to plan, while Georgia and Washington do not, yields evidence supporting the hypothesis that third-wave programs have diverged from first and second wave programs. It also suggests support for the cross-sectional convergence hypothesis, or the notion that programs developed during the same period have similar structures.

As noted previously, Georgia does not mandate the preparation of local comprehensive plans. Instead, Georgia's coordinated planning program authorizes local governments to plan and then withholds certain grant moneys if local governments do not plan and obtain qualified local government status.

> The governing bodies of municipalities and counties are authorized . . . to develop, or to cause to be developed pursuant to a contract or other arrangement approved by the governing body, a comprehensive plan (Georgia Code § 36-70-3). The commissioner [of DCA] shall have and may exercise the power and authority to certify, from time to time, municipalities and counties as qualified local governments (Georgia Code § 50-08-5). "Qualified local government" means a county or municipality which . . . has a comprehensive plan in conformity with the minimum standards and procedures . . . [and] has established regulations consistent with its comprehensive plan and with the minimum standards and procedures . . . (Georgia Code § 50-08-2).

Washington has a complex provision that determines whether a county must plan according to GMA. All cities must plan if located in a county that is required to or chooses to plan. Table 7.1 summarizes the county planning mandate.

Any county that has a decennial population gain of 20 percent or more is required to comply with GMA. The GMA provides an "opt out" provision for counties with populations of fewer than 50,000, but the opt out resolution must have been adopted and filed with the state by December 31, 1990. For counties with populations of 50,000 or more before May 16, 1995, a decennial population increase of 10 percent or more was enough to meet the threshold mandating local planning. On or after May 16, 1995, counties of 50,000 or more that grow by 17 percent or more during the past 10 years are required to comply with provisions of the GMA. Counties can voluntarily "opt in" to GMA (as some counties did) if they pass a resolution making the act applicable. Such action also makes GMA applicable to all cities within that county.

Washington's method of utilizing a population threshold to determine planning mandates requires OFM to annually determine the decennial population changes for each county. If OFM certifies that the population of a county that previously had not been required to plan has increased sufficiently to meet the growth rate threshold, then that county and cities within the county are required to plan according to GMA. Specifically, such counties are required to adopt regulations to conserve resource lands (classification is already mandated), adopt countywide planning policies, designate urban growth areas, adopt comprehensive land use plans, and adopt development regulations to implement comprehensive plans (RCW § 36.70A.040).

In conclusion, the four states exhibit three general types of local planning mandate design: all local governments are required to plan (Florida and Oregon); some (the more fast growing) counties and the cities within are required to plan (Washington); and planning is authorized but not required, while grant money is withheld from those local governments that do not plan according to the state's requirements (Georgia).

An underlying pattern of these three types of mandates is the evolutionary theme that state programs adopted during the third wave exhibit less coercive, more collaborative, approaches to comprehensive planning. Georgia certainly did not follow Florida's mandate that all local governments plan. Washington did not follow Oregon's requirement that all local governments plan, though it did require some local governments to plan. Florida's and Oregon's coercive mandate designs of the first and second eras of program evolution, and Georgia's and Washington's rejection of the coercion-based mandate in designing their third wave programs, provide evidence that supports the cross-sectional convergence and longitudinal divergence hypotheses. I showed in earlier chapters that top-down planning mandates fell out of favor with 1990s-style growth management programs, and the differences in local planning structure highlight a new level of collaboration that distinguishes the third era of state growth management program history from the earlier two eras. The differences between the local mandate designs of Florida-Georgia and Oregon-Washington, however, provide some evidence that tends to refute the hypothesis of regional convergence.

Local planning standards

The four states have adopted administrative rules that describe how local planning is to be performed and what the contents of local comprehensive plans must be. Rulemaking authority of the four states relative to local planning standards is excerpted below.

> The state land planning agency shall, by February 15, 1986, adopt by rule minimum criteria for the review and determination of compliance of the local government comprehensive plan elements required by this [Local Government Comprehensive Planning and Land Development Regulation] act (Florida Statutes § 163.3177). [Rule adopted as chapter 9J-5, FAC]
>
> The department [DCA] shall establish minimum standards and procedures which shall be used by local governments in developing, preparing, and implementing their comprehensive plans (Georgia Code § 50-8-37.1). [Rule adopted as Chapter 110-12-1, Minimum Standards and Procedures for Local Comprehensive Planning].
>
> The commission [LCDC] shall . . . prepare statewide planning guidelines (ORS § 197.040). The department shall prepare and the commission shall adopt goals and guidelines for use by state agencies, local governments and special districts in preparing, adopting, amending and implementing existing and future comprehensive plans (ORS § 197.225).
>
> The department [DCTED] shall . . . [adopt] . . . by rule procedural criteria to assist counties and cities in adopting comprehensive plans and development regulations that meet the goals and requirements of this chapter (RCW § 36.70A.190).

The rulemaking structures for local planning standards deserve further description and comparison (see Figure 7.1). It is interesting to recall

Figure 7.1. Structures of Rulemaking for Local Planning Standards

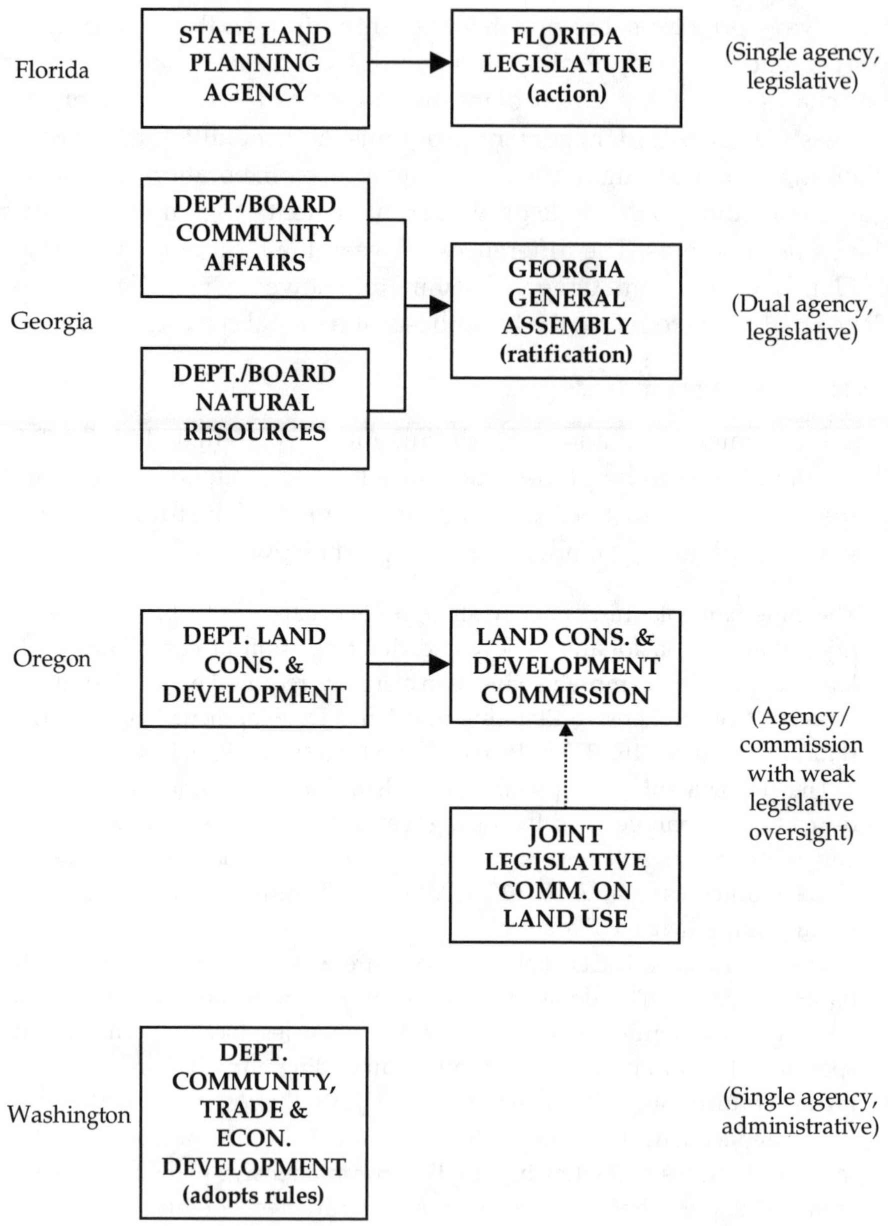

that regional planning standards in Florida are adopted by the governor's office, while local planning standards are adopted by the state land planning agency (i.e., DCA). Florida's legislators retained final authority over the local planning standards. Figure 7.1 characterizes Florida's rulemaking structure for local planning standards as single agency, legislative.

Georgia followed Florida's approach of retaining legislative control over rules, as indicated in the statutory excerpts below.

> Such rules [9J-5 FAC] shall become effective only after they have been submitted to the President of the Senate and the Speaker of the House of Representatives for review by the Legislature no later than 30 days prior to the next regular session of the Legislature. In its review the Legislature may reject, modify, or take no action relative to the rules (Florida Statutes § 163.3177).
>
> The initial minimum standards and procedures promulgated by the department [DCA] pursuant to Code Section 50-8-7.1 shall be submitted by the department to the General Assembly at the next regular session following July 1, 1989, and shall become effective only when ratified by joint resolution of the General Assembly (Georgia Code § 50-8-7.2).

The legislative review of administrative rules for local planning in both Florida and Georgia provides evidence that tends to support the regional convergence hypothesis.

Rulemaking authority in Georgia is split between two state agencies. While DCA promulgates the standards for comprehensive plans, DNR is authorized to (and did) develop minimum standards and procedures for the protection of the natural resources, environment, and vital areas of the state, which are then incorporated into local comprehensive plans (Georgia Code § 12-2-8). Like the local planning standards, the rules for environmental planning adopted by DNR were ratified by the Georgia General Assembly (see Chapter 5). Unlike Florida's law, which enabled the legislature to modify the rules submitted by DCA, Georgia's statute required either ratification or rejection of the local planning rules. Both DCA and DNR are subject to boards (titled the same as the respective departments) that provide overall policy direction to the departments (Georgia Code § 50-8-4). By practice both DCA and DNR send the local planning rules to their boards for approval, even though the Georgia Planning Act does not specifically require it.[4] Georgia's rulemaking structure is characterized in Figure 7.1 as dual agency, legislative.

Oregon and Washington provide rulemaking structures that do not involve final approval by the legislature. This finding offers another piece of evidence that supports the regional convergence and longitudinal divergence hypotheses. Oregon's DLCD has authority to propose rules for local planning. Oregon vests authority to adopt statewide planning goals and guidelines and rules to effectuate those goals and guidelines in LCDC. That authority is, however, subject to oversight by the Joint Legislative Committee on Land Use (ORS § 197.135). Oregon's legislative committee appears not to have ever played a significant oversight role with respect to LCDC's rulemaking. For this reason, Oregon's rulemaking structure for local planning standards is characterized in Figure 7.1 as agency/commission with weak legislative oversight.

Washington vests authority for rulemaking regarding local comprehensive planning in DCTED, with no final legislative approval or legislative committee oversight. Since there is no legislative approval or commission/legislative oversight of state agency rulemaking for local comprehensive planning, Washington's rulemaking structure is characterized in Figure 7.1. as single agency, administrative.

Returning to the hypotheses as depicted in Figure 6.1, the finding that the rulemaking structures are similar in Georgia and Florida supports the hypothesis of regional convergence. Georgia borrowed Florida's rulemaking structure of legislative ratification. On the other hand, Washington did not follow the rulemaking structure established in Oregon (i.e., vesting authority in a commission with limited oversight). Washington's GMA provides no oversight role for the state with regard to rulemaking. This is understandable, since Washington's rulemaking authority is merely "procedural" and was never envisioned by state legislators to authorize DCTED to elaborate substantively on the mandate of GMA (Settle and Gavigan 1993). This finding does not support the hypothesis of an important evolutionary path (i.e., regional convergence) between Oregon and Washington. Again, I attribute the difference in rulemaking structures found in Oregon and Washington to the fact that they were adopted in different eras of time. Washington followed a less coercive and more collaborative mandate design, consistent with 1990s-style growth management practice. This difference between programs in Oregon and Washington therefore yields evidence in support of the longitudinal divergence hypothesis.

Mandatory local plan elements

Either by rule as specified above, in the growth management statute itself, or in both, each of the four states mandates that certain elements be included in local comprehensive plans. It is interesting to compare and contrast the different structures by which the states prescribe the content of local plans. Laws in Florida (Florida Statutes § 163.3177), Georgia (Georgia Code § 50-8-7.1),[5] and Washington (RCW § 36.70A.070) provide broad outlines of the minimum required elements of local comprehensive plans. Each of these states further enunciates the elements of local comprehensive plans by rules separate from the statute (Chapter 9J-5, FAC, Georgia DCA Rules,[6] and Chapter 365-195 WAC, respectively).

Oregon leaves the content of local plans mostly to local governments and ultimately LCDC to decide, but local plan content is actually guided by a complex combination of laws, statewide planning goals and guidelines (adopted by rule), interpretive administrative rules adopted over time by LCDC, and decisions of the Land Use Board of Appeals (LUBA). Oregon's laws and rules do not specifically outline requirements for local plan elements; however, for simplicity, goals can be construed to be individual local plan elements, since all local governments are required to demonstrate consistency with each of the statewide planning goals. The analysis provided in Table 7.2 assumes that Oregon's goals are required local plan elements, even though local comprehensive plans in Oregon are not required to address each goal in separate plan elements. This assumption is necessary in order to fit Oregon's program into the comparative framework provided in Table 7.2.

The conclusions reached in Table 7.2 deserve clarification. First, the comparison of local plan elements of each state is complicated by several factors. The contents of local plans as enunciated by the state do not fit precisely into categories comparable across all four states. Florida, Georgia, and Washington specify the required "elements" of plans, which makes the task of comparing and contrasting the elements relatively easy. Oregon's standards are complex in that they evolve out of a mix of law, goals, interpretive rules, and LUBA decisions.

Second, while Florida, Georgia, and Washington may not specify the content as an element per se, that specific local plan content may nevertheless be: required as a component of a specified element; required by some other statute or rule of the state; or reasonably implied by law or

Table 7.2. Mandatory Elements of Local Comprehensive Plans: Florida, Georgia, Oregon, and Washington

Mandatory Local Plan Element	Florida	Georgia	Oregon	Washington
Population		✔		
Housing	✔	✔	✔ (Goal 10; ORS 197.295; OAR 660-8)	✔
(Future) land use	✔	✔	✔ (Goal 2)	✔
Urban growth boundaries (areas)	(see FAR 9J-5.006)		✔ (Goal 14; ORS 197.015)	(see RCW 36.70A.110)
Rural				✔ (counties only)
Economic development	✔	✔	✔ (Goal 9; ORS 197.712; OAR 660-9)	(optional)
(Conservation element for) natural resources (and/or environment)	✔	✔	✔ (Goal 5; OAR 660-16)	(see discussion of critical areas)
Coastal	✔	✔ (component)		
Shorelines	(via conservation element)			✔
Natural disasters and hazards			✔ (Goal 7)	
Historic resources	(via land use element)	✔	✔ (Goal 5; OAR 660-16)	
Traffic circulation (transportation)	✔	✔ (component)	✔ (OAR 660-12)	✔
General sanitary sewer, solid waste, drainage, potable water, and natural groundwater aquifer recharge element (public utilities)	✔	✔ (component)	✔ (see community facilities and services)	✔

Table 7.2. Mandatory Elements of Local Comprehensive Plans: Florida, Georgia, Oregon, and Washington (Continued)

Mandatory Local Plan Element	Florida	Georgia	Oregon	Washington
Recreation and open space	✔	✔	✔ (Goal 5; OAR 660-16; Goal 8)	(optional, but also see RCW 36.70A.110)
Community facilities and services	(addressed via concurrency provisions)	✔	✔ (Goal 11; ORS 197.712; OAR 660-11)	✔ (lands for public purposes)
Concurrency	(several facilities)			(transportation)
Intergovernmental coordination (but see separate discussion of horizontal consistency)	✔		✔ (ORS 195.020 and 195.065)	
Capital (facilities) improvement	✔	(only if impact fees are charged)	✔ (water, sewer, and roads, OAR 660-11)	✔

Sources: Florida Statutes § 163.3177; Georgia Code § 50-8-7.1 and Rules of the Georgia Department of Community Affairs, Chapter 110 3-2 Minimum Standards and Procedures for Local Comprehensive Planning, Section 110-3-2-.04; Oregon Revised Statutes and Oregon Administrative Rules (various provisions, see Table); Revised Code of Washington, Chapter 36.70A, Sections RCW 36.70A.070, RCW 36.70A.110, and RCW 36.70A.150.

statute and interpreted by state officials as a requirement. This is especially the case for Washington, which specifies local plan elements but then includes several other local plan requirements that could just as easily have been called local plan elements. For these reasons, while I have tried to be comprehensive, the reader should consider the description of required local plan contents in Table 7.2 as being subject to possible errors of omission.

In Table 7.2, a check mark (✔) indicates that the content is specifically characterized as a local plan element or is discernible as a component of a required local plan element. Because Oregon's content requirements for local plans are derived from a mixture of sources, the specific references are provided in Table 7.2. As a staff member of DLCD, I previously compiled from Oregon's statutes and administrative rules the content requirements of local plans. This work draws on that prior unpublished work.

Table 7.3. Similarity Indexes of Required Elements, Local Comprehensive Plans: Florida, Georgia, Oregon, and Washington

	Florida	Georgia	Oregon	Washington
Florida		0.666 (10 of 15)	0.688 (11 of 16)	0.563 (9 of 16)
Georgia			0.600 (9 of 15)	0.375 (6 of 16)
Oregon				0.500 (8 of 16)

Source: Compiled based on data in Table 7.2.

From Table 7.2, I derive indexes of similarity for each state's requirements for local plan elements (see Table 7.3). Of the 16 potential plan elements listed in Table 7.2, each state is compared and frequency counts of those elements in common are made. Note that, if one of the states, or both, requires a particular local plan element, that element is included in the frequency count. If neither state program has a particular element, that element is not counted in the total. Both check marks and asterisks are counted as elements in the similarity indexes provided in Table 7.3. An example illustrates.

To compare Florida and Georgia, one or both of the state programs is required to have 15 of the 16 possible plan elements collectively required by the four states. The denominator for the Georgia-Florida pair is 15. A frequency count of required local plan elements common to Florida and Georgia reveals there are 10 of the same elements required in both states. A proportion of elements in common to the total number of elements possible required (collectively) by the two states yields an index of similarity of 0.666.

The hypotheses about paths of evolutionary learning would predict high similarity indexes between the following pairs of states: Florida-Georgia and Oregon-Washington (i.e., regional convergence), and Florida-Oregon and Georgia-Washington (i.e., cross-sectional convergence). The findings support the existence of three paths of learning suggested to be important in Figure 6.1: between Florida-Georgia, Florida-Oregon, and Oregon-Washington. Each of these pairs of states has a similarity index of at least 0.5. The greatest similarity between the local plan content requirements of the possible pairs of states is between Florida and Oregon (0.688), followed closely by Florida and Georgia (0.666). Surprisingly, and not predicted by the hypotheses, the similarity between the plan elements of Georgia and Oregon (i.e., an index of 0.6) is high.

Both Georgia and Washington have third-wave programs with local plan content requirements that should be similar, according to the cross-sectional convergence hypothesis. In contrast to this proposition, however, the lowest similarity index exists between Georgia and Washington (0.375). I may have introduced some subjectivity to the data in Table 7.2 which were used to calculate the proportions in Table 7.3. The overall findings, however, tend to support my hypotheses that certain paths are important in the evolution of state growth management programs.

Additional and optional local plan elements

Florida specifies two additional local comprehensive plan elements for local governments with populations of 50,000 or more: mass transit and port, aviation, and related facilities. Both Florida and Washington suggest and encourage optional elements for local plans. Florida specifies 12 optional local plan elements, of which four are transportation related (Florida Statutes § 163.3167 and § 163.3177). Washington's law specifies three optional elements (RCW § 36.70A.080) and authorizes other activities as part of a local comprehensive planning effort. The finding that both Florida and Washington encourage optional local plan elements is one more piece of evidence that suggests the Florida and Washington path of learning is more important than the hypotheses suggest.

It is interesting to note that the visioning process has made its way to the list of optional local plan elements in Florida. As elaborated in the passage below, Florida specifically excludes authority by DCA to adopt rules relative to visioning exercises but does require vertical consistency with a state vision. Also note the internal consistency requirement.

> Each local government is encouraged to articulate a vision of the future physical appearance and qualities of its community as a component of its local comprehensive plan . . . A local or regional vision must be consistent with the state vision, when adopted, and be internally consistent with the local or regional plan of which it is a component. The state land planning agency shall not adopt minimum criteria for evaluating or judging the form or content of a local or regional vision (Florida Statutes § 163.3167).

My content analysis reveals that Oregon law does not specify optional elements. This is not surprising given that Oregon's law does not express its requirements in terms of minimum local plan elements. There are two notable exceptions: a provision was added to Oregon's law in 1995 that authorizes local governments to adopt a "public facili-

Figure 7.2. Mandatory and Optional Elements of a Local Comprehensive Plan in Florida

Required elements

1. Housing
2. Land use
3. Economic development
4. Conservation of natural resources
5. Coastal
6. Traffic circulation
7. Sewer/water, etc. (public utilities)
8. Recreation and open space
9. Intergovernmental coordination
10. Capital facilities/concurrency

Optional elements

11. Mass transit
12. Port, aviation, and related facilities
13. Circulation of recreational traffic
14. 10 year transportation concurrency management system
15. Public buildings and related facilities
16. Community design
17. General area redevelopment
18. Safety
19. Hazard mitigation/postdisaster redevelopment
20. Historical and scenic preservation
21. Future vision
22. Countywide marina siting

Source: Florida Statutes § 163.3177

ties strategy" which relates to building moratoria (ORS § 197.768); and another provision provides authority to "convene a land use proceeding to adopt a refinement plan for a neighborhood or community within its jurisdiction and inside the urban growth boundary" (ORS § 197.200).

Georgia's law does not specify optional local plan elements. Georgia's law, however, has an interesting authorization that RDCs may, subject to DCA's approval, require that comprehensive plans within their regions include elements in addition to those established by DCA as minimum standards (Georgia Code § 50-8-35 and Georgia DCA Rule § 110-12-1-.05). This provision is unique to Georgia; it is not found in Florida's law. To my knowledge, this provision of Georgia's statute has not been exercised by any RDC.

It is interesting to highlight the complexity of Florida's local plan content requirements. Including both required and optional plan elements,

Sidebar 7.2. Planning Data by Georgia's OCP: A Worthwhile Mandate and Program?

While I was a planner at Georgia Mountains Regional Development Center, I worked on several local comprehensive plans. I also had the opportunity to review local comprehensive planning data guidebooks prepared for local governments by DCA's Office of Coordinated Planning (OCP). In retrospect, OCP did a fine job responding to the mandate to provide local planning data. OCP inventoried data sources, published guidebooks on how to collect data for local comprehensive planning, trained RDC planners to be familiar with state data sources, and produced a data book for each county and city in Georgia. This is a monumental task indeed given Georgia's nearly 700 local governments. DCA had hired Woods and Poole Economics, Inc. to produce projections of population and economic conditions for each local government.

The data books produced for individual local governments, however, were not very influential in the practice of preparing local plans. In my experience, after viewing several of the data books for counties and cities in the Georgia Mountains RDC region, I had little confidence in the data. I simply did not trust some of the numbers. The economic and population projections were apparently based on very general statewide data and models, and with 700 books to produce, OCP staff and its consultant had little time to examine local conditions to check against the accuracy of such projections. The RDCs in most instances had superior data. Most if not all of the RDCs were state data center "affiliates" and thus were depositories of data from the U.S. Bureau of the Census. Furthermore, through past regional reviews via the "A-95" process and regional economic development planning efforts and preparation of "701" plans, APDCs (the predecessors to RDCs) had compiled much data on local conditions. The RDCs typically produced population projections for their regions that were based on sound studies of local and regional conditions.

Apparently, I was not the only regional planner who lacked confidence in OCP's local planning data books. The topic of using local planning data books was discussed at times during the RDC planners training sessions sponsored by OCP. At one of these sessions I recall a plea by Lynn Thornton, then director of OCP, to regional planners that they "stop telling local governments not to use the data books." I deduced from this plea that other regional planners were suggesting to local governments that the data books were of little value compared to RDC data. Given the specific mandate of

Georgia Code § 50-8-7, it is difficult to second guess why OCP produced the data books. Absent that mandate, if it had it to do over again, OCP probably would have elected not to provide the data books to local government in favor of some other more productive program of local planning technical assistance. In short, OCP complied with the directive of state law, but in the end was not that effective in doing so with regard to the local planning data books. The extent of this implementation failure is small, however, and it does not in any way diminish the overall success of OCP's program of local planning technical assistance.

a local government's comprehensive plan would have to contain nearly two dozen different plan elements to be entirely in accordance with Florida's mandated and suggested plan content requirements (see Figure 7.2).

Local planning data and studies by the state

State agencies participating in the administration of growth management programs must, to some degree, provide data for comprehensive planning and guidance on planning methods and techniques. In Florida, the state land planning agency is required to conduct an affordable housing needs assessment for all local jurisdictions to be used in housing elements of comprehensive plans (Florida Statutes § 163.3177). Also, the executive office is required to produce population estimates of local governmental units as of April 1 of each year, utilizing accepted statistical practices (Florida Statutes § 186.901).

Georgia's planning act is unique among the growth management acts of the four states, because it specifically requires construction of a state-local database networking infrastructure. DCA provides the lead role with the support of other agencies, as indicated in the passage below.

> The department [DCA] shall coordinate and participate in compiling, and other state agencies and local governments shall participate in compiling, a Georgia data base and network to serve as a comprehensive source of information available, in an accessible form, to local governments and state agencies (Georgia Code § 50-8-7).

Statutory provisions of Georgia's planning act go further to elaborate on the directive that DCA provide local planning studies and data.

> The department shall undertake and carry out, and shall coordinate with other state agencies and local governments in undertaking and carrying out, such gathering of information, such distribution of information, and such studies and recommendations as the board or the commissioner may deem necessary for performing local government services and as may be specified by law (Georgia Code § 50-8-7).

As Sidebar 7.2 shows, DCA treated this directive seriously.

Oregon's statute contains some specific references to state data assistance for local land use planning. LCDC is directed to "prepare, collect, provide or cause to be prepared, collected or provided land use inventories" (ORS § 197.040). The Joint Legislative Committee on Land Use also has a role. It is required to "study the availability and adequacy of industrially designated or zoned lands within urban and urbanizable areas" (ORS § 197.135). A third state entity in Oregon is supposed to deliver data for local planning; the Economic Development Department (EDD) is required to "provide a local government with state and national trend information to assist in compliance with ORS 197.712 (2)(a)" (ORS § 197.717).

Oregon's statute appears to lack a specific statutory mandate that DLCD provide local studies and data to local government, but since it is the administrative arm of LCDC, it is fairly implied that DLCD will carry out LCDC's responsibilities. Furthermore, another provision of Oregon law (ORS 195) has recently been used by DLCD to tie long range urban growth management plans to the state economist's population projections.

Washington assigns important responsibilities to OFM, which makes a growth management population projection for each county. Each county, within its designated urban growth areas, must include land and densities sufficient to permit the urban growth that is projected to occur in the county for the succeeding 20-year period (RCW § 36.70A.110). OFM also is required to "maintain a list of those essential state public facilities that are required or likely to be built within the next six years" (RCW § 36.70A.200). Aside from the provision of population projections, RCW 36.70A does not specify that DCTED will play a role in the preparation of data for local planning. Another provision (RCW § 43.63A.550), however, directs DCTED to provide key land use data (Washington Land Use Study Commission 1997).

Consistent with the hypothesis of longitudinal regional convergence, both Florida and Georgia require state agencies to provide data for local planning. Florida specifies roles for the governor's office and the state land planning agency (DCA) in the delivery of local government planning data. Georgia's program establishes a comprehensive state-regional-local data base network with DCA having the lead role.

Oregon's laws require that local planning data be provided by three different participants (LCDC/DLCD, JLCLU, and EDD). Washington requires OFM to prepare population projections that are used to constrain the growth management plans of local government (i.e., counties can only plan for x amount of growth). In 1995, Oregon law was changed to require that cities and counties coordinate population projections (ORS § 195.036), and DLCD has begun to insist that local governments use state-produced county population forecasts as the basis for growth management; this is a rare funding of a reverse evolution of sorts (i.e., a program of the quiet revolution incorporating a feature of a program developed in a later era). Neither Oregon nor Washington specify a major role of the administering agency in providing local planning data; this finding provides evidence supporting the regional convergence hypothesis (i.e., states in the same subnational region have similar program structures). The absence of a role for DCTED in the provision of local data, however, is unexpected; the hypothesis of cross-sectional convergence would suggest that both Georgia and Washington would direct their administering agencies to provide local planning data.

Technical assistance for local comprehensive planning

Technical assistance by the state for local comprehensive planning is an integral component of any state program mandate design, though it is expected to be more prominent in the third wave programs of Georgia and Washington. Technical assistance programs in the four states are addressed in Chapter 10. For diagrams of state technical assistance organization and output, see Figures 10.1 through 10.4. Here, I focus on statutory provisions relative to local planning technical assistance, which can be divided into two types: general provisions and model plan provisions.

Florida's statutes contain both general and model plan provisions. DCA and any other state and regional agencies involved in the growth management program are required to "cooperate and work with units of local government in the preparation and adoption of comprehensive plans, or elements or portions thereof, and of local land development regulations" (Florida Statutes § 163.3204). Florida law also provides that the state land planning agency shall "provide model plans and ordinances and, upon request, other assistance to local governments in the adoption and implementation of their revised local government comprehensive plans" (Florida Statutes § 163.3177). A 1995 addition to Florida's growth management laws also requires that DCA shall promptly prepare model plan elements for utilization by local governments to implement the requirements for intergovernmental coordination elements (Florida Statutes § 163.3177). Hence, Florida's program clearly establishes a role for DCA in providing both general technical assistance and model elements for local comprehensive planning.

Consistent with the hypothesis that the evolutionary path of program development between Florida and Georgia is important, Georgia's statute approximates Florida's law in assigning a major role to DCA to provide technical assistance for local planning.

> The department shall develop, promote, sustain, and assist local governments in the performance of their duties and responsibilities under law to their citizens, including among such duties and responsibilities of local governments coordinated and comprehensive planning (Georgia Code § 50-8-3). The department shall undertake and carry out such planning and technical assistance activities as the board or the commissioner may deem necessary for performing local government services and as may be specified by law. Such planning and technical assistance activities may include, but shall not be limited to, the following: . . . technical assistance to local governments . . . including, but not limited to, preparation and implementation of a comprehensive plan (Georgia Code § 50-8-7).

It is interesting to note here that Georgia's DCA acted upon this provision and produced and circulated a local comprehensive plan for the city of Villa Rica as a minimum example of how to comply with the local planning standards.

Oregon's land use law differs from growth management programs in Florida and Georgia in that it does not specifically enunciate a requirement for DLCD to provide local planning technical assistance. By using the term "may" instead of "shall," Oregon's program is weaker with respect to provision of local planning technical assistance by the state administering agency.

> . . . the department [DLCD] may establish one or more state assistance teams made up of representatives of various agencies and local governments or an

> alternative process for coordinating agency participation in the periodic review of comprehensive plans . . . A local government may arrange with the department for the provision of periodic review planning services and those services may be paid with grant program funds. The department may develop model ordinance provisions to assist local governments in the periodic review plan update process (ORS § 197.639).

On the other hand, Oregon's statute provides that DLCD and participating state agencies must produce technical assistance for planning and zoning land and public facilities for industrial and commercial uses and for preparing public facility plans. Note that the excerpt above authorizes but does not direct DLCD to prepare model ordinances. State law does require DLCD to provide models for streamlining local permit procedures. Furthermore, DLCD and EDD are also required to collaborate on a "joint program to assist rural communities with economic and community development services . . . [which] shall include, but not be limited to, grants, loans, model ordinances and technical assistance" (ORS § 197.717) (also see Figure 10.3).

Washington's GMA is, like Georgia's law, specific with regard to the role the administering agency is supposed to play in the provision of local planning technical assistance. The passage below indicates that directive.

> The department [DCTED] shall establish a program of technical and financial assistance and incentives to counties and cities to encourage and facilitate the adoption and implementation of comprehensive plans and development regulations throughout the state . . . The technical assistance may include, but not be limited to, model land use ordinances, regional education and training programs, and information for local and regional inventories (RCW § 36.70A.190).

In addition to the general directive that DCTED provide local planning assistance, GMA requires the attorney general, in consultation with the Washington Bar Association, to develop a continuing education course relative to property rights (RCW § 36.70A.370). DCTED must also "prepare and circulate to counties and cities such instructional manuals or other information derived from the pilot projects [on environmental review] as will assist all counties and cities . . . in the process of considering comprehensive plans" (RCW § 36.70A.385). Hence, statutes of Washington and Georgia are similar because both direct the administering agencies to provide technical assistance for local planning, including the preparation of model plans or plan elements to assist local governments. This is an important finding that supports the cross-sectional convergence hypothesis.

Funding for local planning

My search of Florida's growth management laws reveals only one specific provision relative to funding of local planning. Grants to assist local governments in the preparation of hazard mitigation/postdisaster redevelopment plans are required to be available through the Emergency Management Preparedness and Assistance Account in the Grants and Donations Trust Fund administered by DCA, if such an account is created by law (Florida Statutes § 163.3177).

Georgia's program designers made choices about local funding that differ from other state programs. Unlike Florida, Oregon, and Washington, all of which provide grants to local governments to meet comprehensive planning mandates, Georgia does not provide direct grants to local governments for planning. Instead, grant money is provided to the state's RDCs, which then deliver comprehensive planning technical assistance to local governments. Somewhat ironically, Georgia provides direct local grants only upon completion of local comprehensive plans and certification of local governments as qualified.

> The department [DCA] shall establish a minimum funding amount for regional development centers . . . (Georgia Code § 50-8-33). The department shall make grants to eligible recipients or qualified local governments . . . The department shall disburse such grants on the basis of criteria which include consideration of matters such as . . . coordinated and comprehensive planning in accordance with minimum standards and procedures . . . and may condition the award of any such grants to a county or municipality upon the county or municipality, as the case may be, being a qualified local government (Georgia Code § 50-8-8).

Oregon's land use law is basically silent with respect to local grant funds for comprehensive planning. Washington's GMA clearly specifies that DCTED will play an active role in financially supporting local comprehensive planning.

> It is also the intent of the legislature that funds be made available to counties and cities beginning July 1, 1990, to assist them in meeting the requirements of this chapter (RCW § 36.70A.180). The department [DCTED] shall develop

> a priority list and establish funding levels for planning and technical assistance grants both for counties and cities that plan under RCW 36.70A.040. The department shall develop and administer a grant program to provide direct financial assistance to counties and cities for the preparation of comprehensive plans under this chapter (RCW § 36.70A.190).

The GMA also establishes a growth management planning and environmental review fund in the state treasury to be managed by DCTED. Moneys in the fund are to be used to make grants to local governments for the purposes set forth in GMA and the State Environmental Policy Act (RCW § 36.70A.490 and § 36.70A.500).

The regional convergence hypothesis suggests that there are important evolutionary parallels between two pairs of states, Florida-Georgia and Oregon-Washington. I also expect to find features that distinguish third wave growth management program states, Georgia and Washington, from Florida and Oregon (i.e., the longitudinal divergence hypothesis). The statutory provisions excerpted above provide evidence that supports the distinct emphasis placed on technical assistance by third-wave programs.

As the evidence here and in Chapter 10 demonstrates, however, Florida's program has also placed a heavy emphasis on technical assistance. This finding contradicts my suggestion that technical assistance is almost exclusively a third-wave program feature. I agree with Burby and May (1997, 56), who find that Florida combined capacity building with coercion in designing its 1980s growth management program. There also is some evidence that Oregon has over time embraced a more collaborative approach to supplement its coercive mandate design. Hence, there may be some convergence of all growth management programs over time toward more collaborative program designs, contrary to the longitudinal divergence hypothesis.

Notes

1. Known generally as population bills, these requirements do not name specific metropolitan areas in the law but instead set a population threshold (e.g., 450,000 in Washington) that effectively only applies to the selected counties or cities.

2. I did not search laws other than those specified in Footnote 1 of Chapter 6. Other provisions relating to regional planning may exist.

3. It was noted previously, however, that Oregon in 1995 instituted an optional regional problem solving process and provided pilot projects. Oregon law provides that "local governments and those special districts that provide urban services may enter into a collaborative regional problem-solving process . . . As used in sections 36a to 36h of this 1995 special session act, "region" means an area of one or more counties, together with the cities within the county, counties, or affected portion of the county (Sections 36a to 36g, Chapter 3, Oregon Laws 1995). It was also already noted that some of the areas selected for regional problem solving pilot projects are subregions of counties, not regions.

4. I did not analyze other state laws (i.e., administrative procedures acts) relative to rulemaking. It is likely that another statute requires the Boards of Community Affairs and Natural Resources to adopt the rules of the department. In that sense, Georgia's approach is similar to Oregon's approach where LCDC adopts rules drafted by DLCD.

5. The Georgia Planning Act provides that "the department shall establish minimum elements which shall be addressed and included in comprehensive plans of local governments which are prepared as part of the coordinated and comprehensive planning process. These elements shall include, but shall not be limited to, housing, human services, natural resources, the environment, vital areas, historic resources, infrastructure, land use other than zoning, recreation, transportation, and economic development." (Georgia Code § 50-8-7.1). This statutory provision is referenced here because it raises an issue of consistency with respect to the state agency administrative rules adopted pursuant to it. Georgia's administrative rules for planning do not specifically include local plan elements for vital areas, human services, and transportation. Given that the Georgia General Assembly ratified the minimum planning standards, however, the legislature had the opportunity to (but did not) object to the rules if they were considered inconsistent with the statutory directive (i.e., certain plan elements specified in the act but not included in the rules).

6. Georgia's rules are officially referred to as follows: Rules of Georgia Department of Community Affairs Chapter 110-12-1 Minimum Standards and Procedures for Local Comprehensive Planning.

CHAPTER

8

Plan Review Structures and Principles

In the two preceding chapters, I identified state, regional, and local roles in state-sponsored programs of land use planning. Roles of the state include specifying the content of local plans, providing data, and delivering technical assistance. From the perspective of the state administering agency, a structure to review local plans must also be in place before local comprehensive plans are completed and submitted. From the perspective of local government, its local comprehensive plan once prepared must be submitted to the state and go through specific processes of review before local adoption.

At this point in the chronology of program evolution, I note that a local plan has been prepared and now it must go through a review and approval process. Then, after plan review and adoption, the local government begins to prepare measures to implement the newly adopted comprehensive plan. At the conclusion of this chapter, I finish the content analysis with a summary of the evidence presented in Chapters 6, 7, and 8 that supports or refutes the three hypotheses about evolutionary paths of program learning.

LOCAL PLAN TRANSMITTAL AND STATE REVIEW REQUIREMENTS

It is important to note a distinction between the transmittal of plans, the review of plans, and authority to approve plans by the region/state. There are statutory provisions relating to the submittal of local plans, and then there are provisions that describe the region/state's authority to review and, in some cases, approve local plans. In other words, to submit a plan does not necessitate review, and to review does not necessarily constitute authority to approve or deny plans.

Table 8.1 provides an oversimplified summary of the complex review structures for comprehensive plans, plan amendments, and plan updates required in the four states. I have tried to be comprehensive in completing Table 8.1, but omissions are possible. The structures for reviewing local comprehensive plans are illustrated in Figure 8.1 (Florida) and Figure 8.2 (Georgia, Oregon and Washington). Figures 8.1 and 8.2 do not capture the complexity of the entire plan review process. I do not include comprehensive plan amendments and comprehensive plan updates in the figures because they would make the diagrams too complicated and difficult to read.

Florida law requires each local government to submit its complete proposed comprehensive plan and plan amendments to the state land planning agency by the date specified in the rule adopted by the state land planning agency (Florida Statutes § 163.3167). State program administrators in Florida and elsewhere realize they cannot review each local government plan simultaneously, so they establish phased or staggered schedules for the review of local plans. Local comprehensive plans and plan amendments must be transmitted to the appropriate RPC and water management district and the Department of Transportation, in addition to DCA (Florida Statutes § 163.3184). See Figure 8.1.

Florida's plan review structure is characterized in Figure 8.1 as a strong dual state agency/weak dual regional agency approach. The state land planning agency has the authority to determine whether a local plan complies with state law and administrative rules and, hence, it may deny a local comprehensive plan. One important reason for the state transportation department to review local plans is to ensure that the level-of-service standards of the state's highways are maintained. Florida's RPCs do not appear to have any significant review authority over plans.

The state land planning agency may review any proposed plan amendment either upon the request of a RPC or upon its own initiative after the agency gives notice to the local government (Florida Statutes § 163.3184). The state land planning agency issues a notice of intent to find that the plan or plan amendment is in compliance or not in compliance. If after a hearing the Administration Commission finds that a

Table 8.1. Local Plan Review Structures: Florida, Georgia, Oregon, and Washington

Review Requirement	Florida	Georgia	Oregon	Washington
Transmit plan to state for review	✔ (163.3184)	✔ (50-8-10)	✔ (197.090, .270)	✔ (36.70A. 040, .106)
Transmit plan to region for review	✔ (163.3184)	✔ (50-8-37)		
Submit plan amendments to state for review	✔ (163.3184)	✔ (110.12-1-.04)	✔ (197.610)	✔ (36.70A.106)
Submit plan amendments to region for review	✔ (163.3184)	✔ (110.12-1)		
Filing of adopted plan with state	✔ (163.3184)	✔ (110.12-1)	✔ (197.270)	✔ (36.70A.040, .106)
Filing of adopted plan with region	✔ (163.3184)	✔ (110.12-1)		
Filing of adopted plan amendments with state	✔ (163.3184)		✔ (197.270, .615)	✔ (36.70A.040)
Filing of adopted plan amendments with region	✔ (163.3184)	✔ (110.12-1)		

Note: I draw on my own experience in Georgia to complete the table. The reference to Georgia Rules (110.12-1) is generalized because I recall these requirements based on state interpretations in practice. The state interpretation draws its authority from this rule.

Source: Compiled from a content analysis of state statutes (see specific references noted in table).

comprehensive plan or plan amendment is not in compliance with state law, the commission specifies remedial actions that would bring the comprehensive plan or plan amendment into compliance (Florida Statutes § 163.3184).

Adopted comprehensive plans and plan amendments must be transmitted to the state land planning agency within 10 working days after adoption, and a copy must be sent to the regional planning agency (Florida Statutes § 163.3184). The state land planning agency also is authorized to adopt by rule a phased schedule for the submittal of local comprehensive plan evaluation and appraisal reports (EARs), or it may

Figure 8.1. Florida's Plan Review Structure

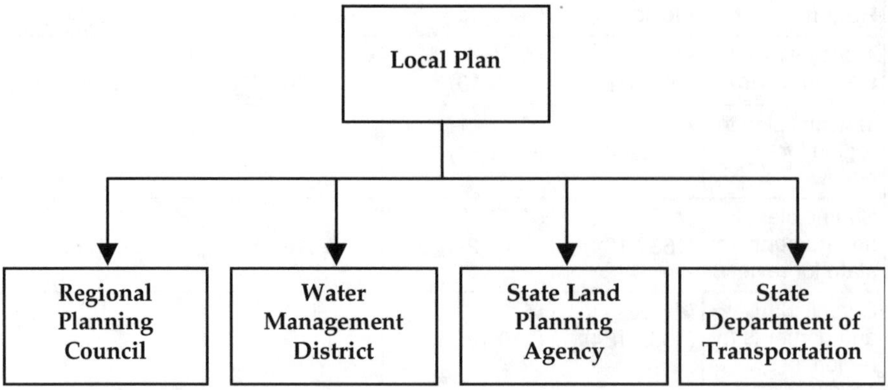

Strong Dual State Agency/Weak Dual Regional Agency Review

elect to delegate the review of such reports to the appropriate RPC (Florida Statutes § 163.3191).

Georgia's plan review structure, which includes regional agencies as well as the state, is very similar to Florida's. The similarity is not surprising, however, given earlier findings in support of the regional convergence hypothesis. It is an example of Georgia's mandate designers' making an effort to simplify Florida's mandate complexity in establishing their own approach.

In Georgia, each municipality and county must submit its local comprehensive plan to its respective RDC for review, comment, and recommendation. See Figure 8.2. The RDC determines whether the adoption or implementation of a local plan would present any conflict, and it may recommend a modification of the local plan to eliminate any conflict or alleviate any problem or difficulty that such conflict may create. Local governments may request reconsideration of any recommendation by the RDC (Georgia Code § 50-8-37). RDCs have review responsibilities and exercise some influence in the preparation of plans, but they do not have any authority to approve or deny local comprehensive plans.

Georgia's DCA also examines and analyzes local government comprehensive plans (Georgia Code § 50-8-7.1). Additionally, DCA "may review, on a continuous basis, the programs and policies including, but not limited to, comprehensive plans of all governments acting within the state to determine their consistency with long-range programs and

Figure 8.2. Plan Review Structures: Georgia, Oregon, and Washington

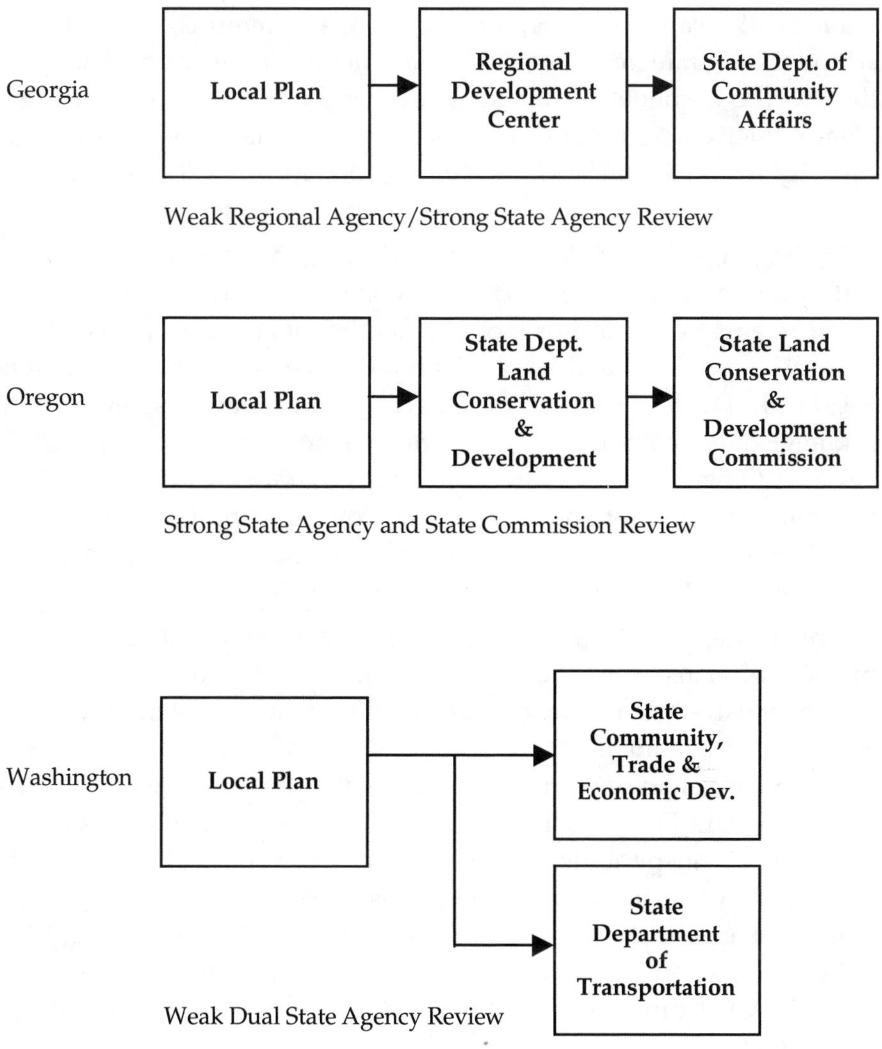

policies of the state" (Georgia Code § 50-8-10). That provision also constitutes Georgia's vertical consistency requirement, albeit without the state plan leading the sequence, as is the case in Florida's program. Georgia's plan review structure is characterized in Figure 8.2 as a weak regional agency/strong state agency approach, because RDCs can only comment on plans, but DCA has authority to withhold "qualified local government" status. See Sidebar 8.1.

It is interesting to note that Georgia's mandate designers chose a different approach to the state's review of local public facilities strategies, which were required by the Service Delivery Strategy Act of 1997. The reader will recall from Chapter 5 that DCA is required to verify local adoption of strategies but shall by law neither approve or disapprove the specific elements or outcomes of local service delivery strategies. Hence, this is a sign that Georgia's lawmakers have softened the state capacity for reviewing the substantive content of local comprehensive plans.

In Oregon, LCDC reviews comprehensive plans for compliance with statewide goals (ORS § 197.040). Oregon's land use law requires local governments to forward proposed amendments to acknowledged comprehensive plans or land use regulations to the Director of DLCD (ORS § 197.610). DLCD's director may participate in and seek review of an acknowledged comprehensive plan or land use regulation (ORS § 197.090). Oregon's plan review structure is characterized in Figure 8.2 as a strong state agency and strong state commission approach, because LCDC holds the authority to find a plan in compliance or not in compliance with the state goals and administrative rules.

Oregon staggers the schedules for local governments to submit comprehensive plans for review (i.e., the periodic review process) so that all comprehensive plan amendments and updates will not have to be reviewed simultaneously by DLCD. The staggered periodic review schedule also enables grant managers to distribute their workload over time. Both DLCD and LCDC review the plans and regulations of local governments in periodic review. Within six months after completing periodic review, a local government must file three copies of its comprehensive plan and land use regulations with DLCD (ORS § 197.270). Other amendments to local plans and regulations also must be submitted to DLCD's director together with the findings adopted by the local government (ORS § 197.615).

Washington requires that a notice of intent to adopt a comprehensive plan and/or land development regulations be submitted to DCTED and allows for a 60-day review period before local adoption (RCW § 36.70A.106). DCTED and other state agencies may provide comments to the county or city on the proposed comprehensive plan, or proposed development regulations, during the public review process (RCW § 36.70A.106). Like the other states, Washington also authorizes DCTED to adopt a schedule to permit phasing of comprehensive plan submittal

Sidebar 8.1. Local Comprehensive Plan Compliance Reviews in Georgia: Does the RDC or DCA Decide?

Georgia's planning act gave RDCs authority to review local comprehensive plans. The RDC's role was to review plans for consistency with regional plans and programs and for compliance with the state's minimum planning standards. It was up to the RDC to decide who at the RDC would review plans; it could be the board of directors of the RDC, a standing committee of the board, the executive director, or the planning director. Regardless of who had the authority at the RDC to review plans, the state required that the executive committee of the RDC board be notified once a determination on a local plan was made.

Initially, DCA wanted to entrust in the RDCs the role of ensuring that local government comprehensive plans complied with all of DCA's minimum standards as adopted by rule. The state agency prepared a local plan review guide, prepared a plan review checklist, and expended resources training regional planners in how to review local plans for compliance with minimum standards. DCA initially intended to provide a "one-time only" review of the joint "prototype" city-county plans that each RDC prepared in 1990 as part of its contractual obligations with DCA. DCA's review would be conducted merely to ensure that contractual obligations were met. DCA hoped that RDCs would deal with compliance issues.

As DCA began to receive RDC plan reviews and the local comprehensive plans themselves, however, state plan reviewers were dissatisfied with many, if not most, of the RDC reviews. Strict compliance with minimum state standards was not being achieved, and DCA frequently overruled RDC compliance determinations. Over time DCA realized that RDCs, whose boards were composed of local elected officials, were unable or unwilling to find plans of member local governments not in compliance. DCA found that RDC plan reviewers were frequently deferring compliance issues to the state because they could not say no to their member local governments. RDCs performed reviews for internal consistency, vertical consistency with regional plans and programs, and compliance with the state's minimum standards for local plan content, but DCA retained for itself the final determination on whether local plans complied with state standards. The state never did get out of the business of reviewing local plans for compliance with state standards, as it had hoped. By 1993, DCA's plan reviewers essentially gave up on the hope that RDCs would determine local plan compliance and conducted compliance reviews themselves. The revised local plan review guide (DCA 1996) indicates that DCA provides the RDC with findings regarding its review of the comprehensive plan for compliance with minimum standards. The RDC then transmits DCA's findings along with its own findings to the local government for consideration.

Sources: Georgia Department of Community Affairs. 1990. Policy Memo Series, Volume 2, Number 1; Local Plan Review Guide, 1996 Edition; and the author's experience.

for counties and cities planning under RCW 36.70A.040 (RCW § 36.70A.045). Unlike Oregon, which allows local governments six months after periodic review to submit adopted plans and regulations, a local government must transmit a copy of its comprehensive plan or development regulations to DCTED within 10 days after final adoption (RCW § 36.70A.106).

Washington's plan review structure is characterized in Figure 8.2 as a weak dual state agency approach, because the state agencies can recommend but cannot enforce compliance with state mandates. The reader will recall that enforcement of the GMA mandate is via recommendation from the applicable Growth Management Hearings Board to the Governor, who may apply sanctions. I add here an observation from a forum of Oregon-Washington growth management scholars and practitioners. Washington's choice of enforcement structure was a deliberate rejection of Oregon's approach and an attempt to "regionalize" the interpretation of GMA, based on the perception in Oregon that Salem lawmakers and bureaucrats were too far removed from the local environment in which decisions about land use are made.[1]

Returning to the research hypotheses, each state exhibits its own unique approach to plan review, though Georgia and Florida have similar plan review structures. This provides some additional evidence in support of the regional convergence hypothesis in the case of Florida and Georgia. These similarities, however, stem largely from the intergovernmental structure already described. The lack of a regional structure to the planning systems in the Pacific Northwest shows some evidence of longitudinal regional convergence and the corollary that regions themselves tend to diverge in their growth management program structures.

I also suggest that there is some cross-sectional convergence evident in the comparison of state plan review structures. Georgia and Washington (i.e., third-wave programs) have much softer local compliance structures: Georgia did not require local planning, and Washington did not vest any authority to make compliance determinations in DCTED. It cannot be discounted, however, that Georgia, once a local government prepares a plan, has authority to withhold qualified local government status if local plans do not sufficiently address state standards. Washington's regional growth management hearings boards are a prime example of its learning from Oregon, in my opinion.

One other observation is worth noting here, relative to how the findings about plan review structures support or refute the research hypotheses. Washington's plan review structure is similar to Florida's in that it provides that plans be reviewed by the state transportation department, as well as, the principal administering state agency. This provides another piece of evidence that suggests the Florida-Washington evolutionary path of learning is important, even though the hypotheses do not predict it to be important.

After completion of the local plan review process, local governments enter what I call the post-planning phase, which focuses on implementation. The degree to which state statutes require transmittal, review, adoption, and enforcement of local land development regulations is the topic I describe next.

REQUIREMENTS FOR LOCAL LAND DEVELOPMENT REGULATIONS

I refer to the requirement to adopt development regulations consistent with local plans as "implementation consistency." Within one year after submission of its revised comprehensive plan, each municipality in Florida must adopt or amend, and enforce, land development regulations that are consistent with and that implement its adopted comprehensive plan. The state land planning agency may require a local government to submit one or more land development regulations, and the agency is required to adopt rules for review of land development regulations (Florida Statutes § 163.3202).

Georgia's law authorizes but does not require local governments to adopt land use regulations that are consistent with their comprehensive plans (Georgia Code § 36-70-3). Although the law does not require land use regulations to be adopted by local governments in Georgia, one provision of state law suggests a different interpretation. The 1989 planning act defines "qualified local government" as "a county or municipality which has a comprehensive plan in conformity with the minimum standards and procedures" and that "has established regulations consistent with its comprehensive plan" (Georgia Code § 50-8-2).

I learned via personal interview in December 1997 with Mike Gleaton, director of Georgia's Office of Coordinated Planning, that DCA now is interpreting that provision as requiring local governments to implement their plans as they themselves suggested in their comprehensive plans. As of about April 1997, local governments that do not implement intended actions as indicated in their comprehensive plans risk losing their qualified local government status (and thus eligibility for certain state grants and loans) if they fail to adopt those regulations.

This new interpretation by DCA does not necessarily suggest, however, that local governments must have land development regulations in order to implement plans. First, local governments still might elect not to plan or not to implement a comprehensive plan. Second, local governments do not have to specify that zoning will be used to implement their comprehensive plans. The new interpretation amounts more to a position that "local governments will do what they said they would do" than to a mandate to adopt local land development regulations.

In Oregon, not only must local governments adopt land use regulations consistent with their comprehensive plans, but their land use decisions also must comply with their acknowledged plans and land use regulations (ORS § 197.175). As with comprehensive plan amendments, proposals to amend local land development regulations must be forwarded to DLCD's director (ORS § 197.610), who may participate in and seek review of local land use regulations (ORS § 197.090). A copy of the adopted text of land use regulations together with the findings adopted by the local government must be submitted to DLCD's director (ORS § 197.615). Hence, Oregon applies much the same review requirements to local regulations as it does to plans.

Washington's law requires that each GMA county and city must adopt development regulations to assure the conservation of agricultural, forest, and mineral resource lands. Further, each local government, not just those required to plan, must adopt development regulations that protect critical areas (RCW § 36.70A.060). GMA counties must adopt regulations designating interim urban growth areas (RCW § 36.70A.110). New local development regulations or amendments to development regulations must be transmitted to DCTED in the same manner as comprehensive plans (RCW § 36.70A.100), which includes a 60-day review process and opportunity for state comment.

LOCAL COMPREHENSIVE PLAN UPDATES

Local planning agencies in Florida must monitor and oversee the effectiveness and status of their comprehensive plans and recommend to the governing body such changes in the comprehensive plans as may be required from time to time (Florida Statutes § 163.3174). That includes preparation of periodic reports on the comprehensive plan, which shall be sent to the governing body and to the state land planning agency at least once every five years after the adoption of the comprehensive plan. Local governing bodies are required to amend their comprehensive plans based on the recommendations contained in adopted evaluation and appraisal reports (EARs) (Florida Statutes § 163.3191). Also, local governments are specifically required to update the future land use, intergovernmental coordination, conservation, and capital improvements elements of their local comprehensive plans (Florida Statutes § 163.3191).

The state land planning agency is required to conduct a sufficiency review of each local EAR to determine whether it has been submitted in a timely fashion and contains the prescribed components (Florida Statutes § 163.3191). Furthermore, Florida law provides that the Executive Office of the Governor shall review EARs (Florida Statutes § 186.007). Hence, in Florida there is a dual agency review procedure for local plan amendments.

Georgia DCA's rules (Chapter 110-12-1-.04, Minimum Local Planning Standards) require comprehensive plan updates at a minimum every 10 years. After five years, however, community leaders are encouraged to determine whether the comprehensive plan needs a major update, based on the degree of change in the community, and amend the comprehensive plan accordingly. Each "short-term work program" of a local comprehensive plan must be updated either annually or every five years. If the local government elects a five-year schedule for updating its short-term work program, it also must submit a "report of plan accomplishments" that identifies the current status of each activity in the previous work program. If a local government no longer desires to undertake a project indicated in its prior work program, it must indicate the reasons it has made that decision.

Georgia's reports of plan accomplishments appear to be similar to Florida's EARs, thus lending additional evidence for the hypothesis of regional convergence. Florida's requirements for EARs, however, are much more detailed than Georgia's requirements. That may be another example of a state's learning to simplify mandate complexity.

Oregon requires that local comprehensive plans be regularly reviewed and, if necessary, amended to keep them consistent with the changing needs and desires of the public (ORS § 197.010). Oregon law institutionalizes a periodic review process to systematically review and revise such plans and regulations.

According to a periodic review schedule of compliance, each local government must revisit and update its comprehensive plan every four to seven years. When engaged in the periodic review process, Oregon's local governments must evaluate their comprehensive plans and land use regulations to determine whether they are achieving the goals, objectives and policies outlined in the comprehensive plan and the statewide planning goals (ORS § 197.633). Local governments are specifically required to amend their comprehensive plans to implement new or amended statewide planning goals, commission administrative rules and land use statutes, if such new goals, rules, and statutes apply to the subject jurisdiction (ORS § 197.646). When DLCD elects to participate in a local government proceeding, it notifies the local government of any concerns it has about the proposal and issues advisory recommendations on actions it considers necessary to address those concerns (ORS § 197.610).

Washington also requires continuous evaluation and review of local comprehensive plans and development regulations. Each county and city initially required to plan under GMA is required to report to DCTED annually for five years, and then every five years thereafter, on its progress made in implementing GMA (RCW § 36.70A.180).

PLAN REVIEW PRINCIPLES

Throughout the previous discussion, I have referred to notions of consistency as they relate to state growth management programs. Notions of consistency refer to the relationships between and among plans of the governments at different levels of the intergovernmental structure. This section further describes the various types of consistency found in the four state growth management statutes. The overall consistency framework is illustrated in Figure 8.3.

Figure 8.3. Consistency Framework

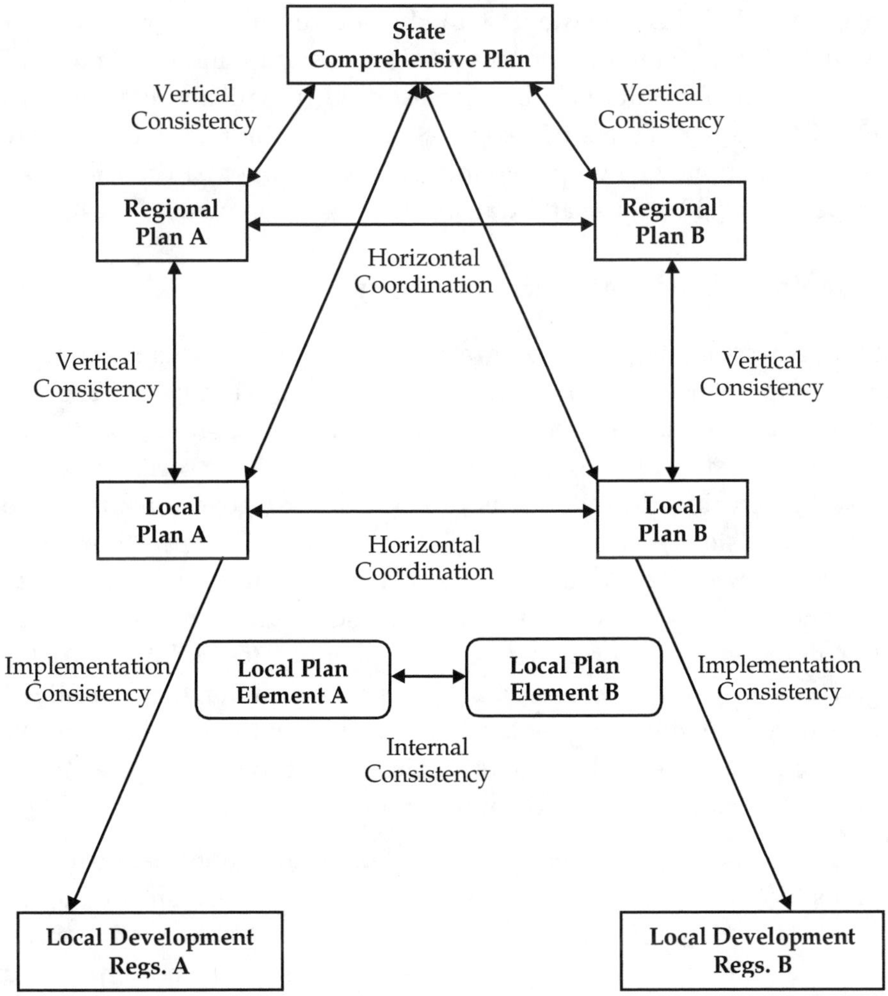

Internal consistency

Three of the four state growth management programs contain a requirement that local government comprehensive plans contain elements that are consistent with one another (i.e., internal consistency). In Florida, local plan elements of the comprehensive plan shall be consistent, and DCA's Rule 9J-5 includes criteria for determining whether elements of the comprehensive plan are related to and consistent with each other (Florida Statutes § 163.3177). In Georgia, RDCs are charged with reviewing local plans for internal consistency (Georgia DCA Rule Chapter 110-12-1-.06, Minimum Procedural Standards). Washington's GMA requires local plans to be internally consistent documents and specifies that all elements shall be consistent with the future land use map (RCW § 36.70A.070). A search of Oregon's land use statute indicates no formal requirement for internal plan consistency. It is likely, however, that DLCD's plan reviewers pay some attention to the internal consistency of local comprehensive plans and plan amendments, especially with respect to local land use and transportation system plans.

Coordination and horizontal consistency

State growth management programs provide mechanisms to coordinate the comprehensive plans of the various local governments. The word "coordination" is favored over the term "horizontal consistency" (Burby and May 1997, 8), because of the difficulties associated with the task of ensuring that the plans of diverse local governments are formally consistent with each other (DiMento 1980). The term "horizontal" refers to government entities on the same or equal level (e.g., cities and counties, or local to local). Incidentally, since counties might have additional roles for the coordination of local planning (as in the cases of Oregon and Washington), some observers might prefer that counties be considered a distinct, higher level of government than cities. Horizontal coordination or consistency requirements exist to some degree in each of the four growth management programs.

Florida places strong emphasis on horizontal coordination of local plans by requiring each local government to prepare an intergovernmental coordination element (ICE). This element shows relationships and states principles and guidelines to be used in coordinating the adopted comprehensive plan with the comprehensive plans of adjacent municipalities, the county, and adjacent counties as well as with the region and state (Florida Statutes § 163.3177). Furthermore, horizontal consistency or coordination is specifically required with regard to land use. A local government must include a policy statement indicating the relationship of the proposed development of the area to the comprehensive plans of adjacent municipalities, the county, and adjacent counties as well as the region and state (Florida Statutes § 163.3177). This finding shows how embedded the horizontal consistency requirement is in Florida's growth management statutes.

In Georgia, horizontal coordination of local comprehensive plans is assigned to RDCs. Pursuant to statute, RDCs notify adjacent local governments, and adjacent RDCs where applicable, of the intent to adopt a comprehensive plan. The RDCs also identify and attempt to address conflicts between local comprehensive plans (Georgia Code § 50-8-37).

Oregon's land use law (ORS 197) appears relatively weak with respect to enunciating coordination requirements among local government plans. Plan coordination requirements, however, were adopted by the legislature in 1993 pursuant to Senate Bill 122 (ORS 195). Oregon's land use statute, nevertheless, broadly defines a plan that is "coordinated" as "when the needs of all levels of governments, semipublic and private agencies and the citizens of Oregon have been considered and accommodated as much as possible" (ORS § 197.015). Oregon's broad definition of a coordinated plan hints at the complexity associated with consistency and coordination issues (DiMento 1980).

Washington's GMA provides for horizontal coordination and consistency as indicated below. Note that this provision also refers to "regional issues," which expresses an intent to go beyond "common borders."

> The comprehensive plan of each county or city that is adopted pursuant to RCW 36.70A.040 shall be coordinated with, and consistent with, the comprehensive plans adopted pursuant to RCW 36.70A.040 of other counties or cities with which the county or city has, in part, common borders or related regional issues (RCW § 36.70A.100).

Vertical consistency

The reader should have a firm grasp by this point on the notion of vertical consistency. As indicated previously, vertical consistency can mean that local plans must be consistent with regional plans and that both local and regional plans must be consistent with a state comprehensive plan (Burby and May 1997, 8). Florida's laws are the most advanced of the four states in defining and applying the principle of vertical consistency. The passages below provide Florida's definitions of consistency, compatibility, and other terms provided by statute to assist in the review of local plans.

> The Legislature finds that in order for the department to review local comprehensive plans, it is necessary to define the term "consistency." Therefore, for the purpose of determining whether local comprehensive plans are con-

> sistent with the state comprehensive plan and the appropriate regional policy plan, a local plan shall be consistent with such plans if the local plan is "compatible with" and "furthers" such plans. The term "compatible with" means that the local plan is not in conflict with the state comprehensive plan or appropriate regional policy plan. The term "furthers" means to take action in the direction of realizing goals or policies of the state or regional plan. For the purposes of determining consistency of the local plan with the state comprehensive plan or the appropriate regional policy plan, the state or regional plan shall be construed as a whole and no specific goal and policy shall be construed or applied in isolation from the other goals and policies in the plans (Florida Statutes § 163.3177).

Florida's law provides a vertical consistency requirement between the growth management element of the state comprehensive plan (which has never been adopted), and the growth management components of local comprehensive plans. Note that vertical consistency between state and regional growth management plans is also addressed in the state planning statute.

> The growth management portion of the state comprehensive plan shall . . . set forth recommendations on when and to what degree local government comprehensive plans must be consistent with the proposed growth management portion of the state comprehensive plan [and] set forth recommendations concerning what degree of consistency is appropriate for the strategic regional policy plans (Florida Statutes § 186.009).

As Burby and May (1997, 9) observe, Georgia "merely encourages" consistency. Indeed, Georgia has a less developed version of vertical consistency, but there is, at face value, a vertical consistency requirement if local governments elect to plan. A relevant passage of Georgia's statute indicates that DCA may review comprehensive plans of all governments acting within the state to determine their consistency with long-range programs and policies of the state (Georgia Code § 50-8-10). This provision seems somewhat out of context, however, because Georgia has yet to adopt a state plan. Perhaps Georgia's mandate designers intended to adopt Florida's vertical consistency requirement, but only in a disguised sort of way, after local governments had completed their own plans (i.e., adopt Florida's vertical consistency mandate without the sequence of Florida's planning). The delayed imposition of vertical consistency in Georgia is an alternative to Florida's combination of vertical consistency and vertical planning sequence.

Oregon's law contains a vertical consistency mandate. It requires consistency of local comprehensive plans and development regulations with statewide planning goals adopted by LCDC (ORS § 197.250). Washington does not enunciate a vertical consistency requirement but, in a manner similar to Oregon, specifies statewide goals that must be used to guide the development of comprehensive plans and development regulations (RCW § 36.70A.020).

In conclusion, each state implements the doctrine of vertical consistency to some degree or another. Approaches to vertical consistency in third-wave programs are decidedly weaker than the coercive designs found in Florida and Oregon. Scholars may not even agree that programs of the third wave contain vertical consistency requirements. Florida has articulated the concept of vertical consistency more clearly, and in greater detail, than the other three states. In the Pacific Northwest, vertical consistency applies to state goals rather than a state comprehensive plan (as in the southern states), but Washington's vertical consistency requirement appears to be much weaker than that found in Oregon. Hence, these findings provide evidence to confirm the longitudinal divergence hypothesis, or that third-wave programs have less coercive, more collaborative, approaches to growth management.

Implementation consistency

Earlier, I introduced implementation consistency, or the concept that regulations and implementing actions of local governments must be consistent with their comprehensive plans. Other scholars have termed this "local internal consistency" (Burby and May 1997, 9). The four state growth management programs require to varying degrees that local government actions and plans be consistent.

Florida law again is the most advanced of the four states with regard to requiring implementation consistency. Florida's growth management statute provides that the local planning rule (9J-5) must include criteria for determining whether elements of local comprehensive plans contain programs and activities to ensure that comprehensive plans are implemented (Florida Statutes § 163.3177). Local planning agencies or commissions must evaluate proposed development regulations for their relationship to the local comprehensive plan (Florida Statutes § 163.3194). The same section further elaborates the notion that land development regulations must be consistent with the adopted comprehensive plan.

> After a comprehensive plan, or element or portion thereof, has been adopted in conformity with this act, all development undertaken by, and all actions taken in regard to development orders by, governmental agencies in regard to land covered by such plan or element shall be consistent with such plan or element as adopted. All land development regulations enacted or amended shall be consistent with the adopted comprehensive plan, or element or portion thereof, and any land development regulations existing at the time of adoption which are not consistent with the adopted comprehensive plan, or element or portion thereof, shall be amended so as to be consistent (Florida Statutes § 163.3194).

Florida law also clearly enunciates an implementation consistency requirement for cities, with its provision that municipalities "shall adopt or amend and enforce land development regulations that are consistent with and implement their adopted comprehensive plan" (Florida Statutes § 163.3202).

Georgia's law does not require implementation consistency. As noted before, the state does not require local land development regulations in order to implement plans, although Georgia's DCA recently has begun to require that local work programs and actions implement local comprehensive plans (as the local governments themselves suggested in their plan that they would do). The consequence of the failure of a governing body to achieve implementation consistency is the loss of its qualified local government status.

Oregon's law clearly enunciates an implementation consistency requirement, perhaps to the degree that Florida's does. Oregon's land use law asserts that the implementation of plans is a matter of statewide concern.

> Implementation and enforcement of acknowledged comprehensive plans and land use regulations are matters of statewide concern (ORS § 197.013). Each city and county in this state shall . . . enact land use regulations to implement their comprehensive plans . . . and make land use decisions and limited land use decisions in compliance with the acknowledged plan and land use regulations (ORS § 197.175).

Washington's GMA has an implementation consistency requirement that indicates "any change to development regulations shall be consistent with and implement the comprehensive plan" (RCW § 36.70A.130). Washington requires counties and cities not planning under GMA to make their land use regulations consistent with their comprehensive plans. State law gave local governments not planning under the act until July 1, 1992, to make their regulations consistent with the comprehensive plan (RCW § 35.63.125). A similar provision applies to "code cities" (RCW § 35A.63.105).

Inverse vertical compatibility

My framework for examining consistency includes four types described above: internal, horizontal, vertical, and implementation. There is another type of consistency that is not talked about in the literature but that exists through the state agency coordination requirements of Oregon's land use program. Once local governments complete plans that have been approved by the state, state agency coordination plans must be compatible with local comprehensive plans. For lack of a better term I call this inverse vertical compatibility, because it is a vertical intergovernmental relationship but it works inversely (local to state) to that which is usually described (state to local). A sequential relationship is also implied in this concept.

Florida's State Comprehensive Planning Act of 1972 describes state agency strategic plans as a "statement of the priority directions" that "shall be consistent with and shall further the goals of the state comprehensive plan" (Florida Statutes § 186.021). This provision does not explicitly require strategic plans for all state agencies. While this provision of Florida law provides for a horizontal consistency of sorts at the state level between agency plans and the state comprehensive plan, it does not explicitly establish an inverse vertical consistency requirement between state agency plans and local comprehensive plans. That is, it does not require that state agency plans be consistent with local plans. This point may be academic, however, in the sense that the law of transitivity applies—local plans must be consistent with the state comprehensive plan and, in turn, agency plans also must be consistent with the state comprehensive plan, therefore, state agency plans must be consistent with local plans. Perhaps it is because of this logic that the state leader in the concept of plan consistency did not enunciate the notion of inverse vertical consistency in its growth management statutes. Florida does mandate state agency coordination, but state agencies are having a difficult time with the coordination mandate in that agency compliance is inconsistent, according to DeGrove (Howe 1991a).

Georgia law authorizes the Governor's Development Council to "establish procedures for, and take action to require, communication and coordination among state agencies in any respect which the council deems necessary or appropriate in order to further the coordination of planning by state agencies" (Georgia Code § 45-12-204). While this provision implies that the Council could require state agency coordination, it does not mandate the preparation of state agency coordination or strategic plans, much less an inverse vertical consistency or compatibility requirement. It is expected, however, that state agency plans will eventually emerge from the Governor's Development Council (Howe 1991a). Furthermore, it is worth noting again that Georgia's unique sequence of local, then regional, then state planning suggests on broad principle that state agency plans, if prepared, will be compatible with adopted local comprehensive plans.

In Oregon, DLCD reviews state agency coordination programs to ensure that they are consistent with the statewide goals and compatible with adopted local comprehensive plans and land use regulations. LCDC was required by law to adopt administrative rules establishing procedures to assure that state agency permits affecting land use are issued in compliance with the goals and compatible with acknowledged comprehensive plans and land use regulations (ORS § 197.180). Oregon has an explicit consistency requirement between state agency plans and acknowledged local comprehensive plans, local regulations, and amendments to local plans and regulations.

"State agencies shall carry out their planning duties, powers and responsibilities and take actions that are authorized by law with respect to programs affecting land use . . . in compliance with goals . . . and in a manner compatible with . . . comprehensive plans and land use regulations . . . [and] amendments to acknowledged comprehensive plans or land use regulations" (ORS § 197.180). That requirement not only is an inverse vertical compatibility requirement, but has an implementation consistency tint to it. That is, by requiring compatibility between state agency plans and local regulations, it goes beyond inverse vertical consistency as described above to include an "inverse vertical implementation consistency" of sorts.

A content search for "state agency" in Washington's growth management law (RCW 36.70A) does not reveal any requirements for state agency coordination plans or consistency or compatibility requirements between state agency actions and local comprehensive plans. Hence, Washington appears to have nothing in its statute that resembles an inverse vertical compatibility requirement.

SANCTIONS AND DISINCENTIVES FOR NONCOMPLIANCE

The four states apply various methods to either ensure that local governments comply with state mandates or encourage them to do so. This section describes those statutory provisions.

Florida has a collection of disincentives and sanctions for noncompliance by local governments. If the Administration Commission, upon a hearing, finds that the comprehensive plan or plan amendment of a local government is not in compliance with state requirements, an order of the Administration Commission can be granted specifying that the local government shall not be eligible for grants administered under various programs, such as community development block grants, recreation development assistance, and others (Florida Statutes § 163.3184). Local governments that fail to adopt local plan elements or amendments required by statute or rule run the risk of having the RPC adopt the respective plan element or amendment for and applicable to that local government (Florida Statutes § 163.3167). State sanctions can be applied for noncompliance by local government in the following respects (not all-inclusive): failing to meet the schedule set for submission of its proposed comprehensive plan by more than 90 days; failure to prepare all of the required elements or plan amendments (Florida Statutes § 163.3167); and failure to implement its local comprehensive plan EAR through timely and sufficient amendments to its local plan (Florida Statutes § 163.3191).

Another remedy available to the state to bring recalcitrant local governments into compliance is the ability of the state land planning agency to require a local government to submit one or more land development regulations, if it has reasonable grounds to believe that a local government has totally failed to adopt any one or more of the land development regulations required by law. The agency may institute an action in circuit court to require adoption of these regulations (Florida Statutes § 163.3202). Hence, Florida's enforcement powers make no attempt to hide the heavy "stick" of state government.

Oregon's LCDC has authority similar to Florida's state land planning agency. Under several instances, LCDC can issue an order requiring a local government to take action necessary to bring its comprehensive plan or land use regulations into compliance with the state goals. Those instances when LCDC can issue an order include, among others, failure to adopt a comprehensive plan or land use regulation according to the compliance schedule; adoption of a plan, program, rule, or regulation that is not in compliance with the state goals; and exercise of a pattern or practice of decision making that violates an acknowledged comprehensive plan or land use regulation (ORS § 197.320).

Local governments in Oregon that fail to submit a required periodic review work program are subject to another set of sanctions, including orders by LCDC that require the local government to apply all or portions of the goals as applicable to land use decisions or that result in forfeiture of all or a portion of the grant money received to conduct a periodic review work program. LCDC also may require the local government to pay the cost of completing the work performed by DLCD (ORS § 197.635). Hence, Oregon's approach also carries a big stick to force compliance by local governments, if and when such sanctions are necessary.

Washington's GMA provides sanctions for failing to adopt a countywide planning policy. If mediation efforts are unsuccessful and local governments still cannot agree on a countywide planning policy, the governor can impose appropriate sanctions from those specified under RCW § 36.70A.340 on the county, city, or cities for failure to reach an agreement (RCW § 36.70A.210). Despite that provision, it is the Growth Management Hearings Boards that are the enforcement arm of Washington's GMA (see Sidebar 8.2). The passage below describes the authority of the hearing boards.

> A growth management hearings board shall hear and determine only those petitions alleging . . . that a state agency, county, or city planning under this chapter is not in compliance with the requirements of this chapter . . . (RCW § 36.70A.280). The board shall issue a final order . . . based exclusively on whether or not a state agency, county, or city is in compliance with the requirements of this chapter . . . (RCW § 36.70A.300). A request for review by the state to a growth management hearings board may be made only by the governor, or with the governor's consent the head of an agency, or by the commissioner of public lands as relating to state trust lands, for the review of whether: (1) A county or city that is required or chooses to plan under RCW 36.70A.040 has failed to adopt a comprehensive plan or development regulations, or county-wide planning policies within the time limits established by this chapter; or (2) a county or city that is required or chooses to plan under this chapter has adopted a comprehensive plan, development regulations, or county-wide planning policies, that are not in compliance with the requirements of this chapter (RCW § 36.70A.310).

Upon receipt of a finding of noncompliance by a Growth Management Hearings Board, the governor may direct OFM to revise its appropriation levels; direct the state treasurer to withhold the portion of revenues to which the county or city is entitled; or file a notice of noncompliance with the secretary of state and the county or city, which temporarily rescinds the county or city's authority to collect the real estate excise tax (RCW § 36.70A.340). These sanctions can be used to force local governments to comply with provisions regarding critical areas, resource lands, other land use regulations, and urban growth area designations (RCW § 36.70A.345).

The reader will recall that Georgia does not mandate local planning and does not have strong sanctions for noncompliance with its local planning mandate. Georgia, however, has used some of the same tools as Florida, Oregon, and Washington have used relative to disincentives. Specifically, Georgia's disincentive for failing to adopt a local comprehensive plan is the loss of the local government's qualified local government status, which if lost makes that local government ineligible to receive several types of state grants and loans. Hence, one again finds evidence to support the proposition that Florida's growth management program served as a model, example, or basis of departure for Georgia's program designers, despite some of the differences already noted.

HYPOTHESES ABOUT EVOLUTIONARY LEARNING

In Chapters 6, 7, and 8, I have discovered that evolutionary paths of learning exist between pairs of states and that certain paths of learning are more important than others in determining how state growth management programs evolve over time. The analysis of the content of state growth management statutes provides evidence that supports three hypotheses: longitudinal regional convergence (Florida-Georgia and Oregon-Washington), which suggests that programs of states in a subnational region will have similar mandate structures, while regions tend to diverge from one another; cross-sectional convergence, which predicts that programs developing during the same period of program history (e.g., Georgia-Washington) move toward similar growth management mandate structures; and longitudinal divergence, or the divergence over time of third-wave programs from first- and second-wave programs and specifically, that there are discernible differences in mandate structures because the state growth management programs were developed during different periods.

Sidebar 8.2. Clark County: Enforcement of GMA in Western Washington

Clark County, across the Columbia River from Portland, Oregon, engaged in a three-year growth management planning processes pursuant to GMA. The process included adoption of countywide planning policies (July 1992), a community framework plan, a comprehensive plan that designated urban growth areas, and development regulations adopted December 29, 1994. "Not unlike the Missoula floods," the Western Washington Growth Management Hearings Board was inundated with an "unprecedented" volume of petitions challenging the county's adoption of its comprehensive plan and development regulations. Some of the challenges applied to the comprehensive plans and development regulations of cities in Clark County, including Battle Ground and Washougal. This sidebar summarizes part of the story about challenging GMA in Clark County.

Approximately one-half of the 85 petitions were property-specific challenges, and nearly all of those challenges were based on GMA's Goal 6, private property rights. The remainder of the challenges set forth more generalized issues. The Western Washington Growth Management Hearings Board found several deficiencies with Clark County's planning process and products, and it issued a final decision and order in 1995 in response to the petitions. First, the county never complied with the requirement to classify, designate, and conserve resources lands and protect critical areas (though a wetlands protection ordinance was adopted).

Anticipating greater restrictions via a GMA comprehensive plan, during a period of "benign neglect" landowners segregated (subdivided via the tax assessor) an estimated 19 square miles of property into "large lot" (five to 20 acres) subdivisions. Those subdivisions were presumptively vested under Washington law. The county adopted a rural designation and provided that all rural lands would have a minimum lot size of five acres. The board found that decision and lot size inconsistent with GMA and the county's own policies, because it ignored what became known as a "rural resource line" that separated relatively undivided resource lands in the north part of the county from rural parcelizations to the south and west. A 10-acre minimum should have been provided north of the rural resource line to protect the resources, the board found. The board also found that "infrastructure costs for rural development are, by definition, more inefficient than for urban." The board noted that the number of rural residential lots available far exceeded the rural population allocation as provided in Clark County's plan. Establishing a five-acre minimum in unsegregated rural areas exacerbated the problem, and the county did not adequately consider the effects of parcelizations and segregations that had occurred since 1990.

In October 1994, I linked up with Portland, Oregon, planning consultant Al Benkendorf. His firm had completed comprehensive plans for the cities of Battle Ground and Washougal in Clark County and needed extra staff to finalize the two comprehensive plans and draft development regulations. Washougal's plan was challenged by Friends of the Columbia River Gorge because it included land that was within the jurisdiction of the Columbia River Gorge National Scenic Area (see discussion in Chapter 4). The board found that the area had densities established by the Gorge Commission, and unless the commission changed the density of one residence for each two acres, the city and county's imposition of an urban growth area was inconsistent with GMA. The board ordered that the land within the scenic area boundary be removed from Washougal's UGA.

I was working on zoning regulations for the city of Battle Ground when we received word of the board's decision in 1995. The comprehensive plan had been prepared by Benkendorf Associates and was awaiting adoption by the city pending the decision of the Growth Management Hearings Board. The city's urban growth area, which had to be established by the county, was ruled to be too large. The board ordered Clark County to reevaluate and reestablish UGAs for all but one city in the county. With respect to Battle Ground's plan and regulations, the board found that the city had no infill policies and was inappropriately relying on concurrency and market conditions to phase urban growth. The board distinguished between infill, which relates to growth phasing and which has as its primary purpose avoiding inefficient sprawl, and concurrency, which is intended to ensure that services were available at the time of or after development. The board found that the omission of infill development policies unduly burdened taxpayers of the city and county and ultimately failed the GMA test. The board also found that Battle Ground's plan failed to provide for a ratio of 60 percent single-family to 40 percent multifamily as suggested in the county's community framework plan. Instead, the city's plan called for a 75/25 ratio. Finding that the affordable housing goal had not been met, the board directed Battle Ground to adopt the 60/40 ratio and to implement policies and development regulations for affordable housing. In response to the board's order, I helped Benkendorf's firm prepare revised regulations for the City of Battle Ground.

Among the regulations we prepared for Battle Ground to seek compliance with the board's order were the following: allowances for attached and detached accessory apartments; establishment of "compatibility standards" for manufactured homes on individual lots (which had not been a permitted use before in all zoning districts); and establishment of an "infill residential development opportunities district overlay," in which developments could qualify for reduced development fees, reduced minimum lot sizes, and the waiver of certain urban improvement standards (e.g., sidewalks and half-street improvements).

The Western Washington Growth Management Hearings Board's order for Clark County exhibits the breadth and strength of the three boards' authority relative to enforcing GMA. The Western board forced Clark County and its cities to reassess and revise their plans and regulations to meet urban growth management, resource protection, and affordable housing goals enunciated in GMA. This review of the board's order illustrates how powerful an enforcement agent the growth management hearings board can be, if petitions are made that allege inconsistencies with GMA and such petitions are found to be valid.

Source: Western Washington Growth Management Hearings Board. 1995. Achen, et. al, Petitioners, vs. Clark County, et. al, Respondents, and Clark County School Districts, et. al., Intervenors. Final Decision and Order No. 95-2-0067. Olympia: Western Washington Growth Management Hearings Board.

There is strong evidence to support the longitudinal regional convergence hypothesis, especially between Florida and Georgia. Both states require a state comprehensive plan, regional planning, development of regional impact programs, and critical areas protection. Although there are major differences between the states, especially the sequence of planning and the visibility and strength of consistency requirements, the underlying structures of their state-sponsored planning programs are similar. I suggest that regional characteristics influence the choices of mandate designers. The southern states, Florida and Georgia, have numerous small counties and interjurisdictional spillovers and conflicts, and mandate designers there have used substate regional planning structures to attain state growth management objectives. Other evidence was presented throughout the three chapters on program structure that supports the regional convergence hypothesis as applied to Florida-Georgia.

The regional convergence hypothesis is also valid with respect to Oregon and Washington. Mandate designers in these two states have converged in their choices of how to structure growth management programs. Similarities between these two states abound, most notably their counties-as-regional-entities approach and their mandates that local governments adopt urban containment programs. There appears to be a particular style of growth management in the Pacific Northwest that distinguishes it from the approaches applied in the southern states. Hence, there is support for my contention that states within subnational regions tend to converge, while subnational regions themselves tend to diverge from one another.

Revisiting Figure 6.1, I discover that there is convergence between state growth management programs developed during the same eras of growth management history. Evidence shows how program structures in Florida and Oregon (i.e., first- and second-wave programs) are alike, while Georgia's and Washington's (i.e., third-wave) programs are similar. I made these contentions in earlier chapters by highlighting the characteristics that distinguish the three eras of growth management history. The findings presented in Chapters 6, 7, and 8 provide further support for the cross-sectional convergence and longitudinal divergence hypotheses.

Two other pairs of states (i.e., possible paths of learning) are not identified as important in the hypotheses—Florida-Washington and Oregon-Georgia. I find some evidence to suggest that the evolutionary path between Florida and Washington is important—the most obvious example is that Washington borrowed Florida's notion of transportation concurrency. I maintain, however, that the program structures are not very similar. Only in the rarest of instances, such as residual similarities from the *Model Land Development Code,* did I find structural linkages between Oregon's land use law and Georgia's coordinated planning program. My evidence is far from conclusive, however, since significant evidence was discovered that tends to refute the hypotheses. If one does not get too absorbed in the details, however, the hypotheses about program evolution and learning are valid. The hypotheses could be tested further by including more state programs, as I note in the concluding chapter, which contains a research agenda.

Note

1. I am referring here to a one-day research forum held in May 1997 at Portland State University on the politics of regional growth management. The forum was sponsored by a research grant from the Lincoln Institute of Land Policy. It was directed by Professors Carl Abbott and Sy Adler and included academics, state agency (DLCD and DCTED) representatives, and local/regional practitioners, including me. A paper on this forum, "Metropolis and Region in the Pacific Northwest: The Politics of Regional Growth Management," was given at the annual meeting of the Association of Collegiate Schools of Planning held in Pasadena, CA in November 1998.

CHAPTER

9

Local Land Use Planning Standards

Mandate designers must contemplate how they will guide local land use planning, or at least articulate some of their expectations for the content of land use plans. This chapter presents an analysis of the statutes and administrative rules specific to the content of local land use plans. Emphasis is placed on the expectations of state plan reviewers regarding how local governments are supposed to address questions of land use and urban growth. Prior to analyzing those content requirements, however, it is important to identify the state planning goals that provide overall direction to local governments in their land use planning and urban growth management activities.

STATE LAND USE AND URBANIZATION GOALS

Excerpted below are the land use planning goals established by the states. Florida and Washington's land use goals are specified by statute, while Georgia and Oregon's land use goals are codified as rules. Both Florida and Georgia refer to "quality of life" in their land use goals. Additionally, both states mention "natural resources" in their land use goals. Florida's goal refers to "preserving" natural resources while Georgia's goal is directed "to allocate" uses that will "accommodate" natural resources. Oregon and Washington both refer to "efficient" land use. All four of the state land use goals refer to public or community facilities and services.

> In recognition of the importance of preserving the natural resources and enhancing the quality of life of the state, development shall be directed to those areas which have in place, or have agreements to provide, the land and water resources, fiscal abilities, and service capacity to accommodate growth in an environmentally acceptable manner (Florida Statutes § 187.201(16)(a)).
>
> To ensure that land resources are allocated for uses that will accommodate and enhance the state's economic development, natural and historic resources, community facilities, and housing and to protect and improve the quality of life of Georgia's residents (DCA Rules § 110-12-1-.04(2)(e)).
>
> Goal 14: Urbanization—To provide for an orderly and efficient transition from rural to urban land use. Urban growth boundaries shall be established to identify and separate urbanizable land from rural land. Establishment and change of the boundaries shall be based upon considerations of the following [selected] factors: (3) Orderly and economic provision for public facilities and services; (4) Maximum efficiency of land uses within and on the fringe of the existing urban area; [and] (5) Environmental, energy, economic and social consequences (OAR § 660-15-000).
>
> (1) Urban growth. Encourage development in urban areas where adequate public facilities and services exist or can be provided in an efficient manner. (2) Reduce sprawl. Reduce the inappropriate conversion of undeveloped land into sprawling, low-density development (RCW § 36.70A.020).

Georgia's land use goal does not provide any direction for managing the state's urban development form. Florida, Oregon, and Washington impose mandates regarding urban development form. In Florida, "development shall be directed . . ." to the most appropriate areas. Oregon's goal calls for the separation of rural and urbanizable lands with UGBs. Washington's land use goal mandates that sprawl be reduced, and state law also mandates that UGAs (i.e., urban containment policies) be established (RCW § 36.70A.110).

Based on the content of statewide land use goals, one would likely predict that Washington would have the most developed rules for reducing urban sprawl. Washington, however, has not developed an administrative rule to elaborate on the goal of reducing sprawl, though in 1997 the legislature did adopt an important amendment to GMA requiring rural elements of comprehensive plans to reduce rural sprawl (RCW § 36.70A.070(5)(c)). Florida is the only state to define urban sprawl and implement a program to assess local land use elements for their ability to discourage urban sprawl land use patterns. Oregon, by mandating UGBs, has a policy of urban containment (i.e., discouragement of urban sprawl), but Oregon's land use law does not employ the term urban sprawl. I now look at the requirements for local land use plan content as specified in state administrative rules.

CONTENT REQUIREMENTS FOR LOCAL LAND USE ELEMENTS

This section provides an analysis of the various local land use plan content requirements of the four states. Generally, state growth management rules for land use elements of comprehensive plans include land use map requirements (both existing and future) according to certain land use categories and a narrative text addressing requirements for land use acreage data (existing, future acreage needed), various land use analyses, and goals, objectives, and policies.

Land use map requirements

Florida requires the map of existing land uses to depict generalized land use for properties adjacent to the local government's jurisdiction (FAC § 9J-5.006(1)(f)), as well as, inside its own jurisdiction. Florida's rule does not define what "adjacent" is, but it is probably interpreted to mean abutting properties only. A future land use map also is required using the same categories (see discussion below) (FAC § 9J-5.006(4)). Local land use elements in Georgia also must include existing and future land use maps and use the state prescribed land use categories. Like in Florida, the expected level of detail for land use maps in Georgia is general, but with a "sufficient scale and accuracy to provide a clear understanding of the general distribution of land uses and their spatial relationships to one another" (Georgia DCA Rule § 110-12-1-.04.3).

Oregon's land use law does not explicitly outline a requirement for comprehensive plan elements, much less a land use element. Oregon's Goal 2 Guidelines, however, specify that "the following elements should be included in the plan: (a) Applicable statewide planning goals; (b) Any critical geographic area designated by the legislature; (c) Elements that address any special needs or desires of the people in the area; and (d) Time periods of the plan, reflecting the anticipated situation at appropriate future intervals." As noted before, these "elements" are not of the same substance as comprehensive plan elements in the other three states.

Oregon includes a land use map requirement by virtue of defining a comprehensive plan and requiring local comprehensive plans. Oregon law defines the comprehensive plan as "a generalized, coordinated land use map and policy statement . . ." (ORS § 197.015). My content analysis of Oregon's land use statute (ORS 197) reveals that the comprehensive plan definition is the only provision of Oregon's land use law that contains a reference to a land use map. Oregon's law does not elaborate on the content requirements of existing and future land use plan maps.

In Washington, the comprehensive plan is referred to in state law as the comprehensive land use plan (RCW § 36.70A.030). Both state law and DCTED's administrative rules specify that local comprehensive plans must contain a land use element that designates the proposed general distribution and general location and extent of the uses of land (RCW § 36.70A.070 and WAC § 365-195-305). These provisions do not specifically include a requirement to map future land use; they specify only that generalized existing land use be mapped. Land use elements, however, must contain a map or maps (WAC § 365-195-300(1)), and "recommendations" for meeting the requirements of the land use element do contain a reference to a future land use map (WAC § 365-195-305(2)). Hence, for all intents and purposes, Washington is considered to require a future land use map as part of its land use element. Therefore, Florida, Georgia, and Washington all require land use elements of comprehensive plans, and local governments in each state are required (if required to or opting to plan) to designate existing and future land uses in generalized map format.

Land use categories

What categories should local governments be required to use to map their existing and future land uses? Mandate designers in Georgia and Florida apparently considered this a more important question than did their counterparts in the Pacific Northwest, because the southern states specify land use categories that must be shown on existing and future land use maps. Georgia's design is especially noteworthy because it specifically requires standardized land use categories, which are then used to construct regional and statewide land use data bases via geographic information systems. There is a provision in Georgia's administrative rules for DCA to grant a local government a variance from the standard classification, but that provision has rarely been requested by local governments and approved by DCA.

Oregon's land use laws and administrative rules are silent on the preferred categories of land uses to include in land use plans. Washington's GMA specifies that a land use element must show the general distribution and general location and extent of the uses of land (RCW § 36.70A.070) (see Table 9.1). Washington's administrative rules, however, were supposed to be procedural rather than substantive in nature and therefore recite but do not elaborate on the statutory list of land uses.

Florida specifies separate lists for existing and future land use maps. The only difference between the two, however, is that transportation concurrency management areas are required to be designated on the future (but not the existing) land use map. Georgia specifies a single classification system suitable for both existing and future land use maps. Washington provides a list of land uses in the state law and reasserts (but does not define or elaborate on) the list in the administrative rules. Oregon's land use law and rules do not provide a classification scheme for mapping existing and future land uses.

Table 9.1 compares the land use categories specified by rules in Florida, Georgia, and Washington. Oregon is excluded because, as described above, its rules do not describe land use categories. Table 9.1 shows that the three states include many of the same land use categories. Those common to the three states include agricultural, residential, commercial, industrial, recreational, and public facilities land uses. In passing, it is worth noting that Florida's rule specifically encourages mixed land uses (FAC § 9J-5.006(4)(c)), while Georgia's rule does not recognize mixed use in its standard land use classification system. Georgia's rule provides that "for mixed- or multi-use sites or planned unit developments (PUDs), the predominant land use should be used to classify the entire site" (Georgia DCA Rule § 110-12-1-.04).

Land use acreage data requirements

Florida's rule (FAC § 9J-5.006(3)(c)) specifically requires in tabular form the acreage and density or intensity for each category of existing land use. Further, the rule (FAC § 9J-5.006(2)(c)) requires an analysis of the amount of land needed to accommodate the population, including estimated gross acreage needed for each category of land use. This requirement is one of land use demand, rather than a statistic that quantifies land uses shown on the future land use map. The distinction is worth further discussion.

Future land use demand is what the local government identifies as being needed to accommodate growth during the planning horizon. This is not the same as the number of acres indicated in each land use category on the future land use map. The two types of information

Table 9.1. Land Use Classifications Required for Local Comprehensive Plans: Florida, Georgia, and Washington

Land Use Category	Florida	Georgia	Washington
Agriculture	✔	✔ (with forestry)	✔
Timber (forestry)		✔ (with agriculture)	✔
Housing (residential)	✔	✔	✔
Commerce	✔	✔	✔
Industry	✔	✔	✔
Recreation	✔	✔ (with conservation)	✔
Open Spaces			✔
Conservation	✔	✔ (with recreation)	
Public utilities (transportation, communication, utilities)		✔	✔
Public facilities (buildings and grounds)	✔	✔	✔
Other public facilities	✔		
Educational	✔		
General aviation airports			✔
Historic resources	✔		
Other land uses			✔
Vacant and undeveloped	✔	✔	
Transportation concurrency management districts (future map)	✔		

Source: Florida Admin. Code § 9J-5; Georgia DCA Rules § 110-12-1-.04 (5)(f)2; RCW § 36.70A.070 and WAC § 365-195-305(1)(a).

could differ considerably in practice. For instance, a local government might find it needs 2,000 acres of single family residential land, but it could—unless state officials object—actually provide 6,000 acres in its future land use map.

Georgia's rule requires estimates of current acreage dedicated to each of the eight standard land use categories and approximate acreage needed in each category to accommodate projected growth during the planning period (Georgia DCA Rule § 110-12-1-.04). Washington's rule recommends but does not require acreage data for existing land uses (WAC § 365-195-305).

Land use analysis requirements

Vacant and/or buildable (i.e., suitable for development) lands inventories are required as a part of the land use analysis specified in Florida's rule (FAC § 9J-5.006(2)(b)). Florida's rule also requires analyses of the need for redevelopment (FAC § 9J-5.006(2)(d)). Georgia's minimum requirements for land use elements include a land use assessment that must consider "blighted areas and transitional areas undergoing shifts in predominant land use" (Georgia DCA Rule § 110-12-1-.04), but the rule does not explicitly require a vacant, buildable lands inventory. Local governments in Georgia are required to quantify the amount of vacant and undeveloped land as part of their land use element because they encompass one of the required land use classifications. This does not, however, constitute a requirement to inventory vacant lands with respect to their physical suitability for development.

Oregon law, as of 1995, requires many of its local governments to conduct buildable lands inventories, study their residential housing patterns, and amend their comprehensive plans to include sufficient buildable lands within their UGBs (ORS § 197.296). Buildable land in Oregon is defined to include both vacant land and developed land likely to be redeveloped (ORS § 197.295). Another provision of Oregon law requires that comprehensive plans and land use regulations provide for an adequate supply of sites for industrial and commercial uses (ORS § 197.712). See Sidebar 9.1.

Washington's rule for the land use element recommends but does not require an inventory of vacant, partially used and underutilized land (WAC § 365-195-305). Also, the rule for UGAs recommends "an inventory of lands within existing municipal boundaries which is available for development, including vacant land, partially used land, and land where redevelopment is likely" (WAC § 365-195-335). Sidebar 9.2 provides an example of drawing an urban growth area for the small town of PeEll, Washington. There also is a requirement specific to highly populated counties in the Puget Sound region to conduct buildable lands inventories.

In 1997 the Washington legislature followed a path similar to that of Oregon and also fulfilled the recommendations of the Land Use Study Commission when it passed Engrossed Senate Bill 6094 (Chapter 429, Washington Laws, 1997). I have not compared the buildable lands statutes of Oregon and Washington. I can assert with some confidence, however, that Washington followed Oregon's legislation. While

Sidebar 9.1. Ensuring Adequate Urban Land Supply I: An Oregon Model

One of the last tasks I worked on while at DLCD was a model work program for local governments to comply with the provisions of ORS 197.296 (House Bill 2709, adopted 1995). I provide below a partial, unofficial work program that relates to the urban growth management tasks of complying with Oregon's 1995 law relative to providing urban lands for housing in UGBs. The excerpts below exclude several important tasks related to housing needs analyses. The source includes descriptions of "products" which have been omitted due to space constraints.

Task 5. Inventory the supply of buildable residential lands

Determine the number of acres of buildable residential land (both vacant and redevelopable) in each residential plan designation in the UGB (including city limits). Summarize data sources; describe methods used in conducting the inventory; provide definitions (vacant land, redevelopable land, etc.); establish assumptions about availability of land; and provide buildable land acreage data in table format, cross-tabulated by residential plan designation and by type of land (vacant, redevelopable). Provide a map or maps showing the location of buildable residential lands, classified according to status (vacant, redevelopable).

Task 6. Inventory the supply of buildable nonresidential lands

Conduct an analysis of nonresidential land needs, including commercial uses, industrial uses, and public and institutional uses. Document assumptions and methods as described in Task 5 above.

Task 7. Identify and evaluate measures to increase likelihood that needed residential development will occur

Identify and evaluate measures that demonstrably increase the likelihood that needed residential development will occur (with, or without a UGB amendment). Measures include: increases in the permitted density on residential land; financial incentives for higher density housing; provision allowing additional density in exchange for amenities and other development features; removal or easing of approval standards or procedures; minimum density ranges; redevelopment and infill strategies; authorization of housing types not previously allowed by the plan or regulations; and adoption of an average residential density standard. The proposed measures should be designed to change densities or housing mix, or both, as necessary, to meet housing needs over the next 20 years. Also as part of this task, ensure that land or needed housing is appropriately located and is zoned at density ranges achievable in the future housing market.

Task 8. Prepare and adopt measures to increase the likelihood that needed residential development will occur

If the city finds (by completing Task 4 described above) that densities, mixes, and characteristics of needed housing types are greater than densities (or different from the mixes and characteristics of housing types found in the analysis) of recent residential development, the city is required to implement measures that demonstrably increase the likelihood that residential development will occur at the housing densities and mixes of housing types and with the qualitative characteristics required to meet housing needs over the next 20 years.

Task 9. Determine land needed for housing

Determine the amount of land acreage needed to accommodate the projection of needed housing units by type of unit. This will be achieved by determining the needed net density range for each residential designation of the comprehensive plan and by determining the number of acres needed in each residential designation of the comprehensive plan.

Task 10. Compare existing residential land supply with trends for residential development at actual densities

Conduct an assessment of whether the residential land supply contains enough vacant and redevelopable land to accommodate the 20-year housing needs, based on the assumption that residential development will continue at the average residential density that has recently occurred. This task entails a comparison of the amount of land needed based on densities of recent construction with the amount of residential land (vacant and redevelopable) available (i.e., the buildable lands analysis) to determine the number of acres of residential land needed to meet 20-year housing needs. Note: If sufficient land is available to meet future housing needs based on densities of recent residential development, the remaining tasks are not required. Task 12, however, is encouraged even if sufficient land is available to meet housing needs.

Task 11. Compare existing residential land supply with the housing needs analysis and the

measures to achieve housing mix, density, and characteristics

Determine if the existing residential land supply will provide for the density, type, characteristics, and land needs of/for future housing.

Task 12. Identify, evaluate, and adopt measures to achieve efficient urban form

Identify, evaluate, and adopt measures that increase the efficiency of land use in the urban area. In addition to those measures designed to increase the likelihood that needed housing will occur (as identified in Task 7 and as adopted in Task 8), consider other methods of increasing the efficiency of the urban area. Such measures may include but are not limited to the following: use of public facility location and phasing policies to direct urban development to locations within or adjacent to urban areas; use of transportation policies to direct urban development to locations within or adjacent to urban areas; and adoption of adequate public facilities requirements.

Task 13. Prioritize lands for UGB expansions

ORS 197.298 establishes priorities for including land in the UGB. For all properties proposed for addition to the UGB for housing needs or nonresidential needs, classify each property as one of the following (in priority order for inclusion in the UGB): urban reserves, exception and nonresource lands adjacent to the UGB, marginal lands, and agriculture and forestry lands.

Task 14. Prepare UGB amendment findings to comply with Goals 2 and 14; prepare and adopt a UGB amendment

To justify the UGB amendment, follow the procedures and requirements as set forth in the land use planning goal (Goal 2) for goal exceptions and as established in Goal 14 and OAR 660, Division 4.

Source: Oregon Department of Land Conservation and Development. 1997b.

Sidebar 9.2. Ensuring Adequate Urban Land Supply I: Drawing a UGA for PeEll, Washington

In 1995, I was working with the town of PeEll, Washington, to prepare its comprehensive plan. This sidebar provides excerpts from a chapter out of the Town of PeEll's comprehensive plan (1996 draft) relating to urban growth areas. It is intended to illustrate one attempt by a small town to comply with Washington's mandate to draw a compact urban growth area.

Vacant and buildable lands inventory

State administrative rules suggest an inventory of vacant, partially used and under-utilized land and an analysis of the extent to which such areas can meet the anticipated growth at the densities selected (WAC 365-195-305(2)(f)). The vacant and buildable lands inventory is needed to meet the state objective of accommodating projected urban growth through "infill" within existing municipal boundaries where possible (WAC 365-195-060(5)). DCD (now DCTED) has prepared a more detailed method for conducting vacant and buildable lands analyses (Enger 1992).

Listed in Table 7.1 [excluded from this text] is an inventory of vacant lots that are determined to be reasonably "buildable." The inventory excludes vacant lots that are probably unbuildable due to flood plain and about a dozen small (6,000 square feet or less) scattered lots, many of which are odd shaped. These latter lots offer potential infill opportunities, but it is highly unlikely these sites will actually be developed. Within the town limits there are approximately 55 buildable lots for residential use, in a variety of lot sizes. There are 23 acres, or almost three-quarters of the vacant land in the town, that are considered vacant and buildable. In addition to these vacant lands, there are 73.5 acres of agriculture, pasture, forest and natural area in PeEll. Given that the vast majority of these lands have not been identified by PeEll as lands of "long term commercial significance," there are opportunities for low-density residential or urban residential development on these sites. Much of this land is flood plain, however. Several single family residences could be accommodated on noncritical agriculture and forest lands, after considering nonresidential needs as well.

Further residential development potential exists if one considers the resubdivision potential of low-density residential lands and redevelopment of other properties. In practice, however, the likelihood for subdivision of these larger lots is limited. PeEll's residents enjoy their low-density residential environment; most do not desire to subdivide their property for additional development, although the right to subdivide is not precluded. Redevelopment is highly unlikely given PeEll's location and low density. Given the existence of vacant, buildable lots, and the impracticality of further subdivision of the larger residential lots, further analysis of these infill and redevelopment possibilities was not conducted. In summary, there are 55 existing platted lots that are determined to be buildable, and there is a potential for additional buildable residential lots through conversion of agricultural lands inside the existing town limits.

"Available" lands inventory

There are vacant buildable lots in the town limits, but they are not necessarily available for residential development. A guidebook prepared by DCTED echos this point, as the passage below indicates:

> "Although vacant, partially-developed and under-utilized land may be suitable for development, it may not be available. In fact, a certain percentage of these lands may never be available for development . . . The amount of land available can be expected to vary from community to community with local conditions and different pressures for growth. In the RERC [Real Estate Research Corporation] survey, which covered a number of different communities, half of the vacant infill parcels surveyed were expected to be on the market within five years . . . Because there are so many unknowns when it comes to land availability, we will never have a definitive answer . . . An understanding of unique local conditions is of key importance" (Washington DCD 1992b).

The town council and residents reviewed the numbers of vacant lots as well as their locations on the map of existing land uses. Concern was raised during the September 1995 meeting that the buildable lots inventory paints an inaccurate picture of adequate residential land supply. According to local sources, these lands are largely not available for residential development because they are held by only a few land owners who are not interested in releasing the properties for development nor developing the properties themselves. Town officials indicated that real estate professionals would show very few (if any) residential lots are on the market and that, if necessary, ownership and land unavailability could be further documented. Given this local information, there is a general perception that the existing town limits will not be sufficient to serve the long-term residential land supply for PeEll, despite the existence of the vacant lots and other residential development potential on agricultural lands.

Given local input concerning the lack of land available for residential development, it is assumed that not all of the buildable residential lots will be available for development during the planning horizon. The drawing of the urban growth area must meet the overall intentions of the state Growth Management Act that a wise use of land inside developed areas be achieved prior to expanding development onto properties outside city limits. The chosen percentage (75 percent) of buildable lands available for development during the planning horizon appears to be a reasonable compromise between state requirements and local conditions in PeEll.

Estimates of additional land supply needed for development

The town's population projections are for an increase of approximately 100 new residents by the year 2015. At the existing household size of approximately 2.3 persons in PeEll, and assuming the need for new dwellings to house the new population (as opposed to "group quarters" or accommodation of new people in existing dwellings), this population projection would result in the need for 43 additional homes (residential lots). Building in a vacancy rate of five percent, to allow for some household mobility within PeEll increases this number to 46 new homes (residential lots) needed.

The county's method, guidelines, and criteria for drawing urban growth areas suggest the need to include a market factor of two times the residential need to provide a built-in safety factor in calculating the land supply needed. Applying this recommended market factor reveals a need for 92 additional residential lots. The existing town limits contains approximately 55 total vacant, buildable lots, and perhaps 30 additional buildable lots after considering conversion of existing agricultural land uses. Applying the assumption that 75 percent of the total vacant, buildable land will be available, approximately 64 lots inside the town can be used for future residential land supply during the planning horizon. This means that land for an additional 28 lots, outside the town limits, is needed. Since the future land use plan provides sufficient institutional, commercial, and industrial lands on properties inside the existing town limits, the inclusion of land outside the town limits in the UGA is needed for residential uses only.

Relevant criteria for drawing Urban Growth Areas (UGAs)

The following criteria, drawn from state guidebooks and recommendations of Lewis County, were used to designate PeEll's urban growth area:

- Territory outside a city may be included only if it is already characterized by urban growth or adjacent to territory already characterized by growth.
- Urban growth should be located first in areas that have public facility and service capabilities and second in areas that will be served by existing and additional needed facilities and services.
- The area is either already developed, firm commitments have been made to develop, or the area is located adjacent to cities or high-intensity population and employment centers.
- Public facilities and services are in place or can be provided at reasonable cost to accommodate urban growth.
- Natural features and land characteristics are capable of supporting urban development without significant environmental degradation.
- The area does not have high current or future value for agriculture, forestry or mineral production and should be able to develop without having a detrimental impact on nearby resource lands.
- Take advantage of physical features such as major drainages, where possible, to help provide a clear separation between urban and rural areas.

Source: The Benkendorf Associates Corporation, 1996. Edited by the author.

employed by DLCD in April 1997, I recall another DLCD employee commenting that Washington officials had requested a copy of Oregon's buildable lands legislation (House Bill 2709, ORS 197.296). A cursory review of Washington's buildable lands legislation suggests that the state adopted what in substance is strikingly similar to Oregon's 1995 law regarding buildable lands. Washington's law passed both houses in late April 1997.

Section 25 of the 1997 law added a requirement, applicable only to counties with populations of 150,000 or more in 1995 and located west of the Cascade Mountains, to conduct a "review and evaluation program" to determine if urban densities within UGAs are being achieved and if sufficient buildable lands are available to accommodate long-range population and employment projections. Furthermore, the counties and cities required to comply with this law must amend their countywide planning policies if they find inconsistencies between what their plans suggest and the development that has actually occurred. Evaluations are due by September 1, 2002, and DCTED must by July 1, 1998, have prepared a list of methods in carrying out the activities required by this new law.

Land use goals, policies, and objectives

Land use elements in Florida must contain goal statements, specific objectives for each goal statement, and policies for each objective that address implementation activities (FAC § 9J-5.006(3)). The rule goes further to specify eleven different policy prescriptions, including "discourage the proliferation of urban sprawl," "encourage the redevelopment and renewal of blighted areas," and "encourage the use of innovative land development regulations." Florida's local governments have no choice regarding urban form; they must combat urban sprawl and promote urban renewal, preferably with innovative land use regulations.

Georgia's rule provides that land use assessments should be considered in the development of needs, goals and policies "as reflected on the future land use map." This statement seems to symbolize the future land use map as the most important expression of local land use policy. Georgia's rules further state, however, that the future land use map is not intended to dictate specific activities on individual parcels of land, and that the map is not enforceable in and of itself.

Oregon defines a comprehensive plan in part as a "policy statement of the governing body" (ORS § 197.015). Goal 2 (land use planning) states that all land use plans shall include "evaluation of alternative courses of action and ultimate policy choices." Guidelines for land use planning indicate that elements of a local comprehensive plan must address the applicable statewide planning goals. Hence, compliance with the statewide planning goals provides the overriding determinant of the organization and content of local comprehensive plans in Oregon.

It is well known that Oregon's law requires local governments to institute UGBs. Oregon's Goal 14 (urbanization) (OAR § 660-15-000) is in itself a major policy prescription for urban containment. Goal 14 guidelines refer to the "growth policy of the area" in designating urbanizable land for further urban expansion. This language implies that there is some discretion in establishing local growth policy as long as UGBs are instituted.

Oregon law has not until recently (1995) specified a planning period of 20 years, though a 20-year time frame for planning has been the convention there and elsewhere. In theory, and most likely in practice, local governments previously could draw and/or maintain a UGB that supplies only enough land for say a 10-year period, thus exercising considerable discretion over local growth policy. ORS § 197.296 (adopted in 1995 and applicable to many but not all local governments) specifically requires a 20-year supply of buildable land inside UGBs, so some of the discretion over growth policy that historically might have been exercised by local governments has now been moderated.

In Washington, countywide planning policies and the designation of urban growth areas are supposed to precede local land use planning. This may not necessarily always be the case in practice. The state's rule for UGAs provides as follows: "The designation of urban growth areas should ultimately be incorporated into the comprehensive plan of each county that plans under the act. However, every effort should be made to complete the urban growth area designation process earlier, so that the comprehensive plans of both the county and the cities can be completed in reliance upon it" (WAC § 365-195-335). Local governments in Washington are subject to the statutory statewide planning goals, and once adopted, countywide planning policies. Where applicable, multi-county planning policies further define the local land use policy framework. The exercise of policy discretion by cities planning under GMA appears, therefore, to be highly constrained. As with the other states, comprehensive plans in Washington must include a descriptive text covering objectives, principles, and standards used to develop the comprehensive plan (WAC § 365-195-300). The specific policy prescriptions mandated by the states for directing urban growth are described in greater detail in the following section.

URBAN FORM AND STATE GROWTH MANAGEMENT POLICY

To what extent do statutes and administrative rules of the four states attempt to guide urban form? The administrative rules provide an opportunity to elaborate on the expectations of mandate designers with respect to local land use plans. Oregon's and Washington's administrative officials have not yet further enunciated specific policies and methods for measuring the extent to which local governments attain desired patterns of urban growth. Georgia's law is basically silent on the issue of what type of urban land use patterns are desired. The only notable provision regarding development patterns in Georgia's rules occurs under the description of a land use assessment, which must include a discussion of "historical factors that have led to current development patterns, to the extent that these can be identified" (Georgia DCA Rule § 110-12-1-.04). Florida's rules, on the other hand, specify the requirements for guiding urban form in what is commonly referred to as the state's "antisprawl" rule (FAC § 9J-5.006(5)). Due to the advanced nature of its antisprawl rule relative to other states, Florida's approach deserves special emphasis here.

Florida's antisprawl rule

To make sure that local comprehensive plans and plan amendments are consistent with provisions of the state comprehensive plan regarding urban form, as well as the state's rule that discourages urban sprawl, plan reviewers must determine whether a plan or plan amendment discourages the proliferation of urban sprawl. This task is facilitated by the rule's establishment of a general method that: (1) defines "urban sprawl;" (2) enunciates a set of "indicators," or those aspects or attributes of a plan or plan amendment which, when present, indicate that the plan or plan amendment may fail to discourage urban sprawl; (3) provides criteria for evaluation of each land use for urban sprawl indicators, and (4) prescribes certain growth management tools designed to mitigate sprawl land use patterns. The definition of urban sprawl is excerpted below, followed by indicators in Table 9.2 and criteria for evaluating land uses in Table 9.3.

> "Urban sprawl" means urban development or uses which are located in predominantly rural areas, or rural areas interspersed with generally low-intensity or low-density urban uses, and which are characterized by one or more of the following conditions: (a) the premature or poorly planned conversion of rural land to other uses; (b) the creation of areas of urban development or uses which are not functionally related to land uses which predominate the adjacent area; or (c) the creation of areas of urban development or uses which fail to maximize the use of existing public facilities or the use of areas within which public services are currently provided. Urban sprawl is typically manifested in one or more of the following land use or development patterns: Leapfrog or scattered development; ribbon or strip commercial or other development; or large expanses of predominantly low-intensity, low-density, or single-use development (FAC § 9J-5.003).

Table 9.2. Florida's Indicators That a Plan or Plan Amendment Does Not Discourage the Proliferation of Urban Sprawl

Number of Indicator in Rule	Description of Indicator
1	Promotes, allows or designates for development substantial areas of the jurisdiction to develop as low-intensity, low-density, or single-use development or uses in excess of demonstrated need.
2	Promotes, allows or designates significant amounts of urban development to occur in rural areas at substantial distances from existing urban areas while leaping over undeveloped lands which are available and suitable for development.
3	Promotes, allows or designates urban development in radial, strip, isolated or ribbon patterns generally emanating from existing urban developments.
4	As a result of premature or poorly planned conversion of rural land to other uses, fails adequately to protect and conserve natural resources, such as wetlands, floodplains, native vegetation, environmentally sensitive areas, natural groundwater aquifer recharge areas, lakes, rivers, shorelines, beaches, bays, estuarine systems, and other significant natural systems.
5	Fails adequately to protect adjacent agricultural areas and activities, including silviculture, and including active agricultural and silvicultural activities as well as passive agricultural activities and dormant, unique and prime farmlands and soils.
6	Fails to maximize use of existing public facilities and services.
7	Fails to maximize use of future public facilities and services.
8	Allows for land use patterns or timing which disproportionately increase the cost in time, money and energy, of providing and maintaining facilities and services, including roads, potable water, sanitary sewer, stormwater management, law enforcement, education, health care, fire and emergency response, and general government.
9	Fails to provide a clear separation between rural and urban uses.
10	Discourages or inhibits infill development or the redevelopment of existing neighborhoods and communities.
11	Fails to encourage an attractive and functional mix of uses.
12	Results in poor accessibility among linked or related land uses.
13	Results in the loss of significant amounts of functional open space.

Source: Florida Administrative Code § 9J-5-006(5).

Table 9.3. Florida's Criteria for Evaluation of Land Uses for Discouraging Urban Sprawl

Number	Evaluation Criteria	Definition
1	Extent.	The amount of development, including the area or size in acres.
2	Location.	(Definition not provided in the rule)
3	Distribution.	The spatial array of land uses throughout an area.
4	Density.	An objective measurement of the number of people or residential units allowed per unit of land, such as residents or employees per acre.
5	Intensity.	An objective measurement of the extent to which land may be developed or used, including the consumption or use of the space above, on or below ground; the measurement of the use of or demand on natural resources; and the measurement of the use of or demand on facilities and services.
6	Compatibility.	A condition in which land uses or conditions can coexist in relative proximity to each other in a stable fashion over time such that no use or condition is unduly negatively impacted directly or indirectly by another use or condition.
7	Suitability.	The degree to which the existing characteristics and limitations of land and water are compatible with a proposed use or development.
8	Functional relationship.	A complementary and interactive relationship among land uses or development, including at a minimum a substantial and positive exchange of human interaction, goods, resources, institutions, services, jobs or workers between land uses or developments.
9	Land use combinations.	(Definition not provided in the rule).
10	Demonstrated need over the planning period.	(Definition not provided in the rule).

Source: Florida Administrative Code § 9J-5.006(5) and § 9J-5.003 (Definitions).

In addition, other relevant terms are defined by Florida's rules: "Pattern means the form of the physical dispersal of development or land use," while "composition means the make up of various land uses by types, extent, intensity, density, or otherwise, which are included in a development or land use category."

Washington's rural sprawl legislation

In 1997, the Washington legislature adopted Chapter 429, Washington Laws, which defines "rural character" (RCW § 36.70A.030) and enunciates what amounts to an antisprawl rule of its own, albeit one applied to rural development. Unexpectedly, it is rural rather than urban sprawl that first received elaboration by statute or rule. The rural sprawl legislation deserves further attention.

GMA established that a rural element was required for counties. GMA includes a goal of reducing sprawl but did not provide details of what constitutes an adequate rural element. With passage of this amendment, the legislature elaborated on the mandate to reduce sprawl, as the excerpt below indicates.

> The rural element shall include measures that apply to rural development and protect the rural character of the area, as established by the county, by: . . . reducing the inappropriate conversion of undeveloped land into sprawling, low-density development in the rural area (RCW § 36.70A.070(5)(c)).

The legislation provides that counties can allow certain limited areas of "more intensive rural development," including facilities and services, of certain types (paraphrased here): infill development and redevelopment of existing areas such as crossroads, shorelines, villages, hamlets, or rural activity centers; new small-scale recreational uses with public facilities but only if they are provided "in a manner that does not permit low-density sprawl;" and isolated cottage industries and businesses "provided in a manner that does not permit low-density sprawl." If a county provides for one of these types of more intensive rural development, the county must impose containment measures and a rural development boundary, as indicated in the following excerpt.

> A county shall adopt measures to minimize and contain the areas or uses of more intensive rural development, as appropriate . . . Lands included in such existing areas or uses shall not extend beyond the logical outer boundary of the existing area or use, thereby allowing a new pattern of low-density sprawl. Existing areas are those that are clearly identifiable

> and contained and where there is a logical boundary delineated predominantly by the built environment, but that may also include undeveloped lands if limited as provided in this subsection. The county shall establish the logical outer boundary of an area of more intensive rural development. In establishing the logical outer boundary the county shall address . . . the ability to provide public facilities and public services in a manner that does not permit low-density sprawl (RCW § 36.70A.070(5)).

The amended legislation resembles Oregon's provisions for unincorporated urban communities (see the next subsection), though it is addressed as more intensive rural development rather than recognized for what it appears to be to me, urban development. This is a paradox in the sense that the "more intensive rural" development with facilities and services is probably "urban" development, but is addressed in the rural element. More intensive rural development differs from the notion of "new fully contained communities" found elsewhere in GMA. This provision of GMA will almost certainly require some elaboration (by rule or case law) of what constitutes more intensive rural development contained by a logical boundary that discourages low-density rural sprawl.

New towns and satellite cities

One method of accommodating future urban growth at the regional scale is to direct future growth into new towns or satellite cities several miles from the core urban area. Florida's rule provides that the concept of a "new town" or "rural activity center," if incorporated into a land use plan, is a method of land use management that will meet the need to discourage urban sprawl (FAC § 9J-5.006(5)). The rule defines "new town" in part as follows:

> "New town" means a new urban activity center and community designated on the future land use map and located within a rural area or at the rural-urban fringe, clearly functionally distinct or geographically separated from existing urban areas and other new towns. A new town shall be of sufficient size, population and land use composition to support a variety of economic and social activities consistent with an urban area designation (FAC § 9J-5.003).

Georgia's rules do not provide any references to managing urban growth, and they are neutral with respect to urban form. Oregon's land use statute and administrative rules do not mention new towns as an option for urban form. Regional land use agencies may still consider satellite cities as an alternative growth management technique, as the Metropolitan Service District (1994) has done for the Portland region UGB.

Though it is not an identical concept, Oregon's administrative rules recognize and address the concept of an "unincorporated urban community" (UUC). Essentially, a UUC is defined as a mixed-use center with at least 150 dwelling units served by community water and sewer (OAR § 660-22-010). Boundaries of UUCs must be shown on the county's comprehensive land use map (OAR § 660-22-020). UUCs are viewed more as preexisting growth conditions to be accommodated in the plan than as new locations for future urban growth. For instance, the unincorporated communities rule provides that "all statewide planning goals applicable to cities shall also apply to UUCs, except for those goal provisions relating to urban growth boundaries and related requirements regarding the accommodation of long-term need for housing and employment growth." The rule also provides, however, that certain UUCs can be expanded to accommodate long-term urban land needs if they meet certain conditions (OAR § 660-22-040).

Hence, in theory, the UUC might serve as a satellite city concept that discourages urban sprawl in much the same way as envisioned in Florida.

Washington's administrative rules are similar to Florida's in that they recognize something similar to satellite cities or new towns—"new fully contained communities" (WAC § 365-195-335). Unlike Oregon's UUCs, which apparently cannot be created anew, counties in Washington may authorize new fully contained communities located outside the UGAs initially designated in their plans. A county doing so, however, must reserve a portion of the 20-year population projection for allocation to such communities and it must reduce the UGA accordingly (WAC § 365-195-335). Hence, Washington's new fully contained communities are more akin to Florida's new towns concept than Oregon's UUCs because new community reserves in Washington must accommodate some of the land supply that would otherwise be provided by UGAs.

Innovative land use management techniques

One of the criticisms of state enabling statutes for planning and zoning is that they are not modern enough (see APA 1996a) to authorize use of the more innovative land use controls now in practice in the United

States. Table 9.4 provides the results of my content search of state statutes and administrative rules for innovative land use and growth management techniques. These techniques deserve some explanation and elaboration.

Florida's rules specifically encourage innovative land use planning techniques, such as urban villages, new towns, satellite communities, cluster subdivisions, and mixed-use development that allows rural and agricultural lands to be developed. These are recognized land use controls for discouraging sprawl (FAC § 9J-5.006(5)). Washington's law also provides for innovative land use techniques such as density bonuses, cluster housing, planned unit developments, and the transfer of development rights (RCW § 36.70A.090). Oregon's land use law does not contain a section on innovative land use techniques, although guidelines for its goals suggest use of similar tools, including fee acquisition, easements, cluster developments, preferential assessment, and development rights acquisition. Georgia's rules do not identify any specific innovative land use regulations.

The results of the content search indicate that, if one excludes Georgia, there is some consistency between and among the states in their prescription or encouragement of innovative land use techniques. Infill development strategies are the only technique provided in the grab bag of growth management tools available to local governments in all four states. Mixing land uses is a technique specifically identified in Florida, Oregon, and Washington. Georgia's rule mentions mixed land uses but tacitly discourages it by not recognizing it as a category in the state's standard land use classification system. Georgia's mandate designers did not intentionally discourage mixed use; this provision was probably included out of concern that local governments could use a mixed category for odd combinations of land use, thereby frustrating the standard land use classification system. Florida, Oregon, and Washington encourage cluster development and PUDs. New towns, a concept discussed in the preceding subsection, is a recognized growth management technique in Florida and Washington.

The concept of "jobs-housing balance" is mentioned in the administrative rules of Florida, Oregon, and Washington, though the concept is not fully developed in any of these states. Essentially, jobs-housing balance means that the number of jobs and the number of houses should be roughly equal (1:1 ratio) in a given community or region. This point, as

Table 9.4. Land Use and Growth Management Techniques Specified in State Statutes and Administrative Rules: Florida, Georgia, Oregon, and Washington

Land Use or Urban Growth Management Technique	Florida	Georgia	Oregon	Washington
Cluster housing, cluster developments	✔	Not found.	✔ Guidelines, Goals 5 and 8; OAR 660-6-02; -12-045, -21-040.	✔ RCW § 36.70A.070, .090. WAC 365-195-310.
Planned unit developments	✔	✷	✔ ORS 197.200, .360. OAR 660-19-005.	✔ RCW 36.70A .030, .090, .360. WAC 365-195-210, -330, -830.
Infill development strategies	✔	✔	✔ ORS 197.296. OAR 660-04 -022, -12-045, 22-040, 22-050.	✔ WAC 365-195-070
Mixed land uses	✔	✷	✔ OAR 660-12-005	✔ WAC 365-195-310
New towns or new fully contained communities	✔	Not found.	Not found. But see OAR 660-22 regarding unincorporated urban communities	✔ RCW 36.70A.350. WAC 365-195-210, -335, -830.
Minimum densities	✔	Not found.	✔ ORS 197.296; OAR 660-12-035	Not found.
Specific, subarea, or refinement plans	Not found.	Not found.	✔ ORS 197.200.	✔ RCW 36.70A.080, .130, .500. WAC 365-195-345.
Urban service areas (infrastructure extension)	✔	Not found.	Not found.	Not found, but see urban growth area.
Urban growth areas or boundaries	✔	Not found.	✔	✔
Urban reserves	Not found.	Not found.	✔ OAR 660-21	✔ WAC 365-195-335
Concurrency provisions	✔	Not found.	Not found.	✔ RCW 36.70A.070, .500. WAC 365-195-510, -835.

Table 9.4. Land Use and Growth Management Techniques Specified in State Statutes and Administrative Rules: Florida, Georgia, Oregon, and Washington (Continued)

Land Use or Urban Growth Management Technique	Florida	Georgia	Oregon	Washington
Jobs-housing balance	✔	Not found.	✔ OAR 660-12-035	✔ RCW 36.70A.350
Transfer of development rights	✔	Not found.	✱✱ Guidelines, Goals 5 and 8.	✔ RCW 36.70A.060, .090. WAC 365-195-400.
Purchase of development rights	✔	Not found.	✱✱ Guidelines, Goals 5 and 8.	✔ RCW 36.70A.060
Traditional neighborhood developments	✔	Not found.	Not found but see OAR 660-12	Not found.

Notes:
✱ Provided only within the context of land use classification—not specifically encouraged as a technique.
✱✱ "development rights acquisition and similar techniques"

Sources: Florida Administrative Code § 9J-5.006(5). Georgia DCA Rule § 110-12-1-.04. Others as noted in table.

well as the proper geographic unit (region, city, subarea) on which to measure the jobs-housing ratio, are subject to scholarly debate.

In Florida, jobs-housing balance is one of several land use management techniques identified by the state as furthering the goal of reducing urban sprawl (FAC § 9J-5.006(5)). Oregon's transportation planning rule (OAR § 660-12-035) requires that local governments in MPO areas of larger than 1,000,000 population (i.e., the Portland region) consider and evaluate jobs-housing balance as an alternative in transportation system planning. Washington's law describes jobs-housing balance within the context of new fully contained communities (RCW § 36.70A.350).

Two of the best known urban growth management tools are UGBs (or UGAs) and concurrency provisions (or adequate public facilities requirements). Oregon's UGBs and Washington's UGAs are urban containment policies. Florida's law identifies UGBs as a land development regulation that will discourage urban sprawl. Florida, however, does not mandate UGBs. There have been discussions of putting UGBs in place, but they "just would not go" in Florida; Martin County appears to be the only county in the state that employs UGBs (Quinn and Noll

Sidebar 9.3. Jobs-Housing Balancing in Oregon: A Worthwhile Policy?

Oregon has a state policy supportive of jobs-housing balances in its communities. The governor's Community Solutions Team has adopted an objective which reads: "Support development that provides for a balance of jobs and housing within a community to reduce the need to commute long distances between home and work; thereby minimizing personal commuting costs and the costs to society of expanding the transportation infrastructure." Moreover, reducing vehicle miles traveled (VMT) is an important objective of Oregon's transportation planning rule. In addition to purported reductions in vehicle miles traveled, other assumed benefits of attaining jobs/housing balances in communities include reduced tail-pipe emissions, reduced urban sprawl, lower energy consumption, promotion of social equity objectives (i.e., reduced class segregation), and "urbanistic benefits" such as the ability to create "interesting, pedestrian-oriented places" (Cervero 1991, 1989).

Oregon has pursued this policy without any significant research that substantiates the underlying logic of the jobs-housing policy. The absence of research prompted me and another graduate student to research the following propositions: (1) Are Oregon's communities balanced with respect to jobs and housing?; and (2) Do jobs/housing balanced communities have shorter (statistically significant) commute times than unbalanced communities?

We composed a data set consisting of 87 cities with populations of 2,500 or more. No precise, accepted, operational definition of jobs/housing balance exists. After conducting a literature review, we concluded that a community should be considered balanced if its jobs/household ratio falls within a range from 1.4:1 to 1.8:1. This range of balanced jobs-household ratios approximates that used by Reid Ewing (1996). Using this range of balanced communities, we found the following: In 1990 there were 11 Oregon cities that were "jobs-rich" (a jobs/households ratio of 1.81:1 or more), including the cities of Beaverton, Bend, Grants Pass, Hood River, Klamath Falls, and Roseburg; 17 cities were "balanced" (a jobs-household ratio of 1.4:1 to 1.8:1), including Corvallis, Eugene, McMinnville, Medford, Portland, and Salem; 46 were "jobs deficient" (ratios of from 0.8:1 to 1.39:1); and 13 were "jobs poor/ bedroom cities" (ratio of less than 0.8:1). The bedroom cities are mostly located in close proximity to regional employment centers and include Cornelius, Keizer, Sutherlin, Talent, West Linn, and Winston.

Jobs-housing balanced communities should have the lowest mean travel times to work. Using 1990 census data for cities, we found statistically significant but weak differences in mean travel times of balanced versus unbalanced communities. For Oregon cities of between 2,500 and 10,000 population in 1990, the mean travel time to work for balanced communities was significantly less, by about two minutes, than the mean travel time to work for unbalanced communities. Although our jobs/households ratio (i.e., the independent variable) is significant, it has low correlation with mean travel time to work (i.e., the dependent variable). The jobs/housing balance variable explained only seven percent of the variation in mean travel time to work among Oregon communities with populations of less than 10,000. Furthermore, the relationship between the variables was not significant for Oregon's cities of more than 10,000. Hence, we were unable to conclude that jobs/housing balances lead to reductions in vehicle miles traveled (using mean commute times as a proxy), but the results of our statistical tests do lend some support to the logic of Oregon's jobs/housing balance policy.

Source: Weitz, Jerry, and Tim Schindler. 1997. "Are Oregon's Communities Balanced? A Test of the Jobs-Housing Balance Policy and the Impact of Balance on Mean Commute Times." Unpublished.

interview, 2/18/98). The city of Stuart, Florida, has drawn a fairly compact line around urban growth, according to Jim Quinn, chief of state planning for DCA. Quinn, however, also notes that Stuart is annexing outside of its UGB, a practice that is prohibited in Washington and, unless a goal exception is achieved, in Oregon. Although UGBs are rare in Florida, some cities and counties use a similar, but certainly not identical tool, urban service boundaries.

The "concurrency" policy lies at the heart of Florida's growth management program. Concurrency is a topic I have written about elsewhere (Weitz 1997a). Washington has borrowed the concurrency concept and applied it to transportation facilities. Oregon's DLCD has studied the concept of concurrency and encourages its use (Henderson, Young & Co. 1996; EcoNorthwest et al. 1995a, 1995b; Oregon DLCD 1992), but it has not mandated that local governments apply concurrency to any of its facilities and services.

A technique that supplements the use of UGBs or UGAs is the urban reserve. The idea behind urban reserves is to identify land outside of a UGB or UGA that is appropriate for long-range urban development and should therefore eventually be included in the UGB when additional land supply is necessary. Oregon's administrative rules (OAR § 660-21) require urban reserves only for certain areas of the state. They are optional in other areas. If designated, urban reserves must generally be contiguous to UGBs (Weitz and Moore 1998).

The concept of zoning has in one sense been "turned on its head" with the notion of establishing minimum rather than maximum development densities. In addition to being concerned about too much bulk and density in various zones, state and local governments are now concerned about the underbuilding of the maximum densities, the underutilization of infrastructure in certain areas, and the inefficiency associated with building at densities less than those prescribed in future land use plans. One response to this problem is to add minimum density regulations to the maximum density provisions traditionally required by local zoning ordinances. Oregon's transportation planning rule identifies minimum densities as a tool to support transportation oriented developments (OAR § 660-12-035). Also, an addition to Oregon's land use law in 1995 (House Bill 2709, ORS § 197.296) suggests that minimum density zoning is one technique to conserve urban land and thereby reduce the need to expand UGBs. Florida's antisprawl rule also lists minimum densities as a tool to discourage urban sprawl. As noted before, Washington's DCTED is required by July 1998 to identify certain measures, within the context of land supplies in UGAs, to ensure consistency between actual development and planned densities. If Washington follows Oregon as it did with its "buildable lands" legislation, then minimum densities will likely be one of the tools identified by DCTED.

The subarea, neighborhood, or in Oregon's case "refinement" plan is a tool recognized in the Pacific Northwest. Oregon's law provides that "a local government may convene a land use proceeding to adopt a refinement plan for a neighborhood or community within its jurisdiction and inside the urban growth boundary" (ORS § 197.200). Washington law indicates subarea plans are an optional element of comprehensive plans, but if prepared subarea plans must be consistent with the comprehensive plan" (RCW § 36.70A.080).

CONCLUSIONS

Each of the four states provides a land use goal to guide the preparation of land use elements of local comprehensive plans. Excluding Oregon, the other three states describe in significant detail that existing and future land use maps must be prepared according to certain specified categories. Plans in all four states are expected to include land use analyses and goals, policies, and objectives.

Georgia's 1989 planning act does not provide any direct or implicit mandate that local governments guide urban form. The lack of a mandate to address urban sprawl, and indeed the absence of a firm mandate that local governments adopt comprehensive plans, is attributed to the state's historically "minimalist" and "deliberately nonintrusive" approach and its strong tradition of local home rule (Whorton 1989). Florida and Washington, on the other hand, have adopted laws that specifically refer to "sprawl" and direct local governments to prevent it. Florida has adopted an antisprawl rule that elaborates substantially on the definition and characteristics of urban sprawl and the types of tools available to discourage it.

Oregon's land use law provides a strong urban containment mandate with its references to UGBs, though it does not use the term urban sprawl. Washington's GMA enunciates a goal to contain urban growth and prevent sprawl. That state recently (1997) required that boundaries be placed around more intensive rural development areas, if counties choose to recognize them in rural elements of comprehensive plans.

A variety of techniques exist to manage land use in a manner that decreases the prospects that sprawl will occur. In addition to containment strategies and concurrency, these include: infill development, mixed uses, jobs-housing balance, new towns, transfer of development rights, urban reserves, and minimum densities.

Florida has adopted administrative rules that make that state an undisputed leader in the movement to combat urban sprawl. No other state has defined urban sprawl, organized a method to determine its existence, identified a comprehensive set of growth management tools to mitigate it, and reviewed local comprehensive plans to determine whether they discourage it. Washington has taken important steps in that direction, with the implementation of UGAs and with new requirements that county rural elements contain sprawl. Washington also is destined to go further in the interpretation of its new rural element requirements. Oregon has had a 25-year history of urban containment but has nevertheless sought new tools to further manage urban growth. It will be interesting to observe how the growth management programs in the four states further evolve in their efforts to guide local land use planning and manage urban growth.

CHAPTER

10

Funding and Technical Assistance

State growth management programs to some extent must build the capacities and capabilities of local governments to prepare comprehensive plans that meet state mandates. Support, consisting mostly of funding and technical assistance to achieve local comprehensive land use planning, is the third and final component of state-sponsored land use planning to be described here. Although support functions are considered simultaneously with other components when designing the program, and can evolve simultaneously with the establishment of program structure and standards, support functions are generally the last of the three program components to evolve. In developing systems of state-sponsored land use planning, the state first establishes the mandate and program structure. Second, the state promulgates standards for planning. Finally, support programs are further defined and implemented.

The local government views funding and technical assistance as incentives or enticements to plan, if not as absolute necessities. Regional planning agencies, where they exist, view local planning mandates and support resources as means to subsist and assert extraterritorial considerations in the planning process. The mandate designer and state program analyst view technical assistance programs as an intergovernmental service delivery system that translates program goals into successful implementation experiences. Here, I attempt to incorporate the perspectives of local, regional, and state participants in the description of the evolution of state technical assistance programs.

Scholars have not studied technical assistance components of state growth management programs to any significant degree. Burby and May's (1997) work, however, signifies an increase in attention to the role of incentive-based mandate designs, of which technical assistance and capacity building are central features. This chapter describes the evolution of the structures and program features that support local and regional comprehensive planning in the four states.

It is worthwhile to summarize here the findings and conclusions about funding and technical assistance that were established in earlier chapters. In Chapter 3, I found that Florida and Oregon provided funding for local planning, but that technical assistance programs were not well developed and local government planning efforts were slow to develop during the quiet revolution. In Florida, during the second wave of program evolution, state funding of local planning was initially insufficient but substantially bolstered after the state revamped its growth management statutes. During the second wave of state growth management program history, state program analysts further recognized the need for state land use inventories and information databases and the necessity of building the capacity of local governments to plan (Chapter 4). In Chapter 5, I concluded that third-wave programs in Georgia and Washington overshadowed their counterparts with an increased emphasis on capacity- and commitment-building features, and that local planning occurred at faster paces than under the coercive approaches implemented in Florida and Oregon. In sum, formalized technical assistance programs and attention to local government capacity-building are hallmarks of the third wave of state growth management program evolution.

My content analysis of state growth management statutes (Chapter 7) indicates that statutes in Florida and Georgia specifically provide for funding of regional plans; only Washington's law enunciates an intention to provide funding of local comprehensive plans; and statutes in Florida, Georgia, and Washington mandate that programs of technical assistance for local planning be provided by the administering state agencies (and in Florida and Georgia, through regional planning agencies). Oregon's law is basically silent regarding funding, and it is only permissive rather than directive with respect to establishing a program of local planning technical assistance.

This chapter further develops my proposition that the provision of technical assistance has increased as state growth management programs have evolved. Georgia's and Washington's programs, as representatives of the third wave of growth management program history, have more formal technical assistance programs that occupy a central position in their incentives-based mandate designs. This heightened awareness of the need for technical assistance is evidenced by the numbers of "how to" documents prepared by Georgia DCA's Office of Coordinated Planning and Washington DCTED's Growth Management Division.

SUPPORT DURING THE QUIET REVOLUTION

Funding for Florida's 1972 land and water legislation

DeGrove (1984, 122-123) finds that funding levels for Florida's 1972 land and water legislation (Florida Statutes Chap. 380) "have not been so low as to seriously cripple the implementation of the law, but they have not been adequate to fully use the policy initiatives embedded in the [state's early] legislation." In 1974, the Bureau of Land and Water Management received funding for 11 new positions (in addition to eleven existing ones), and RPCs received $1 million for DRI functions under Chapter 380 (DeGrove 1984, 125). On the other hand, DeGrove finds that the bureau "has never been staffed adequately to perform the tasks that have been assigned to it" (149), that RPCs were poorly funded (162), and that funding weaknesses resulted in totally inadequate monitoring and enforcement of Chapter 380 activities (171). Accordingly, DeGrove (1984, 166) concludes that it is difficult to determine whether implementation of the land and water legislation received adequate funding and staffing.

Funding for Florida's 1975 local planning requirements

DCA's Division of Technical Assistance in 1977 requested $2 million for the partial funding of the Local Government Comprehensive Planning Act. In making this request, the division noted that that amount was far short of the total cost of implementing the act by local governments, which was estimated at $16 million (Florida DCA 1977b). The 1977 state legislature however, appropriated only $750,000 for local planning funds, which were allocated by DCA to 64 local governments. DCA requested $1.7 million for local government planning grants in fiscal year 1978-79 (Florida DCA 1977c), but again the legislature did not match the request. The 1978 legislature appropriated only $717,000

(Florida DCA 1978a). DCA awarded grants during fiscal year 1978-79 to 73 cities and 12 counties (Florida DCA 1978b).

Technical assistance for Florida's 1975 local planning requirements

After the legislature adopted the Local Government Comprehensive Planning Act (1975), DCA established a Division of Technical Assistance. In 1976 the division sponsored a series of workshops to assist local officials in meeting the requirements of the act. DCA also prepared a 20-minute slide show covering the basic provisions of the act (Florida DCA 1976c, 1976d), a short publication summarizing the requirements of the 1975 act (Florida DCA 1976a), and a more detailed guide to the act for local officials (KRS Associates, Inc. 1976). Hence, DCA immediately followed the 1975 local planning mandate with agency reorganization for technical assistance and production of training sessions and guidebook materials.

Funding for planning in Oregon

The local government comprehensive planning grant program administered by LCDC "lies at the heart of Oregon's land use program" (Oregon JLCLU 1976, 6). Oregon's Governor McCall asked in 1974 for $1.7 million for the land use program, but the legislature appropriated just over $600,000. LCDC, however, has had what most consider adequate start-up funds (DeGrove 1984, 248-249). Also, substantial sums of money were earmarked for local planning grants in Oregon. Two types of local grants were established: planning coordination grants divided equally among counties to coordinate planning by cities and agencies within county boundaries; and planning assistance grants distributed by successful application for comprehensive planning tasks (Oregon JLCLU 1976, 5). By 1976, LCDC had made 152 grants to 123 cities and 29 counties (DeGrove 1984, 261). Oregon was generous with its planning assistance grants to local government during the quiet revolution and in the interlude that followed. For the 1975-1977 biennium, planning assistance grants totaled more than $3 million (Oregon JLCLU 1976, 22). Local comprehensive plans, however, were still slow to develop. Despite some $18 million in planning assistance and coordination grants channeled to local governments by 1980, only 94 (34 percent) of the 277 cities and counties in the state had approved plans (DeGrove 1984, 263).

Leonard (1983, 10) reviews budget summaries for LCDC and finds that approximately $30 million ($18 million from the state and $12 million in federal funds) had been spent on the land use program through 1981, about 80 percent of which was passed on to local governments in the form of planning assistance grants and coordination grants. Administrative costs were on the increase and accounted for 30 percent of the 1981-1983 biennium budget for LCDC due to heavy staff needs to review and acknowledge local plans (Leonard, 1983, 29, note 25).

Leonard's work reveals a high reliance on federal coastal zone management program dollars to fund local planning in Oregon's coastal areas. Florida's program also apparently has made extensive use of coastal zone management program dollars, given its coastal land use requirements and accelerated compliance schedules for coastal jurisdictions. The high reliance on federal coastal funds raises the question whether such federal funds were a prerequisite for the successful implementation of growth management programs in coastal states. Indeed, DeGrove (1984) has noted that virtually all of the state land use programs adopted by the early 1980s were in coastal states.

Technical assistance for planning in Oregon

According to DeGrove (1984, 259), during the first two-thirds of 1975 LCDC spent substantial time considering the appropriate content of a handbook for local governments to use in preparing comprehensive plans. The handbook, titled *Oregon Land Use Handbook*, was distributed in December 1975 to local governments for use in measuring comprehensive plans against state requirements and in applying for extensions and grant funds (Oregon JLCLU 1976, 2). The JLCLU in its 1976 final report expressed satisfaction with the "rapid progress" made by local governments in completing comprehensive plans and the quality of the state's performance in administering the program (Oregon JLCLU 1976, 4). As I have already noted, progress toward adopting local plans actually was quite slow, and the committee's final report was probably designed as a pep talk for local governments and as a justification for continuing the young land use program.

SUPPORT DURING THE SECOND WAVE

Funding for regional planning in Florida

Legislation passed in Florida in 1980 required regional plans. Since no money was provided, however, regional plans were not prepared. Upon passage of the Florida State and Regional Planning Act (1984), the legislature appropriated $5.5 million over three years to assist RPCs in completing their assigned tasks. Comprehensive regional policy plans were due for submission to the Governor's Office of Planning and Budgeting by November 30, 1986 (Florida DCA 1986a). Also in 1984, as a result of the passage of the State and Regional Planning Act, the Florida legislature appropriated substantial additional funds to increase the number of positions and capacities in the state land planning agency (DeGrove 1992, 12).

Funding for local planning in Florida

Compared with the financial assistance provided to local governments for planning under the 1975 act, the Florida legislature's appropriations were much more generous after passage of the 1985 Omnibus GMA. A total of $8.8 million was appropriated for fiscal year 1986-87, including $800,000 specially earmarked for 22 interior rural counties (Lewis 1986). DCA reserved $400,000 of the total appropriation to provide a bonus for early grant application submissions and to fund special projects subject to the DCA secretary's discretion (Florida DCA 1986b). For fiscal year 1987-88, the legislature allocated $9 million for state assistance to local planning programs. Of that total, a reserve fund of $525,295 was available on a discretionary basis for special projects (Florida DCA 1987c). Beginning in September 1987, DCA also began advertising to fill seven new planner positions to provide technical assistance and review plans (Florida DCA 1987d). For fiscal year 1988-89, DCA had $1,830,000 to assist noncoastal municipalities in meeting the requirements of GMA. Of that total, $670,000 was reserved by DCA's secretary for special projects needed to meet the minimum criteria for comprehensive plans (Florida DCA 1988b). As of 1989, DCA's local government comprehensive planning assistance program had awarded $22.6 million to local governments to develop comprehensive plans (Pelham 1989a).

A summary of funding for local planning under the 1985 local planning legislation is provided in Table 10.1 below.[1] As noted in Chapter 4, DCA gave priority to coastal cities and counties (i.e., established earlier deadlines for those areas). It is likely that the funds listed in Table 10.1 include money from the coastal zone management act, given their disaggregation in their original source (see note below Table 10.1).

Scholars also have made note of Florida's funding levels for local comprehensive planning. Fulton (1991) found that approximately $30 million was appropriated to fund local government planning efforts as required by GMA. Funding for DCA was enough to support 40 new full-time positions, 21 for the local planning and land regulation program, 15 for the DRI program, and four for administration of the new Apalachicola Bay Protection Act. A shortage of experienced local and regional planners was anticipated, and the University of Miami recommended direct funding by DCA to train additional planners (Stroud and O'Connell 1986).

Table 10.1. Allocated Funds for Local Comprehensive Planning and Compliance Agreements in Florida: 1985-1988

Fiscal Year	Counties	Coastal Municipalities	Noncoastal Municipalities	Compliance Agreements	Total Allocated Funds
1985-1986	$2,052,289	$0	$0	$0	$2,052,289
1986-1987	$3,460,000	$4,940,000	$0	$0	$8,400,000
1987-1988	$1,472,660	$5,195,669	$1,806,376	$0	$8,474,705
1988-1989	$0	$0	$1,830,000	$340,000	$2,170,000

Notes: Figures do not include funding to newly created communities. Disaggregation of funds by coastal and noncoastal provided in the original are not included here in total. For example, the original source breaks down counties and municipalities in coastal counties by coastal and noncoastal. I suggest that probably was done because it was important to keep account of Coastal Zone Management Act funds which were eligible to be spent only by coastal cities and counties. If that is true, then coastal municipalities obtained both coastal and noncoastal funds for local planning.

Source: Florida Department of Community Affairs, Division of Community Assistance (not dated). One-page summary titled "Allocated funds for local government comprehensive planning and land development regulations," obtained 2/18/98 from Jim Quinn, chief, Bureau of State Planning.

Technical assistance: Florida's 1985 act

As early as March 1986, DCA announced its intentions to provide technical assistance to local governments in meeting the requirements of the act. That year, DCA's Bureau of Local Resource Planning produced a detailed guide to population estimation and projection techniques (Florida DCA 1986c) and a guide to local government comprehensive planning data sources (Florida DCA 1986d). Since then, the comprehensive planning data sources publication has been updated at least twice (e.g., see Florida DCA 1997c).

Model plans and ordinances were proposed to be completed as soon as the legislature adopted the administrative rules for plan review (Florida DCA 1986e). A model plan element for each of the required comprehensive plan elements was produced in 1987, including, for example, the model future land use element for Adams County (Florida DCA

1987a; Einsweiler 1987). Also in 1987, DCA produced a publication on "practical considerations in meeting Florida's local planning requirements" (Florida DCA 1987b). Incidentally, the selected references provided in that "practical considerations" piece are of academic interest because the citations reflect which pieces of land use planning literature were influential in practice. For instance, the publication cites several works including Branch (1988), Burchell and Listokin (1978), Catanese and Synder (1979), Kent (1964; see 1990), Krueckeberg and Silvers (1974), Smith (1979), and perhaps the best known of all, the planning "green book" (So et al., eds. 1979; see 1988). Hence, in just two years DCA produced model elements, population projection techniques, a guide to data sources, and a guide to practical considerations in preparing a local comprehensive plan. One must conclude from these documents, available for review by me, that Florida's technical assistance program for local comprehensive planning did a thorough job of producing resources for local planning.

Funding and technical assistance for local planning in Oregon

As noted in Chapter 4, Oregon's governor appointed a Task Force on Land Use in 1981. Gov. Vic Atiyeh's outline of the charge to the task force included an investigation of the problems of plan implementation, including a discussion of "continued and/or enhanced state financial assistance to local governments" (Oregon Governor's Task Force on Land Use 1982, 4). The task force's final report, which anticipates the postacknowledgment phase, recommends that DLCD "should provide assistance through its county coordinators and/or field representatives" (14). Other relevant recommendations of the task force include that consideration be given to establishing standards of education and experience for planners, developing a shared technical assistance program where unacknowledged jurisdictions receive direct help, and continuing funding for the development, implementation, and monitoring of local plans and plan amendments (24).

Though not addressed indepth, *Planning the Oregon Way* (Abbott, Howe and Adler, eds. 1994) provides a perspective that is critical of the Oregon legislature's commitment to funding LCDC and the land use program. Knaap (1994) finds that Oregon's legislature has appropriated an average of $3.6 million each year to administer the land use program. He also finds that 56 percent of the total state appropriations were passed through to local governments for plans and implementation activities, mostly without strings attached.[2] Knaap (1994, 10-11) notes that local grants were provided at the expense of staffing reviews, monitoring, and research, and he finds that "this pattern of appropriations curtailed the influence of LCDC and preserved the influence of local governments over land use." Abbott (1994) provides some confirmation of the "pattern" found by Knaap, in that he cites an *Oregonian* editorial that criticized the Oregon legislature for cutting DLCD's request for more funds to complete the 1990-1991 urban growth management study. Similarly, Howe (1994) suggests that research programs in Oregon have not evolved because of severe limitations of funds by the legislature.

SUPPORT DURING THE THIRD WAVE

Funding for planning and land development regulations in Florida

In Florida, funding for local comprehensive plans and preparation of the plans themselves were largely complete by the beginning of the third era of program evolution in 1989. For the years 1990 and 1991, the Florida legislature appropriated $1.55 million to RPCs to perform local plan review, review plan amendments, and provide technical assistance, and provided an additional $822,500 for the diverse needs of RPCs. State funding for regional planning, however, was still considered insufficient because of numerous and diverse responsibilities assigned to RPCs (DeGrove 1992, 13-14). On the other hand, through the 1991 legislative session, some $44 million in planning support has gone to Florida's cities and counties.

Table 10.2 summarizes the state funding provided for the preparation of local land development regulations. For fiscal year 1989-90, the Florida legislature appropriated $220,000 to fund compliance agreements and more than $7 million to help prepare land development regulations (Florida DCA 1989e).

Florida's technical assistance for preparing land development regulations

By 1988, DCA already was looking beyond preparation of local comprehensive plans and toward the development of technical assistance for adopting land development regulations also required by the 1985 act. In 1988, DCA provided a grant to Citrus County to produce a set of land development regulations that could serve as a model for other local governments (Florida DCA 1988c). DCA also contracted in 1988 with a

Table 10.2. Allocated Funds for Local Land Development Regulations and Compliance Agreements in Florida: 1989-1991

Fiscal Year	Counties	Coastal Municipalities	Noncoastal Municipalities	Compliance Agreements	Total Allocated Funds
1989-1990	$2,193,428	$5,124,431	$85,125	$220,000	$7,622,984
1990-1991	$911,500	$561,200	$631,300	$480,000	$2,584,000
1991-1992	$698,900	$0	$1,094,100	$459,998	$2,252,998

Notes: Figures do not include funding to newly created communities. Disaggregation of funds by coastal and noncoastal provided in the original not included here in total.

Source: Florida Department of Community Affairs, Division of Community Assistance (not dated). One-page summary titled "Allocated funds for local government comprehensive planning and land development regulations," obtained 2/18/98 from Jim Quinn, chief, Bureau of State Planning.

junior college to establish a land use planning institute in northwest Florida. The institute held two workshops to train local planners in citizen involvement techniques and five workshops for local planning commissioners (Florida DCA 1989f). DCA conducted numerous one-day technical assistance workshops in 1989 to help local governments prepare or revise their land development regulations in accordance with statutory requirements (Florida DCA 1989g). The state agency also sponsored preparation of a model land development code for Florida cities and counties (DCA 1990c) and prepared a technical assistance paper on how to develop adoption ordinances for local comprehensive plans (Florida DCA 1991a).

Furthermore, DCA began publication of a periodical in 1986, known as *Technical Memo* and later renamed *Community Planning,* which announces agency news and publications and provides articles on local planning considerations. DCA's Division of Resource Planning also published a periodical in 1988-89 titled *Planning Notes* which served the same purposes. Perhaps the best known of these, because it was reprinted in DeGrove's (1991) edited collection of articles on growth management, was DCA's 1989 discussion on discouraging urban sprawl in a special issue of *Technical Memo* (Florida DCA 1991b). That special issue is also important because it signals the beginning of Florida DCA's onslaught against urban sprawl (see Pelham 1989b).

Funding for Florida's evaluation and appraisal reports

Upon funding the completion of land development regulations to implement comprehensive plans prepared pursuant to the 1985 act, Florida next required local governments to prepare and submit "evalua-

Figure 10.1. Florida's State-Sponsored Technical Assistance: Organization and Outputs

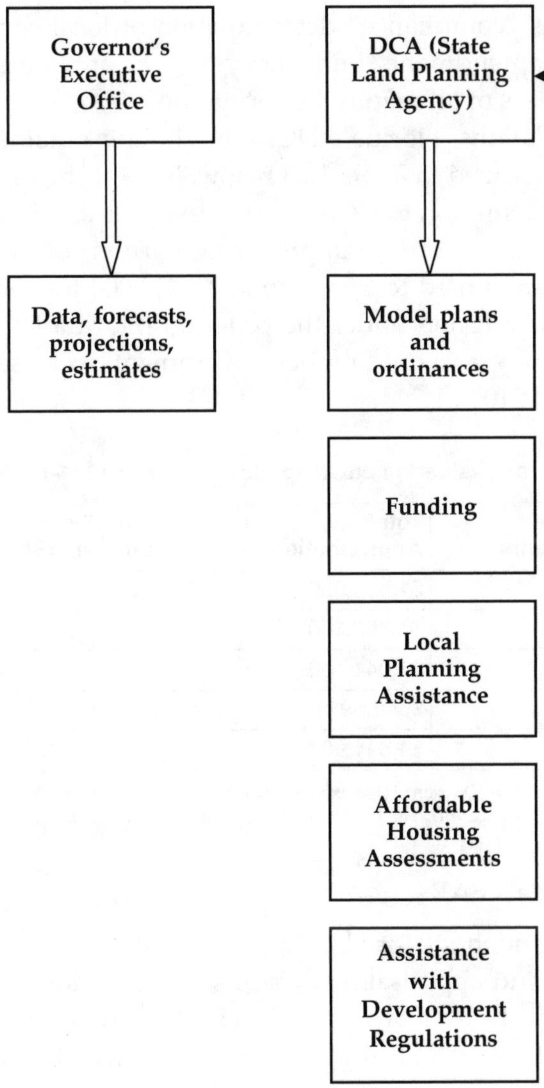

tion and appraisal reports" (EARs). EARs are periodic assessments of the success or failure of local plan implementation activities. DCA conducts "sufficiency" reviews of EARs, though that task can be delegated to the RPC with jurisdiction. The sufficiency review is formally distinguished in Florida from its "compliance" determination of local comprehensive plans and plan amendments. Sufficiency reviews are limited to an analysis of completeness of all required information.

As with plans and regulations, Florida's DCA sought and obtained funding for EARs, as summarized in Table 10.3 below. In 1994 the state legislature appropriated $1.8 million to DCA for the first year of a four-year program to assist local governments in preparing portions of their EARs. This appropriation amounted to approximately $20,000 for each of the 89 local governments affected under the program (Florida DCA 1994). In the next three fiscal years, funding per government decreased to $14,069, as shown in Table 10.3.

Table 10.3. Florida's Funding for Evaluation and Appraisal Reports: 1994-1997

Fiscal Year	Number of Governments	Total Appropriation ($)	Amount Per Government ($)
1994-1995	89	$1,800,000	$20,224
1995-1996	89	$1,252,190	$14,069
1996-1997	74	$1,041,106	$14,069
1997-1998	39	$548,691	$14,069
Total, four years	291	$4,641,987	—

Source: Florida Department of Community Affairs, Division of Resource Planning and Management (not dated). One-page summary titled "EAR Funding Assistance Program: Historical Funding," obtained on 2/18/98 from Jim Quinn, chief, Bureau of State Planning.

Technical assistance: Florida's EARs

In 1995, DCA published a guidebook for Florida's cities and counties on how to prepare evaluation and appraisal reports. A second edition was promptly published (Florida DCA 1996a). A "Checklist for EAR Sufficiency Review" (Florida DCA 1996b) also was prepared, which provides, in effect, a detailed 55-page evaluation form.

Funding Georgia's 1989 planning act

Georgia's OCP initially had broad responsibilities and a "modest" staff of 24, 13 of whom were transferred from other divisions of DCA (DeGrove 1992, 109). Initial funding for the 1989 planning act was close to the governor's request: $290,000 to the Department of Natural

Resources to develop standards and data; $775,000 to DCA to establish OCP; $2.6 million for RDCs; and $1.65 million for local grants (DeGrove 1992, 110).[3] DeGrove finds that funding levels decreased over time (see Table 10.4), leading him to conclude that reductions had cast some doubt on the timely and full implementation of Georgia's growth management program (DeGrove 1992, 113).

Table 10.4. Funding for Georgia's Planning Program: 1990-1992

Year	Funding for DCA	Funding for RDCs
1990	$1,610,268	$1,275,000
1991	$1,437,307	$1,225,014
1992	$888,111	$1,089,163

Source: DeGrove 1992, 113.

Georgia's program of local planning technical assistance

Georgia's OCP engaged in numerous, multifaceted efforts to provide technical assistance to local governments in preparing comprehensive plans. OCP published a set of seven "how to" planning guidebooks in the early 1990s. The titles of the seven initial guidebooks are *Preparing a Local Plan; Why Plan?; How to Organize for Local Planning; Using Data for Local Planning; Planning Assistance; Using Maps for Local Planning;* and *Implementation Tools for Comprehensive Planning* (Georgia DCA 1990a-c; 1991a-c; and 1994). Furthermore, OCP's list of publications expanded into topical areas of planning as well. One area especially emphasized was environmental planning in accordance with the environmental planning rules (discussed in Chapter 5). OCP produced a guidebook on how to address environmental planning criteria in plans (Georgia DCA 1991d), three model ordinances for protection of wetlands, water supply watersheds, and groundwater recharge areas, and other guidebooks on protecting river corridors and managing flood plains. OCP also produced two guidebooks on impact fees and one on mediation. All in all, Georgia's OCP produced more than a dozen guidebooks and three model ordinances to aid local governments in completing comprehensive plans and preparing implementing regulations.[4]

OCP's efforts were hardly limited to the production of guidebooks. Staff planners at OCP prepared a comprehensive plan for the city of Villa Rica to serve as an example of a minimum plan that would be found to comply with the state's local planning standards. As part of its funding scheme and work programs for RDCs, OCP also directed the

Figure 10.2. Georgia's State-Sponsored Technical Assistance: Organization and Outputs

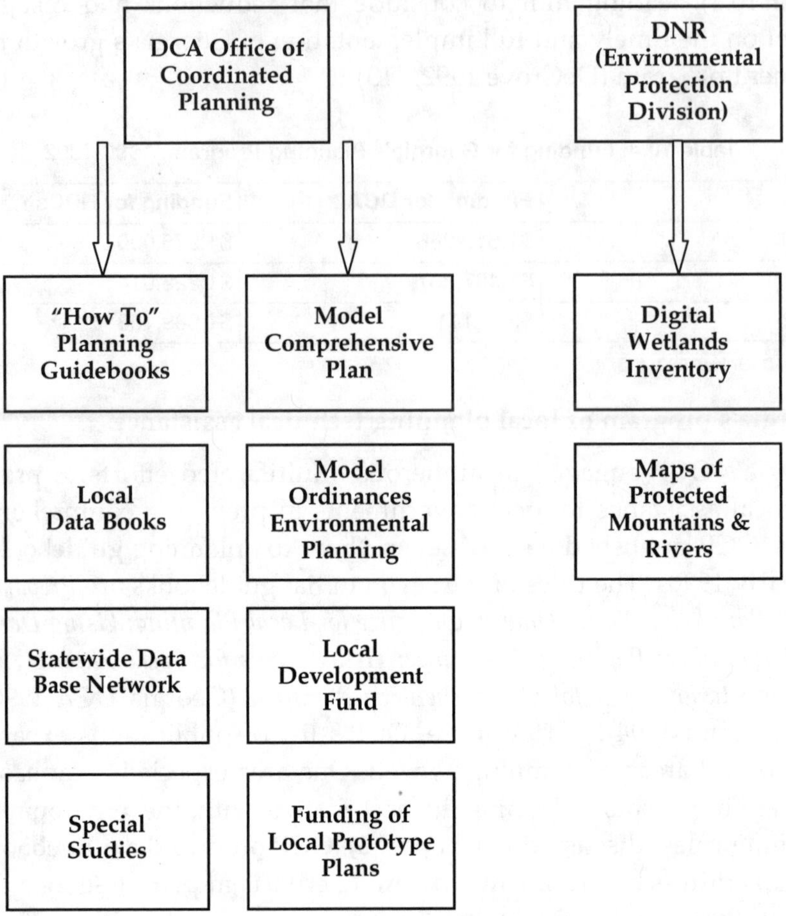

Sidebar 10.1. Financing Local Comprehensive Planning in the Georgia Mountains RDC Region

Georgia's Office of Coordinated Planning (OCP) did not provide direct grants to local governments to prepare plans. Instead, the state agency funded RDCs to provide local planning services. One of the more innovative ideas of OCP was to program the preparation by each RDC of a joint county-city prototype plan in the first years of the coordinated planning program. It was left to the discretion of the RDC as to which county-city(ies) would be selected for the prototype plan. The Georgia Mountains RDC selected Dawson County and Dawsonville for at least two reasons: First, it only had one city, so it was expected that the effort would be superior to a county plan encompassing several cities. Second, Dawson County was experiencing rapid population growth and was ready for local planning, in the judgement of the RDC. The prototype work resulted in the preparation of local comprehensive plans without direct cost to the local governments involved.

The 1989 Georgia Planning Act authorized RDCs to contract with local governments to prepare comprehensive plans. The terms of those contracts were left to the respective RDC and local government(s) to decide. The Georgia Mountains RDC decided early that state funds for local governments and the mandatory local government membership dues were insufficient to complete local comprehensive planning efforts. Other RDCs, incidentally, decided to prepare local plans without additional charge. Some of the counties thought our local planning budget estimates were high and that their membership dues should pay for the RDC to prepare the comprehensive plans. Other RDCs probably experienced similar sentiment and bowed to that argument.

As a result of the Georgia Mountains RDC's decision to charge for services, I (as a regional planner for the RDC) prepared work programs, project budget estimates, and contracts to prepare local comprehensive plans, including joint county-city plans for White, Banks, Franklin, Union, Towns and Hart counties as well as individual comprehensive plans for the cities of Dahlonega, Cumming, and Clarkesville. I recall we had contracts ranging from about $35,000 for White County (excluding the two cities within) in 1991 to approximately $60,000 for Franklin County including plans for its five municipalities in 1994. City contracts ranged from about $10,000 in Dahlonega to about $20,000 for Cumming and Clarkesville. Nearly every one of those budgets was underfunded, in which case the RDC used its general DCA funds to pay for staff time to complete the comprehensive planning programs.

As a nonprofit agency, we expected that our contract budgets would be significantly less than what would be proposed by private consultants. Over time, we gained more experience on actual costs of funding the entire local planning process, and our budget estimates tended to elevate as a result. Two counties in the region selected private consultants instead of RDC-proposed contracts for planning services. In the case of Rabun County and its several small cities, the RDC bid almost $70,000 for the job but lost it to a private consultant who proposed a much smaller budget for the local comprehensive planning effort. In the other case, Hall County and its municipalities, the county (with some reimbursement by cities) expended a total of approximately $350,000 for a team of consultants led by a Florida-based firm. The amount spent by Hall County in preparing the county-city comprehensive plans was more than double what the RDC estimated it would need to complete the project.

production of a "prototype" local comprehensive plan by each of the 18 RDC jurisdictions. For example, in the Georgia Mountains RDC region, Dawson County and the City of Dawsonville were selected by the RDC for preparing the prototype plan (see Sidebar 10.1). OCP's purpose in sponsoring production of the prototype plans was, besides stimulating plan preparation in its first full year of implementation, to ensure that the planning staffs of each RDC would possess the knowledge to prepare local comprehensive plans and to review local plans for compliance with minimum planning standards. To further promote that objective, OCP held training workshops on a quarterly basis for regional planners. Even though local planning was not required, OCP produced a "local planning data book" for each local government (see Sidebar 7.2). Finally, OCP published a "policy memo series" (Georgia DCA, 1991e, 1992b) and various newsletters and fact sheets on the planning program. Hence, Georgia's multifaceted technical assistance program consisted of guidebooks, model ordinances, newsletters, policy memorandums, fact sheets, an example of a comprehensive plan that met minimum standards, local prototype plans, training sessions for regional planners, and data guidebooks for individual local jurisdictions.

A new era of funding in Oregon

Besides DLCD's periodic review funding assistance grants, in 1993 DLCD and ODOT created the Transportation and Growth Management (TGM) Program (see Chapter 5). TGM designed and implemented a local grant program for three categories of activities: transportation system planning in accordance with the transportation planning rule (OAR § 660-12); projects that reexamine and amend local land use plans and ordinances to achieve transportation-efficient land use; and proposals to test and demonstrate new tools for urban growth management. Sidebar 10.2 summarizes representative grant projects sponsored by the TGM Program in its first biennium. As a member of the TGM team from 1994-1997, I managed category 2 and 3 grants and participated in policy development of new urban growth management tools.

Total funding for the TGM program was approximately $7 million for the fiscal 1993-95 biennium. More than 75 percent of the biennium's budget, or about $5.5 million, was from the federal government's Intermodal Surface Transportation Efficiency Act (ISTEA) funds. Twenty percent of the TGM Program's funding, or about $1.4 million, was from lottery proceeds in the 1993-1995 biennium. The remainder of the TGM Program's revenues came from general state funds. About $5 million (71 percent) of the TGM Program's $7 million in budgeted funds for 1993-1995 was distributed to cities, counties, metropolitan planning organizations and councils of governments. Approximately $1 million was expended for urban growth management grants (Oregon TGM Program 1994a).

Technical assistance in Oregon

The reader will recall that during the quiet revolution and the second wave, DLCD was not mandated by law to deliver technical planning assistance to local governments. Given other priorities, DLCD did not formally establish and implement a technical assistance program. DLCD's service delivery philosophy changed during the third wave of program evolution. With the introduction of the TGM Program and changes in the organization of staff, local government capacity-building became a recognized objective. Besides providing grants, TGM also initiated training and technical assistance to local officials and planners, as

Figure 10.3. Oregon's State-Sponsored Technical Assistance: Organization and Outputs

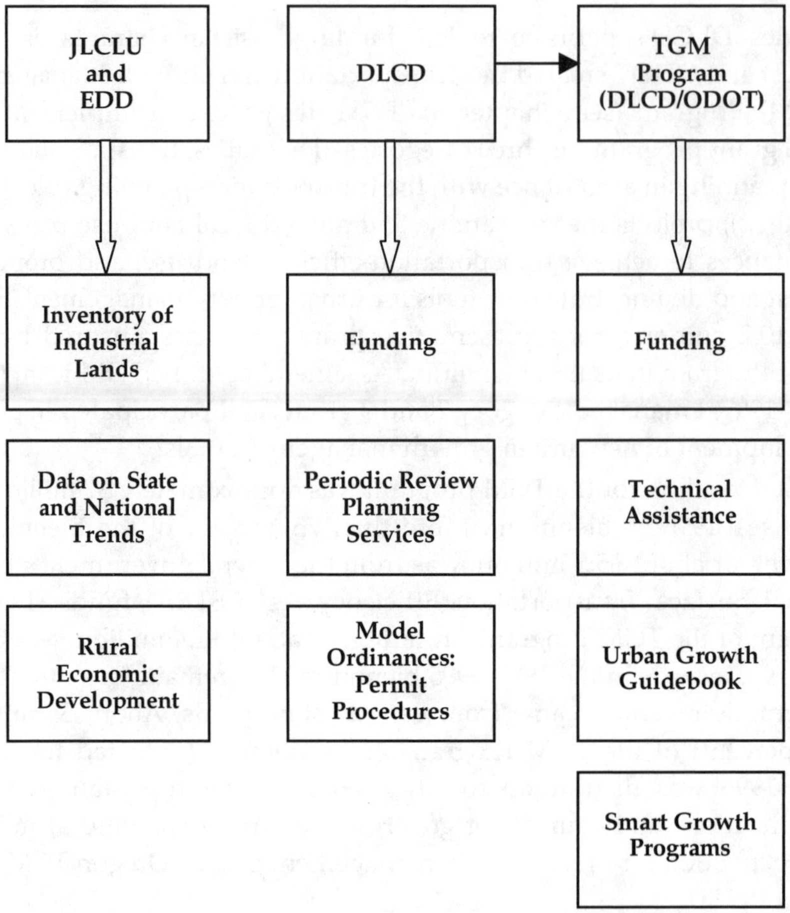

Sidebar 10.2. Summary of Selected TGM Program Grant Projects, 1993-1995

Summarized below are several transportation and growth management grants that the TGM Program provided to local, regional, and special district recipients. Each summary indicates the recipient, the title of the project, a brief description, and products.

Clackamas County, Sunnyside Village Center design plan

Detailed plan of the village center public improvements and transportation connections (transit, bike, pedestrian). Products: Sunnyside Village Area Source Book (design and standards); Funding for Various Street Segments/Sidewalks/Planting Strips and Street Trees.

Metropolitan Service District, parking area inventory

The Metro Regional Parking Plan develops a methodology and includes a count of nonresidential parking supply to meet the transportation planning rule requirement for a 10 percent per capita reduction in parking spaces. The final product arrives at a base count of 0.86 nonresidential parking spaces per capita in the region and includes a detailed set of maps outlining on-street and surface parking for the three-county area. The analysis includes a discussion of parking reduction strategies and support programs to be implemented in a 20-year time frame. Product: Regional Parking Management Program for Portland Metro Area.

Oak Lodge Sanitary District, model urban service agreements

The model agreements define the roles of cities, special districts and county for service delivery in North Clackamas County; define possible future service scenarios; and provide the next steps in SB 122 implementation. Product: North Clackamas Urban Services Agreement Project—Final Report.

Portland, Banfield light rail development opportunity site

This is a market-based master plan for a vacant light rail transit station site. The site is owned by ODOT and is being planned by the Portland Development Commission as a mixed-use transportation-efficient development. Product: Redevelopment Program: NE 60th and Glisan Transit Oriented Development Project.

Sandy, Canby, and North Plains Neighboring Cities 2040 project

This project is a joint effort between the cities of Sandy, Canby, North Plains and the Portland Metro regional government intended to develop agreements to protect the rural reserve areas and green corridors between the cities and the Portland regional UGB, while providing for a balanced growth plan for those neighboring cities. The focus of the project in Sandy is a new town plan with a neotraditional focus based on a "village concept" with mixed-use village cores and greater jobs/ housing balance, a draft transportation system plan, and draft comprehensive plan and ordinance amendments. Critical objectives of the Canby plan are attracting jobs, revising housing density, and evaluating public facility capacity deficiencies and costs. Products: Neighboring Cities 2040 Study; Draft Comprehensive Plan Language, city of Sandy; Draft Municipal Code Language, city of Sandy; Executive Summary—Statewide Planning Rule, city of Sandy; Public Involvement Publications, city of Sandy; Downtown Design Charette, city of Sandy; and Maps of Building Values in Rural Resources: Sandy, Canby, and North Plains.

Albany, North Albany area transportation system plan

This is a local street network plan in compliance with the transportation planning rule. Product: North Albany Street Network Plan; Street Design Standards and Guidelines.

Stayton, City Center revitalization plan

This is a model urban renewal plan and implementing strategies for infill/redevelopment. Products: Report on the Stayton City Center Urban Renewal Plan; Stayton City Center Urban Renewal Plan; Stayton City Center Design Report.

Lane Council of Governments, design principles for mixed uses and increased density

Policies, findings and guidelines for increasing densities for a livable environment with special emphasis on transit "nodal" development. Products: Design Team Citizen Involvement Program Report; Developing and Applying Redevelopment Potential Methodology—Project Report; Eugene-Springfield Metropolitan Area Transportation Plan—Summary Descriptions of Proposed Nodal Development Areas; Nodal Development Strategy Implementation Option—Working Paper; How Do We Grow From Here?—A Guide to Proposed Land Use Strategies and Design Concepts for the Eugene-Springfield Area Transportation Plan; A Comparison of Development Costs in Eugene/ Springfield: Standard Subdivisions vs. Nodal Development; Workshop Process, Key Findings and Recommendations.

Bend (et al.), develop land use alternatives

Growth strategies for less auto use in the cities of Bend and Redmond and Deschutes County and to provide the opportunity for alternative mode usage. The strategies identify techniques appropriate to small to medium cities to integrate transportation and land use policies that promote a balanced transportation system. Products: Resource document that includes a comparative analysis between the typical, post-WWII development pattern and development that employs the "new urbanism."

Source: Oregon Transportation and Growth Management Program. 1996. 1993-1995 Grant Program Catalog. Salem, OR: DLCD.

well as, "smart development" and "quick response" programs. These program components are described briefly below.

TGM hired consultants to conduct research, policy analysis, and grant evaluation on the urban growth management tools and to prepare a technical report and handbook describing urban growth management tools (ECONorthwest et al. 1995a; 1995b). Another consultant was hired to analyze adequate public facilities requirements (Henderson, Young & Co. 1996), prepare a model ordinance, and prepare a pilot test of focused public investment planning as an urban growth management tool in Medford, Oregon. Other policy development efforts and technical assistance activities were completed by TGM to strengthen urban growth management in Oregon's UGBs.

The purpose of the smart development program is to define, educate, advocate, certify, and award developments that are multimodal, pedestrian-friendly and generally transportation/ land use-efficient. The program also includes a component to remove regulatory obstacles and overcome financial obstacles (e.g., lending practices) to smart development. The quick response team is a group of pre-selected, pre-approved consultants who provide rapid response transportation-efficient design alternatives to development proposals. Upon request, a rapid response team is dispatched to assist communities and developers in meeting smart development design objectives (Oregon TGM Program 1994b; See Oregon TGM Program 1998). As noted in Chapter 5, TGM also produced a "how to" guidebook on meeting state legislation on housing needs assessments and buildable lands inventories in UGBs.

Funding Washington's GMA

In connection with GMA II, the Washington legislature appropriated more than $7 million for local comprehensive planning administered by DCD, and it provided another $1 million to DCD to provide planning-related technical assistance (DeGrove 1992, 124). Approximately $1.5 million was appropriated in fiscal year 1991 by the Washington Department of Transportation for the 12 regional transportation planning organizations (RTPOs) that were mandated by GMA and established by 1991. Funding in 1992 for GMA was reduced from the governor's recommendation of $6.8 million to $5.7 by the state legislature.

DCD's technical assistance program was in jeopardy in 1992, but the governor used his line-item veto to restore the allocation for the program along with $1.9 million to begin operating the three growth management hearings boards. Funds for the proposed environmental planning pilot projects, designed to coordinate GMA with the State Environmental Policy Act, were cut completely. DCD also lost two vacant positions in the growth management division, which totaled approximately 20 persons (DeGrove 1992, 134).

Table 10.5 provides a summary of growth management grants to local government awarded between 1991 and 1997. Over that six-year period, DCD/ DCTED provided more than $40 million in local growth management grants. Each county (or if not the county, a particular city within that county) received some amount of financial assistance from the growth management division of DCTED. Figures for individual counties, though not shown in Table 10.5, indicate that grant funding totals provided to individual counties (and the cities within) were in the millions of dollars. DCTED's grants to King County and its numerous municipalities totaled nearly $10 million over six years. During the same period, Pierce County and its cities received over $4 million, Snohomish County and cities more than $3 million, Spokane County and its cities received nearly $3 million, and Clark County and its municipalities received nearly $2 million (Washington DCTED 1997b).

Washington's program of local planning technical assistance

State law (RCW § 43.63A.550) directs DCTED to provide key land use data (Washington Land Use Study Commission 1997). It was noted in Chapter 5 that Washington has produced more than 41 monographs and guidebooks on growth management as of 1994 (Planning Association of Washington 1994). Prior chapters also referred to work by the

Figure 10.4. Washington's State-Sponsored Technical Assistance: Organization and Outputs

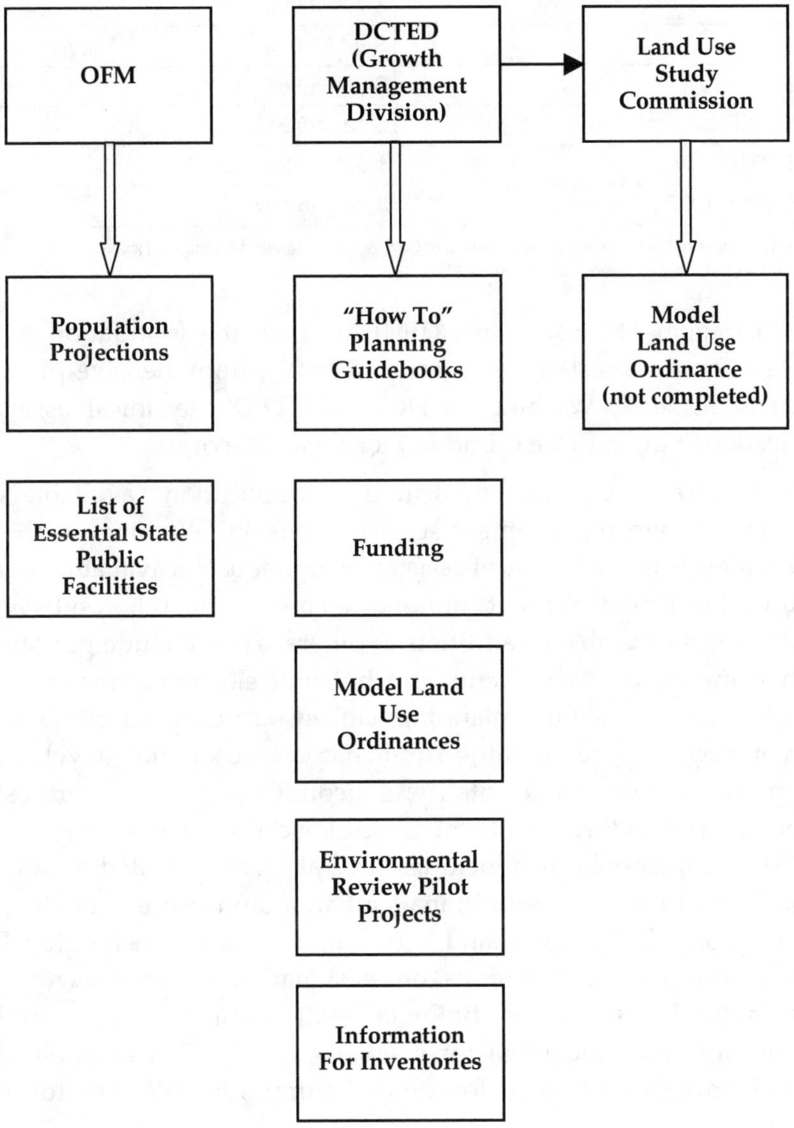

Table 10.5. Growth Management Grants to Local Governments in Washington: 1991-1997

Grant Year(s)	Total Amount
1991	$ 7,399,999
1992	$ 9,145,016
1993	$ 6,825,986
1994-1995	$ 12,063,918
1996-1997	$ 5,644,128
Total, 1991-1997	$ 40,705,547

Source: Web page of the Washington Department of Community, Trade and Economic Development (www.cted.wa.us). Last updated 1/25/97, printed 1/16/98.

Dye Management Group, Inc. (1990) that set the foundation for the state's technical assistance program for local comprehensive planning. In many respects, Washington DCD/ DCTED's technical assistance publications mirror those found in Florida and Georgia.

My review of a composite listing of publications available from DCTED's growth management services division (Washington DCTED 1996) suggests that a technical assistance guidebook is available for each required local plan element, optional element, and other substantive requirements of GMA, in addition to others. They include guidebooks for housing needs assessments and housing elements; transportation elements; capital facilities planning; citizen participation; parks, recreation and open space; defining rural character; economic development and preserving economic vitality; subcounty population forecasting; visioning; and historic preservation. Of special interest to this inquiry, the list of guidebooks also includes several works devoted to land use planning and urban growth management: a land use inventory guide (Washington DCD n.d.), a land use element guide (Washington DCD 1993a), and three publications on designating urban growth areas (Washington DCD 1990; 1992b; Enger 1992).[5] In an attempt to put it all together into one document for smaller cities, DCD also published a model comprehensive plan for small communities (Washington DCD 1993c).

Other products by the state's Growth Management Division include its newsletter, *About Growth* (previously *Implementation Briefs*), comprehensive plan and development regulations review checklists, a guidebook on impact fees, guides on evaluating innovative techniques for resource lands, regulatory reform, integrating growth management and the State Environmental Policy Act, and many others. Hence, one must conclude that Washington has completed an impressive number of technical assistance publications to guide local governments in preparing comprehensive plans and land development regulations.

CONCLUSIONS

Each state has provided funding for local planning, whether directly through local grants, or through the services of regional planning agencies. During the quiet revolution, Oregon's land use program relied heavily on coordination and planning assistance grants to bolster local planning efforts. Oregon spent approximately $18 million for the initial preparation of local plans through 1980. Florida's 1975 act was accompanied by some funding, but not to the same extent as during the second wave, when the state expended approximately $18 million in local planning assistance grants. If one includes funding for regional planning and implementation of the state's land and water legislation, Florida expended millions more.

Georgia's mandate designers elected not to provide direct local planning assistance grants, unlike the program designs of the other three states. Instead, it invested its resources in building the capacity of RDCs, whose employees were trained and whose programs were financed to assist local planning efforts. Although complete funding figures are not readily available, Georgia's RDCs collectively received more than $1 million annually from 1990 to 1992 to conduct local and regional planning activities, and DCA itself invested significantly in the production of technical assistance and training workshops. Between 1991 and 1997, Washington provided more than $40 million in local planning assistance grants to counties and cities planning under GMA.

During the quiet revolution, Oregon did not provide a formal technical assistance program for local government planning. The state's land use law does not direct, but only authorizes, LCDC to conduct a technical assistance program for local planning. Oregon invested in generous planning grants and staffing to provide hands-on assistance to local planners. Furthermore, the style of growth management programs during the quiet revolution was not one of empowerment. Instead, the model was to coerce local governments with a strong mandate and then give them some money to achieve that mandate.

Florida is distinct, because besides funding for local comprehensive plans, it has funded two additional phases of local land use policy implementation: preparation of local land development regulations and preparation of EARs. As Florida's DCA is the first to admit, the money does not pay the full cost of complying with the mandates. Nevertheless, it is significant that Florida directly funded successive local land use policymaking efforts. Georgia, Oregon, and Washington cannot make that claim yet.

The research presented in this chapter confirms the proposition presented earlier—that 1990s-style state growth management programs are distinct because they place greater emphasis on capacity-building and technical assistance. There is one qualification to that proposition, however, that needs to be made based on this more detailed investigation of funding and technical assistance in the four states found in this chapter. Florida's program of technical assistance beginning in 1986 was complete with respect to methods, guides, and models of local planning and land development regulation. It basically set the standard for formal technical assistance that Georgia and Washington built upon. Perhaps the most important feature that distinguishes 1990s-style technical assistance programs from Florida's second-wave style is that the programs instituted during the third wave employ a "how to" approach delivered without the use of coercive measures. Oregon, with the addition of the TGM Program, has similarly moved toward capacity-building and innovative approaches in the spirit of 1990s-style state growth management.

Notes

1. The funding is for "planning" only in the sense that funding for land development regulations, which was provided by DCA in fiscal years 1989-90 through 1991-92, is presented in a separate table. Moreover, funding for "compliance agreements" might be better characterized as negotiation, not planning.

2. The significant difference between the percentage of total LCDC budget passed on to local governments, as found by comparing Leonard (80 percent) and Knaap (56 percent), is probably attributed to Leonard's inclusion of federal (mostly CZMA) funds in his calculation.

3. It is unclear the exact nature of the local planning grants referred to by DeGrove. My experience in Georgia suggests that local governments did not receive direct grants from DCA for local planning, but that RDCs were funded to provide plan preparation and technical assistance. DeGrove is probably referring to Georgia DCA's appropriation to each RDC for the development of local comprehensive "prototype" plans.

4. This information is from an e-mail message to me from Jim Frederick, Assistant Director, Office of Coordinated Planning, Georgia Department of Community Affairs, 12/30/97.

5. These "how to" guidebooks are generally available in hard copy from the state administering agencies (e.g., in the subject case, DCTED). The state planning agencies have not yet made local planning guidebooks accessible to local governments via the Internet. One known exception to this, however, is DLCD's *Tools of the Trade* publication (EcoNorthwest, Pacific Rim Resources, and J. Richard Forester 1995b), which is accessible via that agency's web page (www.lcd.state.or.us). I was the project manager for that publication.

CHAPTER

11

Intergovernmental Frameworks

I contend that the analysis of the content of state growth management statutes presented in Chapters 6, 7, and 8 provides a deeper understanding of intergovernmental structure than is currently found in the literature. In this chapter, I describe various intergovernmental frameworks that have been applied by scholars to state growth management programs, then critique those frameworks based on the content analysis of intergovernmental structures presented in earlier chapters. The question that drives this inquiry is as follows: Given my analysis of the intergovernmental structures of growth management programs, does this evidence tend to support or refute the intergovernmental frameworks (and conclusions drawn from them) found in the growth management literature? I contend that a critical reexamination of existing frameworks and conclusions is needed, and that the content analysis and empirical findings in this work enable me to contribute to that end.

A pair of articles (Gale; Bollens) published in a single issue of the *Journal of the American Planning Association* in 1992 has served as a springboard for other analyses of state growth management programs. Though less well known, there also are frameworks from the policy analysis literature that have been applied to state growth management programs (Ndubisi and Dyer 1992; Durant, Thomas and Haynes 1993). More recently, Burby and May (1997) have advanced the discussion of state growth management program structure with new theory and empirical work. I use the results of the content analysis, where applicable, as evidence to support or refute both the validity and applicability of these intergovernmental frameworks used to describe state growth management programs and the conclusions reached by scholars based on applications of those frameworks.

GALE'S TYPOLOGY OF INTERGOVERNMENTAL STRUCTURES

Dennis Gale, who provides the nomenclature and definition of "state-sponsored" planning that is used in this research, provides a framework of four models or paradigms of state growth management programs. His typology of intergovernmental structure[1] (see Table 11.1) is worthy of further analysis here for several reasons. First, Gale's work deserves honorable mention, because his investigation of state growth management structure provides a template of sorts for this research. Second, it is interesting to compare his content analysis with mine, and to note some differences in our conclusions. Third, some of Gale's conclusions tend to confirm the hypotheses about program learning presented here.

Table 11.1. Gale's Framework of State Growth Management Programs

Model	States Fitting the Model	Description
State-dominant	Florida; Oregon	Hierarchical; mandatory preparation of local plans or local and regional plans; formal state approval of local plans.
Regional-local cooperative	Georgia	Planning ascends cumulatively from lower levels to higher levels of government; less decisive state role than state-dominant model; local planning is voluntary.
Fusion	Washington	Mandatory planning for certain localities; local planning is voluntary for others; no state or regional plan; state review of and comment on local plans, but no formal approval.

Source: Gale 1992.

Generally, my content analysis confirms most of Gale's findings. Gale's research, however, deserves critical reinterpretation. Gale finds that Georgia's program "contrasts sharply" with the state-dominant model, which includes the establishment by higher levels of government of "a template of standards and criteria by which lower levels of government prepare their plans and submit them for review."

I argue that state growth management programs in Florida, Georgia, Oregon, and Washington all have discernible characteristics of the state-dominant model, because their statutes establish structures in which state bureaus have much the same roles. As shown in Chapter 7, statutes of each of the four states establish a rulemaking structure for local comprehensive planning, and each state bureau has adopted minimum local planning standards with procedural and substantive content. Further, Georgia's program provides for DCA to withhold plan approval if a local government plan fails to meet state standards, and both Georgia's DCA and Florida's DCA have exercised that authority. Moreover, Gale finds that Georgia and Florida both apply a similar method of sanction for communities not in compliance with state standards—they withhold state and/or federal funds. I suggest that Georgia's program is still a state-dominant model like Florida's, but that the sequences of planning and consistency requirements differ between the two states. In other words, if one separates the discussion of the sequence of planning and consistency requirements from an analysis of state roles in the program, one comes to conclusions that differ from Gale's about the intergovernmental structures of state growth management programs.

Another example shows that Gale's work deserves critical reinterpretation. Gale suggests that a state-dominated program, such as Florida's, leaves less room for "discretionary judgement" by regional or local bodies than the regional-local cooperative model (i.e., Georgia's program) does. Indeed, Florida's mandate design is frequently characterized as one of the most coercive (Deyle and Smith 1998). It is Florida's program, however, not Georgia's, that contains an informal procedure for negotiating agreements for local compliance with state growth management statutes. Furthermore, Georgia may have enforced its standards, which include a minimum land use classification scheme, much more rigidly than Florida. Also recall the earlier discussion about how Georgia's law permits certain "variances" to the minimum planning standards. In practice, Georgia's DCA has granted few variances to local governments. This contrasts sharply with the negotiated compliance agreements that have evolved in Florida.

There is yet another reason for suggesting a critical reinterpretation of Gale's typology. While I agree with Gale's finding that "Washington borrowed from . . . Georgia," Gale cites Washington's multicounty growth management hearings boards as an example of a program feature that was borrowed from Georgia. Georgia's RDCs, however, do not have authority to recommend sanctions like growth management hearings boards do. In addition, Washington's growth boards do not review local comprehensive plans like RDCs do, except upon appeal. I suggest that Washington's growth boards serve a function that is similar to Oregon's LUBA and LCDC, and that the growth boards are Washington's response to the role of LCDC, albeit a regionalized one.

Despite these critical reinterpretations, other aspects of Gale's work tend to support my hypotheses about program evolution and learning. First, his grouping of Florida and Oregon together as "state-dominant" models tends to confirm my hypothesis that growth management program structures converged during the quiet revolution toward a coercion-based model. Additionally, the similarities found by Gale between Georgia and Washington's structures for local plan updates also support my hypothesis about a convergence of the structures of programs instituted during the third wave.

Second, Gale's finding that both Florida and Georgia have chosen similar dispute resolution techniques (i.e., formal procedures sponsored by the state) tends to support the hypothesis of regional convergence. Additionally, Gale's finding of a similarity between Oregon and Washington's "regional coordination" model, which uses counties as the coordinating unit, provides more evidence that the regional convergence hypothesis is valid in the Pacific Northwest. Third, Gale's findings of differences between Florida and Washington's provisions on local comprehensive plan amendments, and their different ways of applying the consistency doctrine, provide support for the omission (from Figure 6.1) of the Florida-Washington connection as a critical path of learning.

BOLLENS'S INTERGOVERNMENTAL FRAMEWORK

Scott Bollens (1992) has constructed an intergovernmental framework for growth management programs based on prior work by Bosselman and Callies (1971). The framework spotlights only two of the states studied here, Florida and Oregon, but it also includes Georgia, Washington, and other state and regional growth management programs. Table 11.2 summarizes the framework as it relates to Florida, Georgia, Oregon, and Washington.

As with Gale's typology of four models, Bollens's framework of distinct intergovernmental structures deserves critical reinterpretation given my analysis of state growth management statutes in four states. First, contrary to Bollens's typology, Oregon's program has characteristics of the "preemptive/regulatory" intergovernmental structure with its inclusion of LCDC's authority to designate areas of critical state concern. Oregon's program is, on paper, much the same as Florida's 1972 land and water legislation; it is just that Oregon has elected not to use that authority.

Table 11.2. Bollens's Intergovernmental Framework of State and Regional Growth Policies

Intergovernmental Structure	Programs Exhibiting That Structure	Description
Preemptive/ Regulatory	Florida (1972)	Direct state land use regulatory power that preempts local authority and decisions dealing with development.
Conjoint/ Planning	Florida (1985); Oregon; Washington	Local implementation, through required planmaking, of state and regional goals and standards. Penalties and mandates are the primary means of assuring consistency.
Cooperative/ Planning	Georgia	Local implementation, through voluntary planmaking, of state and regional goals and standards. Incentives are the primary means of assuring consistency.

Source: Bollens 1992.

Second, Bollens's "conjoint/planning" framework supposedly includes "integrated" frameworks that characterize second-wave programs enacted since the mid-1980s, yet he includes Oregon's program and others that were adopted in the 1970s in this category. Bollens uses the term "conjoint" because the intergovernmental relationship rests midpoint between preemption and voluntary cooperation.

Third, I question the degree to which Washington's growth management program uses the conjoint/planning intergovernmental structure, as Bollens suggests. Washington's GMA does not apply to all local governments, and hence it also applies a "cooperative/planning" structure where planning is voluntary for some counties. Furthermore, Washington used incentive-based, "carrot" approaches (i.e., funding and technical assistance) to entice those counties not required to plan to complete comprehensive plans. These findings suggest that Washington's program applies more of a cooperative/planning structure.

Finally, Bollens's framework has a major omission in that it ignores the substate regional roles in Florida and Georgia that are an integral part of the intergovernmental structures in those states. His framework might be viewed simply in the context of Peter May's (1993) "coercion-catalytic" dichotomy, with the inclusion of a third category for certain model code provisions. I suggest that combining certain model code provisions with statutory provisions for local planning tends to confuse the analysis and lead to incorrect conclusions about local comprehensive planning.

Bollens's (1992) work, however, supports the longitudinal divergence hypothesis with its finding that "growth laws enacted at different times within the same state (Florida) created contrasting intergovernmental structures." His finding that early programs tend to employ direct regulatory preemption while more recent programs use more "cooperative" intergovernmental planning frameworks has been confirmed and amplified here.

Bollens finds wide differences in the allocation of state-local authority in various programs. This finding and the observation that state growth management programs have "followed divergent policy paths" tends to refute the hypothesis offered here that cross-sectional convergence and longitudinal regional convergence have occurred between programs. Bollens, however, also finds that there has been a more recent "convergence and maturation" of the governance structures and policy objectives of state growth management programs. He concludes that state programs are evolving toward more collaborative planning models, and my research supports that conclusion.

NDUBISI AND DYER'S TYPOLOGY OF REGIONAL INVOLVEMENT

A third model of intergovernmental structure applied to state growth management programs is Ndubisi and Dyer's (1992) five-system, hierarchical typology of regional involvement. This work is of special interest because it includes Florida, Georgia, and Oregon as case studies. According to the authors, regional participation in state growth management programs can be understood as a continuum of five types, with type 1 being the strongest and type 5 being the weakest.

Ndubisi and Dyer find that Florida's program before the 1980 Regional Planning Act was a type 3 or 4 system, because it had a DRI program but local governments could ignore the regional councils' recommendations. Florida's program that was implemented after passage of the 1985 GMA supposedly fits a type 3 model, with mandatory regional councils and regional jurisdiction over certain development activities. The authors characterize Georgia's program as a weak type 3 system, because it mandates RDCs but gives them a relatively weak role with DRIs. Ndubisi and Dyer also find, however, that Georgia's coordinated planning program contains elements of a type 1 system (i.e., substantial regional participation in state policymaking) because RDCs will prepare regional plans that will ultimately be used to prepare a state plan. Oregon's land use program is characterized as a type 4 system because regional councils have only voluntary roles in the land use program, except in the Portland metropolitan area.

Like the works of Gale and Bollens, Ndubisi and Dyer's typology benefits from some critical reinterpretation. Their work is similar to Bollens's in that it attempts to provide an overarching explanation of state growth management structures, including both model code provisions (areas of critical state concern and developments of regional impact) and local comprehensive planning (also see Bollens and Caves 1994). I suggest again that intermingling these two considerations leads to different conclusions than is evident if the focus is exclusively on comprehensive planning.

From my perspective, Ndubisi and Dyer's typology would be a more useful explanation of state-sponsored land use planning programs if it omitted the references to model code provisions and integrated the county-as-regional-entity viewpoint. Their typology is a substate regional model that does not recognize the important "regional" coordination roles that counties play in Oregon's program, as well as, in Washington (which is not included in their work). Oregon's program has always included a county coordination role, especially with respect to UGBs. In both Oregon and Washington, counties are required by law to coordinate the population projections and to approve the UGBs of cities. If one accepts the notion that counties in the Pacific Northwest are "regions," then the regional roles for establishing growth policy in Oregon's and Washington's growth management systems are considerably more powerful than Ndubisi and Dyer's typology suggests.

BURBY AND MAY'S DIMENSIONS OF STATE MANDATES

Burby and May (1997) place each of the four states within a matrix of two key dimensions of state mandates: degree of persuasion and degree of prescription. Table 11.3 reconstructs their matrix and shows how the four sates are placed in the classification scheme.

Table 11.3. Burby and May's Key Dimensions of State Mandates

	Degree of Prescription		
Degree of Persuasion	**Low**	**Moderate**	**High**
Low	Georgia	—	—
Moderate	—	Washington	—
High	—	—	Florida, Oregon

Source: Burby and May, 1997. Table 1.2 (p. 11). Other states provided in original source have been omitted.

Degree of prescription

In their discussion of state prescriptions, Burby and May focus mostly on differences between the states with regard to consistency requirements. They find that there are three kinds of consistency requirements—vertical, horizontal, and internal—and then summarize the extent to which each state employs these consistency concepts. With respect to the four states included here, Burby and May find that Florida's legislation contains all of the consistency requirements; Oregon's law contains all but one (which one is absent, the authors do not specify); Washington's GMA is missing "one or more" types of consistency and does not insist on local consistency with state policy objectives; and Georgia "merely encourages" consistency.

Given my content analysis, Burby and May's assessments appear partially incorrect, and therefore they deserve critical reinterpretation. In Chapter 8, I argue in favor of a different reclassification of consistency requirements than that used by these two planning scholars (see in particular Figure 8.3). Burby and May refer to "internal" consistency as the requirement that local development management activities be consistent with their comprehensive plans. In my opinion, this notion though probably based on DiMento's work (1980) is better labeled "implementation" consistency. Internal consistency, as described here and as distinguished from Burby and May's use of that term, means the degree to which elements of the comprehensive plan are based on the same assumptions and agree with one another in most respects. Since development regulations lie outside, and are separate from, the comprehensive plan itself, it is a misnomer to use the term local "internal" consistency in the context that Burby and May do.

Using Burby and May's conception of internal consistency, which should be relabeled "implementation" consistency, my content analysis shows that Florida requires that development regulations be consistent with comprehensive plans (Florida Statutes § 163.3194). Florida also requires internal (as defined here) consistency (FAC 9J-5 and Florida Statutes § 163.3177), horizontal consistency via the requirement for local intergovernmental coordination elements, and vertical consistency (Florida Statutes § 163.3177). Burby and May are therefore correct in their observation that Florida's statute contains all three (actually four, if one uses my classification) types of consistency.

As noted previously, Burby and May suggest that Oregon's mandate contains all but one of the types of consistency, but they do not specify which type is absent. I have already shown that Oregon has a vertical consistency requirement for both local comprehensive plans and development regulations to be consistent with statewide goals (ORS § 197.250). I also noted that Oregon has an implementation consistency requirement (ORS § 197.175). Furthermore, I mentioned in Chapter 8 that horizontal coordination was weak in Oregon (at least until the adoption of Senate Bill 122 in 1993; see ORS 195) and that a firm requirement for internal consistency as defined here is absent. Under Burby and May's framework, it is horizontal consistency that is missing in Oregon. Under my consistency framework, Oregon's law lacks formal requirements for both internal consistency and horizontal consistency. Hence, two of four rather than one of three types of consistency are missing from Oregon's statute.

According to Burby and May, Washington's GMA lacks a vertical consistency requirement and possibly other types of consistency as well. My content analysis tends to substantiate this assessment -- GMA does not enunciate a formal consistency requirement between state goals and local plans like in Florida's and Oregon's laws. Statewide goals must be used as a guide to develop local plans (RCW § 36.70A.020). If they are not used, the local plans are subject to appeal to the Growth Management Hearings Board.

Vertical consistency still exists in Washington, although it is noticeably weaker than in Florida and perhaps better disguised. That is, there is a subtle vertical consistency requirement that escaped the notice of Burby and May. Washington appears not to have a vertical consistency requirement because DCTED does not automatically review plans for compliance with statewide goals as in Oregon. Plans can be found out-of-compliance in Washington just as they can in Florida and Oregon, it is just that such a determination has to be made "on appeal" by and to a substate regional board (see, for example, Sidebar 8.2) rather than by the routine and automatic review of plans by an agency like Florida's DCA or a commission like Oregon's LCDC. There is no question that Washington's GMA requires internal consistency (RCW § 36.70A.070), horizontal consistency (RCW § 36.70A.100), and implementation consistency (RCW § 36.70A.130). Given the findings of the content analysis, I conclude that Washington's consistency requirements are more specifically enunciated than in Oregon, even though Washington's vertical consistency requirement is noticeably weaker and disguised. This is contrary to the placement of Washington in the "moderate" category by Burby and May (see Table 11.3), if consistency is the litmus test.

I also suggest that Burby and May's assertion about Georgia's consistency requirements is misleading. In Georgia, RDCs are required to review local plans for internal consistency (Georgia DCA Rule § 110-12-1-.06), and the RDCs also hold a meeting prior to local adoption of a comprehensive plan to ensure that the proposed local plan does not conflict with plans of adjacent local governments and regions (Georgia Code § 50-8-37). The meeting requirement, however, may be overkill of the horizontal consistency objective as very few people attend them.

Georgia has not historically required implementation consistency, but it has a hidden provision that allows it to do so (recall the Georgia Planning Act's definition of "qualified local government"). My interview with Mike Gleaton of Georgia's DCA indicates that OCP has recently begun to threaten withdrawing qualified local government status from governments that have failed to adopt the regulations that they themselves suggested they would adopt. Hence, Georgia has slowly fused implementation consistency into its program administration, even though it is a noticeably weaker form since comprehensive plans and zoning regulations are not absolutely required.

As described in Chapter 8, Georgia does not have an overt vertical consistency requirement. Rather, it is a disguised, dormant one that applies if local governments elect to plan. The Georgia Planning Act contains a provision that DCA may review local plans to determine their consistency with state programs and policies (Georgia Code § 50-8-10). This provision is dormant in the sense that Georgia will probably not exercise it until it adopts a state comprehensive plan. Then, in the same manner as with the implementation consistency requirement, Georgia may elect to fuse vertical consistency into the system at the appropriate time. Hence, a careful analysis of Georgia's law and administrative rules shows that each of the four types of consistency exist, it is just that they only come into play if the local government opts to plan (which, indeed, has been the case), and the state adopts a plan as well.

In sum, Burby and May's placement of the four states in their matrix of "prescriptive" mandate features deserves reconsideration given the findings of my content analysis. Florida is unquestionably in the "high" category of prescription, as they suggest. Given the absence of certain consistency requirements in Oregon's law, its program probably should be classified as "moderate." Washington and Georgia have elements of all four types of consistency requirements; they are just not as visible without an in-depth analysis of the content of their statutes and some knowledge of their program implementation experiences. Burby and May's classification needs revision to redefine internal consistency in light of today's growth management statutes and to include both internal and implementation consistency in their overview of the consistency doctrine.

Degree of persuasion

Burby and May (1997, 9) identify two types of tools to convince local governments to prepare plans and implement other state mandates: coercion, such as the use of sanctions; and incentives that enhance local capacity, such as technical assistance and funding. The authors indicate that persuasion by state agencies is weakest in Georgia (and other states), when there is "little oversight and no sanctions imposed" (10). The authors characterize land use programs in Florida and Oregon as having (along with some other states) the strongest set of persuasive features in their planning mandates. Though not specifically characterized as such, four criteria are required for a state program to deserve the distinction of "a high degree of persuasion" (see Table 11.3). Specifically, the state program must: invoke review and approval requirements, make local compliance with state requirements mandatory, impose sanctions for noncompliance, and provide financial and technical assistance (10).

I have analyzed statutory provisions relative to each of these four criteria. My first observation about Burby and May's discussion of persuasion is that they leave out state preemption as a characteristic of "strong persuasion." I noted in earlier chapters that statutes adopted during the quiet revolution were based on a preemption model of mandate—the state will do, or arrange to do, what local governments fail to do. For example, I noted in the section titled "sanctions and disincentives for noncompliance" (Chapter 8) that a regional planning council in Florida may adopt a required local plan element or amendment for the local government if it fails to do so. Given the prominent feature of preemption in statutes of the quiet revolution, it is puzzling that Burby and May overlooked this point and neglected to include preemption as a higher degree of persuasion in their framework.

My content analysis generally supports Burby and May's contentions about a high degree of persuasion used in Florida and Oregon. The reader will recall from Chapter 8 that Florida's state land planning agency can institute an injunction against a local government to require adoption of land development regulations (Florida Statutes § 163.3202), and Oregon's LCDC can issue compliance orders relative to inadequate or insufficient local plans and development regulations (ORS § 197.320). I am less willing to agree, however, that Georgia's and Washington's persuasion rankings should be as low as observed by Burby and May.

In Washington, the governor can impose sanctions on counties and cities for failing to reach agreement on countywide planning policies (RCW § 36.70A.210 and 340). As noted before, Washington has an enforcement agent (regional growth management hearings boards) to ensure compliance with GMA, so it has the ability to impose sanctions for noncompliance like Florida and Oregon do. However, Burby and May are correct in observing that Washington's approach to sanctions is more moderate—it takes the governor himself, only upon an official appeal, to impose a sanction on local government for noncompliance, whereas Oregon's LCDC can issue orders without the concurrence of the state's chief executive.

The historical analysis I have compiled indicates that Georgia's mandate designers deliberately avoided using visible means of imposing sanctions on local governments for noncompliance. Georgia's mandate designers, however, also have used some of the same disincentives that are evident in Florida and Oregon, such as ineligibility to receive certain funds. Georgia and Washington, as third-wave programs, seem to go beyond Florida and Oregon with a more mixed combination of disincentives and incentives. As one example, authorization to adopt development impact fees in Georgia and Washington is extended only to local governments with comprehensive plans that comply with state mandates.

All four of the states "invoke review and approval requirements" for local comprehensive plans, although Washington's DCTED reviews local comprehensive plans but does not have authority to deny them. It appears that Burby and May give Georgia a weak ranking for persuasion because local planning is not absolutely required. If local governments in Georgia decide to prepare comprehensive plans, however, then those plans must be reviewed and approved by the state's DCA. Hence, neither Georgia nor Washington fail to meet the criteria of "review and approval" requirements, though Burby and May's arguments are valid that they appear to be weaker in Georgia and Washington than in Florida and Oregon.

Yet another one of the four criteria for deserving a rank of "high persuasion" assigned by Burby and May is the program feature or statutory provision that local compliance with state requirements is mandatory. Georgia does not require local planning, but if a city or county elects to plan then compliance with minimum standards and time schedules is mandatory. In Washington, certain local governments are not required to plan, but if they do elect to plan under GMA, they must adopt plans that meet minimum procedural standards, including review and comment by DCTED.

The growth management programs adopted by Georgia and Washington also exhibit other absolute mandates that local governments must follow. In Georgia, each local government must be a member of its respective RDC, and financial participation in the RDC is mandatory. Each city and county in Washington, not just those required to adopt comprehensive plans, must adopt critical area protection ordinances and classify resource lands of long-term commercial significance. Hence, although not entirely true for the comprehensive planning mandate, third wave growth management programs nevertheless do contain certain mandatory requirements for all local governments. To the extent that the regional participation and critical area ordinance mandates in Georgia and Washington, respectively, constitute weaker (or less important) mandates than comprehensive planning, Burby and May are correct to leave these two states out of the "high persuasion" ranking.

I have shown that financial and technical assistance have been very important elements of all four growth management programs, though Florida's and Oregon's programs did not provide formal technical assistance programs to any significant degree during the quiet revolution. Georgia may be ranked low in terms of persuasion because local planning grants are not provided directly to local governments. Burby and

May, however, might have overlooked the fact that funding and technical assistance are funneled through Georgia's RDCs to local governments. It is a less visible method of technical assistance and funding, but it is nevertheless similar in extent as in the other states. As of the 1990s, each of the states qualifies with respect to this criterion. Hence, the distinctiveness of Burby and May's "low," "moderate," and "high" rankings of persuasion in state mandates becomes blurred after considering my content analysis of state statutes. Burby and May's rankings also (as reconstructed in Table 11.3) deserve reexamination. Arguments could be made based on my content analysis that Georgia and Washington deserve higher rankings with respect to their programs of persuasion.

I also disagree with Burby and May's statement excerpted below, which serves as a one sentence summary of the types of persuasion.

> We expect comprehensive planning efforts in states where there are strong state provisions, such as Florida and Oregon, to be much more effective in enhancing local government planning than the much weaker programs in states such as California and Georgia. Other states [e.g., Washington] are expected to fall somewhere between these two extremes (Burby and May 1997, 10).

I maintain that third-wave programs in Georgia and Washington achieved very good records of compliance with their local planning mandates with less coercion in shorter times than initially experienced in Florida and Oregon. Burby and May conclude that states need a combination of sanctions and incentives to be effective; another relevant reference is Burby and May's chapter on growth management in Florida, which is subtitled "putting it all together." Local planning in Georgia, however, certainly has been enhanced through the preparation of plans that meet state standards, and Georgia did so, again, without the coercive style of the quiet revolution reform model. Burby and May's own empirical work tends to show that effects of state mandates are "modest at best" and that local planning mandates are "by no means essential tools" (144-5).

Two additional reinterpretations of Burby and May's work are in order. In the chapter on Florida, Burby and May mischaracterize the notion of horizontal consistency in their statement that "Florida's planning mandate pays attention to horizontal consistency by requiring local plans and policies to conform to regional plans (48)." Since there is a hierarchical relationship between local governments and regional entities, the relationship between the two is more accurately referred to as a form of vertical consistency.

In the chapter on Texas and Washington, Burby and May indicate that Washington's GMA "borrowed heavily" from Oregon and Florida (73), but the authors do not cite specific examples of what was borrowed. In fact, they cite two program features that are, by and large, unique to Washington: a program for siting essential public facilities and the mandates for all governments to classify resource lands and protect specified critical areas. Hence, Burby and May argue that a critical path of borrowing exists from Florida and Oregon to Washington. While I concur with the alleged Oregon-Washington connection, the importance of the Florida-Washington path of learning has been de-emphasized here, despite the similarities of the two programs relative to infrastructure concurrency.

Burby and May conclude that Washington has vaulted itself into a leadership position in state comprehensive planning (76), but I contend that it is too early to expect its program to have an impact on other states. Furthermore, there are few signs that the other states included in this study are following its unique model of intergovernmental structure. The influence of Washington's GMA on other state programs, to date, is probably limited to its use in reassessing Oregon's 25-year-old state land use program. Other states, however, can certainly borrow GMA's innovations as new programs are established or existing programs are modified.

In this chapter I have critically reinterpreted various intergovernmental frameworks provided in the state growth management literature in light of the content analysis presented in Chapters 6, 7, and 8. I now turn to the task of offering criticisms and prescriptions regarding state-sponsored land use planning.

Note

1. A fourth model in Gale's (1992) typology, "state-local negotiated," is omitted because it does not apply to the four states studied here. Gale indicates this fourth model applies only to New Jersey.

CHAPTER

12

Lessons, Criticisms, and Prescriptions

The purpose of this chapter is to highlight the lessons learned, critique program designs and implementation experiences, and offer some recommendations and prescriptions about how state growth management programs can be improved. The observations and recommendations are based on my own experience working in three of the four states, findings of this investigation, and the literature that is critical of state growth management programs. Although the limitations of this work are discussed in the concluding chapter, I want to underscore at the outset that this work does not constitute a rigorous application of program evaluation methods. I do not claim that my work constitutes a comprehensive program evaluation or impact assessment of the four state growth management programs.

Have any criteria been established to determine the successes and failures of state growth management programs? Generally, the answer is no. Only scattered evaluations exist to guide me in criticizing the four programs studied here. The American Planning Association's Growing Smart project (APA 1996b), however, has enunciated eleven "statements of philosophy" and other factors and principles developed by an 18-member project directorate to guide its recommendations on reforming state land use statutes. Several of the Growing Smart project directorate's statements of philosophy are relevant here, and I include some of them in the framework for criticizing and prescribing changes to state-sponsored land use planning in Florida, Georgia, Oregon, and Washington. Other observations and criticisms are borrowed from the literature or are offered based on my own experiences.

Table 12.1 summarizes the various observations, lessons, criticisms, and prescriptions made in the remainder of this chapter. The prescriptions are referred to in Table 12.1 as evaluation criteria, which reflects my hope that a more comprehensive system of evaluation can be developed that is uniquely applicable to state growth management programs. Table 12.1 also serves as a scorecard for the four states by attempting to show in summary fashion how the assessment criteria and prescriptions apply to each state. If the state is a clear leader among the four states in meeting that criterion, it receives a double check mark (✔✔). Where this score applies, the state is probably a model for other states to consider in that particular respect. States that otherwise meet the criterion are assigned a single check mark (✔). States that fail to meet a particular criterion are assigned an "x" (✘), and this generally means that improvement of the program is needed. For states that do not clearly meet or fail to meet a particular criterion, they are assigned a diamond (◆). The absence of one of these symbols shown above means that I have elected not make a judgement given limitations on information provided in this study.

GENERAL PRESCRIPTIONS APPLICABLE TO STATUTES AND PROGRAMS

The following criticisms and prescriptions apply to statutes and programs on a general basis.

> "Model statutes should provide for planning that goes beyond the shaping and guidance of physical development" (APA Growing Smart Project Directorate statement of philosophy #2).

Since the subject work focuses on land use and urban development, this suggestion has not been emphasized in this study. This evaluation criterion is nonetheless worthy of inclusion here. Oregon's land use program has been modified over the years to integrate economic development, social considerations (e.g., affordable housing) and intergovernmental coordination. The major emphasis of Oregon's program, however, has always been on physical development and land conservation. Howe (1994) calls for an evaluation of the relationship between Oregon's state planning program and social issues. DeGrove (1984, 170) questions whether Florida's growth management system can be socially

Table 12.1. Summary Application of Evaluation Criteria

Evaluation Criterion (paraphrased, see text)	Florida	Georgia	Oregon	Washington
General Criteria Relative to Statutes and Programs				
The statute goes beyond planning for physical development.	✔✔	◆	✘	◆
The statute accounts for the intergovernmental dimension of planning and development control and builds on the strengths of existing planning organizations.	◆	◆	✘	✘
The statute allows flexibility in planning administration.	✔	✔	✔✔	✔
Governments are empowered with a range of planning tools to manage growth and create quality communities.	✔✔	✘	✔	✔
The program is areally comprehensive.	✔	✘	✔	✘
The program contains all four types of consistency requirements: vertical, horizontal, internal, and implementation.	✔✔	✘	✘	✘
The program is continuously monitored and fine-tuned. Measurable standards are included to evaluate programs, and the program has built-in monitoring systems.	✔✔	✘	✘	◆
The program incorporates both coercion and collaboration in its mandate, but collaboration is more important.	✔✔	✔	✔	✔
Criteria Relative to Land Use Planning Standards				
The statute (or rules) prescribes the substantive content of plans.	✔✔	✔	✘	◆
The content and role of the state comprehensive plan is clearly articulated.	✔✔	✘		
The program avoids a "one-size-fits-all" approach in establishing land use planning standards.	✘	✘	✘	✘
Local planning standards were adopted sufficiently in advance of local planning. Once adopted, the standards were not changed for five years.	✘	✘	✘	✘
Local plan compliance deadlines were not unrealistic or over-ambitious.	✘	✔	✘	✘

Table 12.1. Summary Application of Evaluation Criteria (Continued)

Evaluation Criterion (paraphrased, see text)	Florida	Georgia	Oregon	Washington
Criteria Relative to Land Use Planning Standards (Continued)				
Environmental planning and regulation precede local land use planning, and environmental planning data is a primary objective of the state technical assistance program.	✘	✘	✘	✔
The standards require existing and future land use maps according to a mandatory land use classification system.	✔	✔	✘	✘
Certainty, efficiency, and timeliness in the development review and approval process is improved.			✔	◆
Standards mandate the use of state-constrained population projections for use in local plans.		✘	✔	✔✔
Standards mandate financially constrained local land use plans.	✔	✘	✘	✔
Standards address the issue of regionally difficult-to-site land uses.	✘	✘	✘	✔✔
Special districts are subject to local planning standards, to the extent that they apply.			✔✔	
Criteria Relative to Local Planning Support				
Resources and technical assistance are available to help local governments comply with state mandates.	✔	✔	✔	✔
The state's approach to local funding and technical assistance is efficient.		✔		
The technical assistance program includes data provided by state agencies.	✔	✔	◆	✘
Model plans and ordinances are required and available.	✔✔	✔	◆	✔
The state program provided successive rounds of planning grants.	✔✔		✔	

Notes:

✔ state meets the criterion

✔✔ state is a clear leader, may be a model

✘ state fails to meet the criterion

◆ state does not clearly meet or fails to meet the criterion

no symbol no judgment is made whether state meets or fails to meet the criterion responsive to such needs as affordable housing. Florida's first state plan (1978), however, receives better marks than Oregon's statewide goals do in this respect, because the Florida plan attempted to provide guidance for social and economic planning as well as land use planning, while Oregon's statewide goals primarily address physical land planning problems (Pelham 1979). Pelham (1979, 156) notes that Florida's state plan was initially expected to be a state land development plan in the spirit of the model code, but that the plan "gradually evolved to include a broader range of social and economic issues." Florida's state plan now addresses a whole host of social and economic considerations that makes it the leader of the four states in not limiting planning considerations to physical land use planning. On the other hand, "conspicuously missing" from Oregon's priorities are social concerns such as health, housing, and employment (Pelham 1979, 158).

> "Model statutes should account for the intergovernmental dimension of planning and development control, and they should build on the strengths of existing organizations that undertake and implement planning" (APA Growing Smart Project Directorate statements of philosophy #3 and #5, combined).

Florida's and Georgia's programs included the existing system of regional planning councils within their intergovernmental frameworks. Florida's program, however, contains two substate regional entities (regional planning councils and water management districts), and the latter have not been fully integrated into the growth management program. DeGrove (1984, 173) has called for a merger of Florida's regional planning councils with the water management districts. Furthermore, having two different substate regional systems may result in competition for resources and conflicts over authority. In Georgia, Gov. Zell Miller created substate regional economic development organizations outside the context of the 1989 Georgia Planning Act and the intergovernmental system created by that legislation. The governor's "council of economic development organizations" was a parallel substate regional economic development framework that was not integrated with the 1989 intergovernmental planning framework. Hence, these economic development organizations competed with RDCs by siphoning off some of the funding that would have otherwise gone to the RDCs. It also tended to shift the emphasis of the governor's office away from the planning act and the momentum built toward meeting its goals and objectives.

Oregon and Washington did not firmly recognize and integrate councils of government in their intergovernmental structures. One has to be cognizant, in designing an intergovernmental structure, that intergovernmental approaches produce tension between state, regional, and local levels (DeGrove 1984, 173). The absence of substate regional planning in Oregon and Washington might be excused on the basis that mandate designers needed to respect local authority and avoid intergovernmental tension that might undermine the program. Furthermore, the Pacific Northwest states have compensated to some extent for the lack of substate approaches. Oregon has regional field representatives who have defused "potentially explosive confrontations" (Knaap and Nelson 1992, 216), and regionalized LCDCs of sorts have been developed in Washington in the form of growth management hearings boards. Washington's GMA also has regionalized transportation planning via creation of substate regional transportation planning organizations. Oregon's program nonetheless still lacks a framework for "systematically introducing the regional perspective in multijurisdictional regions outside the Portland area" (Howe 1991a, 35). Oregon and Washington should explore alternatives for better incorporating regional perspectives and planning structures in their growth management programs.

Model statutes should allow flexibility in planning administration.

In *Planning the Oregon Way* (Abbott, Howe and Adler 1994, 297), the editors suggest that if there are no legitimate state interests, local governments should be given more flexibility. They also observe that local governments should be allowed to choose from a variety of ways to achieve state goals. Neuman (1998) suggests that Florida's application of the consistency doctrine and detailed rules leave little room for variation, interpretation, and the negotiation of differences. All four states, however, seem to have moved toward more flexible systems. Florida introduced the concept of negotiated settlement agreements (Burby and May 1997). There is also evidence that Florida's DCA has "selectively implemented" and made a variety of adjustments and compromises in applying Rule 9J-5. DCA overlooked the letter of Rule 9J-5 and focused more on the intent of the legislative mandate (Deyle and Smith 1998). Georgia's authorization that RDCs can require local plan elements unique to their region, subject to DCA's approval, is a good example of how regions can attain the necessary flexibility to deal with unique local planning needs. Unfortunately, this provision of Georgia's planning act has not been exercised to my knowledge.

Oregon shifted from requiring that local governments meet the letter of the goals to a system that allows local governments to demonstrate "substantial," if incomplete, compliance with state goals (Knaap and Nelson 1992, 32-33). Washington's unique approach to critical areas is a good example of a more flexible (i.e., local rather than state) approach to the model code's critical area provisions. With the flexibility of local control over critical areas, however, comes the probability that local jurisdictions will claim they have no such critical areas to regulate. Hence, unequal treatment of similar properties in different jurisdictions may occur (Pivo 1993). Also, Washington's GMA provides for innovative techniques without any general limitations on procedure or substance. Thus, cities and counties in Washington "may freely experiment as they implement GMA" (Settle and Gavigan 1993, 923). These examples from Washington underscore the fact that the goal of flexibility conflicts with the goal of uniformity, and advancements toward one goal tend to work against attainment of the other.

> "Governments . . . [should be] empowered with a range of planning tools to manage growth and change locally to create quality communities" (Part of APA Growing Smart Project Directorate statement of philosophy #10).

With regard to the authorization of land use management techniques, Florida specifies a wide range of urban growth management tools and requires local governments to use some combination of them to contain sprawl. Oregon's program has developed new urban growth management tools, but they have not been integrated entirely into the land use requirements for local plans. Florida has developed a "quality communities" program, while Oregon has also made strides toward that end. Georgia's law does not authorize innovative techniques or promote quality communities, though it does not necessarily hinder these either. Washington's GMA sets forth a few innovative land use techniques but does not really develop and integrate a comprehensive set of urban growth management tools into the program or promote quality communities.

Programs should be areally comprehensive.

In Florida and Oregon, every acre of land has, or is supposed to have, become part of a state-approved local comprehensive plan. While Georgia's mandate design does not assure every acre of land will be subject to a local comprehensive plan, it did mandate regional planning and local participation in RDCs. Hence, Georgia's program is areally comprehensive with respect to regional plans upon their completion. In part because of political controversy, Washington's GMA did not require all local governments to prepare comprehensive plans (Settle and Gavigan 1993, 900), though all are required to comply with mandates to protect critical areas and classify resource lands. Washington's decision not to attain areal comprehensiveness with respect to local planning is justified in part because of the goal of flexibility (i.e., different standards for different types of local governments). I believe, however, after professional experience in Cowlitz County, Washington (a non-GMA county), that GMA exempted from its requirements too many local governments in dire need of comprehensive planning programs.

Programs should contain all types of consistency requirements: vertical, horizontal, internal, and implementation.

While some believe the consistency doctrine has reached its limits, most would agree it is still a necessary objective of state growth management programs. Programs should contain requirements for all four types of consistency: vertical, horizontal, internal, and implementation. Florida's program is an undisputed leader when it comes to the consistency doctrine. Florida law clearly articulates all four consistency objectives, though enunciation in state law does not necessarily imply success has been achieved.

Georgia's program lacks a requirement for implementation consistency, or in other words, local land development regulations that implement comprehensive plans. This omission is understandable given my own experience in that state; Georgia's leaders did not want to erode local home rule or preempt local zoning powers. Georgia's mandate designers, however, should have required implementation consistency for those cities and counties with zoning ordinances and that elected to plan under the 1989 act (see Sidebar 12.1).

Georgia's failure to require implementation consistency seems to have resulted in a crippling effect. The state has spent many resources

Sidebar 12.1. Forsyth County, Georgia: A Lack of Implementation Consistency

Forsyth County, Georgia, which lies within the Atlanta MSA but is part of the Georgia Mountains RDC's jurisdiction, is a rapidly suburbanizing (and, as of 1998, the nation's fastest growing) county which had an old zoning ordinance and a comprehensive plan that had just been completed prior to adoption of the Georgia Planning Act. The zoning was detailed enough to establish residential zoning districts that varied in terms of minimum lot sizes (i.e., density). Professional planning principles would suggest that Forsyth County should have a future land use map and comprehensive plan that provides guidance to the governing body in rezoning parcels of land for future residential development, but the county's plan did not provide such guidance. Based on input from a citizens committee and the governing body, the county's land use plan contained only one residential category and thus did not provide any guidance with regard to residential rezoning decisions.

As a planner with Georgia Mountains RDC, I helped Forsyth County in 1990 to prepare an addendum to its comprehensive plan. Georgia's DCA accepted both the county's comprehensive plan and the addendum. When it came time for Forsyth County to revisit its comprehensive plan (five years from the date of adoption) in the 1990s, I again worked with the county on revisions. Concerned about the county's overgeneralized land use map in light of extensive residential rezonings, I suggested that a parcel-specific future land use map be prepared that incorporated various gradations of residential densities. The county's planning director agreed and arranged to tag all tax parcels via GIS according to a new categorization scheme and land use design. The county planning department produced a map that would have achieved some consistency between future land use map classifications and the county's residential zoning districts. The new map was reviewed and approved by the county planning commission, but when it came time for legislative action, the county board of commissioners rejected the more detailed residential density classification scheme in favor of a single residential land use classification. The governing body simply did not want to limit its options with regard to zoning decisions. And since the state planning act did not require more than one residential land use category, the county's desire for flexibility was allowed to stand even though this meant its comprehensive plan was basically worthless with regard to guiding future residential rezoning decisions.

At least in the case of Forsyth County, I contend that the Georgia Planning Act should have required implementation consistency. State plan reviewers should have disapproved the county's land use element (though admittedly they had little legal authority per the Georgia Planning Act and its rules to do so), because of the inconsistency between the new future land use plan and the existing residential zoning districts. It is not a severe erosion of local home rule for the state to insist that a particular county that already had zoning before it adopted a comprehensive plan make its zoning ordinance implement the comprehensive plan. The county's preexisting authority to adopt a detailed zoning ordinance was left intact, and the resulting comprehensive plan and land use map were destined to be of little value in the residential rezoning process. Every residential rezoning decision by Forsyth County, regardless of density implications, could be found consistent with the single residential land use category. In my opinion, this example is representative of one of the more significant failures of Georgia's planning act.

for local plans without any assurances that new land development regulations will be adopted that reflect and implement those plans. Georgia's DCA has shown some recent signs of "tightening the screws" on local governments by requiring that local governments take actions that they indicated they would undertake in the comprehensive plans. DCA also has pursued compliance with environmental planning criteria, whether or not the criteria are recognized in local plans. For example, Towns County's comprehensive plan found that mountain protection standards promulgated by the state were not needed at the time, yet DCA forced the county to implement the standards (Sparks interview, December 26, 1998). Until it requires implementation consistency, however, the program is destined to have only marginal effects on land development patterns.

For political reasons, Georgia opted for a so-called bottom-up approach in which local plans are prepared first. While this mandate design appears to shun vertical consistency, the program will allow the implementation of vertical consistency if program administrators seek that objective. Georgia's bottom-up mandate design is still flexible enough to implement vertical consistency. Once regional and state plans are completed, local plan updates can be required to implement the goals and objectives of those plans. In the case of Georgia, a delayed implementation of vertical consistency would be better than no vertical consistency at all.

Oregon has strong vertical and implementation consistency requirements, and adequate provisions are made to promote intergovernmental coordination (i.e., horizontal consistency). Oregon needs to enunciate a goal of internal consistency among the various local plan elements (goals). Oregon's plan reviewers need to be more cognizant of internal inconsistencies between plan elements, especially transportation system plans and future land use plans. Other states should consider inverse vertical compatibility as Oregon's law does; state agency coordination programs must be compatible with and implement adopted local comprehensive plans. With inverse vertical compatibility, local governments have one more incentive to prepare a local comprehensive plan.

Washington's GMA has been criticized because it does not provide a strong administrative review of local comprehensive plans for compliance with state standards (Pivo 1993). The administrative machinery of state government is relatively powerless to insist on changes to local plans. Consistency can only be forced upon a local government in Washington by the growth management hearings board with jurisdiction. While removing the enforcement mechanism from sight of local governments may have political benefits, it does precious little to ensure that all local governments plan consistently with state goals and objectives.

Programs need to be continuously monitored and fine-tuned.

Measurable standards should be used to evaluate programs, and the program should have built-in monitoring systems to ensure the standards are met. Strategies for monitoring and evaluation should be an integral part of the growth management program (Knaap and Nelson 1992, 228). Growth management theory needs to validate itself through quantitative measurements of the impacts of growth management techniques, and it needs to develop more adequate definitions of what constitutes successful growth management programs (Harris 1988). Programs take time to mature and must be reevaluated and fine-tuned to maintain effective intergovernmental relationships to manage growth (Porter 1997, 259). Florida's first state comprehensive plan proposed at least one measurable standard for urban form. Unfortunately, this specific objective was politically unacceptable and was removed from the state comprehensive plan initially adopted by the legislature. For preliminary ideas on measures for use in urban growth management evaluations, see Sidebar 12.2.

Of the four states studied here, only Florida has institutionalized a system of continuous assessment and monitoring of the successes and failures of its state growth management program. Other states have engaged in periodic efforts to reexamine program objectives and implementation records, but they have not kept pace with Florida in this respect. Florida alone has acted on the various committee recommendations and modified its program accordingly.

Program assessments in Oregon, such as the report of the Joint Legislative Committee on Land Use (1976) and the Governor's Task Force on Land Use (1982), have been too few and far between. The few evaluations that have been completed of Oregon's program reveal that results have not met urban development objectives (Porter 1997, 260), although there is now some evidence to the contrary (Weitz and Moore 1998). Oregon's mandate designers should critically reexamine the underlying principles and assumptions on which the 1973 land use act was based (Leeman 1997; Weitz 1997b). Statutes should provide for amendment and periodic reexamination of statewide planning goals. Oregon's program specifically provides for amendments to its statewide goals, but the state has not exercised that provision of state law to any degree of regularity.

Georgia's goals, which are specified in administrative rules, are too few and too generalized to be of much value. Mandate designers should strengthen Georgia's planning goals either through the state comprehensive plan or via amendment to the minimum planning standards for local comprehensive plans. Washington has attempted to build program monitoring into its mandate design and has devoted significant resources for study commissions that have recommended changes to GMA. State growth management programs in Georgia and Washington, however, are still too new to determine their impacts.

Programs should incorporate both coercion and collaboration in their mandates, but collaboration is more important.

The coercion model is a hallmark of the quiet revolution. At the end of the quiet revolution, state mandates to prepare local plans were not

Sidebar 12.2. Possible Measures of Excessive Urbanizable Land Conversion

While employed by DLCD in 1995, I tried to establish quantifiable indicators that could be used in evaluating local urban growth management programs. I hoped that these indicators would eventually lead to preliminary ideas for performance standards for growth management. I also thought that if standards could be developed, and it could be shown that local governments failed to attain them, there would be good evidence to suggest that local governments in Oregon needed to adopt more urban growth management tools. This effort was not formally a part of a work program of the TGM Program. I believe, however, that the measures have some merit to practitioners of urban growth management (indeed, some are rather obvious and are already compiled and reviewed by some agencies). Listed below are some indicators that might eventually be developed into a set of standards for excessive urbanizable land conversion.

1. # acres of residential land built upon. This could be obtained for any given period through a combination of subdivision plat approvals, exempted partition recordings, and individual building permits and site plan approvals.

2. # residential acres projected. This is in effect a local plan requirement in Oregon now (cities must prepare land use plans and consider the future residential needs in the plan). Estimates for the appropriate years, however, may need to be required.

3. # subdivision lots exceeding minimum lot size by 20 percent or more. This information is readily derived from approved subdivision plats and exempted partition recordings. It would require classifying each subdivision by zoning district (an easy but potentially time consuming task) and then evaluating the area of each lot in terms of its percentage above the minimum. The 20 percent factor is needed to avoid penalizing for minor deviations from the minimum lot size.

4. # of subdivision lots approved. If this is not already being compiled locally, it should be easy to do by an inventory of subdivision plat approvals and exempted partition recordings for the period to be analyzed.

5. # of multiple family units constructed (approved) and # of multifamily units allowed under maximum densities. Local planning agencies often keep records of multifamily developments, including acreage and number of units. Collecting these data would require pulling and reviewing all approved site plans for multifamily developments, finding the total number of units approved and total acreage of the site, noting the zoning district and maximum permitted density, and doing simple calculations to determine maximum permitted units and to compare with built densities.

6. # of single-family residential permits approved in multifamily zones. This would require a review of all such permits to determine locations by multifamily zoning district. If building permits include the zoning district (as they should), this should not be an extensive effort.

7. Net density of single-family development in multiple-family zones. These data could be derived from subsequent calculations of the data collected in numbers 5 and 6 above.

8. # of infill housing units constructed (approved/permitted). If a vacant lands/buildable land inventory is available as it should be based on planning requirements, this would be a matter of reviewing building permits and site plan approvals within the context of location. "Infill" areas would have to be formally defined and located. Since infill development strategies are not firm planning requirements, this standard may have to be voluntary.

9. Total unit capacity on infill and noninfill sites. This might be tedious to compile. It would be an extension of the vacant/buildable lands inventory. It would require classification of each site by infill/noninfill area, by zoning and appropriate acreage data, and then by individual calculations to determine the maximum densities permitted.

very successful in Florida and Oregon. Remnants of that approach remain today in those states. Third-wave programs in Georgia and Washington discarded the coercive style of Florida's and Oregon's programs and inserted instead a collaboration model that is more accommodating to the status quo of state-local relations. Not coincidentally, Georgia and (to a lesser extent) Washington have achieved better records of compliance with local comprehensive planning mandates in shorter times than experienced initially in Florida and Oregon. Without an absolute mandate to plan, in just seven years almost every local government in Georgia has prepared a local comprehensive plan. While this finding might be written off as mere coincidence or just dumb luck, other scholars suggest that collaborative approaches breed success.

Coercion has been deemphasized as state land use programs have evolved over time, but many local governments will not embrace state goals and objectives without the use of force or strong disincentives. I tend to agree with the observation of Burby and May (1997) that Florida's model of "putting it all together" is desirable in its combination of coercive and collaborative approaches to mandate design. Hence, while collaboration may yield better results, coercive measures of some sort may still be necessary (Deyle and Smith 1998; May and Burby 1996).

CRITERIA RELATIVE TO LAND USE PLANNING STANDARDS

The following prescriptions apply to the "standards" component of state-sponsored land use planning:

> "Model statutes should prescribe the substantive content of plans" (Growing Smart Directorate statement of philosophy #6).

Underlying this statement is the value of uniformity—that each local government should have a comprehensive plan that addresses certain basic considerations as suggested by the state. It should be noted at the outset, however, that this criterion conflicts with the criterion of providing flexibility for local governments in meeting state mandates. Thomas Pelham observed long ago (1979, 6) that much of the new state land use legislation was "process-oriented" and failed to "provide sufficient substantive policy guidance for land-use decision making." At that time, neither Florida's nor Oregon's law provided any significant guidance as to the nature and content of plans (Pelham 1979, 155).

Oregon's goals themselves provide little substantive guidance on how to prepare or evaluate local land use plans (Knaap 1994), and the collection of administrative rules that has developed over time does not provide a clear set of content requirements for local plans. Oregon's guidelines are one attempt to prescribe plan content, but they are not binding on local governments (Pelham 1979, 176). Some of the substantive elements of state land use policy in the Pacific Northwest have been created via judicial interpretations by LUBA in Oregon and the growth management hearings boards in Washington. Pelham (1979, 176) also argued long ago that Oregon should statutorily establish the various required elements of local comprehensive plans, as Florida's 1975 act did. This recommendation still deserves serious consideration. My professional experience in Oregon suggests that local planning could be more easily guided by a consolidation of the numerous local plan content requirements under a single rule.

Washington's GMA specifies elements of local comprehensive plans and enunciates several substantive prescriptions, but GMA's requirements are generally procedural (Settle and Gavigan 1993, 905). Indeed, DCTED found the need to insert substantive requirements even though it was only authorized to adopt procedural criteria. Gary Pivo (1993) has criticized GMA because its "laissez-faire design" allows the state to defer too much to "local parochialism." Hence, GMA and DCTED's rules should be revised to provide additional substantive policy guidance.

If programs include a state comprehensive plan, the content and role of the plan should be clearly articulated.

It is not just local plans that should have specified content. State statutes should also specify the content of state comprehensive plans. Florida's and Georgia's statutes both require a state comprehensive plan. Florida has adopted a state plan as general law, and the law prescribes the content of that plan. Florida has clearly enunciated the purposes, roles, contents, and legal status of the state comprehensive plan, though it did so after the first comprehensive plan failed to win the support of legislators.

Georgia has included state comprehensive planning in its coordinated planning program. Statutory provisions, however, do not exist about the role of the state comprehensive plan, its legal status, its substantive content, and the timing of its adoption and amendment and revision. Georgia's statute needs to enunciate the role and parameters of state comprehensive planning. Now that Georgia has some experience in implementing the 1989 planning act and some base of support for planning, the state's mandate designers should incorporate language regarding state comprehensive planning, using Florida's statute as a model. Reforms or program additions might include the legislative ratification of the state comprehensive plan, just as the 1989 planning act requires approval of local planning standards. Otherwise, Georgia risks repeating the mistake made initially in Florida—preparing a state plan that has little support among state legislators.

Mandate designers should avoid a "one-size-fits-all" approach in establishing land use planning standards.

Douglas Porter (1997, 259) observes that state programs have not recognized the differences in the planning needs of local governments. Despite vast differences among local governments, Florida's 1985 legislation essentially treated all local governments in the same manner (Pelham 1993). Similarly, Oregon adopted a one-size-fits-all approach where the smallest city and the largest county are subject to the same goals and rules. Oregon's transportation planning and public facilities planning rules, however, exempt small urban areas from their requirements (Weitz 1997c), which represents more recent recognition of the problems inherent in the one-size-fits-all approach.

To their credit, Georgia's mandate designers included a provision where different local planning standards could apply to differently situated governments. Georgia never exercised those provisions, however, and by default opted for the one-size-fits-all approach. Washington's law specifically recognizes the need to apply GMA's requirements differently depending on the nature and characteristics of the local government doing the planning, and of course the legislature decided not to require planning for certain slower growth counties. However, DCTED followed the paths of other state agencies and adopted a one-size-fits-all set of procedural criteria for planning. Planning statutes should, where appropriate, provide more than one set of local planning standards. State mandate designers need to consider that local government planning standards should differ on the basis of community size, growth rate, or other planning characteristics.

Local comprehensive planning standards must be adopted sufficiently in advance of local planning. Once adopted, the standards should not be changed for five years.

Local planning standards need to be adopted in advance of local planning, because rules take some time to develop and interpret. In Florida, Secretary of Community Affairs Thomas Pelham admitted that local governments would be handicapped with uncertainty in their local planning efforts, because Rule 9J-5 would not be fully interpreted until after local governments had already prepared plans and submitted them for review (Wallis 1993). Washington also initiated support for local comprehensive programs before establishing its "procedural criteria." Georgia adopted its planning standards, and received ratification by the Georgia General Assembly several months before the first local comprehensive plans were due. Amendments to the local planning standards in 1992 by Georgia's DCA had an undermining effect on certain plans that had been programmed to be completed under the standards that were initially adopted (see Sidebar 12.3).

Similarly, Oregon had to set early limits on adoption of new state goals, and some local governments found it difficult to comply with moving targets created by changes to administrative rules and the creation of new ones. Oregon's continuous additions to administrative rules for local planning, particularly the transportation planning rule, have kept local governments off-balance with respect to expectations and have required continuing adjustments to be made to plans. Mandate designers must develop, well in advance of local planning deadlines, the rules of the game for local governments to follow. Further, mandate designers should stick with those rules and not change them for at least five years, so as to avoid a moving target of compliance and to enable all local governments to plan under the same rules.

Local plan compliance deadlines must not be unrealistic or over-ambitious.

Deadlines that are practically unattainable may impair the quality of local plans (Settle and Gavigan 1993, 930). If local governments are rushed to comply with statutory deadlines, major policy decisions may be simply postponed to the regulatory phase (Porter 1997, 252). Oregon's one-year deadline for local governments to comply with the statewide goals proved to be unrealistic. Similarly, Florida's 1975 law established a "far more realistic" four-year time period for adopting plans (Pelham 1979, 167), but local governments nonetheless failed to meet their compliance deadlines. Short time frames for local planning in Florida have forced local governments to take shortcut and "cookbook" approaches (Porter 1997, 252).

The overambitious deadlines set by program administrators might be attributed in part to an underestimation of the importance of building local capacity and commitment for planning. Another reason for such deadlines is that local plans developed over longer time periods become outdated before they are produced, adopted, and implemented.

Georgia was at least partially successful with regard to this criterion. Georgia's mandate designers tried to address the issue of preparedness for planning by having its RDCs study the readiness of local govern-

Sidebar 12.3. Georgia's Local Planning Standards: The Frustration of a "Moving Target"

In early 1992, Georgia's DCA announced intentions to amend its minimum planning standards that had been adopted in 1990. In retrospect, I can understand why the state needed to make changes: DCA now had some experience with the standards; other agencies were suggesting some changes; and the state had adopted new laws since the standards had been promulgated, such as a development impact fee enabling statute with certain planning requirements and a mountain and river corridor protection act. Some of the changes, however, required additional data be compiled. Specifically, the amended planning standards required 20-year forecasts of employment and income that were not a part of the originally adopted local planning standards. The new planning standards would apply to any plan submitted during or after the final quarter of 1992.

As a Georgia Mountains RDC planner, the proposed additions to the minimum standards for economic development elements concerned me greatly. We had already secured contracts with local governments to prepare plans according to the existing standards. The contracts did not anticipate the substantial additional work implied in DCA's proposed standards. Furthermore, for at least one city and county comprehensive plan, we had already completed the data collection needed for the local economic development element. From my perspective, to modify the standards now was to change the rules after work had already been done (but not yet submitted). At my urging, Georgia Mountains RDC wrote a letter requesting a public hearing and expressing some discontent about the proposed rules.

I was authorized to attend the single public hearing that was to be held by the Georgia Board of Community Affairs prior to its adoption of the amended rules. In April 1992, I traveled from Gainesville in the north part of the state to Waycross in the southeast corner of the state to attend the public hearing. Upon my arrival, Griff Doyle, who was director of OCP at the time, handed me a revised set of rules, presumably modified based on public comments such as my own, and after a few minutes asked if the rules were acceptable. Having little time to digest the modifications, I spoke in opposition to the adoption of the amended rules. Some other local and regional planners joined me in opposing changes to the local planning rules so soon after the original standards had been adopted and without additional hearings. Although our plea that the board not adopt the revised standards resulted in a few dissenting votes, the board voted to adopt the new local planning rules despite our objections. Hence, I maintain that state mandate designers should avoid creating a "moving target" of compliance by amending administrative rules. Each local government should have been able to prepare their plans under the terms of the original rules, which in Georgia were amended just two years later.

ments for planning and make recommendations for the schedule of local plan compliance to be drafted by DCA. This regional analysis of the local readiness for planning seems to have made a positive difference in Georgia—local planning in Georgia proceeded close to its desired compliance schedule. Another possible reason for success is that the policies and planning standards are less rigorous and controversial than those standards found in the other states.

In Washington, GMA II (1991) provided extensions to several GMA I (1990) deadlines, including those for the completion of local comprehensive plans (Settle and Gavigan 1993, 896, 930). With regard to critical area regulations, most local governments met the state-imposed deadline but more than one-fifth did not even meet the extended deadline (Pivo 1993). In closing, it must be understood that mandate designers have to balance the problem of over-ambitious deadlines with the potential damage to resource lands and critical areas if development regulations are delayed (Pivo 1993).

Program designers should consider whether environmental planning and regulation should precede local land use planning, and generating environmental planning data should be one of the first objectives of technical assistance programs.

Washington opted for immediate delineation and protection of critical areas in advance of local planning. In all other states, environmental planning and comprehensive planning occur simultaneously. Unless areas of critical state concern are regulated at the state and/or regional levels, the local comprehensive planning process will generally not provide the consistency of protection needed for sensitive environments of the states. One reason for this is that local governments do not have sufficient information about critical areas in their jurisdictions, and good environmental planning cannot take place simultaneously with comprehensive planning when basic technical assistance is unavailable from the regions or state.

An example from my professional experience is relevant here. Georgia's DNR contracted with a private firm to provide digital information for wetlands on a statewide basis for use by local governments. Due to complications in methodology, gaps in the data, and the late delivery date of the finished product, Georgia DNR's computerized wetlands data base was of essentially no value in the initial round of local plan making. Another example is Georgia's adoption of mountain protection standards in 1992. Some local governments did not adopt mountain protection standards in their plans because the data (elevation maps) were insufficient and/or inaccurate.

There is a third example where Georgia did not have environmental protection sufficiently in place prior to local planning. Georgia also elected to implement its "regionally important resources" program simultaneously with, rather than prior to, local comprehensive planning. Local governments could not be expected to integrate into the first round of local plans the management plans that the state eventually would develop for regionally important resources. Integration of regionally important resources into local plans must therefore occur after the initial round of local planning.

Standards should require a land use classification system for existing and future land use mapping and provide for a data base on land use patterns and changes. The system should then be used to determine the program's impact, effectiveness, and implementation experiences. Programs also should define strong research roles.

The land classification system was pioneered in Hawaii (1961) and advanced in the early 1970s because of Ian McHarg's (1969) influence and work. Washington's 1970s land use legislation failed, but if passed it would have established a state land information data base. Oregon's legislature has provided few resources for monitoring the land use program (Knaap 1994), and the state has no requirement to computerize land use maps. Knaap and Nelson (1992, 227) criticize Oregon's program for its "initial failure to set fundamental mapping, record keeping, and terminology standards, making it difficult to compare and coordinate comprehensive plans." Only Georgia's program is designed to build such a data base for local, regional, and state planning. The other states appear to fall short of this capability, and mandate designers in those states should consider retrofitting their programs with locally compatible data dictionaries, GIS capabilities, and new land use mapping standards. Only then will states be in a position to monitor the effectiveness of land use programs. Oregon and Washington cannot expect to be able to compile and compare local land use data until such requirements are implemented.

> "Certainty and efficiency [and timeliness] in the development review and approval process can be improved" (Growing Smart goal of statutory reform).

Some planners in Oregon find the land use system too law oriented (Sullivan 1994; 1993). Streamlining the permit process in Oregon has been a major goal of the legislature (Knaap and Nelson 1992, 33), however, and it has been largely successful with adoption of the well-known "120-day" rule which establishes a maximum time period during which local governments can act on land use petitions.

Washington, on the other hand, has one of the more confusing sets of planning enabling statutes (Settle 1983). The state's GMA has also been criticized for its complex land use processes. Settle and Gavigan (1993, 932) assert that GMA failed to reform the state's "time-consuming, costly, and cumbersome land use regulatory processes." Washington did not adopt a 120-day rule like Oregon until 1995, when regulatory reform was passed. Mandate designers in that state are still struggling with the task of integrating 1970s state environmental laws with 1990s growth management practices. That goal will apparently evade even the Land Use Study Commission, which went out of existence by the end of 1998 and has not been able to attain all of its regulatory reform objectives.

Standards should mandate the use of state-constrained population projections for local governments.

By state constrained, I mean that the estimates and projections of unincorporated and incorporated populations in a given county equal the total county population estimate/projections, and that the sum of all county population estimates and projections equal those of the state as a whole. Florida's law requires local governments to use population projections that are approved by the state, though local governments may use their own projections if justified. Florida's DCA reviews local population projections to determine if they meet professionally acceptable methodologies (Pelham 1993). It is unclear, however, whether the projections approved by the state are state constrained.

Washington requires that cities and counties planning under GMA use the state's population projections unless an adjustment is accepted by OFM. Settle and Gavigan (1993) note that it is not clear whether the projections are minimums or maximums when applied to planning for urban growth areas. The assumption in practice is that they are maximums. Oregon also has begun to require county population projections and a city-county consensus regarding the allocation of population growth among the various cities and unincorporated areas in a county. Oregon's LCDC has begun to insist on the use of state constrained population projections prepared by the state economist. In Georgia, there is no telling how far off the sum of county plans' population projections would be when compared with the population projection for the state as a whole. Georgia needs to implement a state constrained population projection and allocation model like that employed in the Pacific Northwest. Florida should likewise comply with this recommendation if it has not done so already.

Standards should mandate financially constrained local land use plans.

Florida basically sets the pace in meeting this criterion because of its concurrency provisions. It is land developments, however, not land use plans, that are constrained by capital facilities plans. Washington requires concurrency for transportation facilities. It also requires that, if funding is inadequate for needed facility expansions based on land use assumptions, adequate funding must be identified in the local capital facilities plan. Otherwise, the local land use element must be revised to bring it back in line with available funding (RCW § 36.70A.070; also see Settle and Gavigan 1993, 917). Oregon does not have any significant legal constraints to bring capital improvement plans into line with local land use plans, although the transportation planning rule hints at parity between land use, transportation, and capital facilities within UGBs. Georgia has no provisions that require fiscal constraints when drawing future land use plans for local governments, but the state's mandate designers should consider adopting some in its next update of local planning standards.

Standards should address the issue of regionally difficult-to-site land uses.

Washington is the only one of the four states that has a program for the siting of difficult-to-site land uses that is integrated into its growth management program. Oregon has some specific siting programs, but as indicated earlier, these efforts do not amount to a comprehensive approach. Other states should consider Washington's program if they choose to address the regional NIMBY and LULU syndromes in their planning statutes.

Special districts should be subject to local planning standards, to the extent that they apply.

The drafters of Oregon's 1973 land use law were astute enough to mandate certain activities be undertaken by special districts. Oregon strengthened the planning and coordination requirements of special districts in 1993 via Senate Bill 122 with new mandates for intergovernmental coordination and urban service agreements. Coordination with special districts appears to be only partially realized in Washington. It appears that Florida and Georgia have much smaller numbers of special districts and, therefore, these prescriptions seem less applicable to the southern states. Port districts, special state authorities, and intergovernmental or institutional service providers should be made subject to applicable mandates of growth management programs.

CRITERIA RELATIVE TO LOCAL PLANNING SUPPORT

The following prescriptions refer to state funding and technical assistance for local comprehensive planning:

The legislature should provide a budget that gives local governments the resources to comply with state mandates and provides technical assistance (Abbott, Howe and Adler 1994, 297).

The states often fail to provide adequate funds for local governments to comply with state comprehensive planning mandates. John DeGrove (1993) finds that Florida "failed miserably" in providing funding for its mid-1970s local planning mandate but did much better in supporting those of its 1985 legislation. With regard to concurrency, however, Florida's failure to provide adequate funding "remains a sore point in intergovernmental relations" (Porter 1997, 260). In Washington, DCD "was not prepared to provide technical assistance to local governments immediately after the passage of the GMA because it had not yet developed its assistance capabilities" (Pivo 1993, 1152). Furthermore, Oregon's law does not mandate the funding of local planning efforts, and it is permissive rather than directive regarding DLCD's role in providing local planning technical assistance.

Oregon has not acted on recommendations made in 1982 that the technical assistance program be decentralized, though the Beaver State has consistently maintained its program of local planning grants throughout the years. Mandating that technical assistance be provided, as Georgia and Washington have, sends signals to state administering officials that those objectives are important (Burby and May 1997). While each technical assistance program can be criticized, they all have run fairly well oiled machines when it comes to grant funding and technical assistance programs. Oregon trails the other states with regard to local planning technical assistance, because it has assigned to DLCD a permissive rather than mandatory role with regard to such tasks. That role, however, seems to be changing with activities of the TGM program and other efforts.

The state's approach to local funding and technical assistance is efficient.

Florida, Oregon, and Washington all provided grants directly to local governments for local comprehensive planning. In Washington, counties were the principal recipients for some or all of the grant fund allocations, though many funds were passed on to cities through allocation formulas. Although it is clearly debatable whether it is better to give planning funds directly to local governments or whether those funds should be regionally appropriated, Georgia's funding delivery innovation deserves consideration by other states. Georgia funnels local planning funds to RDCs, which then dispense technical assistance and prepare plans with those state resources. Georgia's innovation, however, was almost a necessity because of its huge number of cities (about 540) and counties (159) and the impracticality of trying to allocate funds directly to that many cities and counties. Oregon and Washington might realize certain efficiencies in grant administration if more of their local planning grants were administered by regional planning organizations and councils of government. Such an arrangement would promote greater consistency of local plans with regional (and probably state) goals.

Technical assistance programs should include the provision of data by state agencies.

Florida and Georgia have assigned roles to various state agencies in the provision of local planning data. In Georgia, local planning data books were prepared for each individual county and distributed to counties and cities before their planning deadlines. I showed that Georgia's local data books were not very effective, but that implementation failure does not diminish the overall success of its effort. Mandate designers in the Pacific Northwest have not recognized this need for agency data. A major role for DLCD or DCTED in the provision of data is not provided for in Oregon's and Washington's statutes, respectively, though such a role should be assigned. Other state agencies in Oregon contribute data for local planning efforts, but these efforts fall short of a comprehensive program of state data for local plan making.

Model plans and ordinances should be required but must be offered with caution.

Experience in Florida indicates that certain local governments tried to adopt model plan elements supplied by DCA without considering the internal consistency of those plan elements. Model plan elements and ordinances are certainly desirable, and state statutes should require them. The state administering agency, however, should guard against certain abuses that might take place, as discovered in Florida.

State programs should provide successive rounds of planning grants.

Florida again provides the model for other states to follow in this respect. My analysis in Chapter 10 shows how Florida's DCA produced successive rounds of funding for local comprehensive planning, land development regulations, and evaluation and appraisal reports (EARs). Oregon also has consistently provided local planning and county coordination grants. Both of these states, however, have been able to use their coastal zone management funds for local planning efforts. Other states will be challenged to make the financial commitment that Florida has to local governments as they enter subsequent stages of the growth management process.

CONCLUSION

I have attempted to offer a number of observations, lessons, criticisms, and prescriptions about the four state growth management programs. They are offered in the interest of improving existing programs and guiding the design of new ones. The list provided in Table 12.1 does not constitute a comprehensive program evaluation system. The limitations of my evaluation approach are further highlighted in the concluding chapter.

CHAPTER

13

Conclusions, Qualifications, and Limitations

This chapter summarizes the major conclusions of preceding chapters and highlights the major limitations of this work. The chapter generally follows a format that provides summaries of the descriptive material presented in earlier chapters, then lists qualifications and limitations. This chapter includes some theorizing about a stage model of state growth management program evolution. It concludes with a research agenda for building a more comprehensive theory of state growth management program evolution.

As this research was conducted, opportunities arose to inquire into other sorts of interesting questions. As with any research effort, tradeoffs and choices were made about what to study, and I focused on a structural analysis to the exclusion of answering other important questions. Some important and interesting questions were omitted from further consideration, either because of time and space constraints on this work or because such questions were simply too difficult to answer given the methods and techniques used in this research. For instance, state political cultures and the influences of interest groups in state policymaking processes are very important considerations that have not been investigated here.

My own critical examination and review of this work by others[1] have revealed the complications and weaknesses of the research. By pointing out unanswered questions, acknowledging biases, highlighting assumptions, noting omissions, and discovering other weaknesses, I hope that the limits of this research will be readily apparent.

EVOLUTION OF STATE-SPONSORED LAND USE PLANNING

I argue that state growth management programs have evolved through three distinct periods of history: the quiet revolution (1969-1976), the second wave (1980-1988), and the third wave (1989-1997). This three-era framework is justified based on several considerations and should replace the "first and second wave" dichotomy that is so pervasive in the literature. As with prior analyses, this one will soon become outdated as state-sponsored programs of land use planning quietly enter yet another (fourth) era of historical development. As this book went to press, a fourth wave of program history, called smart growth, became much more evident.

The quiet revolution

The quiet revolution period (1969-1976) was dominated by environmental concerns, and the *Model Land Development Code* was the primary guide for drafting state land use legislation. Florida and Oregon passed statutes that were based in part on the model code, while Georgia and Washington tried but failed to adopt land use statutes during the quiet revolution. Each of the quiet revolution statutes, both successful and unsuccessful, was based on a coercive or state preemption model of structure and mandate. Some remnants of the preemption model of state mandates remain today in Florida and Oregon.

The second wave

Florida's overhaul of its land use planning mandates in the mid-1980s is the defining event of the second wave of state growth management program history (1980-1988). Florida's landmark growth management act was preceded by a governor's resource management task force (1980), an evaluation of local plans by DCA (1981), appointment of ELMS II (1982), adoption of statutes on regional and state planning (1980, 1984), and a conference on managing growth (1984). Florida perfected a model of program reassessment, and with its sweeping legislative reforms that mandated vertical consistency, concurrency, and compact development, Florida's program was destined to become one of the first programs for other states to consider. Although Oregon reexamined its state land use program in 1982, redirected the program to accommodate economic development and the postacknowledgment phase of program evolution, and sponsored certain program evaluation efforts later in the decade, the state did not systematically examine and then act on that critical assessment by overhauling its land use program. Recently, Oregon's planners are increasingly discussing how to evaluate the program (i.e., the e-mail discussion list on the Oregon Planning Network).

The style of state growth management during the second wave of program history, as exhibited in Florida, was dominated by continuing implementation of model code provisions and a strengthening of the consistency doctrine. Ironically, as Florida introduced its structure to ensure hierarchical (i.e., vertical) consistency among state, regional, and local plans, the consistency framework was being softened. Florida's administrators began to negotiate compliance agreements with local governments, and Oregon's plan reviewers began to seek "substantial" rather than complete consistency with respect to the statewide planning goals.

Rulemaking for local planning standards emerged to distinguish the second wave-programs from quiet revolution reforms. Other hallmarks of the second wave of growth management history are the increasing recognition of the need to build local government capacity and commitment, automate land information systems, and increase linkages between public facilities and land use planning.

The third wave

The third wave of state growth management program history (1989-1997), as represented by new programs in Georgia and Washington and new program directions in Florida and Oregon, is characterized by concerted efforts to: provide better guidance and assistance for local planning; evaluate programs; pay more attention to horizontal (local governmental) coordination; link transportation and land use; and (except in Georgia) combat sprawl development patterns and promote sustainable communities.

Programs in Florida, Oregon, and Washington have been designed or retrofitted during the third wave to promote compact urban growth and combat sprawl. Florida's refinement of its antisprawl rule, Oregon's development of additional urban growth management tools, and Washington's adoption of rural sprawl legislation suggest that the concern over urban form and land development patterns has heightened considerably in the 1990s.

Only in Florida, however, is there a rule that defines urban sprawl, enumerates urban sprawl indicators, provides criteria to evaluate land uses for urban sprawl indicators, and prescribes certain growth management tools to mitigate sprawl. Washington's 1997 law to combat rural sprawl and Oregon's continuing interest in adopting an urbanization rule suggest that other states are following Florida's lead and getting serious about sprawl. There are evolving signs that urban sprawl is back on the political agenda (Leo and colleagues 1998). Florida, Oregon, and Washington have modernized their planning enabling statutes and programs to provide for innovative land use and urban growth management techniques. As part of recent campaign dialogue and the work of the Metropolitan Atlanta Transportation Initiative (McKinsey & Company, Inc. 1998), urban sprawl is indeed back on the political agenda in the Atlanta region as well.

The model code is still pervasive in state growth management programs in the third wave, though its ascendancy has eroded over time. There has been a subtle movement away from the consistency doctrine, even though consistency remains an objective to varying degrees in all four state growth management programs. Neuman (1998) asserts that the doctrine has reached its limits, because its rigidity has clashed with the complexity and pace of change in municipal administration. The consistency doctrine still exists, but program administrators are no longer trying to apply it rigidly under a preemption model of compliance. A more flexible, incentive-based, capacity-building approach is a defining characteristic that distinguishes 1990s-style state growth management programs from statutes and programs adopted during earlier eras.

A STAGE MODEL OF THE EVOLUTION OF PROGRAMS

I hope that a more comprehensive theory of state growth management program evolution can begin to be constructed. One possible element of such a comprehensive theory is a stage model that is based on the general chronology of program development (Table 6.1), historical events (Chapters 3, 4, and 5), and the content analysis of statutes (Chapters 6, 7, and 8) provided in this research. To begin building theory, I offer a stage model of how state growth management programs develop.

State growth management programs evolve, or at least are supposed to evolve, in four stages (i.e., program formulation, local plan preparation, plan implementation, and implementation monitoring). Not many scholars of state growth management programs, Gerrit Knaap (1994) being an exception, have thought about the stages by which growth management programs evolve. Mandate designers of the quiet revolution thought little about what the objectives of programs would be after local comprehensive planning was completed. Early local comprehensive planning mandates (i.e., Florida and Oregon during the quiet revolution) did not fully reflect consideration of how to get local governments to implement as well as adopt plans, and they provide few clues about what was supposed to happen after the plans were completed.

In Table 6.1, I attempt to generalize the chronology of program development in the four states. Charting how programs have developed over time leads me to suggest that there are four distinct but overlapping stages that characterize program design, and to a lesser extent, actual program practice. These four stages are described and then tested to see if programs evolve according to the time frames predicted by the stage model.

My description of program evolution in the form of distinct, linear phases appears logical given the intentions of program designers in the second and third waves. Indeed, the model tends to follow the rather simple linear progression of the local comprehensive planning process (i.e., preparation and adoption, implementation, monitoring, and revision), with mandate design activities leading the sequence. The stage model is expected to be more a reflection of how program designers think programs should evolve than an explanation of how programs actually evolved.

Stage 1: The formative years

The structure of growth management is put into place in the program's first and second (i.e., formative) years. This is true generally of all four states—the mandate is established and the machinery to carry out that mandate is designed and constructed. This means, among other things, that local planning rules are established and institutions are reconstituted or created anew. Florida's comprehensive planning program of the quiet revolution entered stage 1 in 1975, when a comprehensive planning mandate was established from precursor (1969) legislation. Florida's second wave program evolved through stage 1 in 1985 and 1986, when the legislature adopted omnibus growth management legislation and Rule 9J-5. Georgia had local planning rules written and ratified, RDCs reconstituted and funded, technical assistance programs designed and operating, and local governments planning within one year of adoption of the 1989 planning act.

Within two years of adoption of the 1973 act, Oregon adopted statewide planning goals and got LCDC and DLCD established and operating. In Washington, within approximately one year after GMA II was passed, local planning rules were adopted, a technical assistance program was being designed, local planning funds were distributed, and institutions were formulated and/or reconstituted (e.g., DCD, growth management hearings boards, and regional transportation planning organizations). Hence, the four states provide five examples (including Florida's programs of the quiet revolution and second wave) that substantiate my contention that a short, one-to-two-year period of program formulation occurs.[2]

Stage 2: The first round of local planning

Second, programs transition from the formative stage to the local planning phase. Local planning may begin as early as the first year of the program, and therefore overlap stage 1. Schedules for local planning, as well as programs of funding and technical assistance for local planning, tend to follow four-year cycles that begin within one year following establishment of the structure of the program.

Florida's first local planning program had entered stage 2 by the end of the quiet revolution in 1976. A four-year schedule for local planning was established by Florida's Local Government Comprehensive Planning Act of 1975, and some local governments prepared comprehensive plans during the late 1970s, albeit with significant delays and without much success given various program limitations.

Pursuant to the Local Government Comprehensive Planning and Land Development Regulation Act of 1985, all of Florida's cities were supposed to have their revisions to comprehensive plans completed by December 1989. Florida's second-wave program entered stage 2 in 1986 and evolved through that stage by 1988, when most local governments apparently had completed their revisions to local comprehensive plans.[3] Florida's cities and counties had to prepare new comprehensive plans or substantially amend existing plans to comply with the planning standards established by Rule 9J-5. Hence, between 1986 and 1988, some if not most of Florida's local governments were again operating in stage 2, initiating and completing comprehensive planning programs.

Georgia set out a compliance schedule for local governments to prepare and adopt comprehensive plans between 1991 and 1995. Planning in Georgia proceeded according to this schedule and met the expectations of program administrators. In conclusion, both Florida's 1980s program and Georgia's 1990s program fit the model's predictions for stage 2.

Oregon's local governments were supposed to, according to mandate, quickly complete stage 2 in just one year. Local governments in Oregon, however, needed more than four years to complete plans as the stage model would predict. Oregon's program should have entered stage 2 in 1975 and evolved through the plan preparation phase by 1978 but did not. It was not until 1986 that all local governments completed their comprehensive plans. Oregon's experience therefore does not conform to stage 2 as predicted by the model. The extended period of time it took Oregon's program to evolve through stage 2 argues against my contention that stage 2 is a four-year phase of evolution. I cannot offer plausible answers to the question of why Oregon's evolution was stunted during stage 2 because, with one exception (Knaap 1994), the literature on Oregon's land use program (DeGrove 1984; Leonard 1983) does not fully address this question. Furthermore, my research methods were not designed to answer many of the "why" questions.

I am confident the stunted evolution of Oregon's program during stage 2 was not because of a lack of funding. Perhaps it was the tempo (Durant, Thomas and Haynes 1993) at which local governments were required to move—from no plans to rather sophisticated and controversial growth management and zoning (e.g., urban growth boundaries and large lot agricultural zoning). Again, the anomalies tend to be best explained by political theory, which underscores the weaknesses of this work given its inattention to political dynamics.

The stage model of program evolution suggests that local planning in Washington would begin by 1993 and be completed by 1996. Neither prediction, however, appears to be quite correct. Washington's compliance schedule for local governments to meet the local planning mandate was, like Oregon's, overly ambitious. Local governments in Washington had one year to adopt critical area regulations and classify resource lands, and others also had to adopt countywide planning policies. Then, by 1993, local governments were supposed to prepare and adopt comprehensive plans. Hence, Washington's program designers envisioned completing stage 2 in just two years, a difficult task indeed given the complexity and controversial nature of the preceding tasks.

Some local governments, particularly those in the Puget Sound region, did meet these expectations. Several others did not, however, and as in the case of Oregon, compliance with the local planning mandate in Washington lagged behind the ambitious expectations of program administrators.[4] By 1997, four years after local plans were supposed to be completed but in the same year that the stage model predicts local planning would be completed, statistics indicate that three-quarters of the local governments required to prepare comprehensive plans had completed that assignment (see Table 5.3).

Compliance with the local planning mandate in the Evergreen State took longer to achieve than expected by program administrators. It is likely that where delays in the completion of comprehensive planning by other local governments did occur, they can be attributed in part to: (1) the complexity of the mandate and the difficulties associated with adopting controversial growth management policies at the local level; and (2) the lack of a direct and immediately effective administrative mechanism (e.g., such as enforcement orders by the state administering agency rather than judicial remedies via regional boards after action by the governor) to force recalcitrant or tardy local governments to comply with the mandate.

Stage 3: Plan implementation

What happens after local comprehensive plans are completed? Upon completion of all local comprehensive plans, state growth management programs enter, or should have entered, into a postplan adoption, plan implementation phase. The stage model predicts that an approximate four-year time period of local plan implementation will follow, with some overlap, the completion of stage 2. The research presented here provides some evidence to test the validity of stages 1 and 2 of the model. However, little evidence is presented to enable valid tests of the applicability of stages 3 and 4 of the model. Only a few speculative observations can be offered based on this research.

Program designers of the quiet revolution did not fully anticipate a third stage of program evolution, while second- and third-wave program designers were more observant in this respect. Scholarly assessments and my own findings suggest that early state growth management statutes were not designed to accomplish or accommodate a third stage of program evolution. State growth management program designers in Florida and Oregon recognized initially that plan implementation follows plan preparation, and in Oregon's case implementation consistency was required from the outset. Programs of the quiet revolution, however, did not provide the mechanisms needed to transition from planmaking to a plan implementation stage of program development.

Florida's early (1975) program set forth a comprehensive planning mandate but provided little guidance on how to implement local comprehensive plans once prepared. Florida's quiet revolution program should have entered stage 3 by 1979-1980 but it did not, and then the program was overhauled. This omission in program design and shortcomings of the program were corrected in 1985 when the new state growth management legislation more fully anticipated the local plan implementation stage of program evolution. Based on successive cycles of funding provided by Florida's DCA, it appears that land development regulations were prepared by most local governments between 1989 and 1992, the time frame expected by mandate designers and predicted generally by the stage model.

The stage model would predict, and mandate designers would tend to expect, that implementation of local comprehensive plans in Georgia would take place in a four-year time period following, with some overlap, the local compliance schedule. While there are no known statistics available for Georgia's local governments relative to adoption of zoning ordinances in the 1990s, statistics compiled by Georgia's DCA suggest that implementation of environmental planning criteria was under way by 1996. Full implementation of local plans, however, cannot be reasonably expected by program designers given the absence of a mandate to implement local comprehensive plans with land development regulations.

Like Florida, Oregon's quiet revolution program should have entered a postplan, local plan implementation stage by 1978 but did not. Oregon's program did not evolve in a timely fashion through a distinct third stage of local plan implementation, because this stage was not well anticipated in the initial planning mandate and local plans took too long to complete. Oregon's program did not enter stage 3 until 1981, when changes to legislation were made to address the postacknowledgment era of state-sponsored land use planning. Even then, not all local governments had acknowledged comprehensive plans. Oregon's 1973 land use law did not initially contain any references to a postacknowledgment phase of program evolution. Oregon had to retrofit its program to accommodate local plan implementation. The grafting of postacknowledgment legislation onto the land use act in 1981 is an example of how legislators and administrators have to make program adjustments to guide implementation once initial objectives are attained, however tardy the realization of those objectives might have been.

Florida's second-wave, 1980s program entered stage 3 in 1989 when it instituted another four-year cycle of funding and technical assistance, this time to help local governments develop land development regulations. Similarly, there are some signs, though their visibility is much blurrier, that programs in Georgia and Washington have also entered a third stage of program evolution.

Stage 4: Local implementation monitoring and program realignment

With local comprehensive plans and development regulations complete, what is left for state growth management programs to achieve? What happens after the state objective of local plan implementation is realized? The stage model predicts that programs enter a fourth stage of local, as well as state, evaluation, monitoring, and realignment. The state statutes analyzed here provide few clues regarding what the purposes of growth management programs are supposed to be once the objectives of plan adoption and plan implementation are attained. However, Florida's program development since 1993 is nevertheless instructive in this respect.

Florida's experience provides evidence that state growth management programs enter a fourth stage of program evolution. The fourth stage of program evolution consists essentially of local plan monitoring and update activities and overall adjustments to state growth management programs. In the 1990s, Florida's program has been updated to accommodate another phase of program evolution: evaluation and appraisal reports (EARs). Experience in Florida, especially the state funding for local EARs, indicates that programs also move toward a fine-tuning of local comprehensive plans to meet changing state goals and objectives and to emphasize more monitoring and evaluation. There also is evidence in Florida that local program objectives have been realigned by the state to further reduce sprawl and promote quality, sustainable communities.

Oregon seems to follow a stage 4 pattern of evolution as well. The state's periodic review process is specifically designed to bring local comprehensive plans in line with changing state laws and administrative rules. Oregon also matches a stage 4 pattern of evolution in the sense that it has recently emphasized evaluation and monitoring of local plans via the transportation planning rule and has added new program components like Oregon Benchmarks, TGM, the community solutions team, and regional problem solving.

It is reasonable to suggest that programs in Georgia and Washington have begun to or will soon evolve through a fourth stage of program modification and realignment just as Florida and Oregon have. Adoption and implementation of a new mandate for public facilities strategies (1997-1998) in Georgia and a second round of regulatory reform in Washington (1997-1998) are two examples of realignments that have occurred in programs born during the third wave of state growth management program history. There are weak but positive signs that a fourth stage of program evolution is nearly complete in Florida and Oregon and is already taking place in Georgia and Washington. For example, in Georgia a committee has been convened to consider reforming the coordinated planning process, especially DRIs (Sparks interview, December 26, 1998) (also see Preface and Acknowledgments).

LIMITATIONS OF THE HISTORICAL CLASSIFICATION SCHEME AND STAGE MODEL

The stage model presented above relies on the discovery of structured events as depicted in the historical narrative and classification scheme. As the foundations on which the stage model is based, the historical discourse and classification scheme have their limitations. The underlying assumptions implicitly made in constructing the historical framework and delivering the historical narrative may tend to reduce the generalizability of this study's findings. By choosing to describe historical events in chronological order, I have superimposed a linear perspective on program events. Hypotheses, findings, and conclusions all have been shaped to some extent by the objective of describing the evolution of state growth management programs.

Linear accounts of program development may miss much of the program dynamics that have actually taken place. For instance, one cannot discount the possibility that programs develop more in cycles than in linear progressions. Furthermore, program changes probably do not occur in neat increments of time, especially across the various states.

I have argued that there are three distinct waves or eras of state growth management programs, while the literature only recognizes two waves of program history. To posit that there are three waves rather than two is not much more than a historical artifact in the sense that this work is more recent than the literature cited. Indeed, evidence presented here suggests that the purported third wave of state growth management program evolution is in large measure just an extension of many of the same issues and characteristics associated with the second wave of state growth management. Despite my rather meticulous efforts in Chapter 2 to define the proper beginning and ending points of growth management program eras, scholars might still choose to embrace the first and second wave dichotomy that is pervasive in the literature. I maintain that new program directions have manifested themselves during the 1990s, and that these distinctions justify the foregoing historical classification scheme and description of program evolution.

VISIONS OF A FOURTH WAVE

I suggest that a fourth wave of state growth management program history is dawning.[5] If programs have evolved in the ways suggested here and are now moving into a fourth era in the late 1990s, and if the stage model holds any validity, then I should be able to speculate about what directions programs will move in the near future. I suggest that the fourth wave will be characterized by the following:

(1) There will be continued movement toward greater flexibility in the implementation of state growth management program mandates, though I suggest that greater flexibility typically comes at the expense of plan consistency, comparability, and uniformity.

(2) All states will remain engaged to some extent in stage 4 of program evolution. Mandate designers will have to place greater emphasis on reforming existing mandates since administrative rules are now in a condition, due to incremental amendments and additions, such that inconsistencies and conflicts among various provisions are becoming much more likely. Washington's Land Use Study Commission and Oregon's effort to refine its urbanization goal are examples of recently completed and ongoing efforts, respectively. Georgia is considering structural changes to the coordinated planning program a decade after passage of its planning act. Preoccupation with reform, if that happens, may come at the expense of developing nonincremental innovations and taking new program directions. Statutes and rules will probably be revised without the benefit of program evaluations, despite the movement toward the application of benchmarking tools during the third and fourth waves and increasing recognition of the need for program evaluations.

(3) Program officials may choose to further recognize the differences in the planning needs of local governments and therefore modify the one-size-fits-all approach that has tended to characterize programs of the first three waves.

(4) Remnants of the *Model Land Development Code* will persevere despite their ages, but those remnants may be further eroded during the fourth wave as programs are influenced by a new model of state planning enabling legislation advocated by the American Planning Association's Growing Smart program.

(5) The consistency doctrine may fade some with respect to its rigid application to local government planning activities. As this research has shown, however, notions of consistency and compatibility can be further developed and refined. During the fourth wave the consistency doctrine will remain a central tenant of the structure of state growth management programs, though it will probably continue to lose its ascendancy to the collaboration model of state-sponsored land use planning. The last remaining preemption provisions of state statutes adopted during the quiet revolution will be further eroded or ignored altogether as programs move toward more collaborative planning models. It will be even less acceptable during the fourth wave to attempt to implement coercive mandate designs without components of capacity building and programs of technical assistance and funding.

(6) Florida's quality communities program is one example of how programs can take on new components and directions. Oregon's program has shown numerous and significant, if largely unnoticed, innovations that may stimulate new program developments in other states during the fourth wave. Innovations at the state level in Oregon include regional problem solving, a community solutions approach of multiple-agency contact with local government, greater use of benchmarking techniques, and more sophisticated approaches to smart growth and quality communities. Program designers during the fourth wave will continue to discover linkages between transportation, land use, and public facilities and hopefully modify programs to promote greater internal consistency among these local comprehensive plan elements.

As with the past three waves, the directions taken during the smart growth era of program history will depend on contextual factors, including among others the status of federal intergovernmental relations.

STRUCTURE, STANDARDS, AND SUPPORT

State-sponsored land use planning consists of three principal components: structure, standards, and support. I have analyzed the content of state statutes to describe and compare the intergovernmental structures of programs and the sequence of local, regional, and state land use planning. I have also described the various state standards, adopted in statutes and promulgated in rules, that guide local land use planning. Furthermore, this research has described support functions and how they have evolved in Florida, Georgia, Oregon, and Washington.

Support roles (i.e., funding and technical assistance) by the states have increased in importance as state growth management programs have evolved. Programs of the quiet revolution in Florida and Oregon allotted millions of dollars in technical assistance and grants to local government, only to see local plan compliance lag behind the schedules set by program administrators. Florida increased its local planning support capabilities at the state level over time. During the second wave, Florida established the benchmark for other states to follow with respect to funding and technical assistance for local planning. The historical perspective of technical assistance programs for local planning and my content analysis suggest that support systems occupy a central position in the structure of third wave programs.

By posing a formula at the outset of this work (i.e., that state land use planning is a function of structure, standards, and support), I have purposefully oversimplified the ingredients of state growth management programs. The three ingredients are not all-encompassing elements of programs, and the importance of these three components of state land use planning may be elevated to a status undeserved because of my own biases and interests. Future inquiries should think critically about this formula and determine if other major components should be included to further define and describe state growth management programs. For instance, Burby and May (1997) have indicated that the commitment of local governmental officials to state mandates is a key variable in determining the outcomes of program implementation experiences. My formula of the components of state-sponsored land use planning does not accommodate that variable and, perhaps, others that are important in discussions or assessments of growth management programs.

HYPOTHESES ABOUT PATHS OF EVOLUTIONARY LEARNING

In the analysis of the content of state statutes, which includes state, regional, and local planning and plan review structures, I have tried to discover the most important paths of learning between the four state growth management programs. Of six possible pairs of states, or paths of interprogram learning, four are found to be important—Florida-Georgia and Oregon-Washington (i.e., regional convergence) and Florida-Oregon and Georgia-Washington (i.e., cross-sectional convergence). Programs also have diverged over time (i.e., longitudinal divergence), as indicated in the historical narratives. That is, third-wave programs (Georgia and Washington) have diverged from structures and practices of the first and second waves (i.e., Florida and Oregon) of program history. The Florida-Washington path of evolutionary learning is justifiably excluded as an important path of learning, though some key similarities exist. The Oregon-Georgia path of learning appears to be nonexistent, although the Growth Strategies Reassessment Task Force (1998) has recently looked closer at Oregon's model.

There is evidence that tends to confirm these hypotheses. States within the same subnational region tend to adopt similar program structures (i.e., regional convergence), while regional approaches to growth management tend to diverge from one another. Georgia followed Florida's program in several ways, and Washington generally followed Oregon's approach, though admittedly there are important differences that exist between both pairs of states. My account of the evolution of state growth management programs through three historical eras confirms that programs have diverged over time. The emphases of programs have changed from coercion to collaboration, and this change supports the longitudinal divergence hypothesis. While there is evidence to support my hypotheses about interprogram learning, some scattered, somewhat less important findings tend to contradict the hypotheses and argue against their acceptance. Further testing of the general precepts of the hypotheses is needed.

As noted above, the hypotheses are framed within a context of history and a linear perspective. I have not tried to rule out the existence of competing hypotheses, such as a cyclical rather than linear evolution of programs. The learning that has purportedly taken place among officials of the four state programs might have been generated simply by the nature of the task and the relatively limited range of options available to program designers. In the end, the reader is free to debate these hypotheses, which are constructed on broad assumptions that the four state programs have evolved in a linear and connected fashion. I have assumed that programs are developing for the better, and I maintain that the four state programs have evolved in positive ways and that continued improvements are probable.

INTERGOVERNMENTAL FRAMEWORKS

Various scholars have devised and applied intergovernmental frameworks to better understand the structure of state growth management programs. I suggest that certain of these frameworks, while valid and useful, deserve critical reinterpretation based on the analysis of state statutes presented here. The frameworks combine certain program components of the model code (developments of regional impact and areas of critical state concern) with local comprehensive planning mandates and, in doing so, lead to conclusions that differ from the findings presented here about local comprehensive planning and the consistency doctrine. Intermingling analyses of model code provisions and local planning provisions leads to different conclusions than would be evident if the focus is more exclusively on local comprehensive planning. I have found myself also falling into that trap because model code provisions are obvious components of state growth management programs (see Weitz 1999), and it is sometimes difficult to separate out those considerations from local comprehensive planning mandates. The intergovernmental frameworks also provide some support for the research hypotheses about paths of program learning, though it has also been suggested elsewhere that state programs are converging more so than is found by this research. By combining the frameworks that have been applied to state growth management programs with my historical classification scheme and content analysis of state statutes, I believe that an evolutionary theory of state growth management programs is well within reach.

I began this work with lofty ambitions of explaining why programs have evolved the way they have and why mandate designers and program implementing officials made the choices that they did. For instance, readers probably would like to know what the reasons were that the four states embraced statewide land use planning. I pondered a series of "why" questions, but I regret to acknowledge that those questions were eventually eliminated from consideration or left unanswered.

Answering the analytical questions of why programs developed the way they did and why particular mandate design decisions were made requires different methods and sources than I have employed. Extensive interviews with planning pioneers in the four states are needed to document the reasons for such choices. Because I have relied on content analysis to the exclusion of more interviews, the series of "why" questions that the reader may be confronted with must remain until further research is done.

Another limitation of my research is that it lacks discussions of some important contexts about why growth management programs were adopted in the first place. For example, John DeGrove (1984, 1992) sets the context of land use problems and issues and identifies the catalysts leading to adoption of growth management programs. Furthermore, DeGrove's work recognizes some of the political variables that have influenced program implementation over time. My research could be further developed along these lines of inquiry.

EVALUATION OF STRUCTURE, STANDARDS, AND SUPPORT

How much impact do the components of growth management programs have on local government compliance with state mandates? What is the proper mix of structure, standards, and support in designing and implementing state growth management programs? What is the basis for asserting success or failure? My work does not provide a way of quantifying the relative importance of the three major program components. Future research should seek to determine which program components are more influential with respect to improving the degree of local government implementation of state mandates. For example, is it more productive for state program designers to provide increased technical assistance, or would less complex planning standards increase mandate compliance? With the recent publication of an outstanding example of program evaluation specifically applied to state growth management programs (Burby and May 1997), more variables of mandate design and implementation have now been specified.

There is much room beyond this work to answer questions about program effects. I have criticized state growth management program mandate designs and implementation records, but some of the successes need to be more fully described so as not to lose the long-term perspective of how far programs have come since the days of the quiet revolution.

I began this work also with the objective of developing a comprehensive critical framework for evaluating state growth management programs. While the criticisms and prescriptions offered by this work should be valuable, they tend to fall short of the comprehensive normative framework that I wanted to supply and that the profession might desire to have for program evaluations. Rather than providing the organizing normative framework I initially desired, the principles and value judgements presented in Table 12.1 are more of a list of suggestions for program designers to consider. The new variables of program mandate design developed by Burby and May (1997) need to be meshed with my prescriptions into a system that will stimulate the development of more comprehensive approaches for asserting program successes and failures.

My presentation in Chapter 12 of prescriptions and lessons might suggest to the reader that each and every one of the considerations is important to each state. Whether the observations, lessons, criticisms, and prescriptions apply to a particular program or state clearly depends on unique objectives and contextual factors. Hence, I do not intend to implicitly recommend a canon of comprehensiveness, where each state must consider every lesson or prescription presented in Chapter 12.

A RESEARCH AGENDA

In closing, I suggest ways that this work, particularly the stage model of program evolution, can be further refined, expanded, and substantiated to serve its purpose of improving state-sponsored land use planning programs.

Conduct additional content analyses

I describe in the appendix how content analysis methods would enable me to produce more precise, empirical evidence of how programs have evolved over time. Specifically, I could search annotated versions of state statutes in the four states to identify the year legislation was enacted that changed its program features. Codified versions of state statutes indicate the year that legislation was amended, and by searching the annotations of state statutes for various years and then comparing content (or lack thereof) in earlier versions of those statutes, I would be able to precisely indicate which statutory amendments occurred and when they occurred. More content analysis would provide further evidence to substantiate or refute my historical classification scheme, hypotheses about interprogram learning, and the stage model of intraprogram evolution.

Combine interprogram and intraprogram perspectives

My work has been directed primarily toward the task of finding the patterns or paths of evolutionary learning that have occurred between and among the four state growth management programs. The stage theory of intraprogram evolution can be more fully integrated with my hypotheses of interprogram learning. More work is needed to be able to integrate or combine intraprogram and interprogram perspectives.

Apply hypotheses and the stage model to other states

The hypotheses about how state growth management programs converge and/or diverge over time and the broad inductive conclusions about waves and stages of state growth management programs can be further substantiated by including other states in the analysis. For instance, do other growth management states in New England borrow and learn from Vermont's experience to the extent that my regional convergence hypothesis can be confirmed? Do programs and implementation experiences in Rhode Island and Maryland fit generally into the stage model of program evolution? How does the fact that Tennessee has now adopted urban growth boundaries per a 1998 annexation law relate to my hypotheses and stage model? How is it that Tennessee could adopt a tool pioneered in the Pacific Northwest, when Georgia could not or would not? There are rich opportunities to discover whether the evolution of programs in other states fits the frameworks, hypotheses, and the model of stages offered in this study.

Include politics in the analysis of program evolution

Gerrit Knaap (1994) refers to a process of "political integration" throughout stages of program evolution, especially between stage 2 (plan preparation) and stage 3 (plan implementation). Land use politics occurs in different venues at different stages of program evolution, and Knaap has modeled those stages and shown how different political participants influence program evolution at different stages of the planning process. Knaap also observes that an implementation deficit stems from the intergovernmental structure of Oregon's land use program. The political dimension of how interest groups and other institutions influence state program evolution at different time periods needs to be integrated with my stage model of program evolution to deal with political events that confound the outcomes predicted by structural approaches.

My stage model is admittedly incomplete; it is illustrative not definitive. It will take work by scholars of state politics, such as Knaap (1994), to sort out the confounding influences that frustrate the account of program evolution presented here and promoted by state growth management mandate designers. Inserting attention to political dynamics will strengthen any effort to discover a more comprehensive theory of the evolution of state growth management programs.

CONCLUSION

I have focused on land use planning and growth management to the general exclusion of other important considerations in preparing comprehensive plans, such as housing, transportation, and public facilities. By choosing land use specifically or comprehensive planning mandates more generally for study, one must guard against the biased assumption that land use and comprehensive planning are the only or most important types of state mandate. Little evidence exists to suggest that comprehensive planning mandates are superior to collections of single purpose mandates. Additional work along the lines of Burby and May's (1997) pioneering effort will be needed to begin to address that issue.

Each state growth management program has its own advantages and disadvantages. By looking at program structures and implementation experiences, innovations can be discovered and programs can be improved. It will be up to the mandate designers of the twenty-first century to capitalize on windows of opportunity and revise their statutes and standards for the better. I hope that this work contributes significantly toward that end.

Notes

1. I refer here to my dissertation advisory committee at Portland State University, consisting of Professors Sy Adler (chair), Carl Abbott, Deborah Howe, Ethan Seltzer, and Gordon Dodds.

2. Scholars of public policy processes would be quick to note here that stage 1 is often preceded by another phase, a softening-up period (see Durant, Thomas and Haynes 1993), where programs are proposed (some successful but weak, others unsuccessful) until policymakers are softened-up to program policies. This observation underscores an inherent weakness in the stage model—a lack of attention to political dynamics.

3. This conclusion is speculative in the sense that this research effort does not provide any statistics regarding compliance with Florida's local planning mandate as of the late 1980s. The conclusion is more plausible, however, in light of the funding schedules implemented by Florida's Department of Community Affairs.

4. Again, the research did not reveal compliance statistics with respect to the local planning mandate in Washington in 1993, although Pivo's work (1993) has yielded insights into the status of meeting the earlier mandate timeframe for adopting critical area regulations.

5. A fourth wave was not so evident in 1997 and 1998, when I completed my dissertation on the four states. While this book was in production in 1999, however, a fourth began to appear in various states. I have elsewhere called this fourth wave "smart growth" (Weitz 1999). There are now rapid developments in state growth management, for example by (1) publication of a task force report in Georgia with many far-reaching conclusions about turning that program into a true growth management system and (2) adoption of a law by Tennessee requiring local governments to draw urban growth boundaries.

Appendix

Content Analysis Methods

In preparing for this research, I grounded my effort with a review of the literature on content analysis methods (Weber 1985; Rosengren 1981; Krippendorff 1980; Carney 1972). The intent of this literature review was to gain an overall understanding of content analysis as a research method, identify the advantages of content analysis, understand its limitations, and help fashion a method specific to the subject inquiry. A review of the literature on content analysis methods would be an unnecessary departure at this point. Some key points from the content analysis literature, however, underscore that there is a method and certain underlying principles and techniques associated with content analysis.

DEFINITION AND ELABORATION

Content analysis is defined as "a research technique (set of procedures) for making replicable and valid inferences from data to their context" (Krippendorff 1980). Content analysis is a data reduction technique that classifies words, concepts, and/or phrases of text into content categories. The central idea of content analysis is that many words can be classified into much fewer categories. Content analysis is a technique that is fundamentally empirical in orientation, yet it yields exploratory and predictive value and lends itself to qualitative analysis as well. Content analysis often uses simple tabular methods of organizing and displaying text.

ADVANTAGES AND DISADVANTAGES OF CONTENT ANALYSIS

As described above, content analysis is a form of data reduction that helps to overcome the problem of too much information in texts. Content analysis is a flexible method because it is aided by computer (if machine readable text is used) but can also be implemented with human coded methods where necessary. As noted above, the method lends itself to both qualitative and quantitative operations.

In comparison with other social science research methods, content analysis has reliability and validity problems. Researchers are prone to make mistakes by incorrectly generalizing from text to context (i.e., taking things at face value) when reality is otherwise. The method of content analysis needs to be supplemented with reviews by administering officials in the four states to ensure that my generalizations drawn from statutory language reflect actual implementation in practice. I have tried to ensure validity of my generalizations through interviews with program officials in Florida and Georgia, and I trust that my observation of and participation in programs in Georgia, Oregon, and Washington increase the validity of my findings. I also sent preliminary drafts of this work to the administering officials of the four programs in the hope that they would double-check the validity of my own generalizations against actual program practices. That effort, however, went largely unanswered, and hence, I am not relieved of the responsibility for cases where generalizations based on my content analysis may depart from actual practices in the states.

STRATEGIES AND TECHNIQUES OF CONTENT ANALYSIS

As synthesized from the literature, content analysis methodologists generally suggest that researchers should employ a linear process as follows: start with a specific research question(s); consider whether a sampling strategy is necessary; define the recording units/level of aggregation (words, categories, themes, etc.); prepare and validate a content analysis dictionary; construct categories for analysis and theoretically justify them; create and test a coding scheme and assess for reliability; carry out the analysis and code all text; assess reliability and validity achieved; determine whether certain quantifiers are useful and apply relevant quantification techniques; and explain the significance of findings in light of theoretical and substantive concerns.

Specific techniques of content analysis include word frequency counts and lists, key-word-in-context, concordances, and content category counts. These strategies and techniques were considered in analyzing the content of state statutes, as described below.

APPLIED METHOD

I secured machine-readable text of each state law either from computer files from the original source (Florida and Oregon) or from Internet access to state legislation (Georgia and Washington). State administrative rules were also available electronically. After trial and error and field testing of some of the techniques alluded to above, I identified "search" functions (with word processing software) as a viable content analysis technique. For example, using a search mechanism of word processing software (specifically, the "Find and Replace" function in Word Perfect Windows 6.1), I could: (1) classify requirements and standards by degree of authority through searching and coding words such as "requirements," "recommendations," and "guidelines"; (2) identify program support functions by searching for key words such as "grant" and "technical assistance"; and (3) identify the evolution (amendment) of programs by searching for years within the editorial notes included in annotated versions of statutes and rules. The search mechanism is used to supplement where needed a careful reading of the statutes and classification of content, thereby helping me to avoid errors of omission. Word counts and other quantitative techniques of content analysis have only limited applicability given the research design that compares four states. I applied quantitative measures where they appear justified. The search function was applied to the greatest extent in Chapter 9, where I identified and categorized various local growth management techniques.

Bibliography

Abbott, Carl. 1994. "The Oregon Planning Style." In Carl Abbott, Deborah Howe, and Sy Adler, eds., *Planning the Oregon Way: A Twenty Year Evaluation.* Corvallis, OR: Oregon State University Press.

Abbott, Carl, Sy Adler, and Margery P. Abbott. 1997. *Planning a New West: The Columbia River Gorge National Scenic Area.* Corvallis, OR: Oregon State University Press.

Abbott, Carl, Deborah Howe, and Sy Adler, eds. 1994. *Planning the Oregon Way: A Twenty Year Evaluation.* Corvallis, OR: Oregon State University Press.

Adler, Sy. 1994. "The Oregon Approach to Integrating Transportation and Land Use Planning." In Carl Abbott, Deborah Howe, and Sy Adler, eds., *Planning the Oregon Way: A Twenty Year Evaluation.* Corvallis, OR: Oregon State University Press.

_____. 1990. "Environmental Movement Politics, Mandates to Plan, and Professional Planners: The Dialectics of Discretion in Planning Practice." *Journal of Architectural and Planning Research* 7, 4: 315-329.

Alexander, Ernest R., and Andreas Faludi. 1989. "Planning and Plan Implementation: Notes on Evaluation Criteria." *Environment and Planning B: Planning and Design* 16: 127-140.

American Law Institute. 1974. *A Model Land Development Code.* Philadelphia: American Law Institute.

American Planning Association. 1996a. *Modernizing State Planning Statutes: The Growing Smart Working Papers,* Vol. 1. Planning Advisory Service Report No. 462/463. Chicago: American Planning Association.

_____. 1996b. *Growing Smart Legislative Guidebook: Model Statutes for Planning and the Management of Change.* Phase 1 Interim Edition. Chicago: American Planning Association.

_____. 1993. "From the Capitals: Oregon Land Use Law Under Attack." *Planning* 59, 9: 5-6.

_____. 1989. *The Best of Planning: Two Decades of Articles from the Magazine of the American Planning Association.* Chicago: American Planning Association.

American Society of Planning Officials. 1966. *New Directions in Connecticut Planning Legislation: A Study of Connecticut Planning, Zoning and Related Statutes.* Chicago: American Society of Planning Officials.

Ames, Steve. C. 1993. *A Guide to Community Visioning.* Chicago: American Planning Association.

Anderson, Larz T. 1995. *Guidelines for Preparing Urban Plans.* Chicago: American Planning Association.

Association County Commissioners Georgia, Georgia Municipal Association, Georgia Department of Community Affairs, and Carl Vinson Institute of Government, The University of Georgia. 1997. *Charting a Course for Cooperation and Collaboration: An Introduction to the Service Delivery Strategy Act for Local Governments.* Atlanta: Georgia Department of Community Affairs.

Association of Washington Counties. September 1997. *1998 Legislative Issue.*

Audirac, Ivonne, Anne H. Shermyen, and Marc T. Smith. 1990. "Ideal Urban Form and Visions of The Good Life: Florida's Growth Management Dilemma." *Journal of the American Planning Association* 56, 4: 470-82.

Baer, William C. 1997. "General Plan Evaluation Criteria: An Approach to Making Better Plans." *Journal of the American Planning Association* 63, 3: 329-344.

Bagne, Conrad N. 1975. "State Land Use: Writing a Down-to-Earth Bill." In Randall W. Scott, David J. Brower and Dallas D. Miner, eds., *Management and Control of Growth: Issues, Techniques, Problems, Trends.* Washington, DC: Urban Land Institute.

Barrows, Richard L. 1982. *The Roles of Federal, State and Local Governments in Land Use Planning.* Washington, DC: National Planning Conference.

Beckley, Thomas M. 1992. "Leftist Critique of the Quiet Revolution in Land Use Control: Two Cases of Agency Formation." *Journal of Planning Education and Research* 12, 1: 55-66.

The Benkendorf Associates Corporation. 1996. *Town of PeEll, Washington, Comprehensive Plan.* First Complete Draft. Portland, OR: The Benkendorf Associates Corporation.

Berke, Philip R. 1998. "Reducing Natural Hazards Risks through Growth Management." *Journal of the American Planning Association* 64, 1: 76-87.

Berke, Philip R., and Steven P. French. 1994. "The Influence of State Planning Mandates on Local Plan Quality." *Journal of Planning Education and Research* 13, 4: 237-250.

Berke, Philip R., Dale J. Roenigk, Edward J. Kaiser, and Raymond Burby. 1996. "Enhancing Plan Quality: Evaluating the Role of State Planning Mandates for Natural Hazard Mitigation." *Journal of Environmental Planning and Management* 39, 1: 79-96.

Beyle, Thad L., Sureva Seligson, and Deil S. Wright. 1969. "New Directions in State Planning." *Journal of the American Institute of Planners* 35: 334-339.

Bish, Robert L. 1982. *Governing Puget Sound.* Seattle: University of Washington Press.

Bohlen, Sarah, Mary Beth McGuire, and Stuart Meck. 1996. "Getting Started: Initiating the Process of State Planning Law Reform." In *Modernizing State Planning Statutes: The Growing Smart Working Papers,*

Vol. 1. Planning Advisory Service Report No. 462/463. Chicago: American Planning Association.

Bollens, Scott A. 1993a. "Restructuring Land Use Governance." *Journal of Planning Literature* 7, 3: 211-226.

_____. 1993b. "Integrating Environmental and Economic Policies at the State Level." In Jay Stein, ed., *Growth Management: The Planning Challenge of the 1990s.* Newbury Park: Sage.

_____. 1992. "State Growth Management: Intergovernmental Frameworks and Policy Objectives." *Journal of the American Planning Association* 58, 4: 454-466.

Bollens, Scott A., and Roger W. Caves. 1994. "Counties and Land-Use Regionalism: Models of Governance." *International Journal of Public Administration* 17, 5: 851-880.

Bosselman, Fred P. 1986. "State and Local Plans in Hawaii: Lessons for Florida." In John M. DeGrove and Julian C. Juergensmeyer, eds., *Perspectives on Florida's Growth Management Act of 1985.* Cambridge: Lincoln Institute of Land Policy.

Bosselman, Fred, and David Callies. 1971. *The Quiet Revolution in Land Use Control.* Washington, DC: Council on Environmental Quality and Council of State Governments.

Bowman, A., and J. L. Franke. 1984. "The Decline of Substate Regionalism." *Journal of Urban Affairs* 6: 51-63.

Branch, Melville C. 1983. *Comprehensive Planning: General Theory and Principles.* New York: Palisades Publishers.

Brooks, Rusty, and Cindy Searcy. 1995. "Downtowns in Georgia: Where Are We and What Do We Know?" *Small Town* 26, 3: 14-29.

Broussard, Donald. 1987. "Point of View: The Growth Strategies Commission." *Georgia Planner* 2, 4: 9.

Brower, David J., David R. Godschalk, and Douglas R. Porter, eds. 1989. *Understanding Growth Management: Critical Issues and a Research Agenda.* Washington, DC: Urban Land Institute.

Bryson, John M., and R. C. Einsweiler, eds. 1988. *Strategic Planning: Threats and Opportunities for Planners.* Chicago: American Planning Association.

Buchsbaum, Peter A., and Larry J. Smith, eds. 1993. *State and Regional Comprehensive Planning: Implementing New Methods for Growth Management.* Chicago: American Bar Association.

Bunnell, Gene. 1997. "Fiscal Impact Studies as Advocacy and Story Telling." *Journal of Planning Literature* 12, 2: 136-151.

Burby, Raymond J., Philip Berke, Linda C. Dalton, et al. 1993. "Is State-Mandated Planning Effective?" *Land Use Law and Zoning Digest* 45, 10: 3-9.

Burby, Raymond J., and Linda C. Dalton. 1994. "Plans Can Matter! The Role of Land Use Plans and State Planning Mandates in Limiting Development of Hazardous Areas." *Public Administration Review* 54, 3: 229-238.

Burby, Raymond J., and Peter J. May, with Philip R. Berke, Linda C. Dalton, Steven P. French, and Edward J. Kaiser. 1997. *Making Governments Plan: State Experiments in Managing Land Use.* Baltimore: Johns Hopkins University Press.

Burby, Raymond J., Peter J. May, and Robert C. Paterson. 1998. "Improving Compliance with Regulations: Choices and Outcomes for Local Government." *Journal of the American Planning Association* 64, 3: 324-334.

Burchell, Robert W. 1993. "Issues, Actors and Analyses in Statewide Comprehensive Planning." In Peter A. Buchsbaum and Larry J. Smith, eds., *State and Regional Comprehensive Planning: Implementing New Methods for Growth Management.* Chicago: American Bar Association.

Burchell, Robert W., and David Listokin. 1978. *The Fiscal Impact Handbook: Estimating Local Costs and Revenues of Land Development.* Piscataway, NJ: Center for Urban Policy Research.

Bureau of Governmental Research and Service. 1988. *Current and Emerging Roles For COGs in Oregon.* Eugene, OR: Bureau of Governmental Research and Service.

Callies, David L. 1994. "The Quiet Revolution Revisited: A Quarter Century of Progress." *The Urban Lawyer* 26: 197-213.

_____. 1980. "The Quiet Revolution Revisited." *Journal of the American Planning Association* 46: 135-44.

Carney, T. F. 1972. *Content Analysis: A Technique for Systematic Inference from Communications.* Winnipeg: University of Manitoba Press.

Carson, Richard. February 1997. "Is it Time to Reinvent Statewide Land Use Planning?" *Oregon Planners' Journal* 125: 3-4.

Carter, Luther J. 1974. *The Florida Experience: Land and Water Policy in a Growth State.* Baltimore: Johns Hopkins University Press.

Castle, III, Gilbert. H. May 1986. "Making Supermaps." In *The Best of Planning: Two Decades of Articles from the Magazine of the American Planning Association.* Chicago: American Planning Association, 1989.

Catanese, A. J., and J. C. Synder. 1979. *Introduction to Urban Planning.* New York: McGraw Hill.

Cervero, Robert. 1996. "Jobs-Housing Balance Revisited: Trends and Impacts in the San Francisco Bay Area." *Journal of the American Planning Association* 62, 4: 492-511.

_____. 1991. "Jobs/Housing Balance as Public Policy." *Urban Land* 50, 10: 10-14.

_____. 1989. "Jobs-Housing Balancing and Regional Mobility." *Journal of the American Planning Association* 55, 2: 139-150.

Charlier, James. 1991. "Growth Management and Transportation: The Florida Experience." *Carolina Planning* 17, 1: 43-52.

Chinitz, Benjamin. 1990. "Growth Management: Good for the Town, Bad for the Nation?" *Journal of the American Planning Association* 56: 3-8.

Clark, T. A. 1994. "The State-Local Regulatory Nexus in U.S. Growth Management: Claims of Property and Participation in the Localist Resistance." *Environment and Planning C: Government and Policy* 12: 425-447.

Cogan Owens Cogan. 1997. *Working Paper: Goal 14 Analysis.* Salem, OR: Oregon Department of Land Conservation and Development.

Connerly, Charles E., and Nancy A. Muller. 1993. "Evaluating Housing Elements in Growth Management Comprehensive Plans." In Jay Stein, ed., *Growth Management: The Planning Challenge of the 1990s.* Newbury Park, CA: Sage Publications.

Cornish, Robert. September 1987. "Notes on the Master Plan: Coming to Terms." In *The Best of Planning: Two Decades of Articles from the Magazine of the American Planning Association.* Chicago: American Planning Association, 1989.

Corr, O. Casey. 1990. "Seattle in CAPtivity." *Planning* 56, 1: 18-21.

Cortright, Bob, Brian Gregor, John Kelly, et al. January 19, 1993. Interoffice Memorandum Regarding ODOT/DLCD Urban Mobility/Urban Growth Management Program. Salem, OR: Oregon Department of Land Conservation and Development.

Costa, Fernando. 1987. "A Message from the President." *Georgia Planner* 2, 2: 2.

Dalton, Linda C. 1990. "Emerging Knowledge about Planning Practice." *Journal of Planning Education and Research* 9, 1: 29-44.

_____. 1989. "The Limits of Regulation: Evidence from Local Plan Implementation in California." *Journal of the American Planning Association* 55, 2: 151-168.

D'Ambrosi, J. December 1976. *State Land Use Planning: A Selected Annotated Bibliography.* Council of Planning Librarians Exchange Bibliography. Monticello, IL: Council of Planning Librarians.

Daniels, Thomas L., and Arthur C. Nelson. 1986. "Is Oregon's Farmland Preservation Program Working?" *Journal of the American Planning Association* 52: 22-32.

DeAragón, Fernando. 1996. Palm Beach County, Florida: Why Regional Planning Failed. *Planners' Casebook,* 18. Chicago: American Institute of Certified Planners.

DeGrove, John M. 1996. "The Role of the Governor in State Land-Use Reform." In *Modernizing State Planning Statutes: The Growing Smart Working Papers,* Vol. 1. Planning Advisory Service Report No. 462/463.

_____. 1994. "Following in Oregon's Footsteps: The Impact of Oregon's Planning Program on Other States." In Carl Abbott, Deborah Howe, and Sy Adler, eds., *Planning the Oregon Way: A Twenty Year Evaluation.* Corvallis, OR: Oregon State University Press.

_____. 1993. "The Emergence of State Planning and Growth Management Systems: An Overview." In Peter A. Buchsbaum and Larry J. Smith, eds., *State and Regional Comprehensive Planning: Implementing New Meth-*

ods for Growth Management. Chicago: American Bar Association.

_____. 1992. *The New Frontier for Land Policy: Planning and Growth Management in the States.* Cambridge, Ma: Lincoln Institute of Land Policy.

_____. ed. 1991. *Balanced Growth: A Planning Guide for Local Government.* Washington: International City Management Association.

_____. 1989. "Growth Management and Governance." In David J. Brower, David R. Godschalk, and Douglas R. Porter, eds., *Understanding Growth Management: Critical Issues and a Research Agenda.* Washington, DC: Urban Land Institute.

_____. 1988. "Critical Area Programs in Florida: Creative Balancing of Growth and The Environment." *Washington University Journal of Urban and Contemporary Law* 34: 51-97.

_____. 1986. "Beyond the Growth Management Act of 1985." In John M. DeGrove and Julian C. Juergensmeyer, eds., *Perspectives on Florida's Growth Management Act of 1985.* Cambridge: Lincoln Institute of Land Policy.

_____. 1984. *Land Growth and Politics.* Chicago: American Planning Association.

_____. 1983. "The Quiet Revolution 10 Years Later." *Planning* 49, 10: 25-28. Reprinted in *The Best of Planning: Two Decades of Articles from the Magazine of the American Planning Association.* Chicago: American Planning Association, 1989.

DeGrove, John M., and Julian C. Juergensmeyer. 1986. *Perspectives on Florida's Growth Management Act of 1985.* Cambridge: Lincoln Institute of Land Policy.

DeGrove, John M., and Patricia M. Metzger. 1993. "Growth Management and the Integrated Roles of State, Regional and Local Governments." In Jay Stein, ed., *Growth Management: The Planning Challenge of the 1990s.* Newbury Park, CA: Sage Publications.

DeGrove, John M., Thomas Roberts, and Arthur C. Nelson. January 1990. "Statement in Support of Governor Joe Frank Harris to the American Planning Association." *Georgia Planner:* 5.

DeGrove, John M., and Nancy E. Stroud. 1988. "New Developments and Future Trends in Local Government Comprehensive Planning." *Stetson Law Review* 17: 573-605.

_____. 1987. "State Land Planning and Regulation: Innovative Roles in the 1980s and Beyond." *Land Use Law and Zoning Digest* 39, 3: 3-8.

DeHaven-Smith, Lance. 1991. *Controlling Florida's Development.* Wakefield, NH: Hollowbrook Publishing.

_____. 1984. "Regulatory Theory and State Land Use Regulation: Implications from Florida's Experience with Growth Management." *Public Administration Review* 44: 413-420.

Deyle, Robert E., and Richard A. Smith. 1998. "Local Government Compliance with State Planning Mandates: The Effects of State Implementation in Florida." *Journal of the American Planning Association* 64, 4: 457-469.

Diamond, Henry L., and Patrick F. Noonan. 1996. *Land Use in America.* Washington, DC: Island Press.

Dillard, G. Douglas, and Larry M. Dingle, 1990. "Zoning and Land Use Trends Article." In G. D., Dillard, L. M. Dingle, T. D. Brannon, M. B. Davis, J. S. Stokes, and N. V. Toulme, *Major Land Use Laws in Georgia.* Eau Claire, WI: National Business Institute.

DiMento, Joseph. 1986. "Florida's Growth Management Act of 1985: Coping with Consistency." In John M. DeGrove and Julian C. Juergensmeyer, eds., *Perspectives on Florida's Growth Management Act of 1985.* Cambridge: Lincoln Institute of Land Policy.

_____. 1980. *The Consistency Doctrine and the Limits of Planning.* Cambridge: Oelgeschlager, Gunn and Hain.

Downs, Anthony. 1994. *New Visions for Metropolitan America.* Washington, DC: Brookings Institution.

Doyle, Griff. 1992. "Opportunity to Comment on Proposed Revisions to the Minimum Standards and Procedures." *Georgia Planner,* 3, 3.

Durant, Robert F., Larry W. Thomas, and Don Haynes. 1993. "The Politics of Growth Management Reform in the States: A Comparative Analysis." *Policy Studies Review* 12, 3/4: 30-54.

Durkan, T. Ryan. Fall 1996. "Commission Searches for Land Use Treasures." *About Growth: A Quarterly Publication About Growth Management,* 1.

Dye Management Group, Inc. 1990. *Growth Management Data Inventory and Collection Report.* Olympia: Washington State Department of Community Development, Growth Management Division.

EcoNorthwest, David J. Newton Associates, and MLP Associates. 1991. *Urban Growth Management Study: Case Studies Report.* Salem, OR: Oregon Department of Land Conservation and Development.

EcoNorthwest, Pacific Rim Resources, and J. Richard Forester. 1995a. *Evaluation of Policies Recommended by the Urban Growth Management Task Group: Technical Report.* Salem, OR: Oregon Department of Land Conservation and Development.

_____. 1995b. *Tools of the Trade.* Salem, OR: Oregon Department of Land Conservation and Development.

Ehrenhalt, Alan. 1997. "The Great Wall of Portland." *Governing* 10, 8: 20-24.

Einsweiler, L. D. September 1987. "Notes on the Master Plan: Florida: The Rush Is On." In *The Best of Planning: Two Decades of Articles from the Magazine of the American Planning Association.* Chicago: American Planning Association, 1989.

Enger, Susan. 1992. *Issues in Designating Urban Growth Areas, Part I: Providing Adequate Urban Area Land Supply.* Olympia: Washington Department of Community Development, Growth Management Division.

Ewing, Reid. 1996. *Best Development Practices: Doing the Right Thing and*

Making Money at the Same Time. Chicago: American Planning Association.

Fischel, William A. 1991. "Growth Management Reconsidered: Good for the Town, Bad for the Nation?" *Journal of the American Planning Association* 57, 3: 341-344.

Florida Atlantic University/Florida International University Joint Center for Environmental and Urban Problems. 1998. *Eastward Ho! Financial Impediments and Solutions to Development.* Fort Lauderdale: Joint Center.

Florida Department of Community Affairs. 1997a. *Just What Do You Mean . . . "Sustainable?: The Florida Sustainable Communities Demonstration Project.* Tallahassee: Florida Department of Community Affairs.

_____. 1997b. "Sustainable Communities." *Community Planning,* 6, 1.

_____. 1997c. *Data and Information Source Guide.* Tallahassee: Florida DCA.

_____. April 1996a. *Evaluation and Appraisal Reports: A Guidebook for Florida Cities and Counties.* 2nd Ed. Tallahassee: Florida DCA.

_____. 1996b. *Checklist for EAR Sufficiency Review.* Tallahassee: Florida DCA.

_____. 1996c. *Building Partnerships for Florida's Future: Division of Resource Planning and Management Program Guide.* Tallahassee: Florida DCA.

_____. 1995. "Florida Prepares for ICE-age." *Community Planning,* 4, 1.

_____. 1994. "EAR Grant Program Update." *Community Planning* 3, 3.

_____. 1991. "Techniques for Discouraging Sprawl." In John M. DeGrove, ed., *Balanced Growth: A Planning Guide for Local Government.* Washington, DC: International City Management Association. Originally published by the Florida Department of Community Affairs in *Technical Memo* 4, 4, 1989.

_____. 1991a. *Developing Adoption Ordinances for Local Government Comprehensive Plans: A Technical Assistance Paper.* Tallahassee: Florida DCA.

_____. 1991b. "Regional Policy Plan Amendments." *Technical Memo* 6, 2.

_____. 1990a. "Hearing Officer Finds That DCA's Approach to Urban Containment Is Balanced." *Technical Memo* 5, 2.

_____. 1990b. "Comprehensive Planning in Florida: Past, Present, and Future." *Technical Memo* 5, 8.

_____. 1990c. "Unified Land Development Codes Aid Public's Participation in Planning Process." *Technical Memo* 5, 8.

_____. 1989a. *The State Land Development Plan.* Tallahassee: Florida DCA.

_____. 1989b. "Newsbriefs: Revised State Land Development Plan Available." *Planning Notes,* 2, 4.

_____. 1989c. "Report Calls on Locals to Set Urban Service Areas." *Planning Notes* 2, 5.

_____. 1989d. "DCA's Urban Sprawl Conference Scheduled for November 6." *Planning Notes* 2, 7.

_____. 1989e. "Implementing Local Comprehensive Plans Through

Land Development Regulations." *Technical Memo* 4, 4.

_____. 1989f. "Accomplishments of Okaloosa-Walton Land Use Institute." *Technical Memo* 4, 2.

_____. 1989g. "LDR Workshop Calendar." *Planning Notes* 2, 7.

_____. 1989h. "Submission and Review of Plan Amendments." *Planning Notes* 2, 7.

_____. 1989i. "Copying Model Element Language No Substitute for Careful Analyses." *Planning Notes* 2, 3.

_____. 1989j. "Financial Assistance Available." *Planning Notes* 2, 6.

____. 1988a. "Governor's Task Force Studying Urban Growth Patterns." *Planning Notes* 1, 5.

_____. 1988b. "Newsbriefs: Grant Applications." *Planning Notes* 1, 4.

_____. 1988c. "Model LDRs Available Soon." *Planning Notes* 1, 4.

_____. 1987a. "Model Element: Future Land Use." Tallahassee: Florida DCA.

_____. 1987b. *Preparing a Comprehensive Plan: Practical Considerations in Meeting Florida's Local Planning Requirements.* Tallahassee: Florida DCA, Bureau of Local Resource Planning.

_____. 1987c. "$9 Million Available for Local Planning Assistance." *Technical Memo* 2, 2.

_____. 1987d. "Planner Positions Available." *Technical Memo* 2, 2.

_____. 1986a. "Regional Plans Nearing Review." *Technical Memo* 1, 2.

_____. 1986b. "Additional Local Planning Funds Available." *Technical Memo* 1, 2.

_____. 1986c. *Population Estimation and Projection Techniques: A Guide to Methodologies for Forecasting Population Growth for Florida's Local Planning Agencies.* Tallahassee: Florida DCA, Bureau of Local Resource Planning.

_____. 1986d. *A Guide to Local Government Comprehensive Planning Data Sources.* Tallahassee: Florida DCA.

_____. 1986e. "Q And A: Questions and Answers Regarding the Local Government Comprehensive Planning and Land Development Regulation Act." *Technical Memo* 1, 1.

_____. 1978a. "Planning Funds to Be Distributed by Technical Assistance." *Local Government News* 2, 5.

_____. 1978b. "Local Government Comprehensive Planning Assistance Grants Awarded." *Local Government News* 3, 1.

_____. 1977a. "Local Government Comprehensive Planning Act Status as of April 19, 1977." *Local Government News* 1, 7.

_____. 1977b. "DCA Requests Appropriation for Partial Local Government Comprehensive Planning." *Local Government News* 1, 5.

_____. 1977c. "State LGCPA Grants Awarded to 64 Local Governments." *Local Government News* 2, 2.

_____. 1976a. *The Local Government Comprehensive Planning Act.* Tallahassee: Florida DCA, Division of Community Assistance.

_____. 1976b. "Local Government Comprehensive Planning Data." *Local Government News* 1, 4.

_____. 1976c. "LGCPA Workshops Set for Six Areas." *Local Government News* 1, 2.

_____. 1976d. "Local Government Comprehensive Planning Act: Slide Presentation Available." *Local Government News* 1, 4.

Franzen, Robin, and Brent Hunsberger. December 13, 1998. "Have We Outgrown Our Approach to Growth?" *The Sunday Oregonian*. Page A-1.

Frederick, Jim. January 1992. "The ABCs of RIRs." *Georgia Planner* 1.

Freilich, Robert H., and M. Schultz. 1995. *Model Subdivision Regulations: Planning and Law.* Chicago: American Planning Association.

Freilich, Robert H., and Mark S. White. 1996. "State and Regional Roles in Transportation and Land Use." In *Modernizing State Planning Statutes: The Growing Smart Working Papers,* Vol. 1. Planning Advisory Service Report No. 462/463. Chicago: American Planning Association.

Fujii, Tadashi, and Truman A. Hartshorn. 1995. "The Changing Metropolitan Structure of Atlanta, Georgia: Locations of Functions and Regional Structure in a Multinucleated Urban Area." *Urban Geography* 16, 8: 680-707.

Fulton, William. 1991. "The Second Revolution in Land Use Planning." In John M. DeGrove, ed., *Balanced Growth: A Planning Guide for Local Government*. Washington, DC: International City Management Association.

_____. 1990. "Addicted to Growth: Florida Doesn't Want to Become a Congested Mess, but it Isn't Sure How to Prevent It." The State's Growth Management Law May Be its Last Chance. *Governing* 4, 1: 68-70.

_____. 1989. "In Land Use Planning, a Second Revolution Shifts Control to the States." *Governing* 2, 6: 40-45.

Gage, Robert W. 1990. "Key Issues in Intergovernmental Relations in the Post-Reagan Era: Implications for Change." *American Review of Public Administration* 20, 3: 155-174.

Gale, Dennis. E. 1992. "Eight State-Sponsored Growth Management Programs: A Comparative Analysis." *Journal of the American Planning Association* 58, 4: 425-439.

Gay, George E. H. 1996. "State Solutions to Growth Management: Vermont, Oregon and a Synthesis." *Natural Resources & Environment* 10, 3: 73-74.

Georgia Chapter of the American Planning Association. February 29, 1996. "Future Communities Commission Studies Growth Management Tools." *Georgia Planner* 1, 11.

_____. 1992a. "Growth Strategies Update." *Georgia Planner* 9: 6.

_____. 1992b. "Summary of 1992 Georgia General Assembly Action of Planning Issues: Final Report." *Georgia Planner* 6: 1.

_____. March 1991. "1991 Georgia Legislative Session." *Georgia Planner* 1.

_____. February 1990. "Executive Summary: Minimum Planning Standards and Procedures as

Adopted by the Board of Community Affairs January 10, 1990." *Georgia Planner* 1-2.

_____. 1988. "Local Governments Seeking Zoning Reforms from General Assembly." *Georgia Planner* 3, 1: 5.

_____. 1987. "1987 Legislative Report." *Georgia Planner* 2, 2: 1.

Georgia Department of Community Affairs. February 1996a. "Georgia's Growth Strategies Experiment: A Five Year Status Report." *Georgia Planner* 1: 5-9.

_____. July 1996b. *Georgia's Communities: Planning, Growing, Achieving.* Atlanta: Georgia DCA, Office of Coordinated Planning.

_____. December 1996c. *Local Plan Review Guide,* 1996 ed. Atlanta: Georgia DCA, Office of Coordinated Planning.

_____. 1994. *Using Data for Local Planning: A Companion Guidebook to "Data for Planning."* Atlanta: Georgia DCA, Office of Coordinated Planning.

_____. 1992a. "Revised Minimum Planning Standards to Take Effect October 1, 1992." *Georgia Planner* 8: 1.

_____. 1992b. *Policy Memo Series,* Vol. 4, Nos. 1 and 2. Atlanta: Georgia DCA, Office of Coordinated Planning.

_____. 1991a. *How to Organize for Local Planning: A Guidebook.* Atlanta: Georgia DCA, Office of Coordinated Planning.

_____. 1991b. *Planning Assistance: A Guidebook.* Atlanta: Georgia DCA, Office of Coordinated Planning.

_____. 1991c. *Using Maps for Local Planning: A Guidebook.* Atlanta: Georgia DCA, Office of Coordinated Planning.

_____. 1991d. *How to Address "The Environmental Planning Criteria" in Your Local Plan: A Guidebook.* Atlanta: Georgia DCA, Office of Coordinated Planning.

_____. 1991e. *Policy Memo Series,* Vol. 3, Nos. 1 and 2. Atlanta: Georgia DCA, Office of Coordinated Planning.

_____. 1990a. *Preparing a Local Plan: A Guidebook.* Atlanta: Georgia DCA, Office of Coordinated Planning.

_____. 1990b. *Why Plan? A Guidebook for Local Planning.* Atlanta: Georgia DCA, Office of Coordinated Planning.

_____. 1990c. *How to Organize for Local Planning: A Guidebook.* Atlanta: Georgia DCA, Office of Coordinated Planning.

_____. Summer 1990d. *Policy Memo Series,* Vol. 2, No. 1. Atlanta: Georgia DCA, Office of Coordinated Planning.

_____. Fall 1989. *Policy Memo Series,* Vol. 1, No. 1. Atlanta: Georgia DCA, Office of Coordinated Planning.

_____. 1988. *Implementation Strategy for the Coordinated Planning Recommendations.* Atlanta: Georgia DCA.

Gleeson, Michael E., et al. 1976. *Urban Growth Management Systems: An Evaluation of Policy-Related Research.* Chicago: American Society of Planning Officials.

Godschalk, David R. 1992. "In Defense of Growth Management."

Journal of the American Planning Association 58, 4: 422-424.

_____. 1975. "State Growth Management: A Carrying Capacity Policy." In Randall W. Scott, David J. Brower, and Dallas D. Miner, eds., *Management and Control of Growth: Issues, Techniques, Problems, Trends.* Washington, DC: Urban Land Institute.

Godschalk, David R., and David J. Brower. 1989. "A Coordinated Growth Management Research Strategy." In David J. Brower, David R. Godschalk, and Douglas R. Porter, eds., *Understanding Growth Management: Critical Issues and a Research Agenda.* Washington, DC: Urban Land Institute.

Gonzalez, J. L. 1991. "Local Plans Not User-Friendly." *Environmental and Urban Issues* 18, 3: 1-2.

Gordon, Steve C. 1988. "Urban Growth Management Oregon Style." *Public Management* 70, 8: 9-12.

Gottlieb, Paul D. 1995. "The "Golden Egg" as a Natural Resource: Toward a Normative Theory of Growth Management." *Society and Natural Resources* 8: 49-56.

Governor's Growth Strategies Commission. 1988. *Quality Growth Partnership: The Bridge to Georgia's Future.* Final Report. Atlanta: Office of the Governor.

Governor's Task Force on Land Use. 1982. *Report to the Governor.* Salem, OR: Office of the Governor.

Governor's Task Force on Urban Growth Patterns. 1989. *Final Report.* Tallahassee: Florida Department of Community Affairs.

Graham, Jr., Frank. 1981. *The Adirondack Park: A Political History.* Syracuse, NY: Syracuse University Press.

Growth Strategies Reassessment Task Force. 1998. *Georgia's Future: Beyond Growth Strategies.* Atlanta: Georgia Department of Community Affairs.

Hall, Peter. 1988. "The Turbulent Eighth Decade: Challenges to American City Planning." *Journal of the American Planning Association* 55, 3: 275-282.

Harris, Diane Chandler. 1988. "Growth Management Reconsidered." *Journal of Planning Literature* 3, 4: 466-482.

Haworth and Anderson, Inc. 1976. *Land Use Planning in the State of Washington: The Role of Local Government.* Olympia: Washington State Office of Community Development.

Healy, Robert G. August 1983. "Hallmarks of a New Decade in Land Use." In *The Best of Planning: Two Decades of Articles from the Magazine of the American Planning Association.* Chicago: American Planning Association, 1989.

_____. 1976. *Land Use and the States.* Washington, DC: Resources for the Future.

Healy, Robert G., and John S. Rosenburg. 1979. *Land Use and the States,* 2nd Ed. Baltimore: Johns Hopkins University Press.

Helling, Amy. 1998. "Collaborative Visioning: Proceed With Caution! Results From Evaluating Atlanta's Vision 2020 Project." *Journal of the*

American Planning Association 64, 3: 335-349.

Henderson, C., D. Drake, and J. Ross. 1995. "1995 Legislative Update." *Environmental and Urban Issues* 23, 1: 1-6.

Henderson, Young & Company. 1996. *Policy Analysis: Adequate Public Facilities Requirements and Focused Public Investment Plans.* Salem, OR: Oregon Transportation and Growth Management Program.

Hollander, Elizabeth L., Leslie S. Pollock, Jeffry D. Reckinger, and Frank Beal. 1988. "General Development Plans." In Frank So and Judith Getzels, eds., *The Practice of Local Government Planning,* 2nd Ed. Washington, DC: International City Management Association.

Howe, Deborah A. 1994. "A Research Agenda for Oregon Planning: Problems and Practice For the 1990s." In Carl Abbott, Deborah Howe, and Sy Adler, eds., *Planning the Oregon Way: A Twenty Year Evaluation.* Corvallis, OR: Oregon State University Press.

_____. 1993. "Growth Management in Oregon." In Jay Stein, ed., *Growth Management: The Planning Challenge of the 1990s.* Newbury Park, CA: Sage Publications.

_____. 1991a. *Review of Growth Management Strategies Used in Other States.* Salem, OR: Oregon Department of Land Conservation and Development.

_____. 1991b. *Development of a Research Action Plan: Issues and Opportunities.* Salem, OR: Oregon Department of Land Conservation and Development.

Innes, Judith E. 1993. "Implementing State Growth Management in the United States: Strategies for Coordination." In Jay Stein, ed., *Growth Management: The Planning Challenge of the 1990s.* Newbury Park, CA: Sage Publications.

James Duncan and Associates, Van Horn-Gray Associates, Inc., Ivey, Bennett, Harris, and Walls, and Wade-Trim, Inc. 1989a. *The Search for Efficient Urban Growth Patterns: A Study of the Fiscal Impacts of Development in Florida.* Tallahassee: Florida Department of Community Affairs.

_____. 1989b. *The Search for Efficient Urban Growth Patterns: Technical Appendices.* Tallahassee: Florida Department of Community Affairs.

Jeff, Gloria. 1996. "ISTEA and the Clean Air Act Amendments: Implications for State and Local Planning." In *Modernizing State Planning Statutes: The Growing Smart Working Papers,* Vol. 1. Planning Advisory Service Report No. 462/463. Chicago: American Planning Association.

JFK and Associates, Pacific Rim Resources, and SG Resources. 1996. *Accessibility Measure and Transportation Impact Factor Study.* Draft Final Report. Salem, OR: Oregon Transportation and Growth Management Program.

Joint Legislative Committee on Land Use. 1976. *Final Report.* Salem, OR: Joint Legislative Committee on Land Use.

Kaiser, Edward J., and David R. Godschalk. 1995. "Twentieth Century Land Use Planning: A Stalwart Family Tree." *Journal of the American Planning Association* 61, 3: 365-385.

Kaiser, Edward J., David R. Godschalk, and F. Stuart Chapin, Jr. 1995. *Urban Land Use Planning*, 4th Ed. Urbana, IL: University of Illinois Press.

Kelly, Eric Damian. 1994. "The Transportation Land-Use Link." *Journal of Planning Literature*, 9, 4: 128-145.

_____. 1993. *Managing Community Growth: Policies, Techniques and Impacts.* New York: Praeger.

Kent, Denton U. 1983. "The Metropolitan Service District (Metro)." In Gill C. Lim, ed., *Regional Planning: Evolution, Crisis and Prospects.* Totowa, NJ: Allanheld, Osmun and Co. Publishers.

Kent, Jr., T. J. 1990. *The Urban General Plan.* Chicago: American Planning Association.

Kirk, David. June 1990. "Letter from the Georgia Planning Association's President to Jim Higdon, Commissioner, Georgia Department of Community Affairs, May 25, 1990." *Georgia Planner* 4.

Kitzhaber, John. August 28, 1995. "ODOT Must Lead State Growth Plans." *Daily Journal of Commerce* (Guest Column).

Knaap, Gerrit. 1998. "The Determinants of Residential Property Values: Implications for Metropolitan Planning." *Journal of Planning Literature* 12, 3: 267-282.

_____. 1994. "Land Use Politics in Oregon." In Carl Abbott, Deborah Howe, and Sy Adler eds., *Planning the Oregon Way: A Twenty Year Evaluation.* Corvallis, OR: Oregon State University Press.

Knaap, Gerrit, Lewis D. Hopkins, and Kieran P. Donaghy. 1998. "Do Plans Matter? A Game-Theoretic Model for Examining the Logic and Effects of Land Use Planning." *Journal of Planning Education and Research* 18, 1: 25-34.

Knaap, Gerrit, and Arthur C. Nelson. 1992. *The Regulated Landscape: Lessons on State Land Use Planning from Oregon.* Cambridge: Lincoln Institute of Land Policy.

Koenig, John. 1990. "Down to the Wire in Florida." *Planning* 56, 10: 4-11.

Krippendorff, K. 1980. *Content Analysis: An Introduction to its Methodology.* Beverly Hills: Sage.

Krog, Kathleen. 1996. "Muddy Waters." *Planning* 62, 3: 14-17.

KRS Associates, Inc. 1976. *A Local Officials Guide to the Local Government Comprehensive Planning Act.* Tallahassee: Florida DCA, Division of Community Assistance.

Krueckeberg, D. A., and A. L. Silvers. 1974. *Urban Planning Analysis: Methods and Models.* New York: Pergamon Press.

Kundell, James E., Richard W. Campbell, Joseph M. Heikoff, Lawrence R. Hepburn, Robert Klant, and S. Wesley Woolf. 1989. *Land-Use Policy and the Protection of Georgia's Environment.* Athens, GA: University of Georgia, Carl Vinson Institute of Government.

Lawlor, James. 1992. "State of the Statutes." *Planning* 58, 12: 10-14.

Leeman, Wayne. A. 1997. *Oregon Land, Rural or Urban? The Struggle for Control.* Ashland, OR: Millwright Press.

Leo, Christopher, with Mary Ann Beavis, Andrew Carver, and Robyne Turner. 1998. "Is Urban Sprawl Back on the Political Agenda?" *Urban Affairs Review* 34, 2: 179-211.

Leonard, Jeffrey H. 1983. *Managing Oregon's Growth: The Politics of Development Planning.* Washington, DC: Conservation Foundation.

Lewis, Sylvia. 1992. "Goodbye, Ramapo. Hello, Yakima and Isle of Palms." *Planning* 58, 7: 9-16.

Lewis, Jr., Tom. 1986. "Letter from the Secretary to Local Officials." *Technical Memo* 1, 2.

Liberty, Robert L. 1996. "The Battle over Tom McCall's Legacy: The Story of Land Use in the 1995 Oregon Legislature." *Environmental and Urban Issues* 23, 3: 1-14.

_____. 1992. "Oregon's Comprehensive Growth Management Program: An Implementation Review and Lessons for Other States." *Environmental Law Reporter* 22: 10368-10391.

Lim, Gill Chin. 1983. "Regional Planning in Transition." In Gill. Chin Lim, ed., *Regional Planning: Evolution, Crisis and Prospects.* Totowa, NJ: Allanheld, Osmun & Co. Publishers.

Lincoln, Robert. 1996. "Implementing the Consistency Doctrine." In *Modernizing State Planning Statutes: The Growing Smart Working Papers,* Vol. 1. Planning Advisory Service Report No. 462/463. Chicago: American Planning Association.

Liou, K. T., and Todd J. Dicker. 1994. "The Effect of the Growth Management Act on Local Comprehensive Planning Expenditures: The South Florida Experience." *Public Administration Review* 54, 3: 239-244.

Liroff, Robert A., and Gordon G. Davis. 1981. *Protecting Open Space: Land Use Control in the Adirondack Park.* Cambridge: Ballinger.

Little, Charles E. 1974. *The New Oregon Trail: An Account of the Development and Passage of State Land-Use Legislation in Oregon.* Washington, DC: Conservation Foundation.

Mandelker, Daniel R. 1989. "The Quiet Revolution—Success and Failure." *Journal of the American Planning Association* 55: 204-205.

Mann, Richard A., and Mike Miles. 1979. "State Land Use Planning: The Current Status and Demographic Rationale." *Journal of the American Planning Association* 45, 1: 48-61.

May, Peter J. 1994. "Analyzing Mandate Design: State Mandates Governing Hazard-Prone Areas." *Publius: The Journal of Federalism* 24: 1-16.

_____. 1993. "Mandate Design and Implementation: Enhancing Implementation Efforts and Shaping Regulatory Styles." *Journal of Policy*

Analysis and Management 12, 4: 634-663.

May, Peter J., and Raymond J. Burby. 1996. "Coercive Versus Cooperative Policies: Comparing Intergovernmental Mandate Performance." *Journal of Policy Analysis and Management* 15, 2: 171-201.

Mazmanian, Daniel A., and Paul A. Sabatier. 1983. *Implementation and Public Policy.* Lanham, MD: University Press of America.

McCahill, Ed. March 1974. "Florida's Not-So-Quiet Revolution." In *The Best of Planning: Two Decades of Articles from the Magazine of the American Planning Association.* Chicago: American Planning Association, 1989.

McDowell, Bruce D. 1986. "The Evolution of American Planning." In Frank S. So, Irving Hand, and Bruce D. McDowell, eds., *The Practice of State and Regional Planning.* Chicago: American Planning Association.

McHarg, Ian. 1969. *Design with Nature.* Garden City, NY: Natural History Press.

McKay, P. S. 1991. "Fall of 1991: Where Are We? A Status Report on Growth Management Plans in Florida." *Environmental and Urban Issues* 19, 1: 1-7.

McKinsey & Company, Inc. December 28, 1998. "Metro Atlanta Transportation Initiative. The Full Report." *Atlanta Journal-Constitution.* Page E-4.

Meck, Stuart. 1996. "Model Planning and Zoning Enabling Legislation: A Short History." In *Modernizing State Planning Statutes: The Growing Smart Working Papers,* Vol. 1. Planning Advisory Service Report No. 462/463. Chicago: American Planning Association.

Meeks, Jr, Gordon. 1990. "Growth Management: A Renewed Agenda for the States." *Journal of Soil and Water Conservation* 45, 6: 600-604.

Merten, Patrick E. 1997. "Do Statewide Planning and the Consistency Concept Infringe on Home Rule Authority?" *Journal of Planning Literature* 11, 4: 564-573.

Metropolitan Service District. 1994a. *Region 2040: Concepts for Growth.* Portland, OR: Metropolitan Service District.

_____. 1994b. *Region 2040: Recommended Alternative Decision Kit.* Portland, OR: Metropolitan Service District.

Mildner, Gerard, Kenneth Dueker, and Anthony Rufolo. 1996. *Impact of the Urban Growth Boundary on Metropolitan Housing Markets.* Portland, OR: Center for Urban Studies, Portland State University.

Moore, Terry, and Arthur C. Nelson. 1994. "Lessons for Effective Urban Containment and Resource Land Preservation Policy." *Journal of Urban Planning and Development* 120, 4: 157-173.

Moore, Terry, and Paul Thorsnes. 1994. *The Transportation/Land Use Connection: A Framework for Practical Policy.* Planning Advisory Service Report No. 448/449. Chicago: American Planning Association.

Morris, Marya. 1996. "Approaches to Regulating Regional Impacts." In

Modernizing State Planning Statutes: The Growing Smart Working Papers. Planning Advisory Service Report No. 462/463. Chicago: American Planning Association.

_____. 1993. "Oregon's Transportation Planning Rule." *Planning* 59, 3: 13-14.

Murley, James F., Eric Draper, and J. Larry Durrence. 1992. "1992 Legislative Update." *Environmental and Urban Issues* 20, 1: 4-12.

Murley, James F., David L. Powell, and Eric Draper. 1993. "1993 Legislative Update." *Environmental and Urban Issues* 21, 1: 8-15.

Myers, Phyllis. 1974. *Slow Start in Paradise: An Account of the Development, Passage, and Implementation of State Land-Use Legislation in Florida.* Washington, DC: Conservation Foundation.

Nave, Robert. 1988. "Common Problems Found in Comprehensive Plan Elements." *Technical Memo* 3, 3.

Ndubisi, Forster, and Mary Dyer. 1992. "The Role of Regional Entities in Formulating and Implementing Statewide Growth Policies." *State and Local Government Review* 24: 117-127.

Nelson, Arthur C. 1994. "Oregon's Urban Growth Boundary as a Landmark Planning Tool." In Carl Abbott, Deborah Howe, and Sy Adler, eds., *Planning the Oregon Way: A Twenty Year Evaluation.* Corvallis, OR: Oregon State University Press.

_____. 1992. "Preserving Prime Farmland in the Face of Urbanization: Lessons From Oregon." *Journal of the American Planning Association* 58, 4: 467-88.

_____. 1990a. "Blazing New Planning Trails in Oregon." *Urban Land* 49, 8: 32-35. Reprinted in DeGrove 1991.

_____. 1990b. "Growth Strategies: The New Planning Game in Georgia." *Carolina Planning* 16, 1: 4-8.

Nelson, Arthur C., and James B. Duncan, with Clancey J. Mullen and Kirk R. Bishop. 1995. *Growth Management Principles and Practices.* Chicago: American Planning Association.

Nelson, Arthur C., and Terry Moore. 1996. "Assessing Growth Management Policy Implementation: Case Study of the United States' Leading Growth Management State." *Land Use Policy* 13: 241-259.

_____. October 1993. "Assessing Urban Growth Management: The Case of Portland, Oregon, the USA's Largest Urban Growth Boundary." *Land Use Policy:* 293-302.

Neuman, Michael. 1998. "Does Planning Need the Plan?" *Journal of the American Planning Association* 64, 2: 208-220.

Niebanck, Paul. 1986. "Conclusion: The Second Generation of Growth Management." In Douglas R. Porter, ed., *Growth Management: Keeping on Target?* Washington, DC: Urban Land Institute.

Nokes, R. Gregory. December 4, 1998a. "Vote Adds 5,100 Acres to Growth Zone." *The Oregonian.* Page A-1.

_____. December 6, 1998. "Boundary Expansion Won't Be the Last." *The Oregonian.* Page B-1.

Nolon, John R. 1996. "Accommodating Home Rule in State Land Use Reform." In *Modernizing State Planning Statutes: The Growing Smart Working Papers,* Vol. 1. Planning Advisory Service Report No. 462/463. Chicago: American Planning Association.

Northeast Florida Regional Council. 1996. *Northeast Florida Strategic Regional Policy Plan.* (Draft, March). Jacksonville: Northeast Florida Regional Planning Council.

O'Connell, Daniel W. 1986. "New Directions in State Legislation: The Florida Growth Management Act and State Comprehensive Plan." In John M. DeGrove and Julian C. Juergensmeyer, eds., *Perspectives on Florida's Growth Management Act of 1985.* Cambridge: Lincoln Institute of Land Policy.

Oliver, Gordon. 1996. "Oregon Metro Faces the Ultimate Test." *Planning* 62, 6: 11.

_____. 1992. "1000 Friends Are Watching." *Planning* 58, 11: 9-13.

_____. 1989. "Portland Goes for Broke." *Planning* 55, 2: 10-15.

1000 Friends of Washington. 1996a. *Annual Report.* Seattle: 1000 Friends of Washington.

_____. Winter 1996b. "Myths and Facts about Growth Management." *Outlook* 5.

Oregon Department of Land Conservation and Development. November 1998. *Goal 14 Urbanization Bulletin #3: An Update on Proposed Refinements to Goal 14, the Urbanization Goal.*

_____. December 22, 1997a. Memorandum from Director Dick Benner to the Land Conservation and Development Commission Regarding Goal 14 Analysis (Agenda Item 4.0, January 16, 1998, LCDC Meeting).

_____. 1997b. A Model Work Program for Integrating ORS 197.296 Requirements with Goals 1, 10, and 14. (Draft #3, April 25, 1997.)

_____. 1992. Recommendations of the Task Group on Development Inside Urban Growth Boundaries. Salem, OR: DLCD.

_____. 1991. *Urban Growth Management Study: Summary Report.* Salem, OR: DLCD.

Oregon Transportation and Growth Management Program. 1998. *The Principles of Smart Development.* Planning Advisory Service Report No. 479. Chicago: American Planning Association.

_____. 1997. *Planning for Residential Growth: A Workbook for Oregon's Urban Areas.* Salem, OR: DLCD.

_____. 1996. *1993-1995 Grant Program Catalog.* Salem, OR: DLCD.

_____. 1995a. *Problem Documentation Case Study: Bend Urban Growth Boundary Development Time Series Analysis, 1985-1995.* Salem, OR: DLCD.

_____. August 29, 1995b. *Work Program and Budget: 1995-1997 Biennium.* Salem, OR: DLCD.

_____. 1994a. *Annual Report.* December 31, 1994, Draft. Salem, OR: DLCD.

_____. June 28, 1994b. *Revised Work Program and Budget: 1993-1995 Biennium.* Salem, OR: DLCD.

Oregon Progress Board. 1994. *Oregon Benchmarks: Standards for Measuring Statewide Progress and Institutional Performance: Report to the 1995 Legislature.* Salem, OR: Oregon Progress Board.

Patton, H. Milton, and Janet W. Patton. 1975. "Harbingers of State Growth Policies." In Randall W. Scott, David J. Brower, and Dallas D. Miner, eds., *Management and Control of Growth: Issues, Techniques, Problems, Trends.* Washington, DC: Urban Land Institute.

Pelham, Thomas G. 1993. "The Florida Experience: Creating a State, Regional, and Local Comprehensive Planning Process." In Peter A. Buchsbaum and Larry J. Smith, eds., *State and Regional Comprehensive Planning: Implementing New Methods for Growth Management.* Chicago: American Bar Association.

_____. 1989a. "DCA Assists Locals in All Phases of Planning Process." *Technical Memo* 4, 4.

_____. 1989b. "Sound Planning Will Combat Urban Sprawl." *Technical Memo* 4, 4, Special Issue.

_____. 1979. *State Land Use Planning and Regulation: Florida, the Model Code, and Beyond.* Lexington, MA: D. C. Heath and Co.

Pelham, Thomas G., William L. Hyde, and Robert P. Banks. 1985. "Managing Florida's Growth: Toward an Integrated State, Regional, and Local Comprehensive Planning Process." *Florida State University Law Review* 13: 515.

Perloff, Harvey S. 1980. *Planning the Post-Industrial City.* Chicago: American Planning Association.

Peterson, Tracy D. 1990. "Seattle Metro: Regional Solutions to Local Problems." *Government Finance Review* 6, 3: 19-21.

Pivo, Gary. 1993. "Is the Growth Management Act Working? A Survey of Resource Lands and Critical Areas Development Regulations." *University of Puget Sound Law Review* 16, 3: 1141-1179.

Pivo, G., and D. Rose. 1991. *Toward Growth Management Monitoring in Washington State.* Olympia: Washington State Institute for Public Policy.

Planning Association of Washington. 1994. *A Short Course on Local Planning.* Olympia: Washington Department of Community, Trade and Economic Development.

Popper, Frank J. 1989. "Introduction" to Land Use and the Environment. In *The Best of Planning: Two Decades of Articles from the Magazine of the American Planning Association.* Chicago: American Planning Association.

_____. 1988. "Understanding American Land Use Regulation Since 1970: A Revisionist Interpretation." *Journal of the American Planning Association* 54, 3: 291-301.

_____. 1981. "Siting LULUs." *Planning* 47, 4: 12-15.

Poracsky, Joseph, and Michael C. Houck. 1994. "The Metropolitan Portland Urban Natural Resource

Program." In Rutherford H. Platt, Rowan A. Rowntree, and Pamela C. Muick, eds, *The Ecological City: Preserving and Restoring Urban Biodiversity.* Amherst: University of Massachusetts Press.

Porter, Douglas. R. 1997. *Managing Growth in America's Communities.* Washington, DC: Island Press.

_____. ed. 1996. *Performance Standards for Growth Management.* Planning Advisory Service Report No. 461. Chicago: American Planning Association.

_____. 1993. "State Growth Management: The Intergovernmental Experiment." *Pace Law Review* 13, 2: 481-503.

_____. 1991a. "The States Are Coming, the States Are Coming!" *Urban Land* 48, 9: 16-20.

_____. 1991b. "Do State Growth Management Acts Make a Difference? Local Growth Management Measures Under Different State Growth Policies." *Loyola of Los Angeles Law Review* 24, 4: 1015-33.

_____. January 1991c. "Washington State Awakens to Growth Management." *Urban Land* 32-33.

_____. 1989. "Significant Research Needs in the Policy and Practice of Growth Management." In David J. Brower, David R. Godschalk, and Douglas R. Porter, eds., *Understanding Growth Management: Critical Issues and a Research Agenda.* Washington, DC: Urban Land Institute.

_____. ed. 1986. *Growth Management: Keeping on Target?* Washington, DC: Urban Land Institute.

Pressley, Sue Anne. December 4, 1998. "Atlanta's Growth is No Easy Ride." *Washington Post.* Page A-3.

Reinert, Henry. Fall 1996. "Commission Debates More Ways to Simplify Land Use Laws." *About Growth: A Quarterly Publication about Growth Management* 4.

Richard Ragatz Associates, Inc. 1983. *Comprehensive Plan Monitoring: Guidelines and Resources for Oregon Communities.* Salem, OR: Oregon Department of Land Conservation and Development.

Rohse, Mitch, and Peter Watt. 1994. "Siting Regional Public Facilities." In Carl Abbott, Deborah Howe, and Sy Adler, eds., *Planning the Oregon Way: A Twenty Year Evaluation.* Corvallis, OR: Oregon State University Press.

Rosenbaum, Nelson. 1976. *Land Use and the Legislatures: The Politics of State Innovation.* Washington, DC: Urban Institute.

Rosengren, K. E. 1981. *Advances in Content Analysis.* Beverly Hills: Sage.

Rubino, Richard G., and William R. Wagner. 1972. *The State's Role in Land Resource Management.* Lexington, KY: Council of State Governments.

Sadowski, William E. 1992. "Changes Proposed for Florida's Growth Management System." *Technical Memo* 7, 1.

Salkin, Patricia E. 1993. "Statewide Comprehensive Planning: The Next Wave." In Peter A. Buchsbaum and Larry J. Smith, eds., *State and Regional Comprehensive Planning: Implementing New Methods for*

Growth Management. Chicago: American Bar Association.

_____. 1992. "Political Strategies for Modernizing State Land-Use Statutes." *Land Use Law and Zoning Digest* 44, 8: 3-6.

Scott, Randall W., David J. Brower, and Dallas D. Miner, eds. 1975. *Management and Control of Growth: Issues, Techniques, Problems, Trends.* Washington, DC: Urban Land Institute.

Senior, Jeanie. January 25, 1999a. "Gorge Commission to Vote on Bea House Draft Order." *The Oregonian.*

_____. January 26, 1999b. "House in Columbia Gorge Faces Deadline." *The Oregonian.*

_____. April 8, 1999c. "Owners Sue Over Disputed House in Gorge." *The Oregonian.*

_____. May 21, 1999d. "Judge Sets July 26 for Bea House Hearing." *The Oregonian.*

Settle, Richard L. 1983. *Washington Land Use and Environmental Law and Practice.* Seattle: Butterworth Legal Publications.

Settle, R. L, and C. G. Gavigan. 1993. "The Growth Management Revolution in Washington: Past, Present, and Future." *University of Puget Sound Law Review* 16, 3: 867-941.

Settle, R. L., and C. R. White. 1998. "Filling Legislative Gaps in Washington's Growth Management Law." *Land Use Law and Zoning Digest* 50, 2: 3-9.

Shelley, L. L. 1995. "Land Use and Water Planning Task Force Issues Final Report." *Community Planning* 4, 1.

_____. 1993. "ELMS Makes Recommendations." *Community Planning* 2, 1.

Siemon, Charles L. 1997. "Successful Growth Management Techniques: Observations from the Monkey Cage." *Urban Lawyer* 29, 2: 233-250.

_____. 1985. "Florida: Grappling with Growth II." *Urban Land* 44, 9: 36-37.

Silverman, A. 1988. "Planner's Luncheons Focus on Growth Commission, Underground." *Georgia Planner* 3, 1: 2.

_____. 1987. "Planners Luncheon." *Georgia Planner* 2, 2: 4.

Slavin, Matthew I., and Sy Adler. 1996. "Legislative Constraints on Gubernatorial Capacity for State Industrial Policy: Evidence from Oregon's Regional Strategies Program.' *Economic Development Quarterly* 10, 2: 224-238.

Smith, Herbert H. 1979. *The Citizens Guide to Planning.* Chicago: American Planning Association.

Smith, Larry J. 1993. "Planning for Growth, Washington Style." In Peter A. Buchsbaum and Larry J. Smith, eds., *State and Regional Comprehensive Planning: Implementing New Methods for Growth Management.* Chicago: American Bar Association.

So, Frank S. February 1984. "Stategic Planning: Reinventing the Wheel?" In *The Best of Planning: Two Decades of Articles from the Magazine of the American Planning Association.* Chicago: American Planning Association, 1989.

So, Frank S., Irving Hand, and Bruce McDowell, eds. 1986. *The Practice of State and Regional Planning.* Chicago: American Planning Association.

So, Frank S., and Judith Getzels, eds. 1988. *The Practice of Local Government Planning,* 2nd Ed. Washington, DC: International City Management Association.

Starnes, Earl M. 1993. "Substate Frameworks for Growth Management: Florida and Georgia." In Jay M. Stein, ed., *Growth Management: The Planning Challenge of the 1990s.* Newbury Park, CA: Sage Publications.

_____. 1986. "Florida's Minimum Criteria Rule." In John M. DeGrove and Julian C. Juergensmeyer, eds., *Perspectives on Florida's Growth Management Act of 1985.* Cambridge: Lincoln Institute of Land Policy.

Stein, Jay M., ed. 1993. *Growth Management: The Planning Challenge of the 1990s.* Newbury Park, CA: Sage Publications.

Strong, Douglas A. 1984. *Tahoe: An Environmental History.* Lincoln, NE: University of Nebraska Press.

Stroud, Nancy E. 1996. "State Review and Certification of Local Plans." In *Modernizing State Planning Statutes: The Growing Smart Working Papers,* Vol. 1. American Planning Association, Planning Advisory Service Report No. 462/463.

_____. 1983. "Regional Planning Council Reform in Florida." In Gill C. Lim, ed., *Regional Planning: Evolution, Crisis and Prospects.* Totowa, NJ: Allanheld, Osmun And Co. Publishers.

Stroud, Nancy, and John M. DeGrove. 1980. *Oregon's State Urban Strategy.* Washington, DC: National Academy of Public Administration.

Stroud, Nancy, and Daniel W. O'Connell. 1986. "Florida Toughens Up Its Land-Use Laws." *Planning* 52, 1: 12-14.

Stuebing, V. R. 1987. "Is this Planning in 1967 or 1987?" State Experience in Districting Georgia. *Georgia Planner* 2, 4: 1.

Sullivan, Edward J. 1994. "The Legal Evolution of the Oregon Planning System." In Carl Abbott, Deborah Howe, and Sy Adler, eds., *Planning the Oregon Way: A Twenty Year Evaluation.* Corvallis, OR: Oregon State University Press.

_____. 1993. "Oregon Blazes a Trail." In Peter A. Buchsbaum and Larry J. Smith, eds., *State and Regional Comprehensive Planning: Implementing New Methods for Growth Management.* Chicago: American Bar Association.

Talen, Emily. 1996a. "Do Plans Get Implemented? A Review of Evaluation in Planning." *Journal of Planning Literature* 10, 3: 248-259.

_____. 1996b. "After the Plans: Methods to Evaluate the Implementation Success of Plans." *Journal of Planning Education and Research* 16, 2: 79-91.

Thomas, R. 1975. "Florida's Experiment in Land Use Management." *Growth and Change* 6: 29-35.

Thompson, Laura A., and Stuart Meck. 1996. "Appendix A. Reform of State Planning Statutes: A Bibliography." In *Modernizing State*

Planning Statutes: The Growing Smart Working Papers, Vol. 1. American Planning Association, Planning Advisory Service Report No. 462/463.

Thomson, Stephanie. December 1, 1998. "Panel: Gorge Home Breaks Laws." *The Columbian*. Page A-1.

Thornton, Lynn. November 1990. "For Professional Planners: The Planning Game—Georgia Style." *Georgia Planner*.

Turner, Robyne S. 1997. "Sustainable Urban Revitalization: Obstacles and Opportunities in the South Florida Region." *Environmental and Urban Issues* 24, 2: 9-12.

_____. 1990a. "New Rules for the Growth Game: The Use of Rational State Standards in Land Use Policy." *Journal of Urban Affairs* 12, 1: 35-47.

_____. 1990b. "Intergovernmental Growth Management: A Partnership Framework for State-Local Relations." *Publius: The Journal of Federalism* 20, 3: 79-95.

U.S. Department of Commerce, Economics and Statistics Administration, Bureau of the Census. August 1991a. *State and Metropolitan Area Data Book 1991*, 4th Ed. Washington, DC: Bureau of the Census.

_____. August 1991b. *1990 Census of Population and Housing. Summary Population and Housing Characteristics.* Florida (CPH-1-11), Georgia (CPH 1-12), Oregon (CPH-1-39), and Washington (CPH-1-49). Washington, DC: Bureau of the Census.

Walker, T. 1990. "Distinguished Leadership: Gov. Joe Frank Harris." *Planning* 55, 3: 12-13.

Wallis, Allan D. 1993. *Growth Management in Florida*. Cambridge: Lincoln Institute of Land Policy.

Walth, Brent. November 29, 1998. "History of House in Gorge Shows Fumbles on All Sides." *The Oregonian*. Page A-1.

_____. November 1994. "The Birth of the Plan." *Oregon Business* 17: 20-30.

Washington State Department of Community Development. 1993a. *Preparing the Heart of Your Comprehensive Plan: A Land Use Element Guide*. Olympia: Washington DCD.

_____. 1993b. *Issues in Designating Urban Growth Areas, Part II: Suggestions for Criteria and Densities.* Olympia: Washington DCD.

_____. 1993c. *Small Communities Guide to Comprehensive Planning: A Model Comprehensive Plan.* Olympia: Washington DCD.

_____. n. d. *Preparing Your Comprehensive Plan's Foundation: A Land Use Inventory Guide.* Olympia: Washington DCD.

_____. June 1992a. *Implementation Briefs*, 5. Olympia: Washington Department of Community Development, Growth Management Division.

_____. 1992b. *Issues in Designating Urban Growth Areas, Part One: Providing Adequate Urban Land Supply.* Olympia: Washington DCD.

_____. 1990. *Shaping Your Future: A Guide to Designating Urban Growth Areas.* Olympia: Washington DCD.

Washington State Department of Community, Trade and Economic Development. September 16, 1997a. *Growth Management Services: Status Report.* Olympia: Washington DCTED.

_____. 1997b. Growth Management Grants to Local Government by County Region. Olympia: Washington DCTED (Two page table at web site: www.cted.wa.us).

_____. September 12, 1996. *Growth Management Services Publications Directory.* Olympia: Washington DCTED (Found at web site, www.cted.wa.us).

Washington State Department of Community, Trade and Economic Development and League of Women Voters of Washington. 1997. *Growth Management: It's Beginning to Take Shape.* Olympia: The Authors.

Washington State Department of Ecology. 1994. *Shoreline Management Guidebook, 2nd Ed.: Vol. II, Shoreline Master Program Handbook.* Olympia: Washington State Department of Ecology.

Washington State Growth Strategies Commission. 1990. *Final Report: A Growth Strategy for Washington State.* Seattle: Growth Strategies Commission.

Washington State Land Use Study Commission. 1998. *Final Report.* Olympia: Department of Community, Trade and Economic Development.

_____. 1997. *Vision 2003.* Olympia: Department of Community, Trade and Economic Development.

Watterson, W. T. 1993. "Linked Simulation of Land Use and Transportation Systems: Developments and Experience in the Puget Sound Region." *Transportation Research* A 27A, 3: 193-206.

Weber, R. P. 1985. *Basic Content Analysis.* Beverly Hills: Sage.

Weitz, Jerry. 1999. "From Quiet Revolution to Smart Growth: State Growth Management Programs, 1960-1999." Council of Planning Librarians Bibliography 355/356/357. *Journal of Planning Literature* 14, 2.

_____. 1997a. "Concurrency: Evolution and Impacts of an Infrastructure and Growth Management Policy." *Public Works Management and Policy* 2, 1: 51-65.

_____. 1997b. "Oregon Land Use: Reinvention or Progress?" *Oregon Planners' Journal* 14, 9: 6.

_____. 1997c. "Toward a Model Statutory Plan Element: Transportation." *Land Use Law and Zoning Digest* 49, 2: 3-9.

_____. 1996. State Growth Management Policy. Unpublished Research.

_____. 1995. "Letter to the Editor." *Environmental and Urban Issues* 22, 2: 1.

_____. 1992. "A Synopsis of the Mountain Protection Standards." *Georgia Planner* 5: 1-2.

Weitz, Jerry, and Ethan Seltzer. 1998. "Regional Planning and Regional Governance in the United States: 1979-1996." CPL Bibliography 341/342. *Journal of Planning Literature* 12, 3: 361-392.

Weitz, Jerry, and Terry Moore. 1998. "Development Inside Urban Growth Boundaries: Oregon's Empirical Evidence of Contiguous Urban Form." *Journal of the American Planning Association* 64, 4: 424-440.

Weitz, Jerry, and Tim Schindler. 1997. Are Oregon's Communities Balanced? A Test of the Jobs-Housing Balance Policy and the Impact of Balance on Mean Commute Times. Unpublished research, Portland State University.

Wells, Steve. Fall 1996. "GMA Is Foundation for Land Use Regulatory Reform." *About Growth: A Quarterly Publication About Growth Management* 2.

West, Harry. 1992. "The Evolution of Growth Management in Georgia." *Environmental and Urban Issues* 18, 3: 15-27.

Western Washington Growth Management Hearings Board. 1995. Achen, et. al, Petitioners, vs. Clark County, et. al, Respondents, and Clark County School Districts, et. al., Intervenors. Final Decision and Order No. 95-2-0067. Olympia: Western Washington Growth Management Hearings Board.

Whorton, Jr., Joseph W. 1989. "Innovative Strategic Planning: The Georgia Model." *Environmental and Urban Issues* 17, 1: 15-23.

Wickersham, James H. 1994. "The Quiet Revolution Continues: The Emerging New Model For State Growth Management Statutes." *Harvard Environmental Law Review* 18: 489-548.

Zotti, Ed. January 1987. "CADD Takes Hold." In the *Best of Planning: Two Decades of Articles from the Magazine of the American Planning Association.* Chicago: American Planning Association, 1989.

Index

SANDBLAST, K